HUMANKIND

AN INTRODUCTORY READER FOR CULTURAL ANTHROPOLOGY

REVISED FIRST EDITION

Edited by
Loretta A. Cormier and
Sharyn R. Jones

University of Alabama at Birmingham

cognella™
San Diego, CA

First published in the United States of America in 2011 by Cognella, a division of University Readers, Inc.

Trademark Notice: Product or corporate names may be trademarks or registered trademarks, and are used only for identification and explanation without intent to infringe.

15 14 13 12 11   1 2 3 4 5

Printed in the United States of America

ISBN: 978-1-60927-632-4

www.cognella.com 800.200.3908

CONTENTS

PART V: THE FUTURE OF CULTURE

INTRODUCTION

The aim of the *Humankind: An Introductory Reader for Cultural Anthropology* is to introduce students to a variety of theoretical and ethnographically based articles and essays appropriate for undergraduates in introductory level cultural anthropology courses. Efforts were made to provide articles representing diverse cultural settings, a variety of theoretical approaches, and contemporary debates in cultural anthropology. The anthology was originally designed as an adjunct to the text, *Introductory Cultural Anthropology: An Interactive Approach* (Cormier and Jones 2010, National Social Science Press). However, the themes of the reading selections are consistent with the general topics typically addressed in introductory cultural anthropology texts; as such, this volume is a suitable complement to any introductory cultural anthropology textbook.

This book is divided into five broad sections. In Part I, "The Subject of Anthropology," the reader is introduced to the discipline of anthropology through the four fields and the concept of culture through ethnographic narratives. Part II, "Humans as Symbol Makers" focuses on the meaning-centered approach of anthropology. It addresses linguistic anthropology, expressive culture (e.g., music, art, folklore), and the religious experience cross-culturally. In Part II, "Human Social Identities," articles are included that describe the variety of roles and statuses in human social organization cross-culturally. Articles include the broad perspective of variation in systems of marriage, family, and kinship found around the globe as well as social identities mediated by concepts of "race," ethnicity, gender, and sexuality. Part IV, "Humanity in Ecological and Economic Perspective," addresses the more material basis of human existence. Article topics include subsistence practices, traditional plants, economic systems, and the consequences of global economic inequality. In Part V, "The Future of Culture," topics are addressed related to cultural change, cultural survival, and the ethical responsibilities of anthropologists to the cultures that we study.

PART I: THE SUBJECT OF ANTHROPOLOGY

In Part I, "The Subject of Anthropology," the reader is introduced to the discipline of anthropology through the four fields and the concept of culture through several classic ethnographic descriptions. The term "anthropology" translates from Greek as the study of human beings. Anthropologists explore the human experience through space and across time, from the study of the origins of humanity to the study of contemporary peoples across the globe. Anthropology is also a bio-cultural discipline, meaning that we are just as interested in what separates human beings from other species from a biological perspective as we are in contemporary human cultural variation.

Cultural anthropologists study the diversity of the human experience across the globe. One of the key features of humanity that is found in all cultures is our multidimensional symbolic communication through language. The field of linguistic anthropology concentrates on the similarities and differences in human language cross-culturally. Archaeologists specialize in providing time depth to understanding humanity. By excavating the material remains of past cultures, they add to our understanding of human diversity by providing information about how ancient peoples lived and identifying the variables that can help explain culture change over time. For biological anthropologists, two key areas of study are human evolution and primatology. On the one hand, anthropologists interested in human evolution extend the time depth beyond the archaeological record by documenting evidence of the earliest human ancestors through the fossil record. They also study primate populations (monkeys, apes, and prosimians) in order to understand the ways in which humans demonstrate similarities and differences from our primate cousins.

The emphasis of this anthology is on the field of cultural anthropology. However, regardless of field of specialization, anthropologists recognize that the four-field approach is a clear strength of our discipline. Anthropology is unique in that we are the only discipline of scientific inquiry that attempts to take such a broad-based approach to understanding what it means to be human. In Part I, we situate the field of anthropology and orient the reader to how the field of cultural anthropology articulates with the broader discipline of anthropology. While cultural anthropologists have a primary focus on contemporary cultures, the aims of cultural anthropologists articulate with the larger aims of anthropology as a whole.

Robert Kunzig's chapter "Learning to Love Neanderthals" provides a look into the field of paleoanthropology, which explores the fossil record of human ancestors. One ongoing debate in anthropology is the relationship of Neanderthal and Cro Magnon peoples to contemporary humans. The two views are termed the "Out of Africa" hypothesis and the "Multiregional Continuity Hypothesis." The first suggests that modern humans (Cro Magnons) evolved in Africa about 100,000 years ago and migrated into Europe and Asia, replacing the Neanderthals. In this view, the Neanderthals went extinct around 30,000 years ago. The multiregional continuity hypothesis includes the possibility that two groups interbred, so that modern human beings could have ancestry in both Neanderthal and Cro Magnon populations. Kunzig describes the excavation of an interesting fossil in Portugal nicknamed "The Kid" which seems to have mixed Neanderthal and Cro Magnon features.

Part I also includes two ethnographic examples from fieldwork by Clifford Geertz and Renato Rosaldo. Geertz's article "Deep Play: Notes on the Balinese Cockfight" has become a classic in cultural anthropology not only for the methodological contribution of "thick description," but also for relating the difficulties that all cultural anthropologists face as foreigners in gaining acceptance in the cultures they study. Thick description involves describing not only the cultural behaviors and social relationships of members of a group, but describing the context in rich detail. Ideally, the goal is to "read" the culture as if it were a text. Deep Play also describes Geertz's repeated failures to make connections with the Balinese people, despite attempts in many different ways to establish relationships. The article reveals the unanticipated turning point related to the cockfight that led to his gaining acceptance among the Balinese.

Renato Rosaldo's "Grief and a Headhunter's Rage" explores the anthropology of emotion. Rosaldo had been researching an old practice among the Ilongot of the Philippines in which men cut off the head of a victim when a loved one died. The Ilongot explained the practice as a result of the rage of bereavement. Rosaldo attempted to understand their headhunting by applying multiple standard theories of cultural behavior in anthropology, but was unsuccessful. However, when his wife, Michelle Rosaldo died in an accidental fall in the field in the Philippines, Renato Rosaldo identified with the murderous rage of grief experienced by the Ilongot. Rosaldo's work falls within the genre known as "reflexive anthropology," which involves explaining others through the self. He recounts his own personal narrative of the death of his wife and elucidates the Ilongot experience of grief by asking the reader to first identify with his own emotional state.

PART II: HUMANS AS SYMBOL MAKERS

Part II, "Humans as Symbol Makers," focuses on the meaning-centered approach of anthropology. It addresses linguistic anthropology, expressive culture, and the religious experience cross-culturally. While all animals have some form of communication, in anthropology the term "language" refers to the unique form of communication used by humans. One feature that separates human language apart from other communication systems is its symbolic complexity: nothing similar exists in animal communication. Expressive culture involves multiple forms of symbolic representations including art, dance, storytelling, music, and body modification. Manifestations of expressive culture around the world can be seen in creative works that evoke the senses or emotions and often serve as commentary on a culture or society's norms and values. Religion is also a symbolically complicated expression of cultural beliefs. While religion is considered to be a cultural universal, the specific forms of practice are highly variable. That is to say, while some form of religious or magical belief is found in cultures globally, what is specifically believed and how those beliefs are enacted are quite different cross-culturally. Part II will present several articles related to human symbolic thinking in language, art, and religion.

In Deborah Tannen's article "Sex, Lies, and Conversation: Why is it so Hard for Men and Women to Talk to Each Other," the author explores how language must be understood in terms of social context. In linguistic terms, this approach broadly fits into the area of sociolinguistics. Meaning is found not only in the literal meaning of words, but in the broader cultural conditions wherein conversations take place. Tannen goes on to describe gender differences in the conversational styles of speaking among American men and women which lead to miscommunication. The topic is treated more extensively in her book, *You Just Don't Understand,* which was on the *New York Times* best seller list for nearly four years.

Storytelling is another important symbolic way in which a culture's values, norms, and history are conveyed. In Laura Bohannan's "Shakespeare in the Bush," she addresses how it is often taken for granted that our own perceptions are shared by members of other cultures. She describes being involved in a storytelling session among the Tiv of West Africa when she is asked to tell a story. She chooses "Hamlet" believing that the narrative embodies universal human themes. However as she tells the story, she is repeatedly told that she is telling it wrong, and the Tiv "correct" her and alter the story. By the time they are finished, they have changed the entire meaning of the story, inserting Tiv-like characters and motivations. The broader implication of this article is that it reminds us how easy it is to view other peoples ethnocentrically and to judge them through our own lenses.

Zora Neale Hurston is a folklorist and anthropologist who studied under the renowned anthropologist Franz Boas. Her ethnographic research involved collecting and analyzing the folklore of African Americans in the 1920s and 1930s. She was a leader in the "Harlem Renaissance" which, from a literary perspective, involved the rejection of racist stereotypes of African Americans common in novels, plays, and short stories. While Hurston's work did not involve ethnographic accounts, her contribution to literature was based on ethnographic fieldwork and research in folklore. One of her noted short stories is "The Gilded Six-Bits." It is written in an African American dialect and provides a realistic depiction of the complexities of life for a young newlywed couple.

The religious experience is also characterized by multi-layered symbolic meanings. A common shared characteristic of religious life cross-culturally is the experience of altered states of spiritual consciousness and a belief in supernatural forces or supernatural beings such as gods and goddesses. However, religious life is also culturally-specific and may serve to express moral codes, social norms, and other aspects of culture that are not generally shared. One example is Janice Boddy's "Spirits and Selves in Northern Sudan: The Cultural Therapeutics of Possession and Trance." The concept of spirit possession may well be a cultural universal, whether it involves the Christian idea of healing effects of the Holy

Spirit and corruption through demonic possession, or any of the wide variety of forms of spirit possession that exist cross-culturally. In the case study of Northern Sudan, Boddy describes possession by *zar* spirits as causing illness, specifically in married women. More than a physical illness, Boddy describes *zar* possession as a manifestation of social ills related to marital distress and fertility issues, which is perhaps best interpreted as a form of psychotherapy.

Jörg Fachner's article "Wanderer between Worlds: Anthropological Perspectives on Healing Rituals and Music" also draws on the notion of religious healing as psychotherapy, but with an emphasis on music. Popular conceptions of shamans often view these healers as exotic characters in "primitive" cultures who lead group members to altered states of consciousness through hallucinogenic drugs. However, anthropologists find an analogy in the psychotherapist who "heals" by influencing perceptions. In popular thought, less attention is given to the role of music in achieving therapeutic and healing states. Jörg attempts to address this oversight by offering a broader interpretation of the healing effects of music in Western society and cross-culturally, exploring the biological effects of music in altering one's state of mind.

While the seemingly exotic behavior of members of other cultures may be similar to behaviors in our own culture, behaviors that seem similar in other cultures may only be superficially so. In Eric Wolf's "The Virgin of Guadalupe" he describes the adoration of the Virgin Mary in Mexico as rooted in earlier Aztec beliefs. The Virgin of Guadalupe is the national patron saint of Mexico. A shrine was built to her on the Hill of Tepeyac after she appeared to a Mexican indigene, speaking to him in his native Nahuatl (Aztec). Today the shrine is visited by hundreds of thousands of pilgrims each year. However, the shrine to the Virgin of Guadalupe cannot be perceived exclusively as a symbol of the Catholic faith. In fact, in pre-Hispanic times, before the arrival of Catholicism, a shrine to the goddess Tonantzin was located on the Hill of Tepeyac. The Virgin of Guadalupe cannot be clearly differentiated from the Aztec goddess and is best understood as a syncretic (blended) version of the two female supernatural figures.

PART III: HUMAN SOCIAL IDENTITIES

Part III deals with the fascinating and complicated issue of "Human Social identities." An individual's identity is frequently expressed in terms of race, ethnicity, gender, marital status, and rank within a given society. These concepts, and others variously determine one's social role. Identity may be expressed in different ways depending on the social context and a person's position in society. Importantly, identity and status change throughout a person's lifetime as they age, move through rites of passage, and engage in different types of labor and activities. The concept of identity can also be examined at a broader cultural level, in terms of politics, nationalism, history, language, and ethnicity, for example.

Anthropologists have explored social identity at both this broad cultural level and at the locus of the individual. From an analytical perspective, understanding the way humans conceive of, and construct, social identities is critical for explaining human behavior and social interactions between groups.

Like most concepts in anthropology, a precise definition of identity, and agreement upon its mode of formation is lacking. Over time anthropologists have conceived of identity in either somewhat static, deterministic terms (where individual identity expresses social norms and values), or in terms of individuals as social actors who make decisions and express a great degree of variation in personal agendas and preferences. Our modern conception of cultural identity stems from nineteenth-century nationalism in Europe, where most early anthropological works originated. Through time, however, studies of identity have become increasingly diverse and common in the discipline of anthropology as illustrated by a vast body of postmodern and contemporary research on the subject. The articles in Part III present examples that examine group and individual social identity from perspectives of marriage patterns, family structure, ethnicity, tribalism, the concept of race, gender, sexuality, and aggression.

Goldstein's article "When Brothers Share a Wife" discusses cultural identity and marital practices in Tibet. Tibetans engage in *fraternal polyandry*, where multiple brothers marry the same woman. The bride leaves her natal home and moves into the home of the brothers. Fraternal polyandry is common in Tibet, but rarely found in other cultures. Goldstein explains the various marital practices in Tibet, their nuances, and their functions while dispelling myths that have been used to account for these traditions, such as female infanticide, demographic shortages of women, and fear of starvation. Goldstein goes on to present both emic and etic explanations for polyandry in this social context. While reading the paper, consider what the advantages of cooperative domestic arrangements are and why marital practices that are common in the Western world, such as monogamy, would present difficulties for a Tibetan family.

"African Polygyny: Family values and Contemporary Changes," by Philip Kilbride presents another study in plural marriage. Kilbride's paper draws broadly from a range of ethnographic works, and he compares and contrasts norms in various African contexts and also discusses marriage in America. Kilbride challenges the American notion that marriage practices are focused on romantic love and sexual relations, positing that children and community relationships are functionally much more important. He brings up issues of divorce, deadbeat dads, single-parent households and teenage pregnancy to explain the unfortunate byproducts of the American marriage system. A common African perspective on marriage suggests that polygyny is preferable to monogamy. Kilbride argues that this blended family structure is actually much more stable and provides children with more parents and more resources which results in a higher standard of living.

The paper by Vine Deloria, Jr., "Custer Died for Your Sins," is part of a work that was expanded into a book, which addressed Native American Indian stereotypes, challenging whites to critically examine the exploitation of Native Americans, their culture, and their lands. The excerpt reprinted here focuses on the role played by anthropologists in the development of ideas that enforce social marginalization and assimilation while discouraging sovereignty. This paper emphasizes the importance of understanding multiple perspectives and motivations (political, financial, academic, and educational) of various actors in the social dramas surrounding anthropological research. In some ways the paper is a clear critique of the approach taken by authors of cultural theory in the early twentieth century, such as Evans-Pritchard and others who sought to reduce the study of cultures and peoples to a precise analytical enterprise. But the assessment extends to the practice of modern anthropology as well. Deloria asks, "Why should we continue to provide private zoos for anthropologists? Why should tribes have to compete with scholars for funds, when their scholarly productions are so useless and irrelevant to life?" This biting commentary creates a caricature of the anthropologist as an "ideological vulture" (much like the discipline has caricatured "Indians" as folk warriors). Moreover, Deloria's impassioned piece provides cause for reflection and generates questions about the relevancy of the anthropological endeavor. Deloria asks to whom is the work of anthropologists relevant and argues that government schools on reservations brainwash and assimilate rather than educate. At the end of the paper he makes a bold proposal that anthropologists should raise contributions equal to the total budget of their study and donate that to tribal council of the Native Americans. Deloria contends that this would create self-sufficiency among Native Americans and ultimately help to eliminate real social problems.

We have included a current copy of the "American Anthropological Association's Statement on Race." This document was approved in 1998 by the largest organization of anthropologists in the world, the AAA. It was written by a representative committee of American Anthropologists, and approved by the AAA Executive Board and a majority of its members. We hope that students will read this document in order to understand the contemporary scholarly position taken by a majority of anthropologists in regards to the contentious issue of race.

Serena Nanda's paper "Multiple Genders among North American Indians" breaks down false stereotypes about gender and gender variation, emphasizing the complexity of ideology and situational behaviors. This work illustrates that great gender diversity was common in the past, among the Native North American Indians in particular. Moreover, Nanda's work illuminates gender alternatives, which is a pressing contemporary issue as many people struggle for human rights across the globe. This paper and similar research projects in the discipline contributes to our understanding of gender in the present. Nanda introduces the term *variant genders* after pointing out the problematic ethnocentric nature of labels typically used to describe people who do not fit into the Western notion of male or female. She points to current work in the last twenty-five years that suggests occupation and labor practices are much more important features of gender variance than sexuality or biology. Cultural criteria were, and still are, the most important factors defining gender roles and their many variations.

Robert Sapolsky and Lisa Share's article "A Pacific Culture among Wild Baboons: Its Emergence and Transmission" provides a unique perspective in Part III, as they focus on nonhuman primates. Their research offers a rare glimpse at the transmission of social culture (rather than material culture) among a group of Baboons. Sapolsky and Share find that a shift in social structure, from an aggressive environment to an atmosphere of non-aggression, results in positive physiological correlates for this social group. In sum, health and life expectancy increase in the community in relation to attributes that transcend individual social networks and emphasize non-aggressive behavior. There is an obvious lesson in this case study for human primates, and readers might consider how such a transmission could occur in our own society.

PART IV: HUMANITY IN ECOLOGICAL AND ECONOMIC PERSPECTIVE

Part IV includes articles on the role of humans specifically in relation to their association with ecology and economics. Until the mid-1940's American anthropology was firmly grounded in the Boasian approach of Historical Particularism. Like many new theories in anthropology, the work of Julian Steward and Leslie White challenged existing theoretical paradigms. In this case, Steward and White's theories, infused by Marxist thought, were an attack on the criticism of cultural evolutionism of Boas and some of his students. Post-Boasian theorists of the mid-twentieth century created a new, relatively sophisticated cultural evolutionary approach to the study of humans, emphasizing some of the characteristics of humanity that earlier works failed to highlight. For example, Steward sought to understand the adaptation of specific cultures to particular ecological environments via subsistence practices, which he referred to as the "culture core;" this is the theory of *specific evolution*. Anthropologists such as Steward, who were most interested in the impacts of environment on culture, have been labeled *cultural ecologists*. White created a general scheme of cultural evolution, and abandoned the idea of cultural relativism. He believed that energy control, or energy use and efficiency was a standard by which all cultures could be measured and evaluated. White's model is referred to as *general evolution*. George Peter Murdock created the Human Relations Area Files (HRAF), an incredible resource that enables wide scale cross-cultural comparisons and is now available online to many educational institutions. The work of Steward, White, and Murdock formed the foundation for the theoretical schools of *ecological anthropology* and *cultural materialism*.

Cultural materialists view culture, and all its component parts, as a strategy for exploiting material resources and promoting an adaptive optimal advantage. In this vein, Marvin Harris discusses the classic case of cows in India, in his paper, "The Cultural Ecology of India's Sacred Cattle." He argues that there is a logical, economic, material explanation for

Indian Hindu beliefs about the sacredness of cattle, as ideological systems are fundamentally shaped by material needs. The Hindu doctrine of *ahimsa*, meaning the avoidance of violence, assumes the unity of all life and uses cattle as a symbol and prime example. Harris believes that economic and ecological pressures explain why cows are not slaughtered, and *ahimsa* fails to account for the cattle complex in India. While reading this article, consider what Harris describes as the most important use(s) for cattle. Harris's work is synonymous with cultural materialism, which some view as extreme in its application of Western rational or logical etic explanations for all human behaviors. As one of the comments on Harris's article states, the author's underlying criteria for analysis, "… are often vague or culture-bound." In essence, cultural materialist understandings of cultural phenomena ignore tradition and history (for example, centuries of British rule in India), allowing no explanatory power to religious or ideological aspects of culture, while imposing a Western view of logic to create simple explanations for complex behaviors. This paper illustrates one theoretical perspective and one side of an ongoing debate about the nature of human culture. It is important to consider both economic and symbolic approaches in order to truly understand any cultural phenomenon or human behavior; these perspectives are certainly not exclusive and many anthropologists believe that exploring both sides would result in fuller interpretations and greater understanding.

Wade Davis' paper entitled "Hallucinogenic Plants and Their Use in Traditional Societies" provides a comparative study of how and why plant-based drugs are used cross-culturally. Traditionally hallucinogenic plants are used for religious and/or ritual purposes in many cultures. Because hallucinogens are primarily derived from plants, an ecological approach that views the human exploitation of plants to achieve certain ends in a particular culture contexts makes sense. Davis emphasizes that all drugs are used in a highly specific culture context where the so-called, "set" and "setting" are critical elements for consideration. The *set* is an "… individual's expectations of what the drug will do to him; *setting* is the environment—both physical and social—in which the drug is taken." These elements of the drug experience are significant because the active chemical components of the drugs may produce varied effects depending on one's set and setting. Importantly, drugs are used among indigenous groups and American Indians in highly structured ritual settings. This traditional inclusion of drug-taking behavior varies markedly from the nonmedical and recreational consumption of drugs in American culture. Moreover, traditionally hallucinogenic plants are consumed in association with the needs of the group and the collective good. This stands in stark contrast to the typically self-indulgent efforts to relieve boredom or anxiety, which commonly motivate recreational drug users in the United States today.

Warren Hern argues for the *ecopathology hypothesis* in his paper "Is Human Culture Carcinogenic for Uncontrolled Population Growth and Ecological Destruction?" At a basic level, Hern's vehement critique makes the riveting statement that humans are a cancer on the planet, and we are gradually destroying the global ecosystem. A biocultural model is presented along with Hern's hypothesis to account for a range of phenomena (including the uniformity in the structure and range of human communities, and severe environmental changes). It is our unique human culture that has provided us with the key adaptations for survival of our species in any environment or ecological niche. Hern takes a biological perspective to evaluate the human species and our impacts on the earth. For example, in discussing demography he argues that from a broad perspective, humans act as density independent cells, where "humans communicate through culture and form coalitions that defeat limitations posed by ecosystems." Hern predicts that the rapid pace of population expansion will result in auto-extinction of our species. In his conclusion he makes some radical recommendations for dealing with the problem.

The classic article by Marshall Sahlins entitled "The Original Affluent Society" focuses on how anthropology understands and conceptualizes certain modes of subsistence. In an affluent society all people's material wants are easily satisfied, according to Sahlins, and the "Zen road to affluence" would be defined as a case where peoples' wants are few and technical means are adequate. Unlike our own society, hunter-gatherers view material wealth as an oppressive burden, where one's ability to be readily mobile is hindered by material culture. Therefore, the hunter-gatherer view of wealth is very different from the Western concept. While reading this article, consider what a hunter-gatherer's view of poverty might be, and how this compares with your own view. Note how many hours each day or week that the average hunter-gatherers works, and evaluate how this compares with your own life. Sahlins points out a surprising paradox: In our contemporary world, approximately one-half to one-third of humans go to bed hungry each night, and yet we live in an a time of great technological power and in what might be considered a "highly evolved" culture. Sahlins speculates that in the so-called "Stone Age" fewer people were likely starving, and therefore the degree of hunger increases with the evolution of culture.

Richard Lee also discusses the life and ideology of a hunter-gatherer through the lens of his experiences with the "!Kung Bushmen" in his paper "Eating Christmas in the Kalahari." After reading the Sahlins article it is clear why the !Kung think Lee is a "miser" for hoarding a two-month supply of canned goods in his camp. Lee makes the mistake of trying to improve his reputation by purchasing an ox for a Christmas feast. While the gift is culturally appropriate, miscommunication and lack of understanding on many levels cause Lee confusion and discomfort. After Lee figures out how the Bushman tactic of enforced humility works, he speculates that this may be an adaptive characteristic. The paper also illustrates some of the difficulties encountered by anthropologists in a field setting.

The final paper in Part IV is titled "From Jíbaro to Crack Dealer: Confronting the Restructuring of Capitalism in El Barrio" by Philippe Bourgois. Bourgois seeks to understand the underground economy in Spanish Harlem, or New York City's El Barrio, through an economic perspective that utilizes *cultural production theory*, an approach focused on "complex forms of resistance that result in self-destruction and ultimately community trauma." Bourgois wants to understand why people continue to hurt themselves, their families, and those in their communities via self-destructive behavior such as drug dealing. He takes an extremely self-conscious or reflexive stance in order to understand the ugly realities of life in El Barrio and in order to avoid minimizing the deep and complex nature of human suffering he documents. He wants the reader to see and feel life as it is experienced, illuminating the real people involved and providing a deeper insight into the world of East Harlem. Ultimately, Bourgois attempts a sort of advocacy anthropology where he gives voice to "underrepresented victims" and questions the American ideology of racial hierarchy and our common justifications for poverty.

PART V: THE FUTURE OF CULTURE

In Part V, "The Future of Culture," topics are addressed related to cultural change, cultural survival, and the ethical responsibilities of anthropologists to the cultures that we study. While all human cultures are characterized by change, we have seen a trajectory of rapid acceleration in the types of changes in relatively recent times, considering a span of time of several million years of human existence. One of the most significant events in human history was the agricultural revolution, beginning approximately 10,000 years ago, which led to a fundamental change in the ways that human beings related to the environment and to each other. European colonization of the New World was another watershed event that forever changed human ecological and social interactions, introducing many forms of dramatic culture change. Today we are in the midst of increasing globalization of the planet. While immigration brings new people and new ideas into contact, innovations in transportation, communication, and the influence of transnational corporations provide novel modes of human interaction, often with negative consequences, such as the so-called "McDonaldization" of the world. Anthropological fieldwork in such changing contexts is providing new ethical challenges for the role of anthropologists as cultural translators.

One of the most difficult topics that we face in anthropology is understanding the human capacity for atrocities against their fellow human beings. A long-standing question, not only in anthropology, but in philosophy and theology, is whether violence is biologically intrinsic to human nature, or a product of culture and environment. Anthropologists often look to our primate cousins for possible evolutionary explanations. Frans de Waal is a primatologist who has written extensively about differences in non-human primate social behavior. Humans are primate cousins to apes, monkeys, and prosimians. To date, our best scientific evidence places the closest living relatives to the human genus *Homo* with the African ape genus *Pan*. While there is only one contemporary human genus, *Homo sapiens,* two contemporary species exist within the genus *Pan:* the common chimpanzee, *Pan troglodytes* and the bonobo, *Pan paniscus.* De Waal has written extensively on the differences beween bonobos and chimpanzees in resolving conflict. The chimpanzee arguably represents the closest human analogy in the animal world, as chimpanzees engage in organized warfare against members of the same species. The bonobo, by contrast, epitomizes the 60's slogan of making love, not war. Bonobos, as a rule, resolve social conflict through peaceable means which are highly sexualized interactions, be it male-female, same-sex relations, or even adult-juvenile sexual contact. The question remains for humanity: Do we share more in common genetically and biologically with the capacity of chimpanzees for violence and making war or with the capacity of bonobos for love and making peace. Moreover, with our higher level of conscious self-reflection, can we choose how to behave toward our fellow human beings? In "Peace Lessons from an Unlikely Source" De Waal reviews violent and conciliatory behaviors in a number of primate species. He argues that the evidence suggests that both human and nonhuman primate violence have both genetic and cultural components. He also makes the case that far too much attention is given to aggressive behavior instead of understanding complex mechanisms for peace-making in multiple primate species, both human and nonhuman.

The title of Paul Slovic's article comes from a quote from Mother Teresa when she was asked how she coped with large-scale human suffering. She responded by saying, "If I look at the mass, I will never act. If I look at the one, I will." Slovic attempts to explain why a blind eye is often turned to genocide and other forms of suffering. A paradox exists in human behavior that we will often act altruistically with urgency for an individual in danger (such as running into a burning building) but often appear indifferent to large-scale suffering of our fellow human beings. Slovic suggests that one possible explanation lies in human evolutionary psychology. In brief, he argues that while humans have evolved to behave altruistically toward friends and family in an immediate situation, it is difficult for humans to mentally process danger or suffering that is more abstract, involving large numbers of people not in our immediate presence. Ironically, multiplying the number of people suffering actually makes humans less likely to act. Slovic argues that while we can identify with a single person's suffering, if we are asked to contemplate the suffering of thousands, our minds go numb. While we can rationally compute that the suffering of one thousand is worse than the suffering of one, we have not evolved psychologically to be able to empathize with large numbers of strangers.

Omenn's article "Evolution and Public Health" discusses the multiple ways in which human behavior over the last 10,000 years has affected human health. Approximately 10,000 years ago, humans began to radically alter the environment as they moved from a hunting and gathering existence to an agricultural lifestyle, resulting in a number of consequences to human health. One such consequence has been altered patterns of human-animal relations, resulting in changes in either the prevalence of many diseases or the introduction of new "zoonotic" diseases (human diseases acquired from animals). Examples include malaria, various influenzas, and HIV/AIDS. Another consequence is that changes to the human diet have led to the emergence of the so-called "diseases of civilization," including high blood pressure, obesity, diabetes, high cholesterol, auto-immune disorders, and several types of cancers. The diseases are extremely rare among hunter-gatherers, but are chronic in many contemporary populations.

In Nancy Scheper-Hughes "Lifeboat Ethics: Mother Love and Child Death in Northeast Brazil," the author confronts a different type of ethical issue. Scheper-Hughes worked in Northeast Brazil, an area of extreme poverty, which has an extraordinarily high rate of infant mortality. Mothers perceive infants who appear weak as not having "the will to live" and wanting to return to heaven. Believing that these infants are destined to die, mothers withdraw and withhold both physical and emotional support. In effect, the babies are starved to death. Tragically, Scheper-Hughes found that for a number of infants, the child would be listless due to dehydration from a diarrhea-causing infection. In many cases, the dehydration could be treated by very simple means using a salt and sugar solution, or even a Coca-cola. Scheper-Hughes views the maternal withdrawal as a psychological coping mechanism to deal with the grief of the high rate of infant death. Mothers essentially protect themselves emotionally by not forming strong attachments to children that they do not believe will live. A fuller treatment of Scheper-Hughes' research can be found in her book, *Death Without Weeping: The Violence of Everyday Life in Brazil.*

Part V ends with a 1998 document, "Code of Ethics of the American Anthropological Association." It outlines areas of ethical practice for anthropologists in research and teaching. Responsibilities outlined include those toward the people and animals with whom anthropological researchers work and whose lives and cultures they study, to scholarship and science, to students and trainees, and to the public. The goal of the 1998 code is not to provide a list of rules for anthropologists to follow, but rather to raise awareness of the complexity of ethical obligations, promote discussion, and provide general guidelines to assist anthropologists in making ethically responsible decisions.

Students often ask the question: "Why can't anthropologists all agree?" Although the discipline of anthropology is less than 150 years old, we still have a wide array of theoretical approaches. In this anthology, we attempt to give a representative sample of major contributions to theory in anthropology. One reason that we have so many approaches is due to the breadth of the field of anthropology. Since we try to understand humanity in all of its dimensions, it is not surprising that many debates have arisen in attempting to develop a comprehensive understanding of human culture. A second reason is that cultural anthropology deals with understanding thousands of cultures around the globe. While many patterns do emerge demonstrating similarities in human beings everywhere, there is also a tremendous amount of diversity. It is not easy to formulate a single theory to accommodate so many human differences. For example, an ecological theory that explains the behavior of the Inuit in the Arctic may not apply to the Jul'hoansi of the Kalahari desert. Differences in anthropological explanations may not be so much a matter of their being "right" or "wrong" but rather that varying theoretical approaches have varying explanatory power depending on the culturally-specific context. However, the aim of this book is not to prove one theory or another, but to expose the reader to many different ideas and perspectives on the human experience. In cultural anthropology, the goal is often not so much to provide answers but to raise questions. Ultimately, it is hoped that the articles contained in this volume will lead to increased curiosity and understanding about other cultures, and hopefully, a critical examination of how the reader's own culture has shaped his or her values, norms, beliefs, and behaviors.

Part I

The Subject of Anthropology

Learning to Love Neanderthals

By Robert Kunzig

What you want, when you hold a pendant fashioned 35,000 years ago by a Neanderthal—a fox's tooth with a tiny hole for a leather string—what you want is something only the movies can give. A close-up, in the lab's neon light, on the mottled canine between your fingers, the focus so tight you can see the scratches made by the stone tool. The picture fades, and next you see the same tooth in different hands, stronger ones with beefy fingers: the hands of the craftsman. He is piercing the tooth with a sharpened piece of flint. Behind him squats a rough tent of hides stretched over mammoth tusks; behind that the dark mouth of a cave. Before and below him a river meanders lazily between birches and willows. Reindeer graze on the far bank. On an early morning in spring, in northern Burgundy during the Ice Age, the light coming in low over the far bluff catches the craftsman's pale, weathered face. It is a human face. The eyes, under the jutting brow, are human eyes, alive with concentration, with memories of other seasons at this place, with intelligence and hope.

No, hold it: Maybe those Neanderthal eyes are blank as a cat's, all surface, with nothing behind them but dumb instinct and a bit of animal cunning—no memories, no plan, no clue.

Back to spring 1999 and the lab, at a modern campus of the University of Paris. An archeologist named Dominique Baffier holds the tooth. For the past few days newspapers the world over have been reporting the discovery in Portugal of the skeleton of a 4-year-old child, dead for 25,000 years. The discoverers, led by Portuguese archeologist João Zilhão, are making a groundbreaking claim, that the skeleton shows traces of both Neanderthal and modern human ancestry, evidence that modern humans did not simply extinguish the Neanderthals, as many researchers had come to think. Instead the two kinds of human were so alike that in Portugal, at least, they intermingled—and made love—for thousands of years.

The claim is controversial. So, too, and for similar reasons, is the fox tooth Baffier is holding. A collection of such ornaments is arrayed on the table in front of her, along with delicate bone tools—awls for punching through animal hides, needles for sewing or perhaps for pinning up hair. All these artifacts were dug from the mouth of a limestone cave four decades ago at Arcy-sur-Cure, a hundred miles southeast of Paris. Just in the past year, though, the Arcy artifacts have become the subject of heated debate. Zilhão, Baffier, and several French colleagues claim the artifacts show that Neanderthals were not inferior to our ancestors, the Cro-Magnons. Independently, they underwent the same leap into modernity, the same emergence of symbolic thought that millennia later allowed Cro-Magnons to paint on cave walls.

A fox-tooth pendant is not a cave painting, as Baffier well knows, for she studies those paintings too. But it is a symbolic statement. "Oh, it's beautiful," she says quietly, turning the Neanderthal pendant in her fingers, peering at it over her glasses. "It's beautiful and it's moving. A 35,000-year-old bijou—isn't that moving?"

João Zilhão, director of the Portuguese Institute of Archeology, got the call from his wife and fellow archeologist, Cristina Araújo, while he was at a conference in Japan. She had heard from João Maurício and Pedro Souto, coworkers at a Neanderthal cave site. They had heard from a student named Pedro Ferreira, who had gone looking for rock art in the Lapedo Valley, about 90 miles north of Lisbon, and had found some small paintings.

Last November 28, Maurício and Souto went to the Lapedo Valley—which is really a small, steep ravine, a bit over a mile long and a stone's-throw wide. Olive groves and wildflowers, vegetable fields and villages sprawl up to the lip of the canyon, but its cool, lush depths are a world apart. The small stream at the bottom, the Caranguejeira, is hidden by reeds and bushes; the canyon walls themselves are practically hidden by a riot of diverse greenery.

Ferreira showed Maurício and Souto his rock art, and they confirmed that it looked man-made and old (Copper Age, it turned out). Then they looked across the ravine to the south side. Above the treetops they could see a limestone wall leaning out over the canyon. Prehistoric humans liked to take shelter under overhanging rocks like that. Maurício and Souto decided to have a look.

They found a mess, construction debris strewn along the base of the cliff, including an abandoned trailer, an old tractor hood, and a giant section of concrete drainpipe. In a fissure in the wall, just above eye level, Maurício and Souto saw sediments laced with stone tools, lots of animal bones, and black flecks of charcoal—the remains of Paleolithic campfires. But all along the wall they could also see the white gouge marks left by the teeth of a steam shovel. To build a road, the owner of the area had created a flat terrace where before there had been a tall slope of sediment—sediment that had washed off the top of the cliff and collected at the base over tens of millennia. He had used a stream shovel to dig the dirt from the cliff.

In retrospect the demolition man did archeology a big favor. Otherwise, what is now the base of the cliff at Lapedo would still be buried. Maurício saw a rabbit burrow disappearing under the rock. He reached his hand in and pulled out a radius and an ulna—the bones of a human forearm, though he wasn't sure of that at the time.

When the news reached Zilhão, he called Cidália Duarte, a physical anthropologist at the Portuguese Institute of Architectural Heritage. They and Araújo went up to Lapedo the next weekend. While Zilhão examined the stone tools embedded in the cliff face seven feet up. Maurício took the bone lady to the bones in the burrow. "I looked at them," Duarte recalls, "and I said, 'Ooh—this is human! This is a kid!'" Meanwhile, Zilhão was looking at the stratigraphic sequence. He began to add it up: "If the kid is down there, and this up here is Solutrean ..."

Solutrean is the third of four successive cultures—Aurignacian, Gravetian, Solutrean, Magdalenian—of the Upper Paleolithic or Late Stone Age. The Solutrean happened around 20,000 years ago. If the Lapedo Valley kid was seven feet below Solutrean sediments, that suggested he died thousands of years before the Solutrean. Zilhão looked at the bones: They were stained reddish with ochre. Red ochre is one of the things Upper Paleolithic moderns painted caves with, but they also buried their dead with it; the color seems to have had symbolic significance.

"So I immediately recognized that something big was there," says Zilhão. "The question was whether the bulldozing had completely destroyed the burial, and all we had to do was collect the fragments, or if something was still there intact."

The next day, Monday, they went back to their day jobs in Lisbon. The following Friday evening they were back at Lapedo, with Duarte and Araújo digging. "By Sunday evening we were really upset, because all we could find were bits and pieces, fragments of bone, and they didn't even have this reddish color," Duarte recalls. With night falling and spirits crumbling, they started tidying up the dig. Those final offhand brushstrokes did it: The red began to appear. Soon, as Araújo and Duarte gently swept away more dirt, they saw a patch of sediment as red as wine and as large as ... a small child.

Now they faced a paleontological emergency: The skeleton was almost at the surface, exposed to the elements, which in this case included Boy Scouts. A troop had walked by during the weekend and regarded the diggers with ominous curiosity. That week Durate signed up for an unscheduled vacation. Zilhão quietly abandoned his airy director's office and his paperwork at the archeological institute. "I just went away without telling anybody," he says, "so as not to run the risk of a leak."

They started digging in earnest. Right away they realized how lucky they had been: In removing tens of feet of dirt, the steam shovel had missed by just a few inches the body of the child. Unfortunately it had not missed the skull—Duarte could only find fragments of that. One of the first, though, was a beauty: the left half of the lower jaw, including teeth. It had a sharply pointed chin, which is just what you would expect from a Cro-Magnon; Neanderthals had weak chins.

The child was lying on its back, with its head and torso tilted a bit to its left, toward the cliff, and its right hand on its pelvis. Its right side was crushed, but the left side was intact. Ribs, vertebrae, pelvis, fingers, toes, the long bones of the arms and legs—all were there. Duarte and Araújo worked steadily through the Christmas holidays, hiding their work every night under the old tractor hood. Soon they had a new problem: up to 500 visitors a day. Zilhão's desire to keep the excavation secret had run into his desire to have it documented. He had asked Portuguese public television to videotape it, which the TV folk were happy to do—provided they could also run the story. On Christmas Day it opened the evening news: "A Child is Born."

On Christmas Day itself, Duarte was at the site alone. "I wasn't going to leave it there all exposed," she says. The work that day, on the rib cage, was particularly delicate. She was digging with a syringe, squirting acetone around the bones to dissolve the dirt—acetone evaporates quickly, so it doesn't soak the bone—and then removing it with a paintbrush and a plastic spoon. She was squatting, kneeling, and sometimes lying on her side next to the Kid. Earlier, near the clavicle, she had found a tiny seashell, covered with red ochre, with a minute hole. The Kid had worn it as a pendant.

At first Zilhão and Duarte guessed they had excavated a boy. The arms and legs looked robust. But then Erik Trinkaus, a paleoanthropologist at Washington University in St. Louis, had a look at them. He decided the Kid was robust not because he was male, but because he had Neanderthal blood.

Trinkaus is a leading authority on both Neanderthal and early modern human anatomy. When the excavation started, Zilhão let him know right away. "João went out and got a digital camera and started e-mailing me images," Trinkaus says. He got excited too: While Upper Paleolithic skeletons in general are rare, there are no reasonably complete children's skeletons at all. Right after New Year's, while Duarte was still excavating, Trinkaus hopped a plane to Portugal.

He measured all the bones he could, especially the limbs—his specialty. In 1981, Trinkaus published a paper on limb evolution that is still cited. In it he documented a geographic pattern in people today: They get shorter the farther they are from the tropics and the closer they are to the poles. More precisely, their extremities get shorter. Inuits and Lapps have shorter forearms relative to their upper arms and shorter shin-bones relative to their thighbones than do the Masai of East Africa. There is a simple explanation: Shorter, stockier bodies fare better in cold climates because they have less surface area to radiate heat. By measuring fossil limbs, Trinkaus showed that Neanderthals, denizens of Ice Age Europe, were hyperarctic—they had an even smaller shinbone-thighbone ratio than do

Lapps. Early moderns from the Near East and Europe, on the other hand, were decidedly tropical in their legginess, like Africans today.

This was some of the earliest evidence for a theory of human origins that had not even been formulated then, but has since become orthodoxy. The out-of-Africa theory holds that humans today are descended from a small population of (long-legged) early moderns that walked out of Africa around 100,000 years ago. As they spread all over the world, they replaced whatever archaic humans they met, which in Europe were the Neanderthals. In this view, Neanderthals are a distinct population and maybe even a distinct species that went extinct at the hands of our ancestors, leaving no legacy at all.

Two years ago, when a team led by Svante Pääbo, now of the Max Planck Institute for Evolutionary Anthropology in Leipzig, isolated DNA from a Neanderthal bone, many people thought the case had been clinched. The Neanderthal DNA was different enough that there seemed to be no trace of it in modern DNA; it suggested that Neanderthal and modern humans had evolved separately for half a million years and were unlikely to have interbred. Trinkaus was not moved: "There's a general impression that if something comes out of a million-dollar machine, then it's truth, whereas if something comes out of a bunch of dirty old bones that we clean with paintbrushes, then it's vague and ambiguous."

Based on his analysis of dirty bones from the Czech Republic and Croatia, Trinkaus has long favored a sort of watered-down out of Africa, in which the gene pool of modern humans migrating into Europe was seasoned by interbreeding with Neanderthals. The amount of interbreeding would have varied from place to place. One place Trinkaus didn't expect to see much, though, was on the Iberian peninsula, the last refuge of the Neanderthals.

Cro-Magnons reached northern Spain nearly 40,000 years ago, but for some reason they didn't spread south for another 10,000 years. By the time they crossed the Ebro frontier, as Zilhão has dubbed it after the large river in northern Spain, their kind had already executed striking cave paintings. South of the Ebro they encountered Neanderthals who were still making stone tools in the Middle Paleolithic fashion and not making ornaments at all. The better-armed modern invaders would have been almost as tall as the Masai and maybe as black; the indigenes would have been short and as pale as Lapps. It would be easy to picture the former simply wiping out the latter. But it is from this clash of cultures and anatomies, Trinkaus argues, that the Kid was born.

The sharp point of the Kid's chin screamed Cro-Magnon. So did the relatively small front teeth: Neanderthal front teeth were large compared with their molars. So did the red ochre burial style. And so, finally, did the radiocarbon date: At 24,500 years old, it was much younger than the last signs of Neanderthals.

But when Trinkaus measured the angle between the horizontal tooth line and the vertical line from the frontmost tooth down to the chin, the symphyseal angle, he got a clue that this was a strange Cro-Magnon. Instead of jutting forward of the teeth, the chin retreated a shade behind them. Cro-Magnon chins didn't do that, Trinkaus says, but Neanderthal chins did.

Even more significant, he thinks, are the limb proportions. Trinkaus measured the shinbone and the thighbone and found that the ratio fell way over at the Neanderthal end of the curve. He compared the circumference of the bones with their length, and found that the child had leg bones strong enough to support a stocky Neanderthal body. The limb proportions along with the receding chin are enough, Trinkaus says, to prove the child had Neanderthal ancestors as well as Cro-Magnon ones. "It only takes one feature," he says. "We've got two."

But many of his peers are skeptical. Arctic limb proportions don't prove a Neanderthal influence, some argue, since Lapps have them too; maybe the Kid was just an ordinary Cro-Magnon who had adapted to the Ice Age. And the mere fact that the skeleton is that of a child—whose features were still changing, and for whom no good Cro-Magnon comparisons exist—makes some researchers uneasy. "If an adult skeleton had been found, nice and complete, I'm sure we would still have fierce discussions," says Jean-Jacques Hublin of the French National Center for Scientific Research. "But interpreting the remains of a child, of which almost none of the skull is left—that's really a perilous exercise."

This summer, as the dig progresses, Duarte will be looking for more pieces of the child's skull. Finding its two front teeth would be nice (Neanderthals had big ones), or the occipital bone in the rear of the skull (it bulged out in Neanderthals), or even the tiny labyrinth of the inner ear. Hublin has used that feature, and that feature alone, to diagnose a Neanderthal bone at Arcy-sur-Cure.

Duarte also hopes to find the Kid's parents; Upper Paleolithic burials often come in groups. But Trinkaus does not expect she will find a Neanderthal mom and a Cro-Magnon dad. Zilhão's archeological evidence suggests the Kid was born at least two millennia after Neanderthals and Cro-Magnons first met in Portugal. The Kid, Trinkaus argues, must be the product of interbreeding over that entire period, not a one-time hybrid produced by star-crossed lovers. "This is not just two individuals who happened to meet in the bushes," he says.

There is likely to be fierce discussion about that conclusion too. The out-of-Africa model can readily tolerate a little hanky-panky between Neanderthals and Cro-Magnons. "In fact I expect it," says Hublin. A few hybrids would even disprove the view that Neanderthals were a different species. Animals of closely related species can sometimes interbreed, and sometimes the offspring are even fertile.

But if whole populations of Neanderthals and Cro-Magnons were blending, the notion that Neanderthals were replaced by immigrant moderns begins to lose meaning. To out-of-Africa proponents, such blending would conflict with the genetic and fossil evidence, and with the simple observation that people today look like Cro-Magnons and not like Neanderthals. To paleontologists who don't believe the out-of-Africa model, however—

who think modern humans evolved all over the world from interbreeding populations of archaic humans including Neanderthals—Trinkaus's Lapedo kid is welcome news.

Trinkaus himself has never taken sides in this bitter debate. He sees it now moving onto his middle ground: A migration out of Africa happened, sure, but the migrants also interbred to varying degrees with the people they met along the way. Neanderthals are not us, but neither are they an evolutionary dead end—the Kid, if he is right, puts the truth in the middle. "Trinkaus is in the stratosphere," says Zilhão. "He has believed this for a long time. I couldn't care less—they could just as well be different species as far as I'm concerned. This just comes in handy."

It comes in handy as ammunition in a separate fight that is Zilhão's own. That debate concerns how smart Neanderthals were, and it is centered on the cave digs at Arcy. When French archeologists excavated there in the 1950s, they found dozens of animal-tooth pendants, bone tools, and 40 pounds of red ochre spread over the floor. At other sites, such artifacts have been attributed to modern humans. A few years ago, though, after Hublin CT-scanned a skull fragment found alongside the artifacts, and revealed the inner ear, he convinced most people that the bone was that of a Neanderthal, and so were the artifacts.

The conventional explanation is that the Neanderthal craftsmen at Arcy must have been imitating our ancestors. Modern humans were invading western Europe at around the time—35,000 to 45,000 years ago—when the Neanderthals were at Arcy. And whereas the few dozen ornaments found there are practically the only ones attributed to Neanderthals, thousands have been found at Cro-Magnon sites. Many researchers say it is common sense to assume that Neanderthals were "acculturated" by Cro-Magnons. Some even argue that the Neanderthals didn't really understand what they were doing. They copied such modern behaviors as wearing pendants, but they couldn't appreciate the symbolic meaning.

Lurking under all this is the question of why we survived and the Neanderthals didn't: Was it because their brains were inferior? That idea drives Zilhão up the wall. "What's involved here is not the wiring of the brain cells, it's the wiring of the brains into what we call culture," he says. "Forty thousand years ago, people couldn't read or write—are we saying they didn't have the intelligence?"

In a controversial paper published last year with Francesco d'Errico of the University of Bordeaux, and Dominique Baffier, Michele Julien, and Jacques Pelegrin of the University of Paris, Zilhão tried to show that the Neanderthals were intelligent enough to make the Arcy artifacts—and thus the transition to Upper Paleolithic modernity—all by themselves. The Arcy Neanderthals, the researchers argued, made their tools and ornaments using techniques quite unlike those of the moderns—punching a clean hole through a fox tooth, for instance, whereas modern humans did a cruder job of gouging. Zilhão and d'Errico also claim to have proved, through a technical reanalysis of the highly uncertain dates attributed to nearly every relevant site in western Europe, that the Neanderthals couldn't have imitated Cro-Magnons—because they were acting modern thousands of years before any Cro-Magnons were around.

The Lapedo Valley kid drops into the murky waters of this debate like a cannonball. Some researchers say it makes no difference at all if the Kid is a hybrid. But if Trinkaus and Zilhão can prove that modern humans and Neanderthals mixed extensively in Portugal, it would surely affect our view of Neanderthals—by giving us an inkling of the view our ancestors held. Would they really have fraternized with beings who were too dim to understand the purpose of a necklace?

"If you have two populations of hunter-gatherers that are totally different species, that are doing things in very different ways, have different capabilities—they're not going to blend together," Trinkaus says. "They're going to remain separate. So the implication from Portugal is that when these people met, they viewed each other as people. One group may have looked a little funny to the other one—but beyond that they saw each other as human beings. And treated each other as such."

CRITICAL THINKING QUESTIONS

1. Recent physical anthropological theory suggests that modern humans had at least a role in the extinction of the Neanderthals. What new theory do the bones of the four-year-old child excavated in Portugal suggest?

2. What problems did Zilhão and his team face during the excavation of the child?

3. What physical attributes did the child's skeleton exhibit to suggest he may have been a Neanderthal/modern human hybrid?

4. What evidence is being debated regarding the intellectual capacities of the Neanderthals? What significance does this debate have to understanding our own humanity?

Deep Play

Notes on the Balinese Cockfight

Clifford Geertz

THE RAID

Early in April of 1958, my wife and I arrived, malarial and diffident, in a Balinese village we intended, as anthropologists, to study. A small place, about five hundred people, and relatively remote, it was its own world. We were intruders, professional ones, and the villagers dealt with us as Balinese seem always to deal with people not part of their life who yet press themselves upon them: as though we were not there. For them, and to a degree for ourselves, we were nonpersons, specters, invisible men.

We moved into an extended family compound (that had been arranged before through the provincial government) belonging to one of the four major factions in village life. But except for our landlord and the village chief, whose cousin and brother-in-law he was, everyone ignored us in a way only a Balinese can do. As we wandered around, uncertain, wistful, eager to please, people seemed to look right through us with a gaze focused several yards behind us on some more actual stone or tree. Almost nobody greeted us; but nobody scowled or said anything unpleasant to us either, which would have been almost as satisfactory. If we ventured to approach someone (something one is powerfully inhibited from doing in such an atmosphere), he moved, negligently but definitely, away. If seated or leaning against a wall, we had him trapped, he said nothing at all, or mumbled what for the Balinese is the ultimate nonword—"yes." The indifference, of course, was studied; the

Clifford Geertz, "Deep Play: Notes on the Balinese Cockfight," from *Daedalus*, vol. 101; Winter 1972, pp. 1–37. Published by American Academy of Arts and Sciences. Copyright © 1972 by MIT Press. Permission to reprint granted by the rights holder.

villagers were watching every move we made, and they had an enormous amount of quite accurate information about who we were and what we were going to be doing. But they acted as if we simply did not exist, which, in fact, as this behavior was designed to inform us, we did not, or anyway not yet.

This is, as I say, general in Bali. Everywhere else I have been in Indonesia, and more latterly in Morocco, when I have gone into a new village, people have poured out from all sides to take a very close look at me, and, often an all-too-probing feel as well. In Balinese villages, at least those away from the tourist circuit, nothing happens at all. People go on pounding, chatting, making offerings, staring into space, carrying baskets about while one drifts around feeling vaguely disembodied. And the same thing is true on the individual level. When you first meet a Balinese, he seems virtually not to relate to you at all; he is, in the term Gregory Bateson and Margaret Mead made famous, "away."[1] Then—in a day, a week, a month (with some people the magic moment never comes)—he decides, for reasons I have never quite been able to fathom, that you *are* real, and then he becomes a warm, gay, sensitive, sympathetic, though, being Balinese, always precisely controlled, person. You have crossed, somehow, some moral or metaphysical shadow line. Though you are not exactly taken as a Balinese (one has to be born to that), you are at least regarded as a human being rather than a cloud or a gust of wind. The whole complexion of your relationship dramatically changes to, in the majority of cases, a gentle, almost affectionate one—a low-keyed, rather playful, rather mannered, rather bemused geniality.

My wife and I were still very much in the gust-of-wind stage, a most frustrating, and even, as you soon begin to doubt whether you are really real after all, unnerving one, when, Jen days or so after our arrival, a large cockfight was held in the public square to raise money for a new school.

Now, a few special occasions aside, cockfights are illegal in Bali under the Republic (as, for not altogether unrelated reasons, they were under the Dutch), largely as a result of the pretensions to puritanism radical nationalism tends to bring with it. The elite, which is not itself so very puritan, worries about the poor, ignorant peasant gambling all his money away, about what foreigners will think, about the waste of time better devoted to building up the country. It sees cockfighting as "primitive," "backward," "unprogressive," and generally unbecoming an ambitious nation. And, as with those other embarrassments—opium smoking, begging, or uncovered breasts—it seeks, rather unsystematically, to put a stop to it.

Of course, like drinking during Prohibition or, today, smoking marihuana, cockfights, being a part of "The Balinese Way of Life," nonetheless go on happening, and with extraordinary frequency. And, as with Prohibition or marihuana, from time to time the police (who, in 1958 at least, were almost all not Balinese but Javanese) feel called upon to make a raid, confiscate the cocks and spurs, fine a few people, and even now and then expose

---

[1] G. Bateson and M. Mead, *Balinese Character: A Photographic Analysis* (New York, 1942), p. 68.

some of them in the tropical sun for a day as object lessons which never, somehow, get learned, even though occasionally, quite occasionally, the object dies.

As a result, the fights are usually held in a secluded corner of a village in semisecrecy, a fact which tends to slow the action a little—not very much, but the Balinese do not care to have it slowed at all. In this case, however, perhaps because they were raising money for a school that the government was unable to give them, perhaps because raids had been few recently, perhaps, as I gathered from subsequent discussion, there was a notion that the necessary bribes had been paid, they thought they could take a chance on the central square and draw a larger and more enthusiastic crowd without attracting the attention of the law.

They were wrong. In the midst of the third match, with hundreds of people, including, still transparent, myself and my wife, fused into a single body around the ring, a superorganism in the literal sense, a truck full of policemen armed with machine guns roared up. Amid great screeching cries of "pulisi! pulisi!" from the crowd, the policemen jumped out, and, springing into the center of the ring, began to swing their guns around like gangsters in a motion picture, though not going so far as actually to fire them. The superorganism came instantly apart as its components scattered in all directions. People raced down the road, disappeared headfirst over walls, scrambled under platforms, folded themselves behind wicker screens, scuttled up coconut trees. Cocks armed with steel spurs sharp enough to cut off a finger or run a hole through a foot were running wildly around. Everything was dust and panic.

On the established anthropological principle, "When in Rome, my wife and I decided, only slightly less instantaneously than everyone else, that the thing to do was run too. We ran down the main village street, northward, away from where we were living, for we were on that side of the ring. About halfway down another fugitive ducked suddenly into a compound—his own, it turned out—and we, seeing nothing ahead of us but rice fields, open country, and a very high volcano, followed him. As the three of us came tumbling into the courtyard, his wife, who had apparently been through this sort of thing before, whipped out a table, a tablecloth, three chairs, and three cups of tea, and we all, without any explicit communication whatsoever, sat down, commenced to sip tea, and sought to compose ourselves.

A few moments later, one of the policemen marched importantly into the yard, looking for the village chief. (The chief had not only been at the fight, he had arranged it. When the truck drove up he ran to the river, stripped off his sarong, and plunged in so he could say, when at length they found him sitting there pouring water over his head, that he had been away bathing when the whole affair had occurred and was ignorant of it. They did not believe him and fined him three hundred rupiah, which the village raised collectively.) Seeing me and my wife, "White Men," there in the yard, the policeman performed a classic double take. When he found his voice again he asked, approximately, what in the devil did we think we were doing there. Our host of five minutes leaped instantly to our defense, producing an impassioned description of who and what we were, so detailed and so accurate that it was my turn, having barely communicated with a living human being save my landlord and the village chief for more than a week, to be astonished. We had a perfect right to be there, he said, looking the Javanese upstart in the eye. We were American professors; the government had cleared us; we were there to study culture; we were going to write a book to tell Americans about Bali. And we had all been there drinking tea and talking about cultural matters all afternoon and did not know anything about any cockfight. Moreover, we had not seen the village chief all day; he must have gone to town. The policeman retreated in rather total disarray. And, after a decent interval, bewildered but relieved to have survived and stayed out of jail, so did we.

The next morning the village was a completely different world for us. Not only were we no longer invisible, we were suddenly the center of all attention, the object of a great outpouring of warmth, interest, and most especially, amusement. Everyone in the village knew we had fled like everyone else. They asked us about it again and again (I must have told the story, small detail by small detail, fifty times by the end of the day), gently, affectionately, but quite insistently teasing us: "Why didn't you just stand there and tell the police who you were?" "Why didn't you just say you were only watching and not betting?" "Were you really afraid of those little guns?" As always, kinesthetically minded and, even when fleeing for their lives (or, as happened eight years later, surrendering them), the world's most poised people, they gleefully mimicked, also over and over again, our graceless style of running and what they claimed were our panic-stricken facial expressions. But above all, everyone was extremely pleased and even more surprised that we had not simply "pulled out our papers" (they knew about those too) and asserted our Distinguished Visitor status, but had instead demonstrated our solidarity with what were now our covillagers. (What we had actually demonstrated was our cowardice, but there is fellowship in that too.) Even the Brahmana priest, an old, grave, halfway-to-heaven type who because of its associations with the underworld would never be involved, even distantly, in a cockfight, and was difficult to approach even to other Balinese, had us called into his courtyard to ask us about what had happened, chuckling happily at the sheer extraordinariness of it all.

In Bali, to be teased is to be accepted. It was the turning point so far as our relationship to the community was concerned, and we were quite literally "in." The whole village opened up to us, probably more than it ever would have otherwise (I might actually never have gotten to that priest, and our accidental host became one of my best informants), and certainly very much faster. Getting caught, or almost caught, in a vice raid is perhaps not a very generalizable recipe for achieving that mysterious necessity of anthropological field work, rapport, but for me it worked very well. It led to a sudden and unusually complete acceptance into a society extremely difficult for outsiders to penetrate. It gave me the kind of immediate, inside-view grasp of an aspect of "peasant mentality" that anthropologists not fortunate enough to flee headlong with their subjects from armed authorities normally do not get. And, perhaps most important of all, for the other things might have come in other ways, it put me very quickly on to a combination emotional explosion, status war, and philosophical drama of central significance to the society whose inner nature I desired to understand. By the time I left I had spent about as much time looking into cockfights as into witchcraft, irrigation, caste, or marriage.

OF COCKS AND MEN

Bali, mainly because it is Bali, is a well-studied place. Its mythology, art, ritual, social organization, patterns of child rearing, forms of law, even styles of trance, have all been microscopically examined for traces of that elusive substance Jane Belo called "The Balinese Temper."[2] But, aside from a few passing remarks, the cockfight has barely been noticed, although as a popular obsession of consuming power it is at least as important a revelation of what being a Balinese "is really like" as these more celebrated phenomena.[3] As much of America surfaces in a ball park, on a golf links, at a race track, or around a poker table, much of Bali surfaces in a cock ring. For it is only apparently cocks that are fighting there. Actually, it is men.

To anyone who has been in Bali any length of time, the deep psychological identification of Balinese men with their cocks is unmistakable. The double entendre here is deliberate. It works in exactly the same way in Balinese as it does in English, even to producing the same tired jokes, strained puns, and uninventive obscenities. Bateson and Mead have even suggested that, in line with the Balinese conception of the body as a set of separately animated parts, cocks are viewed as detachable, self-operating penises, ambulant genitals with a life of their own.[4] And while I do not have the kind of unconscious material either to confirm or disconfirm this intriguing notion, the fact that they are masculine symbols

---

[2] J. Belo, "The Balinese Temper," in *Traditional Balinese Culture,* ed. J. Belo (New York, 1970) (originally published in 1935), pp. 85–110.

[3] The best discussion of cockfighting is again Bateson and Mead's *Balinese Character,* pp. 24–25, 140; but it, too, is general and abbreviated.

[4] Ibid., pp. 25–26. The cockfight is unusual within Balinese culture in being a single-sex public activity from which the other sex is totally and expressly excluded. Sexual differentiation is culturally extremely played down in Bali and most activities, formal and informal, involve the participation of men and women on equal ground, commonly as linked couples. From religion, to politics, to economics, to kinship, to dress, Bali is a rather "unisex" society, a fact both its customs and its symbolism clearly express. Even in contexts where women do not in fact play much of a role—music, painting, certain agricultural activities—their absence, which is only relative in any case, is more a mere matter of fact than socially enforced. To this general pattern, the cockfight, entirely of, by, and for men (women—at least *Balinese* women—do not even watch), is the most striking exception.

par excellence is about as indubitable, and to the Balinese about as evident, as the fact that water runs downhill.

The language of everyday moralism is shot through, on the male side of it, with rooster-ish imagery. *Sabung,* the word for cock (and one which appears in inscriptions as early as A.D. 922), is used metaphorically to mean "hero," "warrior," "champion," "man of parts," "political candidate," "bachelor," "dandy," "lady-killer," or "tough guy." A pompous man whose behavior presumes above his station is compared to a tailless cock who struts about as though he had a large, spectacular one. A desperate man who makes a last, irrational effort to extricate himself from an impossible situation is likened to a dying cock who makes one final lunge at his tormentor to drag him along to a common destruction. A stingy man, who promises much, gives little, and begrudges that, is compared to a cock which, held by the tail, leaps at another without in fact engaging him. A marriageable young man still shy with the opposite sex or someone in a new job anxious to make a good impression is called "a fighting cock caged for the first time,"[5] Court trials, wars, political contests, inheritance disputes, and street arguments are all compared to cockfights.[6] Even the very island itself is perceived from its shape as a small, proud cock, poised, neck extended, back taut, tail raised, in eternal challenge to large, feckless, shapeless Java.[7]

But the intimacy of men with their cocks is more than metaphorical. Balinese men, or anyway a large majority of Balinese men, spend an enormous amount of time with their favorites, grooming them, feeding them, discussing them, trying them out against one another, or just gazing at them with a mixture of rapt admiration and dreamy self-absorption. Whenever you see a group of Balinese men squatting idly in the council shed or along the road in their hips down, shoulders forward, knees up fashion, half or more of them will have a rooster in his hands, holding it between his thighs, bouncing it gently up and down to strengthen its legs, ruffling its feathers with abstract sensuality, pushing it out against a neighbor's rooster to rouse its spirit, withdrawing it toward his loins to calm it again. Now and then, to get a feel for another bird, a man will fiddle this way with someone else's cock for a while, but usually by moving around to squat in place behind it, rather than just having it passed across to him as though it were merely an animal.

---

[5] C Hooykaas, *The Lay of the Jaya Prana* (London, 1958), p. 39. The lay has a stanza (no. 17) with the reluctant bridge groom use. Jaya Prana, the subject of a Balinese Uriah myth, responds to the lord who has offered him the loveliest of six hundred servant girls: "Godly King, my Lord and Master/I beg you, give me leave to go/such things are not yet in my mind;/like a fighting cock encaged/indeed I am on my mettle/I am alone/as yet the flame has not been fanned."

[6] For these, see V. E. Korn, *Het Adatmcht van Bali,* 2d ed. (The Hague 1932) index under *toh.*

[7] There is indeed a legend to the effect that the separation of Java and Bali is due to the action of a powerful Javanese religious figure who wished to protect himself against a Balinese culture hero (the ancestor of two Ksatria castes) who was a passionate cockfighting gambler. See C. Hooykaas, *Agama Tinha* (Amster dam, 1964), p. 184.

In the houseyard, the high-walled enclosures where the people live, fighting cocks are kept in wicker cages, moved frequently about so as to maintain the optimum balance of sun and shade. They are fed a special diet, which varies somewhat according to individual theories but which is mostly maize, sifted for impurities with far more care than it is when mere humans are going to eat it, and offered to the animal kernel by kernel. Red pepper is stuffed down their beaks and up their anuses to give them spirit. They are bathed in the same ceremonial preparation of tepid water, medicinal herbs, flowers, and onions in which infants are bathed, and for a prize cock just about as often. Their combs are cropped, their plumage dressed, their spurs trimmed, and their legs massaged, and they are inspected for flaws with the squinted concentration of a diamond merchant, A man who has a passion for cocks, an enthusiast in the literal sense of the term, can spend most of his life with them, and even those, the overwhelming majority, whose passion though intense has not entirely run away with them, can and do spend what seems not only to an outsider, but also to themselves, an inordinate amount of time with them. "I am cock crazy," my landlord, a quite ordinary *officionado* by Balinese standards, used to moan as he went to move another cage, give another bath, or conduct another feeding. "We're all cock crazy."

The madness has some less visible dimensions, however, because although it is true that cocks are symbolic expressions or magnifications of their owner's self, the narcissistic male ego writ out in Aesopian terms, they are also expressions—and rather more immediate ones—of what the Balinese regard as the direct inversion, aesthetically, morally, and metaphysically, of human status: animality.

The Balinese revulsion against any behavior regarded as animal like can hardly be overstressed. Babies are not allowed to crawl for that reason. Incest, though hardly approved, is a much less horrifying crime than bestiality. (The appropriate punishment for the second is death by drowning, for the first being forced to live like an animal.)[8] Most demons are represented—in sculpture, dance, ritual, myth—in some real or fantastic animal form. The main puberty rite consists in filing the child's teeth so they will not look like animal fangs. Not only defecation but eating is regarded as a disgusting, almost obscene activity, to be conducted hurriedly and privately, because of its association with animality. Even falling down or any form of clumsiness is considered to be bad for these reasons. Aside from cocks and a few domestic animals—oxen, ducks—of no emotional significance, the Balinese are aversive to animals and treat their large number of dogs not merely callously but with a phobic cruelty. In identifying with his cock, the Balinese man is identifying not just with his ideal self, or even his penis, but also, and at the same time,

[8] An incestuous couple is forced to wear pig yokes over their necks and crawl to a pig trough and eat with their mouths there. On this, see J. Belo, "Customs Pertaining to Twins in Bali," in *Traditional Balinese Culture*, ed. J. Belo, p. 49; on the abhorrence of animality generally, Bateson and Mead, *Balinese Character*, p. 22.

with what he most fears, hates, and ambivalence being what it is, is fascinated by—"The Powers of Darkness."

The connection of cocks and cockfighting with such Powers, with the animalistic demons that threaten constantly to invade the small, cleared-off space in which the Balinese have so carefully built their lives and devour its inhabitants, is quite explicit. A cockfight, any cockfight, is in the first instance a blood sacrifice offered, with the appropriate chants and oblations, to the demons in order to pacify their ravenous, cannibal hunger. No temple festival should be conducted until one is made. (If it is omitted, someone will inevitably fall into a trance and command with the voice of an angered spirit that the oversight be immediately corrected.) Collective responses to natural evils—illness, crop failure, volcanic eruptions—almost always involve them. And that famous holiday in Bali, "The Day of Silence" *(Njepi),* when everyone sits silent and immobile all day long in order to avoid contact with a sudden influx of demons chased momentarily out of hell, is preceded the previous day by large-scale cockfights (in this case legal) in almost every village on the island.

In the cockfight, man and beast, good and evil, ego and id, the creative power of aroused masculinity and the destructive power of loosened animality fuse in a bloody drama of hatred, cruelty, violence, and death. It is little wonder that when, as is the invariable rule, the owner of the winning cock takes, the carcass of the loser—often torn limb from limb by its enraged, owner—home to eat, he does so with a mixture of social embarrassment, moral satisfaction, aesthetic disgust, and cannibal joy. Or that a man who has lost an important fight is sometimes driven to wreck his family shrines and curse the gods, an act of metaphysical (and social) suicide. Or that in seeking earthly analogues for heaven and hell the Balinese compare the former to the mood of a man whose cock has just won, the latter to that of a man whose cock has just lost.

THE FIGHT

Cockfights (*tetadjen; sabungan*) are held in a ring about fifty feet square. Usually they begin toward late afternoon and run three or four hours until sunset. About nine or ten separate matches (*sehet*) comprise a program. Each match is precisely like the others in general pattern: there is no main match, no connection between individual matches, no variation in their format, and each is arranged on a completely ad hoc basis. After a fight has ended and the emotional debris is cleaned away—the bets have been paid, the curses cursed, the carcasses possessed—seven, eight, perhaps even a dozen men slip negligently into the ring with a cock and seek to find there a logical opponent for it. This process, which rarely takes less than ten minutes, and often a good deal longer, is conducted in a very subdued, oblique, even dissembling manner. Those not immediately involved give it at best but disguised, sidelong attention; those who, embarrassedly, are, attempt to pretend somehow that the whole thing is not really happening.

A match made, the other hopefuls retire with the same deliberate indifference, and the selected cocks have their spurs *(tadji)* affixed—razor-sharp, pointed steel swords, four or five inches long. This is a delicate job which only a small proportion of men, a half-dozen or so in most villages, know how to do properly. The man who attaches the spurs also provides them, and if the rooster he assists wins, its owner awards him the spur-leg of the victim. The spurs are affixed by winding a long length of string around the foot of the spur and the leg of the cock. For reasons I shall come to presently, it is done somewhat differently from case to case, and is an obsessively deliberate affair. The lore about spurs is extensive—they are sharpened only at eclipses and the dark of the moon, should be kept out of the sight of women, and so forth. And they are handled, both in use and out, with the same curious combination of fussiness and sensuality the Balinese direct toward ritual objects generally.

The spurs affixed, the two cocks are placed by their handlers (who may or may not be their owners) facing one another in the center of the ring.[9] A coconut pierced with a small hole is placed in a pail of water, in which it takes about twenty-one seconds to sink, a period known as a *tjeng* and marked at beginning and end by the beating of a slit gong. During these twenty-one seconds the handlers *(pengangkeb)* are not permitted to touch their roosters. If, as sometimes happens, the animals have not fought during this time, they are picked up, fluffed, pulled, prodded, and otherwise insulted, and put back in the center of the ring and the process begins again. Sometimes they refuse to fight at all, or one keeps running away, in which case they are imprisoned together under a wicker cage, which usually gets them engaged.

Most of the time, in any case, the cocks fly almost immediately at one another in a wing-beating, head-thrusting, leg-kicking explosion of animal fury so pure, so absolute, and in its own way so beautiful, as to be almost abstract, a Platonic concept of hate. Within moments one or the other drives home a solid blow with his spur, The handler whose cock has delivered the blow immediately picks it up so that it will not get a return blow, for if he does not the match is likely to end in a mutually mortal tie as the two birds wildly hack each other to pieces. This is particularly true if, as often

---

[9] Except for unimportant, small-bet fights (on the question of fight "importance," see below) spur affixing is usually done by someone other than the owner. Whether the owner handles his own cock or not more or less depends on how skilled he is at it, a consideration whose importance is again relative to the importance of the fight. When spur affixers and cock handlers are someone other than the owner, they are almost always a quite close relative—a brother or cousin—or a very intimate friend of his. They are thus almost extensions of his personality, as the fact that all three will refer to the cock as "mine," say "I" fought So-and-So, and so on, demonstrates. Also, owner-handler-affixer triads tend to be fairly fixed, though individuals may participate in several and often exchange roles within a given one.

happens, the spur sticks in its victim's body, for then the aggressor is at the mercy of his wounded foe.

With the birds again in the hands of their handlers, the coconut is now sunk three times after which the cock which has landed the blow must be set down to show that he is firm, a fact he demonstrates by wandering idly around the ring for a coconut sink. The coconut is then sunk twice more and the fight must recommence.

During this interval, slightly over two minutes, the handler of the wounded cock has been working frantically over it, like a trainer patching a mauled boxer between rounds, to get it in shape for a last, desperate try for victory. He blows in its mouth, putting the whole chicken head in his own mouth and sucking and blowing, fluffs it, stuffs its wounds with various sorts of medicines, and generally tries anything he can think of to arouse the last ounce of spirit which may be hidden somewhere within it. By the time he is forced to put it back down he is usually drenched in chicken blood, but, as in prize fighting, a good handler is worth his weight in gold. Some of them can virtually make the dead walk, at least long enough for the second and final round.

In the climactic battle (if there is one; sometimes the wounded cock simply expires in the handler's hands or immediately as it is placed down again), the cock who landed the first blow usually proceeds to finish off his weakened opponent. But this is far from an inevitable out come, for if a cock can walk, he can fight, and if he can fight, he can kill, and what counts is which cock expires first. If the wounded one can get a stab in and stagger on until the other drops, he is the official winner, even if he himself topples over an instant later.

Surrounding all this melodrama—which the crowd packed tight around the ring follows in near silence, moving their bodies in kinesthetic sympathy with the movement of the animals, cheering their champions on with wordless hand motions, shiftings of the shoulders, turnings of the head, falling back en masse as the cock with the murderous spurs careens toward one side of the ring (it is said that spectators sometimes lose eyes and fingers from being too attentive), surging forward again as they glance off toward another—is a vast body of extraordinarily elaborate and precisely detailed rules.

These rules, together with the developed lore of cocks and cockfighting which accompanies them, are written down in palm-leaf manuscripts (*lontar; rontal*) passed on from generation to generation as part of the general legal and cultural tradition of the villages. At a fight, the umpire (*saja komong; djuru kembar*)—the man who manages the coconut—is in charge of their application and his authority is absolute. I have never seen an umpire's judgment questioned on any subject, even by the more despondent losers, nor have I ever heard, even in private, a charge of unfairness directed against one, or, for that matter, complaints about umpires in general. Only exceptionally well trusted, solid, and, given the complexity of the code, knowledgeable citizens perform this job, and in fact men will bring their cocks only to fights presided over by such men. It is also the umpire to whom accusations of cheating, which, though rare in the extreme, occasionally arise, are referred; and it is he who in the not infrequent cases where the cocks expire virtually together decides which (if either, for, though the Balinese do not care for such an outcome, there can be ties) went first. Likened to a judge, a king, a priest, and a policeman, he is all of these, and under his assured direction the animal passion of the fight proceeds within the civic certainty of the law. In the dozens of cockfights I saw in Bali, I never once saw an altercation about rules. Indeed, I never saw an open altercation, other than those between cocks, at all.

This crosswise doubleness of an event which, taken as a fact of nature, is rage un-trammeled and, taken as a fact of culture, is form perfected, defines the cockfight as a sociological entity. A cockfight is what, searching for a name for something not vertebrate enough to be called a group and not structureless enough to be called a crowd, Erving Goffman has called a "focused gathering"—a set of persons engrossed in a common flow of activity and relating to one another in terms of that flow.[10] Such gatherings meet and disperse; the participants in them fluctuate; the activity that focuses them is discrete—a particulate process that reoccurs rather than a continuous one that endures. They take their form from the situation that evokes them, the floor on which they are placed, as Goffman puts it; but it is a form, and an articulate one, nonetheless. For the situation, the floor is itself created, injury deliberations, surgical operations, block meetings, sit-ins, cockfights, by the cultural preoccupations—here, as we shall see, the celebration of status rivalry—which not only specify the focus but, assembling, actors and arranging scenery, bring it actually into being.

In classical times (that is to say, prior to the Dutch invasion of 1908), when there were no bureaucrats around to improve popular morality, the staging of a cockfight was an explicitly societal matter. Bringing a cock to an important fight was, for an adult male, a compulsory duty of citizenship; taxation of fights, which were usually held on market day, was a major source of public revenue; patronage of the art was a stated responsibility of princes; and the cock ring, or *wantilan,* stood in the center of the village near those other monuments of Balinese civility—the council house, the origin temple, the marketplace, the signal tower, and the banyan tree. Today, a few special oc-casions aside, the newer rectitude makes so open a statement of the connection between the excitements of collective life and those of blood sport impossible, but, less directly expressed, the connection itself remains intimate and intact. To expose it, however, it is necessary to turn to the aspect of cockfighting around which all the others pivot, and through which they exercise their force, an aspect I have thus far studiously ignored. I mean, of course, the gambling.

---

[10] E. Goffman. *Encounters: Two Studies in the Sociology of Interaction* (Indianapolis, 1961), pp. 9–10.

Odds and Even Money

The Balinese never do anything in a simple way that they can contrive to do in a complicated one, and to this generalization cockfight wagering is no exception.

In the first place, there are two sorts of bets, or *toh*.[11] There is the single axial bet in the center between the principals (*toh ketengah*), and there is the cloud of peripheral ones around the ring between members of the audience (*toh kesasi*). The first is typically large; the second typically small. The first is collective, involving coalitions of bettors clustering around the owner; the second is individual, man to man. The first is a matter of deliberate, very quiet, almost furtive arrangement by the coalition members and the umpire huddled like conspirators in the center of the ring; the second is a matter of impulsive shouting, public offers, and public acceptances by the excited throng around its edges. And most curiously, and as we shall see most revealingly, *where the first is always, without exception, even money, the second, equally without exception, is never such.* What is a fair coin in the center is a biased one on the side.

The center bet is the official one, hedged in again with a webwork of rules, and is made between the two cock owners, with the umpire as overseer and public witness.[12] This bet, which, as I say, is always relatively and sometimes very large, is never raised simply by the owner in whose name it is made, but by him together with four or five, sometimes seven or eight, allies—kin, village mates, neighbors, close friends. He may, if he is not especially well-to-do, not even be the major contributor; though, if only to show that he is not involved in any chicanery, he must be a significant one.

Of the fifty-seven matches for which I have exact and reliable data on the center bet, the range is from fifteen ringgits to five hundred, with a mean at eighty-five and with the distribution being rather noticeably tri-modal: small fights (15 ringgits either side of 35) accounting for about 45 percent of the total number; medium ones (20 ringgits either side of 70) for about 25 percent; and large (75 ringgits either side of 175) for about 20 percent,

---

[11] This word, which literally means an indelible stain or mark, as in a birthmark or a vein in a stone, is used as well for a deposit in a court case, for a pawn, for security offered in a loan, for a stand-in for someone else in a legal or ceremonial context, for an earnest advanced in a business deal, for a sign placed in a field to indicate its ownership is in dispute, and for the status of an unfaithful wife from whose lover her husband must gain satisfaction or surrender her to him. See Korn, *Ret Adatrecht van Bali;* Th. Pigeaud, *Javaans-Nederlands Hand-woordenboek* (Groningen, 1938); H. H, Juynboll, *Oudjavaansche-Nederlandsche Woordenlijst* (Leiden, 1923).

[12] The center bet must be advanced in cash by both parties prior to the actual fight. The umpire holds the stakes until the decision is rendered and then awards them to the winner, avoiding, among other things, the intense embarrassment both winner and loser would feel if the latter had to pay off personally following his defeat. About 10 percent of the winner's receipts are subtracted for the umpire's share and that of the fight sponsors.

with a few very small and very large ones out at the extremes. In a society where the normal daily wage of a manual laborer—a brickmaker, an ordinary farmworker, a market porter—was about three ringgits a day, and considering the fact that fights were held on the average about every two-and-a-half days in the immediate area I studied, this is clearly serious gambling, even if the bets are pooled rather than individual efforts.

The side bets are, however, something else altogether. Rather than the solemn, legalistic pactmaking of the center, wagering takes place rather in the fashion in which the stock exchange used to work when it was out on the curb. There is a fixed and known odds paradigm which runs in a continuous series from ten-to-nine at the short end to two-to-one at the long: 10-9, 9-8, 8-7, 7-6, 6-5, 5-4, 4-3, 3-2, 2-1. The man who wishes to back the *underdog cock* (leaving aside how favorites, *kebut,* and underdogs, *ngai,* are established for the moment) shouts the short-side number indicating the odds he wants *to be given.* That is, if he shouts *gasal,* "five," he wants the underdog at five-to-four (or, for him, four-to-five); if he shouts "four," he wants it at four-to-three (again, he putting up the "three"); if "nine," at nine-to-eight, and so on. A man backing the favorite, and thus considering giving odds if he can get them short enough, indicates the fact by crying out the color-type of that cock—"brown," "speckled," or whatever.[13]

As odds-takers (backers of the underdog) and odds-givers (backers of the favorite) sweep the crowd with their shouts, they begin to focus in on one another as potential betting pairs, often from far across the ring. The taker tries to shout the giver into longer

---

[13] Actually, the typing of cocks, which is extremely elaborate (I have collected more than twenty classes, certainly not a complete list), is not based on color alone, but on a series of independent, interacting, dimensions, which include—besides color—size, bone thickness, plumage, and temperament. (But *not* pedigree The Balinese do not breed cocks to any significant extent, nor, so tar as 1 have been able to discover, have they ever done so. The *mil,* or jungle cock, which is the basic fighting strain everywhere the sport is found, is native to southern Asia, and one can buy a good example in the chicken section of almost any Balinese market for anywhere from four or five rmggits up to fifty or more. The color element is merely the one normally used as the type name, except when the two cocks of different types-as on principle they must bejiavethe same color, in which case a secondary indication from one of the other dimensions ("large speckled" v. "small speckled," etc.) is added. The types are coordinated with various cosmological ideas which help shape the making of matches, so that, for example, you fight a small, headstrong, speckled brown-on-white cock with flat-lying feathers and thin legs from the east side of the ring on a certain dav of the complex Balinese calendar, and a large, cautious, all-black cock with tufted feathers and stubby legs from the north side on another day, and so on. All this is again recorded in palm-leaf manuscripts and endlessly discussed by the Balinese (who do not all have identical systems), and a full-scale fomponential-cum-symbolic analysis of cock classifications would be extremely valuable both as *in* adjunct to the description of the cockfight and in itself. But my data on the subject, though extensive and varied, do not seem to be complete and systematic enough to attempt such an analysis here. For Balinese cosmological ideas more generally see Belo, ed., *Traditional Balinese Culture,* and J. L. Swellengrebel, ed., *Bali: Studies in Life, Thought, and Ritual* (The Hague, 1960)

odds, the giver to shout the taker into shorter ones.[14] The taker, who is the wooer in this situation, will signal how large a bet he wishes to make at the odds he is shouting holding a number of fingers up in front of his face and vigorously waving them. If the giver, the wooed, replies in kind, the bet is made; if he does not, they unlock gazes and the search goes on.

The side betting, which takes place after the center bet has been made and its size announced, consists then in a rising crescendo of shouts as backers of the underdog offer their propositions to anyone who will accept them, while those who are backing the favorite but do not like the price being offered, shout equally frenetically the color of the cock to show they too are desperate to bet but want shorter odds.

Almost always odds-calling, which tends to be very consensual in that at any one time almost all callers are calling the same thing, starts off toward the long end of the range—five-to-four or four-to-three—and then moves, also consensually, toward the short end with greater or lesser speed and to a greater or lesser degree. Men crying "five" and finding themselves answered only with cries of "brown" start crying "six," either drawing the other callers fairly quickly with them or retiring from the scene as their too-generous offers are snapped up. If the change is made and partners are still scarce, the procedure is repeated in a move to "seven," and so on, only rarely, and in the very largest fights, reaching the ultimate "nine" or "ten" levels. Occasionally, if the cocks are clearly mismatched, there may be no upward movement at all, or even a movement down the scale to four-to-three, three-to-two, very, very rarely two-to-one, a shift which is accompanied by a declining number of bets as a shift upward is accompanied by an increasing number. But the general pattern is for the betting to move a shorter or longer distance up the scale toward the, for side bets, nonexistent pole of even money, with the overwhelming majority of bets falling in the four-to-three to eight-to-seven range.[15]

---

[14] For purposes of ethnographic completeness, it should be noted that it is possible for the man backing the favorite-the odds-giver-to make a bet £ which he wins if his cock wins or there is a tie, a slight shortening of the odds (I do not have enough cases to be exact, but ties seem to occur about once every fifteen or twenty matches). He indicates his wish to do this by shouting *sapih* ("tie") rather than the cock-type, but such bets are in fact infrequent.

[15] The precise dynamics of the movement of the betting is one of the most intriguing, most complicated, and, given the hectic conditions under which it occurs, most difficult to study, aspects of the fight. Motion picture recording plus multiple observers would probably be necessary to deal with it effectively. Even impressionistically—the only approach open to a lone ethnographer caught in the middle of all this—it is clear that certain men lead both in determining the favorite (that is, making the opening cock-type calls which always initiate the process) and in directing the movement of the odds, these "opinion leaders" being the more accomplished cockfighters-cum-solid-citizens to be discussed below. If these men begin to change their calls, others follow; if they begin to make bets, so do others and—though there are always a large number of frustrated bettors crying for shorter or longer odds to the end—the

As the moment for the release of the cocks by the handlers approaches, the screaming, at least in a match where the center bet is large, reaches almost frenzied proportions as the remaining unfulfilled bettors try desperately to find a last-minute partner at a price they can live with. (Where the center bet is small, the opposite tends to occur: betting dies off, trailing into silence, as odds lengthen and people lose interest.) In a large-bet, well-made match—the kind of match the Balinese regard as "real cockfighting"—the mob scene quality, the sense that sheer chaos is about to break loose, with all those waving, shouting, pushing, clambering men is quite strong, an effect which is only heightened by the intense stillness that falls with instant suddenness, rather as if someone had turned off the current, when the slit gong sounds, the cocks are put down, and the battle begins.

When it ends, anywhere from fifteen seconds to five minutes later, *all bets are immediately paid.* There are absolutely no IOUs, at least to a betting opponent. One may, of course, borrow from a friend before offering or accepting a wager, but to offer or accept it you must have the money already in hand and, if you lose, you must pay it on the spot, before the next match begins. This is an iron rule, and as I have never heard of a disputed umpire's decision (though doubtless there must sometimes be some), I have also never heard of a welshed bet, perhaps because in a worked-up cockfight crowd the consequences might be, as they are reported to be sometimes for cheaters, drastic and immediate. It is, in any case, this formal asymmetry between balanced center bets and unbalanced side ones that poses the critical analytical problem for a theory which sees cockfight wagering as the link connecting the fight to the wider world of Balinese culture. It also suggests the way to go about solving it and demonstrating the link.

The first point that needs to be made in this connection is that the higher the center bet, the more likely the match will in actual fact be an even one. Simple considerations of rationality suggest that. If you are betting fifteen ringgits on a cock, you might be willing to go along with even money even if you feel your animal somewhat the less promising. But if you are betting five hundred you are very, very likely to be loathe to do so. Thus, in large-bet fights, which of course involve the better animals, tremendous care is taken to see that the cocks are about as evenly matched as to size, general condition, pugnacity, and so on as is humanly possible. The different ways of adjusting the spurs of the animals are often employed to secure this. If one cock seems stronger, an agreement will be made to position his spur at a slightly less advantageous angle—a kind of handicapping, at which spur affixers are, so it is said, extremely skilled. More care will be taken, too, to employ skillful handlers and to match them exactly as to abilities.

In short, in a large-bet fight the pressure to make the match a genuinely fifty-fifty proposition is enormous, and is consciously felt as such. For medium fights the pressure is somewhat less, and for small ones less yet, though there is always an effort to make things

---

movement more or less ceases. But a detailed understanding of the whole process awaits what, alas, it is not very likely ever to get: a decision theorist armed with precise observations of individual behavior.

at least approximately equal, for even at fifteen ringgits (five days' work) no one wants to make an even money bet in a clearly unfavorable situation. And, again, what statistics I have tend to bear this out. In my fifty-seven matches, the favorite won thirty-three times overall, the underdog twenty-four, a 1.4 : 1 ratio. But if one splits the figures at sixty ringgits center bets, the ratios turn out to be 1.1 : 1 (twelve favorites, eleven underdogs) for those above this line, and 1.6 : 1 (twenty-one and thirteen) for those below it. Or, if you take the extremes, for very large fights, those with center bets over a hundred ringgits the ratio is 1 ; 1 (seven and seven); for very small fights, those under forty ringgits, it is 1.9 : 1 (nineteen and ten).[16]

Now, from this proposition—that the higher the center bet the more exactly a fifty-fifty proposition the cockfight is—two things more or less immediately follow; (1) the higher the center bet is, the greater the pull on the side betting toward the short-odds end of the wagering spectrum, and vice versa; (2) the higher the center bet is, the greater the volume of side betting, and vice versa.

The logic is similar in both cases. The closer the fight is in fact to even money, the less attractive the long end of the odds will appear and, therefore, the shorter it must be if there are to be takers. That this is the case is apparent from mere inspection, from the Balinese's own analysis of the matter, and from what more systematic observations I was able to collect. Given the difficulty of making precise and complete recordings of side betting, this argument is hard to cast in numerical form, but in all my cases the odds-giver, odds-taker consensual point, a quite pronounced mini-max saddle where the bulk (at a guess, two-thirds to three-quarters in most cases) of the bets are actually made, was three or four points further along the scale toward the shorter end for the large-center-bet fights than for the small ones, with medium ones generally in between. In detail, the fit is not, of course, exact, but the general pattern is quite consistent: the power of the center bet to pull the side bets toward its own even-money pattern is directly proportional to its size, because its size is directly proportional to the degree to which the cocks are in fact evenly matched. As for the volume question, total wagering is greater in large-center-bet fights because such fights are considered more "interesting," not only in the sense that they are less predictable, but, more crucially, that more is at stake in them—in terms of

---

[16] Assuming only binomial variability, the departure from a fifty-fifty expectation in the sixty-ringgits-and-below case is 1.38 standard deviations, or (in a one direction test) an eight in one hundred possibility by chance alone; for the be-low-Forty-ringgits case it is 1.65 standard deviations, or about five in one hundred. The fact that these departures though real are not extreme merely indicates, again, that even in the smaller fights the tendency to match cocks at least reasonably evenly persists. It is a matter of relative relaxation of the pressures toward equalization, not their elimination. The tendency for high-bet contests to be coin-flip propositions is, of course, even more striking, and suggests the Balinese know quite well what they are about.

money, in terms of the quality of the cocks, and consequently, as we shall see, in terms of social prestige.[17]

The paradox of fair coin in the middle, biased coin on the outside is thus a merely apparent one. The two betting systems, though formally incongruent, are not really contradictory to one another, but are part of a single larger system in which the center bet is, so to speak, the "center of gravity," drawing, the larger it is the more so, the outside bets toward the short-odds end of the scale. The center bet thus "makes the game," or perhaps better, defines it, signals what, following a notion of Jeremy Bentham's, I am going to call its "depth."

The Balinese attempt to create an interesting, if you will, "deep," match by making the center bet as large as possible so that the cocks matched will be as equal and as fine as possible, and the outcome, thus, as unpredictable as possible. They do not always succeed. Nearly half the matches are relatively trivial, relatively uninteresting—in my borrowed terminology, "shallow"—affairs. But that fact no more argues against my interpretation than the fact that most painters, poets, and playwrights are mediocre argues against the view that artistic effort is directed toward profundity and, with a certain frequency, approximates it. The image of artistic technique is indeed exact: the center bet is a means, a device, for creating "interesting," "deep" matches, *not* the reason, or at least not the main reason, *why* they are interesting, the source of their fascination, the substance of their depth. The question of why such matches are interesting—indeed, for the Balinese, exquisitely absorbing—takes us out of the realm of formal concerns into more broadly sociological and social-psychological ones, and to a less purely economic idea of what "depth" in gaming amounts to.[18]

---

[17] The reduction in wagering in smaller rights (which, of course, feeds on itself, one of the reasons people find small-fights uninteresting is that there is less wagering in them, and contrariwise for large ones) takes place in three mutually reinforcing ways. First, there is a simple withdrawal of interest as people wander off to have a cup of coffee or chat with a friend. Second, the Balinese do not mathematically reduce odds, but bet directly in terms of stated odds as such. Thus for a nine-to-eight bet, one man wagers nine ringgits, the other eight; tor five-to-four, one wagers five, the other four. For any given currency unit, like the ringgit, therefore, 6.3 times as much money is involved in a ten-to-nine bet as in a two-to-one bet, for example, and, as noted, in small fights betting settles toward the longer end. Finally, the bets which are made tend to be one-rather than two-, three-, or in some of the very largest fights, four-or five-finger ones. (The fingers indicate the *multiples* of the stated bet odds at issue, not absolute figures. Two fingers in a six-to-five situation means a man wants to wager ten ringgits on the underdog against twelve, three in an eight-to-seven situation, twenty-one against twenty-four, and so on.)

[18] Besides wagering there are other economic aspects of the cockfight, especially its very close connection with the local market system which, though secondary both to its motivation and to its function, are not without importance. Cockfights are open events to which anyone who wishes may come, sometimes from quite distant areas, but well over 90 percent, probably over 95, are very local affairs, and the locality concerned is defined not by the village, nor even by the administrative district, but by the rural market

PLAYING WITH FIRE

Bentham's concept of "deep play" is found in his *The Theory of Legislation.*[19] By it he means play in which the stakes are so high that it is, from his utilitarian standpoint, irrational for men to engage in it at all. If a man whose fortune is a thousand pounds (or ringgits) wages five hundred of it on an even bet, the marginal utility of the pound he stands to win is clearly less than the marginal disutility of the one he stands to lose. In genuine deep play, this is the case for both parties. They are both in over their heads. Having come together in search of pleasure they have entered into a relationship which will bring the participants, considered collectively, net pain rather than net pleasure. Bentham's conclusion was, therefore, that deep play was immoral from first principles and, a typical step for him, should be prevented legally.

But more interesting than the ethical problem, at least for our concerns here, is that despite the logical force of Bentham's analysis men do engage in such play, both passionately and often, and even in the face of law's revenge. For Bentham and those who think as he does (nowadays mainly lawyers, economists, and a few psychiatrists), the explanation is, as I have said, that such men are irrational—addicts, fetishists, children, fools, savages, who need only to be protected against themselves. But for the Balinese, though naturally they do not formulate it in so many words, the explanation lies in the fact that in such play, money is less a measure of utility, had or expected, than it is a symbol of moral import, perceived or imposed.

It is, in fact, in shallow games, ones in which smaller amounts of money are involved, that increments and decrements of cash are more nearly synonyms for utility and disutility, in the ordinary, unexpanded sense—for pleasure and pain, happiness and unhappiness. In

---

system. Bali has a three-day market week with the familiar "solar-system"-type rotation. Though the markets themselves have never been very highly developed, small morning affairs in a village square, it is the microregion such rotation rather generally marks out—ten or twenty square miles, seven or eight neighboring villages (which in contemporary Bali is usually going to mean anywhere from five to ten or eleven thousand people) from which the core of any cockfight audience, indeed virtually all of it, will come. Most of the fights are in fact organized and sponsored by small combines of petty rural merchants under the general premise, very strongly held by them and indeed by all Balinese, that cockfights are good for trade because "they get money out of the house, they make it circulate." Stalls selling various sorts of things as well as assorted sheer-chance gambling games (see below) are set up around the edge of the area so that this even takes on the quality of a small fair. This connection of cockfighting with markets and market sellers is very old, as, among other things, their conjunction in inscriptions [R, Goris, *Prasasti Bali,* 2 vols. (Bandung, 1954)] indicates. Trade has followed the cock for centuries in rural Bali, and the sport has been one of the main agencies of the island's monetization.

[19] The phrase is found in the Hildreth translation, International Library of Psychology (1931), note to p. 106; see L, L. Fuller, *The Morality of Law* (New Haven, 1964), p. 6 ff.

deep ones, where the amounts of money are great, much more is at stake than material gain: namely, esteem, honor, dignity, respect—in a word, though in Bali a profoundly freighted word, status.[20] It is at stake symbolically, for (a few cases of ruined addict gamblers aside) no one's status is actually altered by the outcome of a cockfight; it is only, and that momentarily, affirmed or insulted. But for the Balinese, for whom nothing v is more pleasurable than an affront obliquely delivered or more painful than one obliquely received—particularly when mutual acquaintances, undeceived by surfaces, are watching—such appraisive drama is deep indeed.

This, I must stress immediately, is *not* to say that the money does not matter, or that the Balinese is no more concerned about losing five hundred ringgits than fifteen. Such a conclusion would be absurd. It is because money *does,* in this hardly unmaterialistic society, matter and matter very much that the more of it one risks, the more of a lot of other things, such as one's pride, one's poise, one's dispassion, one's masculinity, one also risks, again only momentarily but again very publicly as well. In deep cockfights an owner and his collaborators, and, as we shall see, to a lesser but still quite real extent also their backers on the outside, put their money where their status is.

It is in large part *because* the marginal disutility of loss is so great at the higher levels of betting that to engage in such betting is to lay one's public self, allusively and metaphorically, through the medium of one's cock, on the line. And though to a Benthamite this might seem merely to increase the irrationality of the enterprise that much further, to the Balinese what it mainly increases is the meaningfulness of it all. And as (to follow Weber rather than Bentham) the imposition of meaning on life is the major end and primary condition of human existence, that access of significance more than compensates for the economic costs involved.[21] Actually, given the even-money quality of the larger matches, important changes in material fortune among those who regularly participate in them seem virtually nonexistent, because matters more or less even out over the long run. It is, actually, in the

---

[20] Of course, even in Bentham, utility is not normally confined as a concept to monetary losses and gains, and my argument here might be more carefully put in terms of a denial that for the Balinese, as for any people, utility (pleasure, happiness …) is merely identifiable with wealth. But such terminological problems are in any case secondary to the essential point: the cockfight is not roulette.

[21] M. Weber, *The Sociology of Religion* (Boston, 1963). There is nothing specifically Balinese, of course, about deepening significance with money, as Whyte's description of corner boys in a working-class district of Boston demonstrates: "Gambling plays an important role in the lives of Cornerville people. Whatever game the corner boys play, they nearly always bet on the outcome. When there is nothing at stake, the game is not considered a real contest. This does not mean that the financial element is all-important. I have frequently heard men say that the honor of winning was much more important than the money at stake. The corner boys consider playing for money the real test of skill and, unless a man performs well when money is at stake, he is not considered a good competitor." W. E Whyte, *Street Corner Society,* 2d ed. (Chicago, 1955), p. 140.

smaller, shallow fights, where one finds the handful of more pure, addict-type gamblers involved—those who *are* in it mainly for the money—that "real" changes in social position, largely downward, are affected. Men of this sort, plungers, are highly dispraised by "true cockfighters" as fools who do not understand what the sport is all about, vulgarians who simply miss the point of it all. They are, these addicts, regarded as fair game for the genuine enthusiasts, those who do understand, to take a little money away from—something that is easy enough to do by luring them, through the force of their greed, into irrational bets on mismatched cocks. Most of them do indeed manage to ruin themselves in a remarkably short time, but there always seems to be one or two of them around, pawning their land and selling their clothes in order to bet, at any particular time.[22]

This graduated correlation of "status gambling" with deeper fights and, inversely, "money gambling" with shallower ones is in fact quite general. Bettors themselves form a sociomoral hierarchy in these terms. As noted earlier, at most cockfights there are, around the very edges of the cockfight area, a large number of mindless, sheer-chance-type gambling games (roulette, dice throw, coin-spin, pea-under-the-shell) operated by concessionaires. Only women, children, adolescents, and various other sorts of people who do not (or not yet) fight cocks-the extremely poor, the socially despised, the personally idiosyncratic—play at these games, at, of course, penny ante levels. Cockfighting men would be ashamed to go anywhere near them. Slightly above these people in standing are those who though they do not themselves fight cocks, bet on the smaller matches around the edges. Next, there are those who fight cocks in small, or occasionally medium matches, but have not the status to join in the large ones, though they may bet from time to time on the side in those. And finally, there are those, the really substantial members of the community, the solid citizenry around whom local life revolves, who fight in the larger fights and bet on them around the side. The focusing element in these focused gatherings, these men generally dominate and define the sport as they dominate and define the society. When a Balinese male talks, in that almost venerative way, about "the true cockfighter," the *bebatoh* ("bettor") or *djuru kurung* ("cage keeper"), it is this sort of person, not those who bring the mentality of the pea-and-shell game into the quite different, inappropriate

---

[22] The extremes to which this madness is conceived on occasion to go—and the fact that it is considered madness—is demonstrated by the Balinese folk tale *I/Tuhung Kuning*. A gambler becomes so deranged by his passion that, leaving on a trip, he orders his pregnant wife to take care of the prospective newborn if it is a boy but to feed it as meat to his fighting cocks if it is a girl. The mother gives birth to a girl, but rather than giving the child to the cocks she gives them a large rat and conceals the girl with her own mother. When the husband returns, the cocks, crowing a jingle, inform him of the deception and, furious, he sets out to kill the child. A goddess descends from heaven and takes the girl up to the skies with her. The cocks die from the food given them, the owner's sanity is restored, the goddess brings the girl back to the father, who reunites him with his wife. The story is given as "Geel Komkommertje" in J. Hooykaas-van Leeuwen Boomkamp, *Sprookjes en Verhalen van Bali* (The Hague, 1956), pp, 19-25.

context of the cockfight, the driven gambler (*potét,* a word which has the secondary meaning of thief or reprobate), and the wistful hanger-on, that they mean. For such a man, what is really going on in a match is something rather closer to an *affaire d'honneur* (though, with the Balinese talent for practical fantasy, the blood that is spilled is only figuratively human) than to the stupid, mechanical crank of a slot machine.

What makes Balinese cockfighting deep is thus not money in itself, but what, the more of it that is involved the more so, money causes to happen: the migration of the Balinese status hierarchy into the body of the cockfight. Psychologically an Aesopian representation of the ideal/demonic, rather narcissistic, male self, sociologically it is an equally Aesopian representation of the complex fields of tension set up by the controlled, muted, ceremonial, but for all that deeply felt, interaction of those selves in the context of everyday life. The cocks may be surrogates for their owners' personalities, animal mirrors of psychic form, but the cockfight is—or more exactly, deliberately is made to be—a simulation of the social matrix, the involved system of cross-cutting, overlapping, highly corporate groups—villages, kingroups, irrigation societies, temple congregations, "castes"—in which its devotees live,[23] And as prestige, the necessity to affirm it, defend it, celebrate it, justify it, and just plain bask in it (but not, given the strongly ascriptive character of Balinese stratification, to seek it), is perhaps the central driving force in the society, so also—ambulant penises, blood sacrifices, and monetary exchanges aside—is it of the cockfight. This apparent amusement and seeming sport is, to take another phrase from Erving Goffman, "a status bloodbath."[24]

The easiest way to make this clear, and at least to some degree to demonstrate it, is to invoke the village whose cockfighting activities I observed the closest—the one in which the raid occurred and from which my statistical data are taken.

Like all Balinese villages, this one—Tihingan, in the Klungkung region of southeast Bali—is intricately organized, a labyrinth of alliances and oppositions. But, unlike many, two sorts of corporate groups, which are also status groups, particularly stand out, and we may concentrate on them, in a part-for-whole way, without undue distortion.

First, the village is dominated by four large, patrilineal, partly endogamous descent groups which are constantly vying with one another and form the major factions in the village. Sometimes they group two and two, or rather the two larger ones versus the two smaller ones plus all the unaffiliated people; sometimes they operate independently. There are also subfactions within them, subfactions within the subfactions, and so on to rather fine levels of distinction. And second, there is the village itself, almost entirely endogamous,

---

[23] For a fuller description of Balinese rural social structure, see C. Geertz, "Form and Variation in Balinese Village Structure," *American Anthropologist* 61 (1959): pp. 94–108; "Tihingan, A Balinese Village," in R. M. Koentjaraningrat, *Villages in Indonesia* (Ithaca, 1967), pp. 210–243; and, though it is a bit off the norm as Balinese villages go, V. E. Korn, *De Dorpsrepubliek tnganan Pagringsingan* (Santpoort, Netherlands, 1933).

[24] Goffman, *Encounters,* p. 78.

which is opposed to all the other villages round about in its cockfight circuit (which, as explained, is the market region), but which also forms alliances with certain of these neighbors against certain others in various supravillage political and social contexts. The exact situation is thus, as everywhere in Bali, quite distinctive; but the general pattern of a tiered hierarchy of status rivalries between highly corporate but various based groupings (and, thus, between the members of them) is entirely general.

Consider, then, as support of the general thesis that the cockfight, and especially the deep cockfight, is fundamentally a dramatization of status concerns, the following facts, which to avoid extended ethnographic description I shall simply pronounce to be facts—though the concrete evidence, examples, statements, and numbers that could be brought to bear in support of them, is both extensive and unmistakable:

1. A man virtually never bets against a cock owned by a member of his own kingroup. Usually he will feel obliged to bet for it, the more so the closer the kin tie and the deeper the fight. If he is certain in his mind that it will not win, he may just not bet at all, particularly if it is only a second cousin's bird or if the fight is a shallow one. But as a rule he will feel he must support it and, in deep games, nearly always does. Thus the great majority of the people calling "five" or "speckled" so demonstratively are expressing their allegiance to their kinsman, not their evaluation of his bird, their understanding of probability theory, or even their hopes of unearned income.

2. This principle is extended logically. If your kingroup is not involved you will support an allied kingroup against an unallied one in the same way, and so on through the very involved networks of alliances which, as I say, make up this, as any other, Balinese village.

3. So, too, for the village as a whole. If an outsider cock is fighting any cock from your village, you will tend to support the local one. If, what is a rarer circumstance but occurs every now and then, a cock from outside your cockfight circuit is fighting one inside it, you will also tend to support the "home bird."

4. Cocks which come from any distance are almost always favorites, for the theory is the man would not have dared to bring it if it was not a good cock, the more so the further he has come. His followers are, of course, obliged to support him, and when the more grand-scale legal cockfights are held (on holidays, and so on) the people of the village take what they regard to be the best cocks in the village, regardless of ownership, and go off to support them, although they will almost certainly have to give odds on them and to make large bets to show that they are not a cheapskate village. Actually, such "away games," though infrequent, tend to mend the ruptures between village members that the constantly occurring "home games," where village factions are opposed rather than united, exacerbate.

5. Almost all matches are sociologically relevant. You seldom get two outsider cocks fighting, or two cocks with no particular group backing, or with group backing

which is mutually unrelated in any clear way. When you do get them, the game is very shallow, betting very slow, and the whole thing very dull, with no one save the immediate principals and an addict gambler or two at all interested.

6. By the same token, you rarely get two cocks from the same group, even more rarely from the same subfaction, and virtually never from the same sub-subfaction (which would be in most cases one extended family) fighting. Similarly, in outside village fights two members of the village will rarely fight against one another, even though, as bitter rivals, they would do so with enthusiasm on their home grounds.

7. On the individual level, people involved in an institutionalized hostility relationship, called *puik,* in which they do not speak or otherwise have anything to do with each other (the causes of this formal breaking of relations are many: wife-capture, inheritance arguments, political differences) will bet very heavily, sometimes almost maniacally, against one another in what is a frank and direct attack on the very masculinity, the ultimate ground of his status, of the opponent.

8. The center bet coalition is, in all but the shallowest games, *always* made up by structural allies—no "outside money" is involved. What is "outside" depends upon the context, of course, but given it, no outside money is mixed in with the main bet; if the principals cannot raise it, it is not made. The center bet, again especially in deeper games, is thus the most direct and open expression of social opposition, which is one of the reasons why both it and matchmaking are surrounded by such an air of unease, furtiveness, embarrassment, and so on.

9. 9. The rule about borrowing money—that you may borrow *for* a bet but not *in* one—stems (and the Balinese are quite conscious of this) from similar considerations; you are never at the *economic* mercy of your enemy that way. Gambling debts, which can get quite large on a rather short-term basis, are always to friends, never to enemies, structurally speaking.

10. When two cocks are structurally irrelevant or neutral so far as *you* are concerned (though, as mentioned, they almost never are to each other) you do not even ask a relative or a friend whom he is betting on, because if you know how he is betting and he knows you know, and you go the other way, it will lead to strain. This rule is explicit and rigid; fairly elaborate, even rather artificial precautions are taken to avoid breaking it. At the very least you must pretend not to notice what he is doing, and he what you are doing.

11. There is a special word for betting against the grain, which is also the word for "pardon me" *(mpura).* It is considered a bad thing to do, though if the center bet is small it is sometimes all right as long as you do not do it too often. But the larger the bet and the more frequently you do it, the more the "pardon me" tack will lead to social disruption.

12. In fact, the institutionalized hostility relation, *puik,* is often formally initiated (though its causes always lie elsewhere) by such a "pardon me" bet in a deep

fight, putting the symbolic fat in the fire. Similarly, the end of such a relationship and resumption of normal social intercourse is often signalized (but, again, not actually brought about) by one or the other of the enemies supporting the other's bird,

13. In sticky, cross-loyalty situations, of which in this extraordinarily complex social system there are of course many, where a man is caught between two more or less equally balanced loyalties, he tends to wander off for a cup of coffee or something to avoid having to bet, a form of behavior reminiscent of that of American voters in similar situations.[25]

14. The people involved in the center bet are, especially in deep fights, virtually always leading members of their group—kinship, village, or whatever. Further, those who bet on the side (including these people) are, as I have already remarked, the more established members of the village—the solid citizens. Cockfighting is for those who are involved in the everyday politics of prestige as well, not for youth, women, subordinates, and so forth.

15. So far as money is concerned, the explicitly expressed attitude toward it is that it is a secondary matter. It is not, as I have said, of no importance; Balinese are no happier to lose several weeks' income than anyone else. But they mainly look on the monetary aspects of the cock fight as self-balancing, a matter of just moving money around, circulating it among a fairly well-defined group of serious cockfighters. The really important wins and losses are seen mostly in other terms, and the general attitude toward wagering is not any hope of cleaning up, of making a killing (addict gamblers again excepted), but that of the horse player's prayer: "Oh, God, please let me break even." In prestige terms, however, you do not want to break even, but, in a momentary, punctuate sort of way, win utterly. The talk (which goes on all the time) is about fights against such-and-such a cock of So-and-So which your cock demolished, not on how much you won, a fact people, even for large bets, rarely remember for any length of time, though they will remember the day they did in Pan Loh's finest cock for years.

16. You must bet on cocks of your own group aside from mere loyalty considerations, for if you do not people generally will say, "What! Is he too proud for the likes of us? Does he have to go to Iava or Den Pasar [the capital town] to bet, he is such an important man?" Thus there is a general pressure to bet not only to show that you are important locally, but that you are not so important that you look down on everyone else as unfit even to be rivals. Similarly, home team people must bet against outside cocks or the outsiders will accuse them—a serious charge—of just

---

[25] B. R. Berelson, P. F. Lazersfeld, and W. N. McPhee, *Voting; A Study of Opinion Formation in a Presidential Campaign* (Chicago, 1954).

collecting entry fees and not really being interested in cockfighting, as well as again being arrogant and insulting.

17. Finally, the Balinese peasants themselves are quite aware of all this and can and, at least to an ethnographer, do state most of it in approximately the same terms as I have. Fighting cocks, almost every Balinese I have ever discussed the subject with has said, is like playing with fire only not getting burned. You activate village and kingroup rivalries and hostilities, but in "play" form, coming dangerously and entrancingly close to the expression of open and direct interpersonal and intergroup aggression (something which, again, almost never happens in the normal course of ordinary life), but not quite, because, after all, it is "only a cockfight."

More observations of this sort could be advanced, but perhaps the general point is, if not made, at least well-delineated, and the whole argument thus far can be usefully summarized in a formal paradigm:

THE MORE A MATCH IS …

1. Between near status equals (and/or personal enemies)
2. Between high status individuals

THE DEEPER THE MATCH.

THE DEEPER THE MATCH …

1. The closer the identification of cock and man (or, more properly, the deeper the match the more the man will advance his best, most closely-identified-with cock).
2. The finer the cocks involved and the more exactly they will be matched.
3. The greater the emotion that will be involved and the more the general absorption in the match.
4. The higher the individual bets center and outside, the shorter " the outside bet odds will tend to be, and the more betting there will be overall,
5. The less an "economic" and the more a "status" view of gaming will be involved, and the "solider" the citizens who will be gaming.[26]

Inverse arguments hold for the shallower the fight, culminating, in a reversed-signs sense, in the coin-spinning and dice-throwing amusements For deep fights there are no

---

[26] As this is a formal paradigm, it is intended to display the logical, not the causal, structure of cockfighting Just which of these considerations leads to which, in what order, and by what mechanisms, is another matter—one 1 nave attempted to shed some light on in the general discussion.

absolute upper limits, though there are of course practical ones, and there are a great many legend like tales of great Duel-in-the-Sun combats between lords and princes in classical times (for cockfighting has always been as much an elite concern as a popular one), far deeper than anything anyone, even aristocrats, could produce today anywhere in Bali.

Indeed, one of the great culture heroes of Bali is a prince, called after his passion for the sport, "The Cockfighter," who happened to be away at a very deep cockfight with a neighboring prince when the whole of his family—father, brothers, wives, sisters—were assassinated by commoner usurpers. Thus spared, he returned to dispatch the upstart, regain the throne, reconstitute the Balinese high tradition, and build its most powerful, glorious, and prosperous state. Along with everything else that the Balinese see in fighting cocks—themselves, their social order, abstract hatred, masculinity, demonic power—they also see the archetype of status virtue, the arrogant, resolute, honor-mad player with real fire, the ksatria prince.[27]

---

[27] In another of Hooykaas-van Leeuwen Boomkamp's folk tales ("De Gast," *Sprookjes en Verhalen van Bali*, pp. 172–180), a low caste *Sudra*, a generous, pious, and carefree man who is also an accomplished cockfighter, loses, despite his accomplishment, fight after fight until he is not only out of money but down to his last cock. He does not despair, however—"I bet," he says, "upon the Unseen World."

His wife, a good and hard-working woman, knowing how much he enjoys cockfighting, gives him her last "rainy day" money to go and bet. But, filled with misgivings due to his run of ill luck, he leaves his own cock at home and bets merely on the side. He soon loses all but a coin or two and repairs to a food stand for a snack, where he meets a decrepit, odorous, and generally unappetizing old beggar leaning on a staff. The old man asks for food, and the hero spends his last coins to buy him some. The old man then asks to pass the night with the hero, which the hero gladly invites him to do. As there is no food in the house, however, the hero tells his wife to kill the last cock for dinner. When the old man discovers this fact, he tells the hero he has three cocks in his own mountain hut and says the hero may have one of them for fighting. He also asks for the hero's son to accompany him as a servant, and, after the son agrees, this is done.

The old man turns out to be Siva and, thus, to live in a great palace in the sky, though the hero does not know this. In time, the hero decides to visit his son and collect the promised cock. Lifted up into Siva's presence, he is given the choice of three cocks. The first crows: "I have beaten fifteen opponents." The second crows, "I have beaten twenty-five opponents." The third crows, "I have beaten the king." "That one, the third, is my choice," says the hero, and returns with it to earth.

When he arrives at the cockfight, he is asked for an entry fee and replies, "I have no money; I will pay after my cock has won." As he is known never to win, he is let in because the king, who is there fighting, dislikes him and hopes to enslave him when he loses and cannot pay off. In order to insure that this happens, the king matches his finest cock against the hero's. When the cocks are placed down, the hero's flees, and the crowd, led by the arrogant king, hoots in laughter. The hero's cock then flies at the king himself, killing him with a spur stab in the throat. The hero flees. His house is encircled by the king's men. The cock changes into a Garuda, the great mythic bird of Indie legend, and carries the hero and his wife to safety in the heavens.

FEATHERS, BLOOD, CROWDS, AND MONEY

"Poetry makes nothing happen," Auden says in his elegy of Yeats, "it survives in the valley of its saying … a way of happening, a mouth." The cockfight too, in this colloquial sense, makes nothing happen. Men go on allegorically humiliating one another and being allegorically humiliated by one another, day after day, glorying quietly in the experience if they have triumphed, crushed only slightly more openly by it if they have not. *But no one's status really changes.* You cannot ascend the status ladder by winning cockfights; you cannot, as an individual, really ascend it at all. Nor can you descend it that way.[28] All you can do is enjoy and savor, or suffer and withstand, the concocted sensation of drastic and momentary movement along an aesthetic semblance of that ladder a kind of behind-the-mirror status jump which has the look of mobility without its actuality.

Like any art form—for that, finally, is what we are dealing with—the cockfight renders ordinary, everyday experience comprehensible by presenting it in terms of acts and objects which have had their practical consequences removed and been reduced (or, if you prefer, raised) to the level of sheer appearances, where their meaning can be more powerfully articulated and more exactly perceived. The cockfight is "really real" only to the cocks—it does not kill anyone, castrate anyone, reduce anyone to animal status, alter the hierarchical relations among people, or refashion the hierarchy; it does not even redistribute income in any significant way. What it does is what, for other peoples with other temperaments and other conventions, *Lear* and *Crime and Punishment* do; it catches up these themes—death, masculinity, rage, pride, loss, beneficence, chance—and, ordering them into an encompassing structure, presents them in such a way as to throw into relief a particular view of their essential nature. It puts a construction on them, makes them, to those historically positioned to appreciate the construction, meaningful—visible, tangible, graspable—"real," in an ideational sense, An image, fiction, a model, a metaphor, the cockfight is a means of expression; its function is neither to assuage social passions nor to heighten them (though, in its playing-with-fire way it does a bit of both), but, in a medium of feathers, blood, crowds, and money, to display them.

When the people see this, they make the hero king and his wife queen and they return as such to earth. Later their son, released by Siva, also returns and the hero-king announces his intention to enter a hermitage. ("I will fight no more cockfights. I have bet on the Unseen and won.") He enters the hermitage and his son becomes king.

[28] Addict gamblers are really less declassed (for their status is, as everyone else's, inherited) than merely impoverished and personally disgraced. The most prominent addict gambler in my cockfight circuit was actually a very high caste *satria* who sold off most of his considerable lands to support his habit. Though everyone privately regarded him as a fool and worse (some, more charitable, regarded him as sick), he was publicly treated with the elaborate deference and politeness due his rank. On the independence of personal reputation and public status in Bali, see above, Chapter 14.

The question of how it is that we perceive qualities in things—paintings, books, melodies, plays—that we do not feel we can assert literally to be there has come, in recent years, into the very center of aesthetic theory.[29] Neither the sentiments of the artist, which remain his, nor those of the audience, which remain theirs, can account for the agitation of one painting or the serenity of another. We attribute grandeur, wit, despair, exuberance to strings of sounds, lightness, energy, violence, fluidity to blocks of stone. Novels are said to have strength, buildings eloquence, plays momentum, ballets repose. In this realm of eccentric predicates, to say that the cockfight, in its perfected cases at least, is "disquietful" does not seem at all unnatural, merely, as I have just denied it practical consequence, somewhat puzzling.

The disquietfulness arises, "somehow," out of a conjunction of three attributes of the fight: its immediate dramatic shape; its metaphoric content; and its social context. A cultural figure against a social ground, the fight is at once a convulsive surge of animal hatred, a mock war of symbolical selves, and a formal simulation of status tensions, and its aesthetic power derives from its capacity to force together these diverse realities. The reason it is disquietful is not that it has material effects (it has some, but they are minor); the reason that it is disquietful is that, joining pride to selfhood, selfhood to cocks, and cocks to destruction, it brings to imaginative realization a dimension of Balinese experience normally well-obscured from view. The transfer of a sense of gravity into what is in itself a rather blank and unvarious spectacle, a commotion of beating wings and throbbing legs, is effected by interpreting it as expressive of something unsettling in the way its authors and audience live, or, even more ominously, what they are.

As a dramatic shape, the fight displays a characteristic that does not seem so remarkable until one realizes that it does not have to be there: a radically atomistical structure.[30] Each

---

[29] For four, somewhat variant, treatments, see S. Langer, *Feeling and Form* (New York, 1953); R. Wollheim, *Art and Its Objects* (New York, 1968); N. Goodman, *Languages of Art* (Indianapolis, 1968); M. Merleau-Ponty, "The Eye and the Mind," in his *The Primacy of Perception* (Evanston, 111., 1964), pp. 159-190.

30 British cockfights (the sport was banned there in 1840) indeed seem to have lacked it, and to have generated, therefore, a quite different family of shapes. Most British fights were "mains," in which a preagreed number of cocks were aligned into two teams and fought serially. Score was kept and wagering took place both on the individual matches and on the main as a whole There were also "battle Royales," both in England and on the Continent, in which a large number of cocks were let loose at once with the one left standing at the end the victor. And in Wales, the so-called Welsh main followed an elimination pattern, along the lines of a present-day tennis tournament, winners proceeding to the next round As a genre, the cock fight has perhaps less compositional flexibility than, say Latin comedy, but it is not entirely without any. On cockfighting more generally, see A. Ruport, *The Art of Cockfighting* (New York, 1949), OR. Scott *History of Cockfighting* (London, 1957); and L. Fitz-Barnard, *Fighting Sports* (London, 1921)

match is a world unto itself, a particulate burst of form. There is the matchmaking, there is the betting, there is the fight, there is the result—utter triumph and utter defeat—and there is the hurried, embarrassed passing of money. The loser is not consoled. People drift away from him, look around him, leave him to assimilate his momentary descent into nonbeing, reset his face and return, scarless and intact, to the fray. Nor are winners congratulated, or events rehashed; once a match is ended the crowd's attention turns totally to the next, with no looking back. A shadow of the experience no doubt remains with the principals, perhaps even with some of the witnesses of a deep fight, as it remains with us when we leave the theater after seeing a powerful play well-performed; but it quite soon fades to become at most a schematic memory—a diffuse glow or an abstract shudder—and usually not even that. Any expressive form lives only in its own present—the one it itself creates. But, here, that present is severed into a string of flashes, some more bright than others, but all of them disconnected, aesthetic quanta. Whatever the cockfight says, it says in spurts.

But, as I have argued lengthily elsewhere, the Balinese live in spurts![31] Their life, as they arrange it and perceive it, is less a flow, a directional movement out of the past, through the present, toward the future than an on-off pulsation of meaning and vacuity, an arhythmic alternation of short periods when "something" (that is, something significant) is happening, and equally short ones where "nothing" (that is, nothing much) is—between what they themselves call "full" and "empty" times, or, in another idiom, "junctures" and "holes." In focusing activity down to a burning-glass dot, the cockfight is merely being Balinese in the same way in which everything from the monadic encounters of everyday life, through the clanging pointillism of *gamelan* music, to the visiting-day-of-the-gods temple celebrations are. It is not an imitation of the punctuateness of Balinese social life, nor a depiction of it, nor even an expression of it; it is an example of it, carefully prepared.[32]

If one dimension of the cockfight's structure, its lack of temporal directionality, makes it seem a typical segment of the general social life, however, the other, its flat-out, head-to-head (or spur-to-spur) aggressiveness, makes it seem a contradiction, a reversal, even a subversion of it. In the normal course of things, the Balinese are shy to the point of obsessiveness of open conflict. Oblique, cautious, subdued, controlled, masters of indirection and dissimulation—what they call *aim,* "polished," "smooth"—they rarely face what they can turn away from, rarely resist what they can evade. But here they portray themselves as wild and murderous, with manic explosions of instinctual cruelty. A powerful rendering of life as the Balinese most deeply do not want it (to adapt a phrase Frye has used of

---

[31] Above, pp. 391–398.

[32] For the necessity of distinguishing among "description," "representation," "exemplification," and "expression" (and the irrelevance of "imitation" to all of them) as modes of symbolic reference, see Goodman, *Languages of Art,* pp. 61–110, 45–91, 225–241.

Gloucester's blinding) is set in the context of a sample of it as they do in fact have it.[33] And, because the context suggests that the rendering, if less than a straightforward description, is nonetheless more than an idle fancy; it is here that the disquietfulness—the disquietfulness of the *fight*, not (or, anyway, not [oo] necessarily) its patrons, who seem in fact rather thoroughly to enjoy it—emerges. The slaughter in the cock ring is not a depiction of how things literally are among men, but, what is almost worse, of how, from a particular angle, they imaginatively are.[34]

The angle, of course, is stratificatory. What, as we have already seen, the cockfight talks most forcibly about is status relationships, and what it says about them is that they are matters of life and death. That prestige is a profoundly serious business is apparent everywhere one looks in Bali—in the village, the family, the economy, the state. A peculiar fusion of Polynesian title ranks and Hindu castes, the hierarchy of pride is the moral backbone of the society. But only in the cockfight are the sentiments upon which that hierarchy rests revealed in their natural colors. Enveloped elsewhere in a haze of etiquette, a thick cloud of euphemism and ceremony, gesture and allusion, they are here expressed in only the thinnest disguise of an animal mask, a mask which in fact demonstrates them far more effectively than it conceals them. Jealousy is as much a part of Bali as poise, envy as grace, brutality as charm; but without the cockfight the Balinese would have a much less certain understanding of them, which is, presumably, why they value it so highly.

Any expressive form works (when it works) by disarranging semantic contexts in such a way that properties conventionally ascribed to certain things are unconventionally ascribed to others, which are then seen actually to possess them. To call the wind a cripple, as Stevens does, to fix tone and manipulate timbre, as Schoenberg does, or, closer to our case, to picture an art critic as a dissolute bear, as Hogarth does, is to cross conceptual

---

[33] N. Frye, *The Educated Imagination* (Bloomington, Ind, 1964), p. 99.

[34] There are two other Balinese values and disvalues which, connected with punctuate temporality on the one hand and unbridled aggressiveness on the other, reinforce the sense that the cockfight is at once continuous with ordinary social life and a direct negation of it: what the Balinese call *rami,* and what they call *paling. Rami* means crowded, noisy, and active, and is a highly sought-after social state: crowded markets, mass festivals, busy streets are all *ramè,* as, of course, is, in the extreme, a cockfight. *Ramè* is what happens in the "full" times (its opposite, *sepi,* "quiet," is what happens in the "empty" ones). *Paling* is social vertigo, the dizzy, disoriented, lost, turned-around feeling one gets when one's place in the coordinates of social space is not clear, and it is a tremendously disfavored, immensely anxiety-producing state. Balinese regard the exact maintenance of spatial orientation ("not to know where north is" is to be crazy), balance, decorum, status relationships, and so forth, as fundamental to ordered life *(krama)* and *paling,* the sort of whirling confusion of position the scrambling cocks exemplify as its profoundest enemy and contradiction. On *ramè,* see Bateson and Mead, *Balinese Character,* pp. 3, 64; on *paling,* ibid., p. 11, and Belo, ed., *Traditional Balinese Culture,* p. 90 ff.

wires; the established conjunctions between objects and their qualities are altered, and phenomena—fall weather, melodic shape, or cultural journalism—are clothed in signifiers which normally point to other referents.[35] Similarly, to connect—and connect, and connect—the collision of roosters with the divisiveness of status is to invite a transfer of perceptions from the former to the latter, a transfer which is at once a description and a judgment. (Logically, the transfer could, of course, as well go the other way; but, like most of the rest of us, the Balinese are a great deal more interested in understanding men than they are in understanding cocks.)[36]

What sets the cockfight apart from the ordinary course of life, lifts it from the realm of everyday practical affairs, and surrounds it with an aura of enlarged importance is not, as functionalist sociology would have it, that it reinforces status discriminations (such reinforcement is hardly necessary in a society where every act proclaims them), but that it provides a metasocial commentary upon the whole matter of assorting human beings into fixed hierarchical ranks and then organizing the major part of collective existence around that assortment. Its function, if you want to call it that, is interpretive: it is a Balinese reading of Balinese experience, a story they tell themselves about themselves.[37]

SAYING SOMETHING OF SOMETHING

To put the matter this way is to engage in a bit of metaphorical refocusing of one's own, for it shifts the analysis of cultural forms from an endeavor in general parallel to dissecting an organism, diagnosing a symptom, deciphering a code, or ordering a system—the dominant

---

[35] The Stevens reference is to his 'The Motive for Metaphor" ("You like it under the trees in autumn,/ Because everything is half dead./The wind moves like a cripple among the leaves/And repeats words without meaning") [Copyright 1947 by Wallace Stevens, reprinted from *The Collected Poems of Wallace Stevens* by permission of Alfred A. Knopf, Inc., and Faber and Faber Ltd.]; the Schoenberg reference is to the third of his *Five Orchestral Pieces* (Opus 16), and is borrowed from H. H. Drager, 'The Concept of Tonal Body,'" in *Reflections on Art*, ed. S. Langer (New York, 1961), p. 174. On Hogarth, and on this whole problem—there called "multiple matrix matching"—see E. H. Gombrich, 'The Use of Art for the Study of Symbols," in *Psychology and the Visual Arts*, ed. J. Hogg (Baltimore, 1969), pp. 149–170. The more usual term for this sort of semantic alchemy is "metaphorical transfer," and good technical discussions of it can be found in M. Black, *Models and Metaphors* (Ithaca, N.Y., 1962), p. 25 ff; Goodman, *Language as Art*, p. 44 ff; and W. Percy, "Metaphor as Mistake," *Sewanee Review* 66 (1958); 78–99.

[36] The tag is from the second book of the *Organon, On Interpretation*. For a discussion of it, and for the whole argument for freeing "the notion of text … from the notion of scripture or writing" and constructing, thus, a general hermeneutics, see P. Rieoeur, *Freud and Philosophy* (New Haven, 1970), p. 20 ff.

[37] Ibid.

analogies in contemporary anthropology—to one in general parallel with penetrating a literary text. If one takes the cockfight, or any other collectively sustained symbolic structure, as a means of "saying something of something" (to invoke a famous Aristotelian tag), then one is faced with a problem not in social mechanics but social semantics.[38] For the anthropologist, whose concern is with formulating sociological principles, not with promoting or appreciating cockfights, the question is, what does one learn about such principles from examining culture as an assemblage of texts?

Such an extension of the notion of a text beyond written material, and even beyond verbal, is, though metaphorical, not, of course, all that novel. The *interpretatio naturae* tradition of the middle ages, which, culminating in Spinoza, attempted to read nature as Scripture, the Nietszchean effort to treat value systems as glosses on the will to power (or the Marxian one to treat them as glosses on property relations), and the Freudian replacement of the enigmatic text of the manifest dream with the plain one of the latent, all offer precedents, if not equally recommendable ones.[37] But the idea remains theoretically undeveloped; and the more profound corollary, so far as anthropology is concerned, that cultural forms can be treated as texts, as imaginative works built out of social materials, has yet to be systematically exploited.[38]

In the case at hand, to treat the cockfight as a text is to bring out a feature of it (in my opinion, the central feature of it) that treating it as a rite or a pastime, the two most obvious alternatives, would tend to obscure: its use of emotion for cognitive ends. What the cockfight says it says in a vocabulary of sentiment—the thrill of risk, the despair of loss, the pleasure of triumph. Yet what it says is not merely that risk is exciting, loss depressing, or triumph gratifying, banal tautologies of affect, but that it is of these emotions, thus exampled, that society is built and individuals are put together. Attending cockfights and participating in them is, for the Balinese, a kind of sentimental education. What he learns there is what his culture's ethos and his private sensibility (or, anyway, certain aspects of them) look like when spelled out externally in a collective text; that the two are near enough alike to be articulated in the symbolics of a single such text; and—the disquieting part—that the text in which this revelation is accomplished consists of a chicken hacking another mindlessly to bits.

Every people, the proverb has it, loves its own form of violence. The cockfight is the Balinese reflection on theirs: on its look, its uses, its force, its fascination. Drawing on almost every level of Balinese experience, it brings together themes—animal savagery, male

---

[38] Lévi-Strauss' "structuralism" might seem an exception. But it is only an apparent one, for rather than taking myths, totem rites, marriage rules, or whatever as texts to interpret, Lévi-Strauss takes them as ciphers to solve, which is very much not the same thing. He does not seek to understand symbolic forms in terms of how they function in concrete situations to organize perceptions (meanings, emotions, concepts, attitudes); he seeks to understand them entirely in terms of their internal structure, *independent de tout sujet, de tout objet, et de toute contexts*. See above, Chapter 13.

narcissism, opponent gambling, status rivalry, mass excitement, blood sacrifice—whose main connection is their involvement with rage and the fear of rage, and, binding them into a set of rules which at once contains them and allows them play, builds a symbolic structure in which, over and over again, the reality of their inner affiliation can be intelligibly felt. If, to quote Northrop Frye again, we go to see *Macbeth* to learn what a man feels like after he has gained a kingdom and lost his soul, Balinese go to cockfights to find out what a man, usually composed, aloof, almost obsessively self-absorbed, a kind of moral autoeosm, feels like when, attacked, tormented, challenged, insulted, and driven in result to the extremes of fury, he has totally triumphed or been brought totally low. The whole passage, as it takes us back to Aristotle (though to the *Poetics* rather than the *Hermeneutics)*, is worth quotation:

> But the poet [as opposed to the historian], Aristotle says, never makes any real statements at all, certainly no particular or specific ones. The poet's job is not to tell you what happened, but what happens: not what did take place, but the kind of thing that always does take place. He gives you the typical, recurring, or what Aristotle calls universal event. You wouldn't go to *Macbeth* to learn about the history of Scotland—you go to it to learn what a man feels like after he's gained a kingdom and lost his soul. When you meet such a character as Micawber in Dickens, you don't feel that there must have been a man Dickens knew who was exactly like this: you feel tj that there's a bit of Micawber in almost everybody you know, including o yourself. Our impressions of human life are picked up one by one, and remain for most of us loose and disorganized. But we constantly find things in literature that suddenly coordinate and bring into focus a great many such impressions, and this is part of what Aristotle means by the typical or universal human event.[39]

It is this kind of bringing of assorted experiences of everyday life to focus that the cockfight, set aside from that life as "only a game" and reconnected to it as "more than a game," accomplishes, and so creates what, better than typical or universal, could be called a paradigmatic human event—that is, one that tells us less what happens than the kind of thing that would happen if, as is not the case, life were art and could be as freely shaped by styles of feeling as *Macbeth* and *David Copperfield* are.

Enacted and re-enacted, so far without end, the cockfight enables the Balinese, as, read and reread, *Macbeth* enables us, to see a dimension of his own subjectivity, As he watches fight after fight, with the active watching of an owner and a bettor (for cockfighting has no more interest as a pure spectator sport than does croquet or dog racing), he grows familiar with it and what it has to say to him, much as the attentive listener to string quartets or

---

[39] Frye, *The Educated Imagination,* pp. 63–64.

the absorbed viewer of still life grows slowly more familiar with them in a way which opens his subjectivity to himself.[40]

Yet, because—in another of those paradoxes, along with painted feelings and unconsequenced acts, which haunt aesthetics—that subjectivity does not properly exist until it is thus organized, art forms generate and regenerate the very subjectivity they pretend only to display. Quartets, still lifes, and cockfights are not merely reflections of a pre-existing sensibility analogically represented; they are positive agents in the creation and maintenance of such a sensibility. If we see ourselves as a pack of Micawbers, it is from reading too much Dickens (if we see ourselves as unillusioned realists, it is from reading too little); and similarly for Balinese, cocks, and cockfights. It is in such a way, coloring experience with the light they cast it in, rather than through whatever material effects they may have, that the arts play their role, as arts, in social life.[41]

In the cockfight, then, the Balinese forms and discovers his temperament and his society's temper at the same time. Or, more exactly, he forms and discovers a particular facet of them. Not only are there a great many other cultural texts providing commentaries on status hierarchy and self-regard in Bali, but there are a great many other critical sectors of Balinese life besides the stratificatory and the agonistic that receive such commentary. The ceremony consecrating a Brahmana priest, a matter of breath control, postural immobility, and vacant concentration upon the depths of being, displays a radically different, but to the Balinese equally real, property of social hierarchy—its reach toward the numinous transcendent. Set not in the matrix of the kinetic emotionality of animals, but in that of the static passionlessness of divine mentality, it expresses tranquillity not disquiet. The

---

[40] The use of the, to Europeans, "natural" visual idiom for perception—"see," "watches," and so forth—is more than usually misleading here, for the fact that, as mentioned earlier, Balinese follow the progress of the fight as much (perhaps, as fighting cocks are actually rather hard to see except as blurs of motion, more) with their bodies as with their eyes, moving their limbs, heads, and trunks in gestural mimicry of the cocks' maneuvers, means that much of the individual's experience of the fight is kinesthetic rather than visual. If ever there was an example of Kenneth Burke's definition of a symbolic act as "the dancing of an attitude" [*The Philosophy of Literary Form,* rev, ed. (New York, 1957), p. 9] the cock fight is it. On the enormous role of kinesthetic perception in Balinese life, Bate-son and Mead, *Balinese Character,* pp. 84–88; on the active nature of aesthetic perception in general, Goodman. *Language of Art,* pp. 241–244.

[41] All this coupling of the occidental great with the oriental lowly will doubt less disturb certain sorts of aestheticians as the earlier efforts of anthropologists to speak of Christianity and totemism in the same breath disturbed certain sorts of theologians. But as ontological questions are (or should be) bracketed in the sociology of religion, judgmental ones are (or should be) bracketed in the sociology of art. In any case, the attempt to deprovincialize the concept of art is but part of the general anthropological conspiracy to deprovincialize all important social concepts—marriage, religion, law, rationality—and though this is a threat to aesthetic theories which regard certain works of art as beyond the reach of sociological analysis, it is no threat to the conviction, for which Robert Graves claims to have been reprimanded at his Cambridge tripos, that some poems are better than others.

mass festivals at the village temples, which mobilize the whole local population in elaborate hostings of visiting gods—songs, dances, compliments, gifts—assert the spiritual unity of village mates against their status inequality and project a mood of amity and trust.[42] The cockfight is not the master key to Balinese life, any more than bullfighting is to Spanish, What it says about that life is not unqualified nor even unchallenged by what other equally eloquent cultural statements say about it. But there is nothing more surprising in this than in the fact that Racine and Moliére were contemporaries, or that the same people who arrange chrysanthemums cast swords.[43]

The culture of a people is an ensemble of texts, themselves ensembles, which the anthropologist strains to read over the shoulders of those to whom they properly belong. There are enormous difficulties in such an enterprise, methodological pitfalls to make a Freudian quake, and some moral perplexities as well. Nor is it the only way that symbolic forms can be sociologically handled. Functionalism lives, and so does psychologism. But to regard such forms as "saying something of something," and saying it to somebody, is at least to open up the possibility of an analysis which attends to their substance rather than to reductive formulas professing to account for them.

As in more familiar exercises in close reading, one can start anywhere in a culture's repertoire of forms and end up anywhere else. One can stay, as I have here, within a single, more or less bounded form, and circle steadily within it. One can move between forms in search of broader unities or informing contrasts. One can even compare forms from different cultures to define their character in reciprocal relief. But whatever the level at which one operates, and however intricately, the guiding principle is the same: societies, like lives, contain their own interpretations. One has only to learn how to gain access to them.

---

[42] For the consecration ceremony, see V. E. Korn, "The Consecration of the Priest," in Swellengrebel, ed., *Bali: Studies,* pp. 131–154; for (somewhat exaggerated) village communion, R. Goris, "The Religious Character of the Balinese Village," ibid., pp. 79–100.

[43] That what the cockfight has to say about Bali is not altogether without perception and the disquiet it expresses about the general pattern of Balinese life is not wholly without reason is attested by the fact that in two weeks of December 1965, during the upheavals following the unsuccessful coup in Djakarta, between forty and eighty thousand Balinese (in a population of about two million) were killed, largely by one another—the worst outburst in the country. (J, Hughes, *Indonesian Upheaval* (New York, 1967), pp. 173–183. Hughes' figures are, of course, rather casual estimates, but they are not the most extreme.] This is not to say, of course, that the killings were caused by the cockfight, could have been predicted on the basis of it, or were some sort of enlarged version of it with real people in the place of the cocks—all of which is nonsense. It is merely to say that if one looks at Bali not just through the medium of its dances, its shadow-plays, its sculpture, and its girls, but—as the Balinese themselves do—also through the medium of its cockfight, the fact that the massacre occurred seems, if no less appalling, less like a contradiction to the laws of nature. As more than one real Gloucester has discovered, sometimes people actually get life precisely as they most deeply do not want it.

GRIEF AND A HEADHUNTER'S RAGE

Renato Rosaldo

If you ask an older Ilongot man of northern Luzon, Philippines, why he cuts off human heads, his answer is brief, and one on which no anthropologist can readily elaborate; He says that rage, born of grief, impels him to kill his fellow human beings. He claims that he needs a place "to carry his anger." The act of severing and tossing away the victim's head enables him, he says, to vent and, he hopes, throw away the anger of his bereavement. Although the anthropologist's job is to make other cultures intelligible, more questions fail to reveal any further explanation of this man's pithy statement. To him, grief, rage, and headhunting go together in a self-evident manner. Either you understand it or you don't. And, in fact, for the longest time I simply did not.

In what follows, I want to talk about how to talk about the cultural force of emotions.[1] The *emotional force* of a death, for example, derives less from an abstract brute fact than from a particular intimate relation's permanent rupture. It refers to the kinds of feelings one experiences on learning, for example, that the child just run over by a car is one's own and not a stranger's. Rather than speaking of death in general, one must consider the subject's position within a field of social relations in order to grasp one's emotional experience.[2]

My effort to show the force of a simple statement taken literally goes against anthropology's classic norms, which prefer to explicate culture through the gradual thickening of symbolic webs of meaning. By and large, cultural analysts use not *force* but such terms as *thick description, multivocality, polysemy, richness,* and *texture.* The notion of force, among other things, opens to question the common anthropological assumption that the greatest human import resides in the densest forest of symbols and that analytical detail, or "cultural depth," equals enhanced explanation of a culture, or "cultural elaboration." Do people always in fact describe most thickly what matters most to them?

THE RAGE IN ILONGOT GRIEF

Let me pause a moment to introduce the Ilongots, among whom my wife, Michelle Rosaldo, and I lived and conducted field research for thirty months (1967–69, 1974), They number about 3,500 and reside in an upland area some 90 miles northeast of Manila, Philippines.[3] They subsist by hunting deer and wild pig and by cultivating rain-fed gardens (swiddens) with rice, sweet potatoes, manioc, and vegetables. Their (bilateral) kin relations are reckoned through men and women. After marriage, parents and their married daughters live in the same or adjacent households. The largest unit within the society, a largely territorial descent group called the *bertan,* becomes manifest primarily in the context of feuding. For themselves, their neighbors, and their ethnographers, head-hunting stands out as the Ilongots' most salient cultural practice.

When Ilongots told me, as they often did, how the rage in bereavement could impel men to headhunt, I brushed aside their one-line accounts as too simple, thin, opaque, implausible, stereotypical, or otherwise unsatisfying. Probably I naively equated grief with sadness. Certainly no personal experience allowed me to imagine the powerful rage Ilongots claimed to find in bereavement. My own inability to conceive the force of anger in grief led me to seek out another level of analysis that could provide a deeper explanation for older men's desire to headhunt.

Not until some fourteen years after first recording the terse Ilongot statement about grief and a headhunter's rage did I begin to grasp its overwhelming force. For years I thought that more verbal elaboration (which was not forth-coming) or another analytical level (which remained elusive) could better explain older men's motives for headhunting. Only after being repositioned through a devastating loss of my own could I better grasp that Ilongot older men mean precisely what they say when they describe the anger in bereavement as the source of their desire to cut off human heads. Taken at face value and granted its full weight, their statement reveals much about what compels these older men to headhunt.

In my efforts to find a "deeper" explanation for headhunting, I explored exchange theory, perhaps because it had informed so many classic ethnographies. One day in 1974, I explained the anthropologist's exchange model to an older Ilongot man named Insan. What did he think, I asked, of the idea that headhunting resulted from the way that one death (the beheaded victim's) canceled another (the next of kin). He looked puzzled, so I went on to say that the victim of a beheading was exchanged for the death of one's own kin, thereby balancing the books, so to speak. Insan reflected a moment and replied that he imagined somebody could think such a thing (a safe bet, since I just had), but that he and other Ilongots did not think any such thing. Nor was there any indirect evidence for my exchange theory in ritual, boast, song, or casual conversation.[4]

In retrospect, then, these efforts to impose exchange theory on one aspect of Ilongot behavior appear feeble. Suppose I had discovered what I sought? Although the notion of balancing the ledger does have a certain elegant coherence, one wonders how such bookish dogma could inspire any man to take another man's life at the risk of his own.

My life experience had not as yet provided the means to imagine the rage that can come with devastating loss. Nor could I, therefore, fully appreciate the acute problem of meaning that Ilongots faced in 1974. Shortly after Ferdinand Marcos declared martial law in 1972, rumors that firing squads had become the new punishment for headhunting reached the Ilongot hills. The men therefore decided to call a moratorium on taking heads. In past epochs, when headhunting had become impossible, Ilongots had allowed their rage to dissipate, as best it could, in the course of everyday life. In 1974, they had another option; they began to consider conversion to evangelical Christianity as a means of coping with their grief. Accepting the new religion, people said, implied abandoning their old ways, including headhunting. It also made coping with bereavement less agonizing because they could believe that the deceased had departed for a better world. No longer did they have to confront the awful finality of death.

The force of the dilemma faced by the Ilongots eluded me at the time. Even when I correctly recorded their statements about grieving and the need to throw away their anger, I simply did not grasp the weight of their words. In 1974, for example, while Michelle Rosaldo and I were living among the Ilongots, a six-month-old baby died, probably of pneumonia. That afternoon we visited the father and found him terribly stricken. "He was sobbing and staring through glazed and bloodshot eyes at the cotton blanket covering his baby."[5] The man suffered intensely, for this was the seventh child he had lost. Just a few years before, three of his children had died, one after the other, in a matter of days. At the time, the situation was murky as people present talked both about evangelical Christianity (the possible renunciation of taking heads) and their grudges against lowlanders (the contemplation of headhunting forays into the surrounding valleys).

Through subsequent days and weeks, the man's grief moved him in a way I had not anticipated. Shortly after the baby's death, the father converted to evangelical Christianity. Altogether too quick on the inference, I immediately concluded that the man believed that the new religion could somehow prevent further deaths in his family. When I spoke my mind to an Ilongot friend, he snapped at me, saying that "I had missed the point: what the man in fact sought in the new religion was not the denial of our inevitable deaths but a means of coping with his grief. With the advent of martial law, headhunting was out of the question as a means of venting his wrath and thereby lessening his grief. Were he to remain in his Ilongot way of life, the pain of his sorrow would simply be too much to bear."[6] My description from 1980 now seems so apt that I wonder how I could have written the words and nonetheless failed to appreciate the force of the grieving man's desire to vent his rage.

Another representative anecdote makes my failure to imagine the rage possible in Ilongot bereavement all the more remarkable. On this occasion, Michelle Rosaldo and I were urged by Ilongot friends to play the tape of a headhunting celebration we had witnessed some five years before. No sooner had we turned on the tape and heard the boast of a man who had died in the intervening years than did people abruptly tell us to shut off the recorder. Michelle Rosaldo reported on the tense conversation that ensued:

> As Insan braced himself to speak, the room again became almost uncannily electric. Backs straightened and my anger turned to nervousness and something more like fear as I saw 'that Insan's eyes were red: Tukbaw, Renato's Ilongot "brother," then broke into what was a brittle silence, saying he could make things clear. He told us that it hurt to listen to a headhunting celebration when people knew that there would never be another. As he put it: "The song pulls at us, drags our hearts, it makes us think of our dead uncle." And again: "It would be better if I had accepted God, but I still am an Ilongot at heart; and when I hear the song, my heart aches as it does when I must look upon unfinished bachelors whom I know that I will never lead to take a head." Then Wagat, Tukbaw's wife, said with her eyes that all my questions gave her pain, and told me: "Leave off now, isn't that enough? Even I, a woman, cannot stand the way it feels inside my heart."[7]

From my present position, it is evident that the tape recording of the dead man's boast evoked powerful feelings of bereavement, particularly rage and the impulse to headhunt. At the time I could only feel apprehensive and diffusely sense the force of the emotions experienced by Insan, Tukbaw, Wagat, and the others present.

The dilemma for the Ilongots grew out of a set of cultural practices that, when blocked, were agonizing to live with. The cessation of headhunting called for painful adjustments to other modes of coping with the rage they round in bereavement. One could compare their dilemma with the notion that the failure to perform rituals can create anxiety.[8] In the Ilongot case, the cultural notion that throwing away a human head also casts away the anger creates a problem of meaning when the headhunting ritual cannot be performed. Indeed, Max Weber's classic problem of meaning in *The Protestant Ethic and the Spirit of Capitalism* is precisely of this kind.[9] On a logical plane, the Calvinist doctrine of predestination seems lawless: God has chosen the elect, but his decision can never be known by mortals. Among those whose ultimate concern is salvation, the doctrine of predestination is as easy to grasp conceptually as it is impossible to endure in everyday life (unless one happens to be a "religious virtuoso"). For Calvinists and Ilongots alike, the problem of meaning resides in practice, not theory. The dilemma for both groups involves the practical matter of how to live with one's beliefs, rather than the logical puzzlement produced by abstruse doctrine.

HOW I FOUND THE RAGE IN GRIEF

One burden of this introduction concerns the claim that it took some fourteen years for me to grasp what Ilongots had told me about grief, rage, and headhunting. During all those years I was not yet in a position to comprehend the force of anger possible in bereavement, and now I am. Introducing myself into this account requires a certain hesitation both because of the discipline's taboo and because of its increasingly frequent violation by essays laced with trendy amalgams of continental philosophy and autobiographical snippets. If classic ethnography's vice was the slippage from the ideal of detachment to actual indifference, that of present-day reflexivity is the tendency for the self-absorbed Self to lose sight altogether of the culturally different Other. Despite the risks involved, as the ethnographer I must enter the discussion at this point to elucidate certain issues of method.

The key concept in what follows is that of the positioned (and repositioned) subject.[10] In routine interpretive procedure, according to the methodology of hermeneutics, one can say that ethnographers reposition themselves as they go about understanding other cultures. Ethnographers begin research with a set of questions, revise them throughout the course of inquiry, and in the end emerge with different questions than they started with. One's surprise at the answer to a question, in other words, requires one to revise the question until lessening surprises or diminishing returns indicate a stopping point. This interpretive approach has been most influentially articulated within anthropology by Clifford Geertz."

Interpretive method usually rests on the axiom that gifted ethnographers learn their trade by preparing themselves as broadly as possible. To follow the meandering course of ethnographic inquiry, field-workers require wide-ranging theoretical capacities and finely tuned sensibilities. After all, one cannot predict beforehand what one will encounter in the field. One influential anthropologist, Clyde Kluckhohn, even went so far as to recommend a double initiation: first, the ordeal of psychoanalysis, and then that of fieldwork. All too often, however, this view is extended until certain prerequisites of field research appear to guarantee an authoritative ethnography. Eclectic book knowledge and a range of life experiences, along with edifying reading and self-awareness, supposedly vanquish the twin vices of ignorance and insensitivity.

Although the doctrine of preparation, knowledge, and sensibility contains much to admire, one should work to under mine the false comfort that it can convey. At what point can people say that they have completed their learning or their life experience? The problem with taking this mode of pre paring the ethnographer too much to heart is that it can lend a false air of security, an authoritative claim to certitude and finality that our analyses cannot have. All interpretations are provisional; they are made by positioned subjects who are prepared to know certain things and not others. Even when knowledge-able, sensitive, fluent in the language, and able to move easily in an alien cultural world, good ethnographers still have their limits, and their analyses always are incomplete. Thus, I began to fathom the force of what Ilongots had been telling me about their losses through my own loss, and not through any systematic preparation for field research.

My preparation for understanding serious loss began in 1970 with the death of my brother, shortly after his twenty-seventh birthday. By experiencing this ordeal with my mother and father, I gained a measure of insight into the trauma of a parent's losing a child. This insight informed my account, partially described earlier, of an Ilongot man's reactions to the death of his seventh child. At the same time, my bereavement was so much less than that of my parents that I could not then imagine the overwhelming force of rage possible in such grief. My former position is probably similar to that of many in the discipline. One should recognize that ethnographic knowledge tends to have the strengths and limitations given by the relative youth of field-workers who, for the most part, have not suffered serious losses and could have, for example, no personal knowledge of how devastating the loss of a long-term partner can be for the survivor.

In 1981 Michelle Rosaldo and I began field research among the Ifugaos of northern Luzon, Philippines. On October 11 of that year, she was walking along a trail with two Ifugao companions when she lost her footing and fell to her death some 65 feet down a sheer precipice into a swollen river be-low. Immediately on finding her body I became enraged. How could she abandon me? How could she have been so stupid as to fall? I tried to cry. I sobbed, but rage blocked the tears. Less than a month later I described this moment in my journal: "I felt like in a nightmare, the whole world around me expanding and contracting, visually and viscerally heaving. Going down I find a group of men, maybe seven or eight, standing still, silent, and I heave and sob, but no tears," An earlier experi-ence, on the fourth anniversary of my brother's death, had taught me to recognize heaving sobs without tears as a form of anger. This anger, in a number of forms, has swept over me on many occasions since then, lasting hours and even days at a time. Such feelings can be aroused by rituals, but more often they emerge from unexpected reminders (not unlike the Ilongots' unnerving encounter with their dead uncle's voice on the tape recorder).

Lest there be any misunderstanding, bereavement should not be reduced to anger, neither for myself nor for anyone else. Powerful visceral emotional states swept over me, at times separately and at other times together. I experienced the deep cutting pain of sorrow almost beyond endurance, the cadaverous cold of realizing the finality of death, the trembling beginning in my abdomen and spreading through my body, the mourn-ful keening that started without my willing, and frequent tearful sobbing. My present purpose of revising earlier understandings of Ilongot headhunting, and not a general view of bereavement, thus focuses on anger rather than on other emotions in grief.

Writings in English especially need to emphasize the rage in grief. Although grief therapists routinely encourage awareness of anger among the bereaved, upper-middle-class Anglo-American culture tends to ignore the rage devastating losses can bring. Paradoxically, this culture's conventional wisdom usually denies the anger in grief at the same time that therapists encourage members of the invisible community of the bereaved to talk in detail about how angry their losses make them feel. My brother's death in combination with what I learned about anger from Ilongots (for them, an emotional state more publicly celebrated than denied) allowed me immediately to recognize the experience of rage.[13]

Ilongot anger and my own overlap, rather like two circles, partially overlaid and partially separate. They are not identical. Alongside striking similarities, significant differences in tone, cultural form, and human consequences distinguish the "anger" animating our respective ways of grieving. My vivid fantasies, for example, about a life insurance agent who refused to recognize Michelle's death as job-related did not lead me to kill him, cut off his head, and celebrate afterward. In so speaking, I am illustrating the discipline's methodological caution against the reckless attribution of one's own categories and experiences to members of another culture. Such warnings against facile notions of universal human nature can, however, be carried too far and harden into the equally pernicious doctrine that, my own group aside, everything human is alien to me. One hopes to achieve a balance between recognizing wide-ranging human differences and the modest truism that any two human groups must have certain things in common.

Only a week before completing the initial draft of an earlier version of this introduction, I rediscovered my journal entry, written some six weeks after Michelle's death, in which I made a vow to myself about how I would return to writing anthropology, if I ever did so, "by writing Grief and a Headhunter's Rage ..." My journal went on to reflect more broadly, on death, rage, and headhunting by speaking of my "wish for the Ilongot solution; they are much more in touch with reality than Christians. So, I need a place to carry my anger—and can we say a solution of the imagination is better than theirs? And can we condemn them when we napalm villages? Is our rationale so much sounder than theirs?" All this was written in despair and rage.

Not until some fifteen months after Michelle's death was I again able to begin writing anthropology. Writing the initial version of "Grief and a Headhunter's Rage" was in fact cathartic, though perhaps hot in the way one would imagine. Rather than following after the completed composition, the catharsis occurred beforehand. When the initial version of this introduction was most acutely on my mind, during the month before actually beginning to write, I felt diffusely depressed and ill with a fever. Then one day an almost literal fog lifted and words began to flow. It seemed less as if I were doing the writing than that the words were writing themselves through me.

My use of personal experience serves as a vehicle for making the quality and intensity of the rage in Ilongot grief more readily accessible to readers than certain more detached modes of composition. At the same time, by invoking personal experience as an analytical category one risks easy dismissal. Unsympathetic readers could reduce this introduction to an act of mourning or a mere report on my discovery of the anger possible in bereavement. Frankly, this introduction is both and more. An act of mourning, a personal report, *and* a critical analysis of anthropological method, it simultaneously encompasses a number of distinguishable processes, no one of which cancels out the others. Similarly, I argue in what follows that ritual in general and Ilongot headhunting in particular form the intersection of multiple coexisting social processes. Aside from revising the ethnographic record, the paramount claim made here concerns how my own mourning and consequent reflection on Ilongot bereavement, rage, and headhunting raise methodological issues of general concern in anthropology and the human sciences.

DEATH IN ANTHROPOLOGY

Anthropology favors interpretations that equate analytical "depth" with cultural "elaboration." Many studies focus on visibly bounded arenas where one can observe formal and repetitive events, such as ceremonies, rituals, and games. Similarly, studies of word play are more likely to focus on jokes as programmed monologues than on the less scripted, more free-wheeling improvised interchanges of witty banter. Most ethnographers prefer to study events that have definite locations in space with marked centers and outer edges. Temporally, they have middles and endings. Historically, they appear to repeat identical structures by seemingly doing things today as they were done yesterday. Their qualities of fixed definition liberate such events from the untidiness of everyday life so that they can be "read" like articles, books, or, as we now say, *texts*.

Guided by their emphasis on self-contained entities, ethnographies written in accord with classic norms consider death under the rubric of ritual rather than bereavement. Indeed, the subtitles of even recent ethnographies on death make the emphasis on ritual explicit. William Douglas's *Death in Murelaga* is subtitled *Funerary Ritual in a Spanish Basque Village;* Richard Huntington and Peter Metcalf's *Celebrations of Death* is subtitled *The Anthropology of Mortuary Ritual;* Peter Metcalf's *A Borneo Journey into Death* is subtitled *Berawan Eschatology from Its Rituals.*[14] Ritual itself is defined by its formality and routine; under such descriptions, it more nearly resembles a recipe, a fixed program, or a book of etiquette than an open-ended human process.

Ethnographies that in this manner eliminate intense emotions not only distort their descriptions but also remove potentially key variables from their explanations. When anthropologist William Douglas, for example, announces his project in *Death in Murelaga,* he explains that his objective is to use death and funerary ritual "as a heuristic device with which to approach the study of rural Basque society."[15] In other words, the primary object of study is social structure, not death, and certainly not bereavement. The author begins his analysis by saying, "Death is not always fortuitous or unpredictable."[16] He goes on to describe how an old woman, ailing with the infirmities of her age, welcomed her death. The description largely ignores the perspective of the most bereaved survivors, and instead vacillates between those of the old woman and a detached observer.

Undeniably, certain people do live a full life and suffer so greatly in their decrepitude that they embrace the relief death can bring. Yet the problem with making an ethnography's major case study focus on "a very easy death"[17] (I use Simone de Beauvoir's title with irony, as she did) is not only its lack of representativeness but also that it makes death in general appear as routine for the survivors as this particular one apparently was for the deceased. Were the old woman's sons and daughters untouched by her death? The case study shows less about how people cope with death than about how death can be made to appear routine, thereby fitting neatly into the author's view of funerary ritual as a mechanical programmed unfolding of prescribed acts. "To the Basque," says Douglas, "ritual is order and order is ritual."[18]

Douglas captures only one extreme in the range of possible deaths. Putting the accent on the routine aspects of ritual conveniently conceals the agony of such unexpected early deaths as parents losing a grown child or a mother dying in childbirth. Concealed in such descriptions are the agonies of the survivors who muddle through shifting, powerful emotional states. Although Douglas acknowledges the distinction between the bereaved members of the deceased's domestic group and the more public ritualistic group, he writes his account primarily from the viewpoint of the latter. He masks the emotional force of bereavement by reducing funerary ritual to Orderly routine.

Surely, human beings mourn both in ritual settings *and* in the informal settings of everyday life. Consider the evidence that willy-nilly spills over the edges in Godfrey Wilson's classic anthropological account of "conventions of burial" among the Nyakyusa of South Africa:

> That some at least of those who attend a Nyakyusa burial are moved by grief it is easy to establish. I have heard people talking regretfully in ordinary conversation of a man's death; I have seen a man whose sister had just died walk over alone towards her grave and weep quietly by himself without any parade of grief; and I have heard of a man killing himself because of his grief for a dead son.[19]

Note that all the instances Wilson witnesses or hears about happen outside the circumscribed sphere of formal ritual. People converse among themselves, walk alone and silently weep, or more impulsively commit suicide. The work of grieving, probably universally, occurs both within obligatory ritual acts and in more everyday settings where people find themselves alone or with close kin.

In Nyakyusa burial ceremonies, powerful emotional states also become present in the ritual itself, which is more than a series of obligatory acts. Men say they dance the passions of their bereavement, which includes a complex mix of anger, fear, and grief:

> "This war dance *(ukukina),*" said an old man, "is mourning, we are mourn-ing the dead man. We dance because there is war in our hearts. A passion of grief and fear exasperates us *(ilyyojo likutusila)."* ... *Elyojo* means a passion or grief, anger or fear; *ukusila* means to annoy or exasperate beyond endurance. In explaining *ukusila* one man put it like this: "If a man continually insults me then he exasperates me *(ukusila)* so that I want to fight him." Death is a fearful and grievous event that exasperates those men nearly concerned and makes them want to fight.[20]

Descriptions of the dance and subsequent quarrels, even killings, provide ample evidence of the emotional intensity involved. The articulate testimony by Wilson's informants makes it obvious that even the most intense sentiments can be studied by ethnographers.

Despite such exceptions as Wilson, the general rule seems to be that one should tidy things up as much as possible by wiping away the tears and ignoring the tantrums. Most anthropological studies of death eliminate emotions by assuming the position of the most detached observer.[21] Such studies usually conflate the ritual process with the process of mourning, equate ritual with the obligatory, and ignore the relation between ritual and everyday life. The bias that favors formal ritual risks assuming the answers to questions that most need to be asked. Do rituals, for example, always reveal cultural depth?

Most analysts who equate death with funerary ritual assume that rituals store encap-sulated wisdom as if it were a microcosm of its encompassing cultural macrocosm. One recent study of death and mourning, for example, confidently begins by affirming that rituals embody "the collective wisdom of many cultures."[22] Yet this generalization surely requires case-by-case investigation against a broader range of alternative hypotheses.

At the polar extremes, rituals either display cultural depth or brim over with platitudes. In the former case, rituals indeed encapsulate a culture's wisdom; in the latter instance, they act as catalysts that precipitate processes whose unfolding occurs over subsequent months or even years. Many rituals, of course, do both by combining a measure of wisdom with a comparable dose of platitudes.

My own experience of bereavement and ritual fits the platitudes and catalyst model better than that of microcosmic deep culture. Even a careful analysis of the language and symbolic action during the two funerals for which I was a chief mourner would reveal precious little about the experience of bereavement.[23] This statement, of course, should not lead anyone to derive a universal from somebody else's personal knowledge. Instead, it should encourage ethnographers to ask whether a ritual's wisdom is deep or conventional, and whether its process is immediately transformative or but a single step in a lengthy series of ritual and everyday events.

In attempting to grasp the cultural force of rage and other powerful emotional states, both formal ritual and the informal practices of everyday life provide crucial insight. Thus, cultural descriptions should seek out force as well as thickness, and they should extend from well-defined rituals to * myriad less circumscribed practices.

GRIEF, RAGE, AND ILONGOT HEADHUNTING

When applied to Ilongot headhunting, the view of ritual as a storehouse of collective wisdom aligns headhunting with expiatory sacrifice. The raiders call the spirits of the potential victims, bid their ritual farewells, and seek favorable omens along the trail. Ilongot men vividly recall the hunger and deprivation they endure over the days and even weeks it takes to move cautiously toward the place where they set up an ambush and await the first person who happens along. Once the raiders kill their victim, they toss away the head rather than keep it as a trophy. In tossing away the head, they claim by analogy to cast away their life burdens, including the rage in their grief.

Before a raid, men describe their state of being by saying that the burdens of life have made them heavy and entangled, like a tree with vines clinging to it. They say that a successfully completed raid makes them feel light of step and ruddy in complexion. The collective energy of the celebration with its song, music, and dance reportedly gives the participants a sense of well-being. The expiatory ritual process involves cleansing and catharsis.

The analysis just sketched regards ritual as a timeless, self-contained process. Without denying the insight in this approach, its limits must also be considered. Imagine, for example, exorcism rituals described as if they were complete in themselves, rather than being linked with larger processes unfolding before and after the ritual period. Through what processes does the afflicted person recover or continue to be afflicted after the ritual? What are the social consequences of recovery or its absence? Failure to consider such questions diminishes the force of such afflictions and therapies for which the formal ritual is but a phase. Still other questions apply to differently positioned subjects, including the person afflicted, the healer, and the audience. In all cases, the problem involves the delineation of processes that occur before and after, as well as during, the ritual moment.

Let us call the notion of a self-contained sphere of deep cultural activity the *microcosmic view,* and an alternative view *ritual as a busy intersection.* In the latter case, ritual appears as a place where a number of distinct social processes intersect. The crossroads simply provides a space for distinct trajectories to traverse, rather than containing them in complete encapsulated form. From this perspective, Ilongot headhunting stands at the confluence of three analytically separable processes.

The first process concerns whether or not it is an opportune time to raid. Historical conditions determine the possibilities of raiding, which range from frequent to likely to unlikely to impossible. These conditions include American colonial efforts at pacification, the Great Depression, World War II, revolutionary movements in the surrounding low-lands, feuding among Ilongot groups, and the declaration of martial law in 1972. Ilongots use the analogy of hunting to speak of such historical vicissitudes. Much as Ilongot hunts-men say they cannot know when game will cross their path or whether their arrows will strike the target, so certain historical forces that condition their existence remain beyond their control. My book *Ilongot Headhunting, 1883–1974* explores the impact of historical factors on Ilongot headhunting.

Second, young men coming of age undergo a protracted period of personal turmoil during which they desire nothing so much as to take a head. During this troubled period, they seek a life partner and contemplate the traumatic dislocation of leaving their families of origin and entering their new wife's household as a stranger. Young men weep, sing, and burst out in anger because of their fierce desire to take a head and wear the coveted red hornbill earrings that adorn the ears of men who already have, as Ilongots say, arrived *(tabi)*. Volatile, envious, passionate (at least according to their own cultural stereotype of the young unmarried man *[buintaw]*), they constantly lust to take a head. Michelle and I began fieldwork among the Ilongots only a year after abandoning our unmarried youths; hence our ready empathy with youthful turbulence. Her book on Ilongot notions of self explores the passionate anger of young men as they come of age.

Third, older men are differently positioned than their younger counterparts. Because they have already beheaded somebody, they can wear the red hornbill earrings so coveted by youths. Their desire to headhunt grows less from chronic adolescent turmoil than from more intermittent acute agonies of loss. After the death of somebody to whom they are closely attached, older men often inflict on themselves vows of abstinence, not to be lifted until the day they participate in a successful headhunting raid. These deaths can cover a range of instances from literal death, whether through natural causes or beheading, to social death where, for example, a man's wife runs off with another man. In all cases, the rage born of devastating loss animates the older men's desire to raid. This anger at abandonment is irreducible in that nothing at a deeper level explains it. Although certain analysts argue against the dreaded last analysis, the linkage of grief, rage, and headhunting has no other known explanation.

My earlier understandings of Ilongot headhunting missed the fuller significance of how older men experience loss and rage. Older men prove critical in this context because they, not the youths, set the processes of headhunting in motion. Their rage is intermittent, whereas that of youths is continuous. In the equation of headhunting, older men are the variable and younger men are the constant. Culturally speaking, older men are endowed with knowledge and stamina that their juniors have not yet attained, hence they care for *(saysay)* and lead *(bukur)* the younger men when they raid.

In a preliminary survey of the literature on headhunting, I found that the lifting of mourning prohibitions frequently occurs after taking a head. The notion that youthful anger and older men's rage lead them to take heads is more plausible than such commonly reported "explanations" of headhunting as the need to acquire mystical "soul stuff" or personal names.[24] Because the discipline correctly rejects stereotypes of the "bloodthirsty savage," it must investigate how headhunters create an intense desire to decapitate their fellow humans. The human sciences must explore the cultural force of emotions with a view to delineating the passions that animate certain forms of human conduct.

SUMMARY

The ethnographer, as a positioned subject, grasps certain human phenomena better than others. He or she occupies a position or structural location and observes with a particular angle of vision. Consider, for example, how age, gender, being an outsider, and association with a neo-colonial regime influence what the ethnographer learns. The notion of position also refers to how life experiences both enable and inhibit particular kinds of insight. In the case at hand, nothing in my own experience equipped me even to imagine the anger possible in bereavement until after Michelle Rosaldo's death in 1981. Only then was I in a position to grasp the force of what Ilongots had repeatedly told me about grief, rage, and headhunting. By the same token, so-called natives are also positioned subjects who have a distinctive mix of insight and blindness. Consider the structural positions of older versus younger Ilongot men, or the differing positions of chief mourners versus those less involved during a funeral. My discussion of anthropological writings on death often achieved its effects simply by shifting from the position of those least involved to that of the chief mourners.

Cultural depth does not always equal cultural elaboration. Think simply of the speaker who is filibustering. The language used can sound elaborate as it heaps word on word, but surely it is not deep. Depth should be separated from the presence or absence of elaboration. By the same token, one-line explanations can be vacuous or pithy. The concept of force calls attention to an enduring intensity in human conduct that can occur with or without the dense elaboration conventionally associated with cultural depth. Although relatively without elaboration in speech, song, or ritual, the rage of older Ilongot men who have suffered devastating losses proves enormously consequential in that, foremost among other things, it leads them to behead their fellow humans. Thus, the notion of force involves both affective intensity and significant consequences that unfold over a long period of time.

Similarly, rituals do not always encapsulate deep cultural wisdom. At times they instead contain the wisdom of Polonius. Although certain rituals both reflect and create ultimate values, others simply bring people together and deliver a set of platitudes that enable them to go on with their lives. Rituals serve as vehicles for processes that occur both before and after the period of their performance. Funeral rituals, for example, do not "contain" all the complex processes of bereavement. Ritual and bereavement should not be collapsed into one another because they neither fully encapsulate nor fully explain one another. Instead, rituals are often but points along a number of longer processual trajectories; hence, my image of ritual as a crossroads where distinct life processes intersect.[25]

The notion of ritual as a busy intersection anticipates the critical assessment of the concept of culture developed in the following chapters. In contrast with the classic view, which posits culture as a self-contained whole made up of coherent patterns, culture can arguably be conceived as a more porous array of intersections where distinct processes crisscross from within and beyond its borders. Such heterogeneous processes often derive from differences of age, gender, class, race, and sexual orientation.

This book argues that a sea change in cultural studies has eroded once-dominant conceptions of truth and objectivity. The truth of objectivism—absolute, universal, and timeless—has lost its monopoly status. It now competes, on more nearly equal terms, with the truths of case studies and colored by local perceptions. The agenda for social analysis has shifted to include not only eternal verities and law like generalizations but also political processes, social changes, and human differences. Such terms as *objectivity, neutrality,* and *impartiality* refer to subject positions once endowed with great institutions but they are arguably neither more nor less valid than those of more engaged, yet equally perceptive, knowledgeable social actors. Social analysis must now grapple with the realization that its objects of analysis are also analyzing subjects who critically interrogate ethnographers— their writings, their ethics, and their politics.

PART II

HUMANS AS SYMBOL-MAKERS

Sex, Lies, and Conversation
Why Is It So Hard for Men and Women to Talk to Each Other?

Deborah Tannen

Most divorced women cite poor communication as a major contributor to their divorces. Few men even mention it as a factor. How is it that men and women perceive their communication so differently? According to the linguist Deborah Tannen, the discrepancy takes root in childhood and reflects the different roles played by verbal communication in men's and women's lives. This selection, adapted from Tannen's 1995 book *You Just Don't Understand: Women and Men in Conversation,* helps us understand the opposite gender and its very different conversational culture.

I was addressing a small gathering in a suburban Virginia living room—a women's group that had invited men to join them. Throughout the evening, one man had been particularly talkative, frequently offering ideas and anecdotes, while his wife sat silently beside him on the couch. Toward the end of the evening, I commented that women frequently complain that their husbands don't talk to them. This man quickly concurred. He gestured toward his wife and said, "She's the talker in our family." The room burst into laughter; the man looked puzzled and hurt. "It's true," he explained. "When I come home from work I have nothing to say. If she didn't keep the conversation going, we'd spend the whole evening in silence."

This episode crystallizes the irony that although American men tend to talk more than women in public situations, they often talk less at home. And this pattern is wreaking havoc with marriage.

The pattern was observed by political scientist Andrew Hacker in the late '70s. Sociologist Catherine Kohler Riessman reports in her new book *Divorce Talk* that most of the women she interviewed-but only a few of the men gave lack of communication as the reason for their divorces. Given the current divorce rate of nearly 50 percent, that amounts to millions of cases in the United States every year-a virtual epidemic of failed conversation.

In my own research, complaints from women about their husbands most often focused not on tangible inequities such as having given up the chance-' for a career to accompany a husband to his, or doing far more than their share of daily life-support work like cleaning, cooking, social arrangements, and errands. Instead, they focused on communication: "He doesn't listen to me," "He doesn't talk to me." I found, as Hacker observed years before, that most wives want their husbands to be, first and foremost, conversational partners, but few husbands share this expectation of their wives.

In short, the image that best represents the current crisis is the stereotypical cartoon scene of a man sitting at the breakfast table with a newspaper held up in front of his face, while a woman glares at the back of it, wanting to talk.

LINGUISTIC BATTLE OF THE SEXES

How can women and men have such different impressions of communication in marriage? Why the widespread imbalance in their interests and expectations?

In the April [1990] issue of *American Psychologist*, Stanford University's Eleanor Maccoby reports the results of her own and others' research showing that children's development is most influenced by the social structure of peer interactions. Boys and girls tend to play with children of their own gender, and their sex-separate groups have different organizational structures and interactive norms.

I believe these systematic differences in childhood socialization make talk between women and men like cross-cultural communication, heir to all the attraction and pitfalls of that enticing but difficult enterprise. My research on men's and women's conversations uncovered patterns similar to those described for children's groups.

For women, as for girls, intimacy is the fabric of relationships, and talk is the thread from which it is woven. Little girls create and maintain friendships by exchanging secrets; similarly, women regard conversation as the cornerstone of friendship. So a woman expects her husband to be a new and improved version of a best friend. What is important is not the individual subjects that are discussed but the sense of closeness, of a life shared, that emerges when people tell their thoughts, feelings, and impressions.

Bonds between boys can be as intense as girls', but they are based less on talking, more on doing things together. Since they don't assume talk is the cement that binds a relationship, men don't know what kind of talk women want, and they don't miss it when it isn't there.

Boys' groups are larger, more inclusive, and more hierarchical, so boys must struggle to avoid the subordinate position in the group. This may play a role in women's complaints that men don't listen to them. Some men really don't like to listen, because being the listener makes them feel one down, like a child listening to adults or an employee to a boss.

But often when women tell men, "You aren't listening," and the men protest, "I am," the men are right. The impression of not listening results from misalignment in the mechanics of conversation. The misalignment begins as soon as a man and a woman take physical positions. This became clear when I studied videotapes made by psychologist Paul Dorval of children and adults talking to their same-sex best friends. I found that at every age, the girls and women faced each other directly, their eyes anchored on each other's faces. At every age, the boys and men sat at angles to each other and looked elsewhere in the room, periodically glancing at each other. They were obviously attuned to each other, often mirroring each other's movements. But the tendency of men to face away can give women the impression they aren't listening even when they are. A young woman in college was frustrated: Whenever she told her boyfriend she wanted to talk to him, he would lie down on the floor, close his eyes, and put his arm over his face. This signaled to her, "He's taking a nap." But he insisted he was listening extra hard. Normally, he looks around the room, so he is easily distracted. Lying down and covering his eyes helped him concentrate on what she was saying.

Analogous to the physical alignment that women and men take in conversation is their topical alignment. The girls in my study tended to talk at length about one topic, but the boys tended to jump from topic to topic. The second-grade girls exchanged stories about people they knew. The second grade boys teased, told jokes, noticed things in the room, and talked about finding games to play. The sixth-grade girls talked about problems with a mutual friend. The sixth-grade boys talked about fifty-five different topics, none of which extended over more than a few turns.

LISTENING TO BODY LANGUAGE

Switching topics is another habit that gives women the impression men aren't listening, especially if they switch to a topic about themselves. But the evidence of the tenth-grade boys in my study indicates otherwise. The tenth grade boys sprawled across their chairs with bodies parallel and eyes straight ahead, rarely looking at each other. They looked as if they were riding in a car, staring out the windshield. But they were talking about their feelings. One boy was upset because a girl had told him he had a drinking problem, and the other was feeling alienated from all his friends.

Now, when a girl told a friend about a problem, the friend responded by asking probing questions and expressing agreement and understanding. But the boys dismissed each other's problems. Todd assured Richard that his drinking was "no big problem" because "sometimes you're funny when you're off your butt." And when Todd said he felt left out, Richard responded, "Why should you? You know more people than me."

Women perceive such responses as belittling and unsupportive. But the boys seemed satisfied with them. Whereas women reassure each other by implying, "You shouldn't feel bad because I've had similar experiences," men do so by implying, "You shouldn't feel bad because your problems aren't so bad."

There are even simpler reasons for women's impression that men don't listen. Linguist Lynette Hirschman found that women make more listener-noise, such as "mhm," "uhuh," and "yeah," to show "I'm with you." Men, she found, more often give silent attention. Women who expect a stream of listener noise interpret silent attention as no attention at all.

Women's conversational habits are as frustrating to men as men's are to women. Men who expect silent attention interpret a stream of listener noise as overreaction or impatience. Also, when women talk to each other in a close, comfortable setting, they often overlap, finish each other's sentences, and anticipate what the other is about to say. This practice, which I call "participatory listenership," is often perceived by men as interruption, intrusion, and lack of attention.

A parallel difference caused a man to complain about his wife, "She just wants to talk about her own point of view. If I show her another view, she gets mad at me. When most women talk to each other, they assume a conversationalist's job is to express agreement and support. But many men see their conversational duty as pointing out the other side of an argument. This is heard as disloyalty by women, and refusal to offer the requisite support. It is not that women don't want to see other points of view, but that they prefer them phrased as suggestions and inquiries rather than as direct challenges.

In his book *Fighting for Life*, Walter Ong points out that men use "agonistic" or warlike, oppositional formats to do almost anything; thus discussion becomes debate and conversation becomes a competitive sport. In contrast, women see conversation as a ritual means of establishing rapport. If Jane tells a problem and June says she has a similar one, they walk away feeling closer to each other. But this attempt at establishing rapport can backfire when used with men. Men take too literally women's ritual "troubles talk," just as women mistake men's ritual challenges for real attack.

THE SOUNDS OF SILENCE

These differences begin to clarify why women and men have such different expectations about communication in marriage. For women, talk creates intimacy. Marriage is an orgy of closeness: you can tell your feelings and thoughts, and still be loved. Their greatest fear is being pushed away. But men live in a hierarchical world, where talk maintains independence and status. They are on guard to protect themselves from being put down and pushed around.

This explains the paradox of the talkative man who said of his silent wife, "She's the talker." In the public setting of a guest lecture, he felt challenged to show his intelligence and display his understanding of the lecture. But at home, where he has nothing to prove and no one to defend against, he is free to remain silent. For his wife, being home means she is free from the worry that something she says might offend someone, or spark disagreement, or appear to be showing off; at home she is free to talk.

The communication problems that endanger marriage can't be fixed by mechanical engineering. They require a new conceptual framework about the role of talk in human relationships. Many of the psychological explanations that have become second nature may not be helpful, because they tend to blame either women (for not being assertive enough) or men (for not being in touch with their feelings). A sociolinguistic approach by which male-female conversation is seen as cross-cultural communication allows us to understand the problem and forge solutions without blaming either party.

Once the problem is understood, improvement comes naturally, as it did to the young woman and her boyfriend who seemed to go to sleep when she wanted to talk. Previously, she had accused him of not listening, and he had refused to change his behavior, since that would be admitting fault. But then she learned about and explained to him the differences in women's and men's habitual ways of aligning themselves in conversation. The next time she told him she wanted to talk, he began, as usual, by lying down and covering his eyes. When the familiar negative reaction bubbled up, she reassured herself that he really was listening. But then he sat up and looked at her. Thrilled, she asked why, He said, You like me to look at you when we talk, so I'll try to do it." Once he saw their differences as cross-cultural rather than right and wrong, he independently altered his behavior.

Women who feel abandoned and deprived when their husbands won't listen to or report daily news may be happy to discover their husbands trying to adapt once they understand the place of small talk in women's relationships. But if their husbands don't adapt, the women may still be comforted that for men, this is not a failure of intimacy. Accepting the difference, the wives may look to their friends or family for that kind of talk. And husbands who can't provide it shouldn't feel their wives have made unreasonable demands. Some couples will still decide to divorce, but at least their decisions will be based on realistic expectations.

In these times of resurgent ethnic conflicts, the world desperately needs cross-cultural understanding. Like charity, successful cross-cultural communication should begin at home.

SHAKESPEARE IN THE BUSH

Laura Bohannan

Communication is an essential characteristic of human social life. Through language we socialize our children and pass down cultural values from generation to generation, Communication forms and defines relations among individuals as well as among groups. Because communication is so natural, we seldom ask a critical question: When we speak, does the listener understand?

At a minimum, communication involves a sender, a receiver, and a shared code for exchanging information. When an individual or a group sends a message, the sender anticipates that those who receive the message will interpret and understand the message in the way the sender intended. Miscommunication is, of course, an unfortunately common phenomenon that can lead to fist fights, divorces, and wars.

What most of us do not appreciate is the degree to which culture affects our interpretation of messages. As Laura Bohannan tells the tale of Hamlet, we gradually discover how particular behaviors or events can have very different meanings in different places. What is interesting is that the miscommunication of interpretational differences is not a result of poor language or translation abilities. Miscommunication is not a result of speaking too quickly or not loudly enough. It reflects cultural differences.

As you read this selection, ask yourself the following questions:

- *What were the author's original beliefs about the universality of the classics—such as Hamlet?*
- *How did the Tiv elders react to the marriage of Hamlet's mother to his uncle? How was this different from Hamlet's own emotional reaction?*
- *Why do the Tiv believe that a chief should have more than one wife?*
- *As the author tells the story, consider how the elders interpret various actions to fit Tiv culture and in so doing redefine the central meaning of the play.*

The following terms are discussed in this selection:

age grade	*levirate*
agnatic	*polygyny*
chiefdom	*socialization*
cultural relativism	

Just before I left Oxford for the Tiv in West Africa, conversation turned to the season at Stratford. "You Americans," said a friend, "often have difficulty with Shakespeare. He was, after all, a very English poet, and one can easily misinterpret the universal by misunderstanding the particular."

I protested that human nature is pretty much the same the whole world over; at least the general plot and motivation of the greater tragedies would always be clear—everywhere—although some details of custom might have to be explained and difficulties of translation might produce other slight changes. To end an argument we could not conclude, my friend gave me a copy of *Hamlet* to study in the African bush: it would, he hoped, lift my mind above its primitive surroundings, and possibly I might, by prolonged meditation, achieve the grace of correct interpretation.

It was my second field trip to that African tribe, and 1 thought myself ready to live in one of its remote sections—an area difficult to cross even on foot. I eventually settled on the hillock of a very knowledgeable old man, the head of a homestead of some hundred and forty people, all of whom were either his close relatives or their wives and children. Like the other elders of the vicinity, the old man spent most of his time performing ceremonies seldom seen these days in the more accessible parts of the tribe. I was delighted. Soon there would be three months of enforced isolation and leisure, between the harvest that takes place Just before the rising of the swamps and the clearing of new farms when the water goes down. Then, I thought, they would have even more time to perform ceremonies and explain them to me.

I was quite mistaken. Most of the ceremonies demanded the presence of elders from several homesteads. As the swamps rose, the old men found it too difficult to walk from one homestead to the next, and the ceremonies gradually ceased. As the swamps rose even higher, all activities but one came to an end. The women brewed beer from maize and millet. Men, women, and children sat on their hillocks and drank it.

People began to drink at dawn. By midmorning the whole homestead was singing, dancing, and drumming. When it rained people had to sit inside their huts: there they drank and sang or they drank and told stories. In any case, by noon or before, 1 either had to join the party or retire to my own hut and my books, "One does not discuss serious matters when there is beer. Come, drink with us," Since I lacked their capacity for the thick native beer, I spent more and more time with *Hamlet.* Before the end of the second month, grace descended on me. I was quite sure that *Hamlet* had only one possible interpretation, and that one universally obvious.

Early every morning in the hope of having some serious talk before the beer party, 1 used to call on the old man at his reception hut—a circle of posts supporting a thatched roof above a low mud wall to keep out wind and rain. One day I crawled through the low doorway and found most of the men of the homestead sitting huddled in their ragged clothes on stools, low plank beds, and reclining chairs, warming themselves against the chill of the rain around a smoky fire. In the center were three pots of beer. The party had started.

The old man greeted me cordially. "Sit down and drink." I accepted a large calabash full of beer, poured some into a small drinking gourd, and tossed it down. Then I poured some more into the same gourd for the man second in seniority to my host before I handed my calabash over to a young man for further distribution. Important people shouldn't ladle beer themselves.

"It is better like this," the old man said, looking at me approvingly and plucking at the thatch that ad caught in my hair. "You should sit and drink with us more often. Your servants tell me that when you are not with us, you sit inside your hut looking at a paper."

The old man was acquainted with four kinds of "papers;" tax receipts, bride price receipts, court fee receipts, and letters. The messenger who brought him letters from the chief used them mainly as a badge of office, for he always knew what was in them and. told the old man. Personal letters for the few who had relatives in the government or mission stations were kept until someone went to a large market where there was a letter writer and reader. Since my arrival, letters were brought to me to be read. A few men also brought me bride price receipts, privately, with requests to change the figures to a higher sum. 1 found moral arguments were of no avail, since in-laws are fair game, and the technical hazards of forgery difficult to explain to an illiterate people, I did not wish them to think me silly enough to look at any such papers for days on end, and. I hastily explained that my "paper" was one of the "things of long ago" of my country.

"Ah," said the old man. "Tell us."

I protested that 1 was not a storyteller. Storytelling is a skilled art among them; their standards are high and the audiences critical—and vocal in their criticism. I protested in vain. This morning they wanted, to hear a story while they drank. They threatened, to tell me no more stories until I told them one of mine. Finally, the old man promised that no one would criticize my style "for we know you are struggling with our language." "But," put in one of the elders, "you must explain what we do not understand, as we do when we tell you our stories." Realizing that here was my chance to prove Hamlet universally intelligible, I agreed.

The old man handed me some more beer to help me on with my storytelling. Men filled their long wooden pipes and knocked coals from the fire to place in the pipe bowls; then, puffing contentedly, they sat back to listen. I began in the proper style, "Not yesterday, not yesterday, but long ago, a thing occurred. One night three men were keeping watch outside the homestead of the great chief, when suddenly they saw the former chief approach them."

"Why was he no longer their chief?"

"He was dead," I explained., "That is why they were troubled and afraid when they saw him."

"Impossible," began one of the elders, handing his pipe on to his neighbor, who Interrupted, "Of course it wasn't the dead chief. It was an omen sent by a witch. Go on."

Slightly shaken, I continued. "One of these three was a man who knew things"—the closest translation for scholar, but unfortunately it also meant witch. The second elder looked triumphantly at the first. "So he spoke to the dead chief saying, 'Tell us what we must do so you may rest in your grave,' but the dead chief did not answer. He vanished, and they could see him no more. Then the man who knew things—his name was Horatio—said this event was the affair of the dead chief's son, Hamlet."

There was a general shaking of heads round the circle. "Had the dead chief no living brothers? Or was this son the chief?"

"No," I replied, "That is, he had one living brother who became the chief when the elder brother died."

The old men muttered: such omens were matters for chiefs and elders, not for youngsters; no good could come of going behind a chief's back; clearly Horatio was not a man who knew things.

"Yes, he was," I insisted, shooing a chicken away from my beer. "In our country the son is next to the father. The dead chief's younger brother had become the great chief. He had also married his elder brother's widow only about a month after the funeral."

"He did well," the old man beamed and announced to the others, "I told you that if we knew more about Europeans, we would find they really were very like us. In our country also," he added to me, "the younger brother marries the elder brother's widow and becomes the father of his children. Now, if your uncle, who married your widowed mother, is your father's full brother, then he will be a real father to you. Did Hamlet's father and uncle have one mother?"

His question barely penetrated my mind; I was too upset and thrown off balance by having one of the most important elements of *Hamlet* knocked straight out of the picture. Rather uncertainly I said that I thought they had the same mother, but I wasn't sure-tine story didn't say. The old man told me severely that these genealogical details made all the difference and that when I got home I must ask the elders about it, He shouted out the door to one of his younger wives to bring his goatskin bag,

Determined to save what I could of the mother motif, I took a deep breath and began again, "The son Hamlet was very sad because his mother had married, again so quickly. There was no need for her to do so, and it is our custom for a widow not to go to her next husband until she has mourned for two years,"

"Two years is too long," objected the wife, who had appeared with the old man's battered goatskin bag. "Who will hoe your farms for you while you have no husband?"

"Hamlet," I retorted without, thinking, "was old enough to hoe his mother's farms himself. There was no need for her to remarry." No one looked convinced, I gave up. "His mother and the great chief told Hamlet not to be sad, for the great chief himself would be a father to Hamlet. Furthermore, Hamlet would be the next chief; therefore he must stay to learn the things of a chief, Hamlet agreed to remain, and all the rest went off to drink beer."

While I paused, perplexed at how to render Hamlet's disgusted soliloquy to an audience convinced that Claudius and Gertrude had behaved in the best possible manner, one of the younger men asked me who had married, the other wives of the dead chief.

"He had no other wives," I told him.

"But a chief must have many wives! How else can he brew beer and prepare food for all his guests?"

I said firmly that in our country even chiefs had only one wife, that they had servants to do their work, and that they paid them, from tax money.

It was better, they returned, for a chief to have many wives and sons who would help him hoe his farms and feed his people; then everyone loved the chief who gave much and took nothing—taxes were a bad thing.

I agreed with the last comment, but for the rest fell back on their favorite way of fobbing off my questions; "That is the way it is done, so that is how we do it,"

I decided to skip the soliloquy. Even if Claudius was here thought quite right to marry his brother's widow, there remained the poison motif, and I knew they would disapprove of fratricide. More hopefully I resumed, "That night Hamlet kept watch with the three who had seen his dead father. The dead chief again appeared, and although the others were afraid, Hamlet followed his dead father off to one side, When they were alone, Hamlet's dead father spoke."

"Omens can't talk!" The old man was emphatic.

"Hamlet's dead father wasn't an omen. Seeing him might have been an omen, but he was not," My audience looked as confused as I sounded, "It was Hamlet's dead father. It was a thing we call a 'ghost.'" 1 had to use the English word, for unlike many of the neighboring tribes, these people didn't believe in the survival after death of any individuating part of the personality.

"What is a 'ghost'? An omen?"

"No, a 'ghost' is someone who is dead but who walks around and can talk, and people can hear him and see him but not touch him."

They objected. "One can touch zombis."

"No, no! It was not a dead body the witches had animated to sacrifice and eat. No one else made Hamlet's dead father walk, He did it himself."

"Dead men can't walk," protested my audience as one man,

I was quite willing to compromise. "A 'ghost' is the dead man's shadow,"

But again they objected. "Dead men cast no shadows."

"They do in my country" I snapped,

The old "man quelled the babble of disbelief that arose immediately and told me with that insincere, but courteous, agreement one extends to the fancies of the young, ignorant, and superstitious, "No doubt in your country the dead can also walk without being zombis." From the depths of his bag he produced a withered fragment of kola nut, bit off one end to show it wasn't poisoned, and handed me the rest as a peace offering.

"Anyhow," I resumed, "Hamlet's dead father said that his own brother, the one who became chief, had poisoned him. He wanted Hamlet to avenge him. Hamlet believed this in his heart, for he did not like his father's brother." 1 took another swallow of beer. "In the country of the great chief, living in the same homestead, for it was a very large one, was an important elder who was often with the chief to advise and help him. His name was Polonius. Hamlet was courting his daughter, but her father and her brother…, (I cast hastily about for some tribal analogy) warned her not to let Hamlet visit her when she was alone on her farm, for he would be a great chief and so could not marry her."

"Why not?" asked the wife, who had settled down on the edge of the old man's chair. He frowned at her for asking stupid questions and growled, "They lived in the same homestead."

"That was not the reason," I informed them, "Polonius was a stranger who lived in the homestead because he helped the chief, not because he was a relative."

"Then why couldn't Hamlet marry her?"

"He could have," 1 explained, "but Polonius didn't think he would. After all, Hamlet was a man of great importance who ought to many a chief's daughter, for in his country a man could have only one wife. Polonius was afraid that if Hamlet made love to his daughter, then no one else would give a high price for her."

"That might be true," remarked one of the shrewder eiders, "but a chief's son would give Ms. mistress's father enough presents and patronage to more than make up the difference. Polonius sounds like a fool to me."

"Many people think he was," I agreed. "Meanwhile Polonius sent his son Laertes off to Paris to learn the things of that country, for it was the homestead of a very great chief indeed. Because he was afraid that Laertes might waste a lot of money on beer and women and gambling, or get into trouble by fighting, he sent one of his servants to Paris secretly, to spy out what Laertes was doing. One day Hamlet came upon Polonius's daughter Ophelia. He behaved so oddly he frightened her. Indeed" I was fumbling for words to express the dubious quality of Hamlet's madness—"the chief and many others had also noticed that when Hamlet talked one could understand the words but not what they meant. Many people thought that he had become mad." My audience suddenly became more attentive. "The great chief wanted to know what was wrong with Hamlet, so he sent for two of Hamlet's age mates (school friends would have taken long explanation) to talk to Hamlet and find out what troubled his heart. Hamlet, seeing that they had been bribed by the chief to betray him, told them nothing. Polonius, however, insisted that Hamlet was mad because he had been forbidden to see Ophelia, whom he loved."

"Why," inquired a bewildered voice, "should anyone bewitch Hamlet on that account?"

"Bewitch him?"

"Yes, only witchcraft can make anyone mad, unless, of course, one sees the beings that lurk in the forest."

I stopped being a storyteller, took out my notebook and demanded to be told more about these two causes of madness. Even while they spoke and I jotted notes, I tried to calculate the effect of this new factor on the plot. Hamlet had not been exposed to the beings that lurk in the forest. Only his relatives in the male line could bewitch him. Barring relatives not mentioned by Shakespeare, it had to be Claudius who was attempting to harm him. And, of course, it was.

For the moment I staved off questions by saying that the great chief also refused to believe that Hamlet was mad for the love of Ophelia and nothing else. "He was sure that something much more important was troubling Hamlet's heart."

"Now Hamlet's age mates," I continued, "had brought with them a famous storyteller. Hamlet decided to have this man tell, the chief and all his homestead a story about a man who had poisoned his brother because he desired his brother's wife and wished to be chief himself. Hamlet was sure the great chief could not hear the story without making a sign if he was indeed guilty, and then he would discover whether his dead father had told him the truth,"

The old man interrupted, with deep cunning, "Why should a father lie to his son?" he asked.

I hedged: "Hamlet wasn't sure that it really was his dead father." It was impossible to say anything, in that language, about devil-inspired visions,

"You mean," he said, "it actually was an omen, and he knew witches sometimes send false ones, Hamlet was a fool not to go to one skilled in reading omens and divining the truth in the first place. A man-who-sees-the-truth could have told him how his father died, if he really had been poisoned, and if there was witchcraft in it; then Hamlet could have called the elders to settle the matter,"

"The shrewd elder ventured to disagree. "Because his father's brother was a great chief, one-who-sees-the-truth might therefore have been afraid to tell it. I think it was for that reason that a friend of Hamlet's father—a witch and an elder—sent an omen so his friend's son would know. Was the omen true?"

"Yes," I said, abandoning ghosts and the devil; a witch-sent omen it would have to be. "It was true, for when the storyteller was telling his tale before all the homestead, the great chief rose in fear. Afraid that Hamlet knew his secret, he planned to have him killed."

The stage set of the next bit presented some difficulties of translation. I began cautiously. "The great chief told Hamlet's mother to find out from her son what he knew. But because a woman's children are always first in her heart, he had the important elder Polonius hide behind a cloth that hung against the wall of Hamlet's mother's sleeping hut. Hamlet started to scold his mother for what she had done."

There was a shocked murmur from everyone. A man should never scold his mother.

"She called out in fear, and Polonius moved behind the cloth. Shouting, 'a rat!' Hamlet took his machete and slashed through the cloth." I paused for dramatic effect. "He had killed Polonius!"

The old men looked at each other in supreme disgust. "That Polonius truly was a fool and a man who knew nothing! What child would not know enough to shout, 'It's me!'" With a pang, I remembered that these people are ardent hunters, always armed with bow, arrow, and machete; at the first rustle in the grass an arrow is aimed and ready, and the hunter shouts "Game!" If no human voice answers immediately, the arrow speeds on its way. Like a good hunter Hamlet had shouted, "A rat!"

I rushed in to save Folonius's reputation. "Polonius did speak. Hamlet heard him. But he thought it was the chief and wished to kill him to avenge his father. He had meant to kill him earlier that evening. …" I broke down, unable to describe to these pagans, who had no belief in individual afterlife, the difference between dying at one's prayers and dying "unhousell'd, disappointed, unaneled."

This time I had shocked my audience seriously. "For a man to raise his hand against his father's brother and the one who has become his father—that is a terrible thing. The elders ought to let such a man be bewitched."

I nibbled at my kola nut in some perplexity, then pointed out that after all the man had killed Hamlet's father.

"No," pronounced the old man, speaking less to me than to the young men sitting behind the elders. "If your father's brother has killed your father, you must appeal to your father's age mates; *they* may avenge him. No man may use violence against his senior relatives." Another thought struck him. "But if his father's brother had indeed been wicked enough to bewitch Hamlet and make him mad that would be a good story indeed, for it would be his fault that Hamlet, being mad, no longer had any sense and thus was ready to kill his father's brother."

There was a murmur of applause. *Hamlet* was again a good story to them, but it no longer seemed quite the same story to me. As I thought over the coming complications of plot and motive, I lost courage and decided to skim over dangerous ground quickly.

"The great chief," I went on, "was not sorry that Hamlet had killed Polonius. It gave him a reason to send Hamlet away, with his two treacherous age mates, with letters to a chief of a far country, saying that Hamlet should be killed. But Hamlet changed the writing on their papers, so that the chief killed his age mates instead," I encountered a reproachful glare from one of the men whom I had told undetectable forgery was not merely immoral but beyond human skill. I looked the other way.

"Before Hamlet could return, Laertes came back for his father's funeral. The great chief told him Hamlet had killed Polonius. Laertes swore to kill Hamlet because of this, and because his sister Ophelia, hearing her father had been killed by the man she loved, went mad and drowned in the river."

"Have you already forgotten what we told you?" The old man was reproachful. "One cannot take vengeance on a madman; Hamlet killed Polonius in his madness. As for the girl, she not only went mad, she was drowned. Only witches can make people drown. Water itself can't hurt anything. It is merely something one drinks and bathes in."

I began to get cross. "If you don't like the story, I'll stop."

The old man made soothing noises and himself poured me some more beer. "You tell the story well, and we are listening. But it is clear the elders of your country have never told you what the story really means. No, don't interrupt! We believe you when you say your marriage customs are different, or your clothes and weapons. But people are the same everywhere; therefore, there are always witches and it is we, the elders, who know how witches work. We told you it was the great chief who wished to kill Hamlet, and now your own words have proved us right. Who were Ophelia's male relatives?"

"There were only her father and her brother." Hamlet was clearly out of my hands.

"There must have been many more; this also you must ask of your elders when you get back to your country. From what you tell us, since Polonius was dead, it must have been Laertes who killed Ophelia, although I do not see the reason for it."

We had emptied one pot of beer, and the old men argued the point with slightly tipsy interest. Finally one of them demanded of me, "What did the servant of Polonius say on his return?"

With difficulty I recollected Reynaldo and his mission. "I don't think he did return before Polonius was killed."

"Listen," said the elder, "and I will tell you how it was and how your story will go, then you may tell me if I am right. Polonius knew his son would get into trouble, and so he did. He had many fines to pay for fighting, and debts from gambling. But he had only two ways of getting money quickly. One was to marry off his sister at once, but it is difficult to find a man who will marry a woman desired by the son of a chief. For if the chief's heir commits adultery with your wife, what can you do? Only a fool calls a case against a man who will someday be his judge. Therefore Laertes had to take the second way: he killed his sister by witchcraft, drowning her so he could secretly sell her body to the witches."

I raised an objection. "They found her body and buried it. Indeed Laertes jumped into the grave to see his sister once more—so, you see, the body was truly there. Hamlet, who had just come back, jumped in after him."

"What did I tell you?" The elder appealed to the others. "Laertes was up to no good with his sister's body. Hamlet prevented him, because the chief's heir, like a chief, does not wish any other man to grow rich and powerful. Laertes would be angry, because he would have killed his sister without benefit to himself. In our country he would try to kill Hamlet for that reason. Is this not what happened?"

"More or less," I admitted. "When the great chief found Hamlet was still alive, he encouraged Laertes to try to kill Hamlet and arranged a fight with machetes between them. In the fight both the young men were wounded to death. Hamlet's mother drank the poisoned beer that the chief meant for Hamlet in case he won the fight. When he saw his mother die of poison, Hamlet, dying, managed to kill his father's brother with his machete."

"You see, I was right!" exclaimed the elder.

"That was a very good story," added the old man, "and you told it with very few mistakes. There was just one more error, at the very end. The poison Hamlet's mother drank was obviously meant for the survivor of the fight, whichever it was. If Laertes had won, the great chief would have poisoned him, for no one would know that he arranged Hamlet's death. Then, too, he need not fear Laertes' witchcraft; it takes a strong heart to kill one's only sister by witchcraft.

"Sometime," concluded the old man, gathering his ragged toga about him, "you must tell us some more stories of your country. We, who are elders, will instruct you in their true meaning, so that when you return to your own land your elders will see that you have not been sitting in the bush, but among those who know things and who have taught you wisdom."

The Gilded Six-Bits

Zora Neale Hurston

I t was a Negro yard around a Negro house in a Negro settlement that looked to the payroll of the G. and G. Fertilizer works for its support.

But there was something happy about the place. The front yard was parted in the middle by a sidewalk from gate to door-step, a sidewalk edged on either side by quart bottles driven neck down into the ground on a slant. A mess of homey flowers planted without a plan but blooming cheerily from their helter-skelter places. The fence and house were whitewashed. The porch and steps scrubbed white.

The front door stood open to the sunshine so that the floor of the front room could finish drying after its weekly scouring. It was Saturday, Everything clean from the front gate to the privy house. Yard raked so that the strokes of the rake would make a pattern, Fresh newspaper cut in fancy edge on the kitchen shelves.

Missie May was bathing herself in the galvanized washtub in the bedroom. Her dark-brown skin glistened under the soapsuds that skittered down from her wash rag. Her stiff young breasts thrust forward aggressively like broad-based cones with the tips lacquered in black.

She heard men's voices in the distance and glanced at the dollar clock on the dresser.

"Humph! Ah'm way behind time t'day! Joe gointer be heah 'fore Ah git man clothes on if Ah don't make haste."

She grabbed the clean meal sack at-hand and dried herself hurriedly and began to dress. But before she could tie her slippers, there came the ring of singing metal on wood. Nine times.

Missie 'May grinned with delight. She had not seen the big tall man come stealing in the gate and creep up the walk grinning Happily at the joyful mischief he was about to commit. But she knew that it was' her husband throwing silver dollars in the door for her to pick up and pile beside her plate at dinner. It was this way every Saturday afternoon. The nine dollars hurled into the open door, he scurried to a hiding place behind the cape jasmine bush and waited.

Missie May promptly appeared at the door in mock alarm.

"Who dat chunkin' money in mah do'way?" she demanded. No answer from the yard. She leaped off the porch and began to search the shrubbery. She peeped under the porch and hung over the gate to look up and down the road. While she did this, the man behind the jasmine darted to the china berry tree. She spied him and gave chase.

"Nobody ain't gointer be chunkin' money at me and Ah not do 'em nothin'," she shouted in mock anger. He ran around the house with Missie May at his heels. She overtook him at the kitchen door. He ran inside but could not close it after him before she crowded in and locked with him in a rough and tumble. For several minutes the two were a furious mass of male and female energy. Shouting, laughing, twisting, turning, tussling, tickling each other in the ribs; Missie May clutching onto Joe and Joe trying, but not too hard, to get away.

"Missie May, take yo'' hand out mah pocket!" Joe shouted out between laughs.

"Ah ain't, Joe, not lessen you gwine gimme what eve' it is good you got in yo' pocket. Turn it go, Joe, do Ah'll tear yo' clothes."

"Go on tear 'em. You de one dat pushes de needles round heah. Move yo' hand Missie May."

"Lemme git dat paper sack out yo' pocket. Ah bet it's candy kisses.''

"Tain't. Move yo' hand. Woman ain't got no business in a man's clothes nohow. Go way." Missie May gouged way down and gave an upward jerk and triumphed.

"Unhhunhl Ah got it. It 'tis so candy kisses. Ah knowed you had somethin' for me in yo' clothes. Now Ah got to see whut's in every pocket you got."

Joe smiled indulgently and let his wife go through all of his pockets and take out the things that he had hidden there for her to find. She bore off the chewing gum, the cake of sweet soap, the pocket handkerchief as if she had wrested them from him, as if they had not been bought for the sake of this friendly battle.

"Whew! dat play-fight done got me all warmed up," Joe exclaimed. "Got roe some water in de kittle?"

"Yo' water is on de fire and yo' clean things is cross de bed. Hurry up and wash yo'self and git changed so we kin eat. Ah'm hongry." As Missie said this, she bore the steaming kettle into the bedroom.

"You ain't hongry, sugar," Joe contradicted her. "Youse jes' a little empty. Ah'm de one whut's hongry. Ah could eat up camp meetin', back off 'ssociation, and drink Jurdan dry. Have it on de table when Ah git out de tub."

"Don't you mess wid mah business, man. You git in yo' clothes. Ah'm a real wife, not no dress and breath. Ah might not look lak one, but if you burn me, you won't git a thing but wife ashes."

Joe splashed in the bedroom and Missie May fanned around in the kitchen. A fresh red and white checked cloth on the table. Big pitcher of buttermilk beaded with pale drops of butter from the chum. Hot fried mullet, crackling bread, ham hock atop a mound of string beans and new potatoes, and perched on the window-sill a pone of spicy potato pudding.

Very little talk during the meal but that little consisted of banter that pretended to deny affection but in reality flaunted it. Like when Missie May reached for a second helping of the tater pone. Joe snatched it out of her reach.

After Missie May had made two or three unsuccessful grabs at the pan, she begged, "Aw, Joe gimme some mo' dat tater pone."

"Nope, sweetenin' is for us men-folks. Y'all pritty lil frail eels don't need notfiin' lak dis. You too sweet already."

"Please, Joe."

"Naw, naw. Ah don't want you to git no sweeter than whut you is already. We goin' down de road a lil piece t'night so you go put on yo' Sunday-go-to-meetin' things."

Missie May looked at her husband to see if he was playing some prank. "Sho nuf, Joe?"

"Yeah. We goin' to de ice cream parlor."

"Where de ice cream parlor at, Joe?"

"A new man done come heah from Chicago and he done got a place and took and opened it up for a ice cream parlor, and bein' as it's real swell, Ah wants you to be one de first ladies to walk in dere and have some set down,"

"Do Jesus, Ah ain't knowed nothin' 'bout it. Who de man done it?"

"Mister Otis D. Slemmons, of spots and places—Memphis, Chicago, Jacksonville, Philadelphia and so on."

"Dat heavy-set man wid his mouth full of gold teethes?"

"Yeah. Where did you see 'im at?"

"Ah went down to de sto' tuh git a box of lye and Ah seen 'im standin' on de corner talkin' to some of de mens, and Ah come on back and went to scrubbin' de floor, and he passed and tipped his hat whilst Ah was scourin' de steps. Ah thought Ah never seen *him* befo'."

Joe smiled pleasantly. "Yeah, he's up to date. He got de finest domes Ah ever seen on a colored man's back."

"Aw, he don't look no better in his clothes than you do in yourn. He got a puzzlegut on 'im and he so chuckle-headed, he got a pone behind his neck."

Joe looked down at his own abdomen and said wistfully, " Wisht Ah had a build on me lak he got. He ain't puzzle-gutted, honey. He jes' got a corperation. Dat make 'm look lak a rich white man, All rich mens is got some belly on 'em."

"Ah seen de pitchers of Henry Ford and he's a spare-built man and Rockefeller look lak he ain't got but one gut. But Ford and Rockefeller and dis Slemmons and all de rest kin be as many-gutted as dey please, Ah'm satisfied wid you jes lak you is, baby. God took pattern after a pine tree and built you noble. Youse a pritty man, and if Ah knowed any way to make you mo" pritty stili Ah'd take and do it."

Joe reached over gently and toyed with Missie May's ear. "You jes' say dat cause you love me, but Ah know Ah can't hold no light to Otis D. Slemmons. Ah ain't never been nowhere and Ah ain't got nothin' but you."

Missie May got on his lap and kissed him and he kissed back in kind. Then he went on. "All de womens is crazy 'bout 'im everywhere he go."

"How you know dat, Joe?"

"He tole us so hisself."

"Dat don't make it so. His mouf is cut cross-ways, ain't it? Well, he kin lie jes' lak anybody else."

"Good Lawd, Missie! You womens sho is hard to sense into things. He's got a five-dollar gold piece for a stick-pin and he got a ten-dollar gold piece on his watch chain and his mouf is jes' crammed full of gold teethes. Sho wisht it wuz mine. And whut make it so cool, he got money 'cumulated. And womens give it all to 'im."

"Ah don't see whut de womens see on 'im. Ah wouldn't give 'im a wink if de sheriff wuz after 'im."

"Well, he tole us how de white womens in Chicago give 'im all dat gold money. So he don't 'low nobody to touch it at all. Not even put dey finger on it. Dey tole 'im not to. You kin make 'miration at it, but don't tetch it."

"Whyn't he stay up dere where dey so crazy 'bout 'im?"

"Ah reckon dey done made "im vast-rich and he wants to travel some. He say dey wouldn't leave 'im hit a lick of work. He got mo' lady people crazy 'bout him than he kin shake a stick at."

"Joe, Ah hates to see you so dumb. Dat stray nigger jes' tell y'all anything and y'all b'lieve it."

"Go 'head on now, honey and put on yo' clothes. He talkin' 'bout his pritty womens— Ah want 'im to see *mine.*"

Missie May went off to dress and Joe spent the time, trying to make his stomach punch out like Slemmons' middle. He tried the rolling swagger of the stranger, but found that his tall bone-and-muscle stride fitted ill with it. He just had time to drop back into his seat before Missie May came in dressed to go.

On the way home that night Joe was exultant "Didn't Ah say ole Otis was swell? Can't he talk Chicago talk? Wuzn]t dat funny whut he said when great big fat ole Ida Armstrong come in? He asted me, 'Who is dat broad wid de forte shake?' Dat's a new word. Us always thought forty was a set of riggers but he showed us where it means a whole heap of things. Sometimes he don't say forty, he jes' say thirty-eight and two and dat mean de same thing.

Know whut he tole me when Ah wuz payin' for our ice cream? He say, 'Ah have to hand it to you, Joe. Dat wife of yours is jes' thirty-eight and two. Yessuh, she's forte!' Ain't he killin'?"

"He'll do in case of a rush. But he sho'is got uh heap uh gold on 'im. Dat's de first time Ah ever seed gold money. It lookted good on him sho nuff, but it'd look a whole heap better.on you."

"Who, me? Missie May youse crazy! Where would a po' man lak me git gold money from?"

Missie May was silent for a minute, then she said, "Us might find some goin' long de road some time. Us could."

"Who would be losin' gold money round heah? We ain't even seen none dese white folks wearin' no gold money on dey watch chain. You must be figgerin' Mister Packard or Mister Cadillac goin" pass through heah."

"You don't know whut been lost 'round heah. Maybe somebody way back in memorial times lost they gold money and went on off and it ain't never been found. And then if we wuz to find it, you could wear some 'thout havin' no gang of womens lak dat Slemmons say he got."

Joe laughed and hugged her. "Don't be so wishful 'bout me. Ah'm satisfied de way Ah is. So long as Ah be yo' husband, Ah don't keer 'bout nothin' else. Ah'd ruther all de other womens in de world to be dead than for you to have de toothache. Less we go to bed and git our night rest."

It was Saturday night once more before Joe could parade his wife in Slemmons' ice cream parlor again. He worked the night shift and Saturday was his only night off. Every other evening around six o'clock he left home, and dying dawn saw him hustling home around the lake where the challenging sun flung a flaming sword from east to west across the trembling water.

That was the best part of life—going home to Missie May. Their white-washed house, the mock battle on Saturday, the dinner and ice cream parlor afterwards, church on Sunday nights when Missie out-dressed any woman in town—all, everything was right.

One night around eleven the acid ran out at the G. and G. The foreman knocked off the crew and let the steam die down. As Joe rounded the lake on his way home, a lean moon rode the lake in a silver boat. If anybody had asked Joe about the moon on the lake, he would have said he hadn't paid it any attention. But he saw it with his feelings. It made him yearn painfully for Missie. Creation obsessed him, He thought about children. They had been married more than a year now. They had money put away. They ought to be making little feet for shoes. A little boy child would be about right.

He saw a dim light in the bedroom and decided to come in through the kitchen door. He could wash the fertilizer dust off himself before presenting himself to Missie May. It would be nice for her not to know that he was there until he supped into his place in bed and hugged her back. She always liked that.

He eased the kitchen door open slowly and silently, but when he went to set his dinner bucket on the table he bumped it into a pile of dishes, and something crashed to the floor. He heard his wife gasp in fright and hurried to reassure her.

"Iss me, honey. Don't git skeered."

There was a quick, large movement in the bedroom. A rustle, a thud, and a stealthy silence. The light went out.

What? Robbers? Murderers? Some varmint attacking his helpless wife, perhaps. He struck a match, threw himself an guard and stepped over the door-sill into the bedroom.

The great belt on the wheel of Time slipped and eternity, stood still. By the match light he could see the man's legs fighting with his breeches in his frantic desire to get them on. He had both chance and time to kill the intruder in his helpless condition— half in and half out of his pants—but he was too weak to take action, The shapeless enemies of humanity that live in the hours of Time had waylaid Joe. He was assaulted in his weakness. Like Samson awakening after his haircut. So he just opened his mouth and laughed.

The match went out and he struck another and lit the lamp. A howling wind raced across his heart, but underneath its fury he heard his wife sobbing and Slemmons pleading for his life. Offering to buy it with all that he had. "Please, suh, don't kill me. Sixty-two dollars at de sto.' Gold money."

Joe just stood. Slemmons looked at the window, but it was screened. Joe stood out like a rough-backed mountain between him and the door. Barring him from escape, from sunrise, from life.

He considered a surprise attack upon the big clown that stood there laughing like a chessy cat. But before his fist could travel an inch, Joe's own rushed out to crush him like a battering ram, Then Joe stood over him.

"Git into yo' damn rags, Slemmons, and dat quick."

Slemmons scrambled to his feet and into his vest and coat. As he grabbed his hat, Joe's fury overrode his intentions and he grabbed at Slemmons with his left hand and struck at him with his right. The right landed, The left grazed the front of his vest. Slemmons was knocked a somersault into the kitchen and fled through the open door. Joe found himself alone with Missie May, with the golden watch charm clutched in his left fist. A short bit of broken chain dangled between his fingers.

Missie May was sobbing. Wails of weeping without words. Joe stood, and after awhile he found out that he had something in his hand. And then he stood and felt without thinking and without seeing with his natural eyes. Missie May kept on crying and Joe kept on feeling so much and not knowing what to do with all his feelings, he put Slemmons' watch charm in his pants pocket and took a good laugh and went to bed.

"Missie May, whut you cryin' for?"

"Cause Ah love you so hard and Ah know you don't love *me* no mo'."

Joe sank his face into the pillow for a spell then he said huskily, "You don't know de feelings of dat yet, Missie May."

"Oh Joe, honey, he said he wuz gointer give me dat gold money and he jes' kept on after me—"

Joe was very still and silent for a long time. Then he said, "Well, don't cry no mo', Missie May. Ah got yo' gold piece for you."

The hours went past on their rusty ankles. Joe still and quiet on one bed-rail and Missie May wrung dry of sobs on the other. Finally the sun's tide crept upon the shore of night and drowned all its hours. Missie May with her face stiff and streaked towards the window saw the dawn come into her yard. It was day. Nothing more. Joe wouldn't be coming home as usual. No need to fling open the front door and sweep off the porch, making it nice for Joe. Never no more breakfast to cook; no more washing and starching of Joe's jumper-jackets and pants. No more nothing. So why get up?

With this strange man in her bed, she felt embarrassed to get up and dress. She decided to wait till he had dressed and gone. Then she would get up, dress quickly and be gone forever beyond reach of Joe's looks and laughs. But he never moved. Red light turned to yellow, then white.

From beyond the no-man's land between them came a voice. A strange voice that yesterday had been Joe's.

"Missie May, ain't you gonna fix me no breakfus'?"

She sprang out of bed. "Yeah, Joe. Ah didn't reckon you wuz hongry."

No need to die today. Joe needed her for a few more minutes anyhow.

Soon there was a roaring fire in the cook stove. Water bucket full and two chickens killed. Joe laved fried chicken and rice. She didn't deserve a thing and good Joe was letting her cook him some breakfast. She rushed hot biscuits to the table as Joe took his seat.

He ate with his eyes in his plate. No laughter, no banter.

"Missie May, you ain't earon' yo' breakfus'."

"Ah don't choose none, Ah thank yuh."

His coffee cup was empty. She sprang to refill it. When she turned from the stove and bent to set the cup beside Joe's plate, she saw the yellow coin on the table between them.

She slumped into her seat and wept into her arms.

Presently Joe said calmly, "Missie May, you cry too much. Don't look back lak Lot's wife and turn to salt."

The sun, the hero of every day, the impersonal old man that beams as brightly on death as on birth, came up every morning and raced across the blue dome and dipped into the sea of fire every evening. Water ran down hill and birds nested.

Missie knew why she didn't leave Joe. She couldn't. She loved him too much, but she could not understand why Joe didn't leave her. He was polite, even kind at times, but aloof.

There were no more Saturday romps. No ringing silver dollars to stack beside her plate. No pockets to rifle. In fact the yellow coin in his trousers was like a monster hiding in the cave of his pockets to destroy her.

She often wondered if he still had it, but nothing could have induced her to ask nor yet to explore his pockets to see for herself. Its shadow was in the house whether or no.

One night Joe came home around midnight and complained of pains in the back. He asked Missie to rub him down with liniment. It had been three months since Missie had touched his body and it all seemed strange. But she rubbed him. Grateful for the chance. Before morning, youth triumphed and Missie exulted. But the next day, as she joyfully made up their bed, beneath her pillow she found the piece of money with the bit of chain attached.

Alone to herself, she looked at the thing with loathing, but look she must. She took it into her hands with trembling and saw first thing that it was no gold piece. It was a gilded half dollar. Then she knew why Slemmons had forbidden anyone to touch his gold. He trusted village eyes at a distance not to recognize his stick-pin as a gilded quarter, and his watch charm as a four-bit piece.

She was glad at first that Joe had left it there. Perhaps he was through with her punishment, They were man and wife again, Then another thought came clawing at her. He had come home to buy from her as if she were any woman in the long house. Fifty cents for her love. As if to say that he could pay as well as Slemmons. She slid the coin into his Sunday pants pocket and dressed herself and left his house.

Half way between her house and the quarters she met her husband's mother, and after a short talk she turned and went back home. Never would she admit defeat to that woman who prayed for it nightly. If she had not the substance of marriage she had the outside show. Joe must leave *her*. She let him see she didn't want his old gold four-bits too.

She saw no more of the coin for some time though she knew that Joe could not help finding it in his pocket, But his health kept poor, and he came home at least every ten days to be rubbed.

The sun swept around the horizon, trailing its robes of weeks and days. One morning as Joe came in from work, he found Missie May chopping wood. Without a word he took the ax and chopped a huge pile before he stopped.

"You ain't got no business choppin' wood, and you know it."

"How come? Ah been choppin' it for de last longest."

"Ah ain't blind. You makin' feet for shoes."

"Won't you be glad to have a lil baby chile, Joe?"

"You know dat 'thout astin' me."

"Iss gointer be a boy chile and de very spit of you."

"You reckon, Missie May?"

"Who else could it look lak?"

Joe said nothing, but he thrust his hand deep into his pocket and fingered something there.

It was almost six months later Missie May took to bed and Joe went and got his mother to come wait on the house.

Missie May was delivered of a fine boy. Her travail was over when Joe came in from work one morning. His mother and the old women were drinking great bowls of coffee around the fire in the kitchen.

The minute Joe came into the room his mother called him aside.

"How did Missie May make out?" he asked quickly.

"'Who, dat gal? She strong as a ox. She gointer have plenty mo'. We done fixed her wid de sugar and lard to sweeten her for de nex' one."

Joe stood silent awhile.

"You ain't ast 'bout de baby, Joe. You oughter be mighty proud cause he sho is de spittin' image of yuh, son. Dat's yourn all right, if you never git another one, dat un is yourn. And you know Ah'm mighty proud too, son, cause Ah never thought well of you mar-ryin' Missie May cause her ma used tuh fan her foot round right smart and Ah been mighty skeered dat Missie May wuz gointer git misput on her road."

Joe said nothing. He fooled around the house till late in the day then just before he went to work, he went and stood at the foot of the bed and asked his wife how she felt. He did this every day during the week.

On Saturday he went to Orlando to make his market. It had been a long time since he had done that.

Meat and lard, meal and flour, soap and starch. Cans of corn and tomatoes. All the staples. He fooled around town for awhile and bought bananas and apples. Way after while he went around to the candy store.

"Hello, Joe," the clerk greeted him, "Ain't seen you in a long time."

"Nope, Ah ain't been heah. Been round in spots and places."

"Want some of them molasses kisses you always buy?"

"Yessuh," He threw the gilded half dollar on the counter. "Will dat spend?"

"Whut is it, Joe? Well, I'll be doggone! A gold-plated four-bit piece. Where'd you git it, Joe?"

"Offen a stray nigger dat come through Eatonville. He had it on his watch chain for a charm—goin' round making out iss gold money, Ha ha! He had a quarter on his tie pin and it wuz all golded up too. Tryin' to fool people. Makin' out he so rich and everything. Ha! Ha! Tryin' to tole off folkses wives from home."

"How did you git it, Joe? Did he fool you, too?"

"Who, me? Naw suh! He ain't fooled me none. Know whut Ah done? He come round me wid his smart talk. Ah hauled off and knocked 'im down and took his old four-bits way from 'im. Gointer buy my wife some good ole lasses kisses wid it. Gimme fifty cents worth of dem candy kisses."

"Fifty cents buys a mighty lot of candy kisses, Joe, Why don't you split it up and take some chocolate bars, too. They eat good, too."

"Yessuh, dey do, but Ah wants all dat in kisses. Ah got a lil boy chile home now. Tain't a week old yet, but he kin suck a sugar tit and maybe eat one them kisses hisself."

Joe got his candy and left the store. The clerk turned to the next customer. "Wisht I could be like these darkies. Laughin' all the time. Nothin' worries 'em."

Back in Eatonville, Joe reached his own front door. There was the ring of singing metal on wood. Fifteen times. Missie May couldn't run to the door, but she crept there as quickly as she could.

"Joe Banks, Ah hear you chunkin' money in mah do'way. You wait till Ah got mah strength back and Ah'm gointer fix you for dat."

Spirits and Selves in Northern Sudan

The Cultural Therapeutics of Possession and Trance

Janice Boddy

Examination of cultural and social factors surrounding zar spirit possession diagnoses in Northern Sudan suggests that a major issue addressed by the cult is the cultural overdetermination of women's selfhood. Circumcision and infibulation operate to establish in women a sense of self congruent with the cultural image of woman as reproducer. When experiences and expectations fail to mesh, some women fall ill and are ultimately diagnosed as possessed. Through acceptance of the possession diagnosis and participation in curing rites involving trance, a patient is given scope to expand and regenerate her sense of self and recontextualize her experiences.

The following concepts are discussed in this selection:

ethnomedicine	*spirit possession*
women	*the self*
Sudan	*gender identity*

I n Northern Arabic-speaking Sudan, numerous women—and very few men—are diagnosed to be suffering at some point in their lives from illness attributed to *zar*, a type of spirit possession. In Hofriyat, a village on the Nile some kilometers

Janice Boddy, "Spirits and Selves in Northern Sudan: The Cultural Therapeutics of Possession and Trance," from *American Ethnologist*, Vol. 15, No. 1; February 1988, pp. 4–27. Published by American Anthropological Association, 1988. Copyright © by American Anthropological Association and Janice Boddy. Permission to reprint granted by the rightsholder.

downstream from Khartoum, I found that in different years, 42 percent (1977) and 47 percent (1984) of women ever married and over the age of 15 have succumbed to this affliction.[1] Marital status is a significant factor in possession illness. *Zairan* (*zar* spirits), Hofriyati assert, rarely trouble themselves with the unwed—with women whose fertility has yet to be activated. Most affected are those between the ages of 35 and 55, among whom two-thirds acknowledge themselves to be possessed. The latter proportion is due to a cumulative effect: once possessed, a woman is always possessed thereafter.[2]

This paper offers an interpretation, grounded in the Hofriyati world, of the *zar* cult and women's participation in it. My concern is to avoid viewing possession phenomena in terms that, though our culture finds them accessible, are foreign to Hofriyati—whether biochemical reactions to nutritional deficiency (cf. Kehoe and Geletti 1981), or women's instrumental efforts to assuage their subordinate status by acquiring goods or garnering attention (cf. Lewis 1971, 1986). Such approaches may prove fruitful in assessing and translating specific cases of possession illness,[3] but since they neither account for possession forms, nor adequately credit the taken-for-grantedness of spirits in the everyday lives of the possessed, ultimately they distort and impoverish what they propose to understand. If the aim of the enterprise is to comprehend the scope of possession phenomena, to situate them in their cultural contexts, ethnographers must attend to their informants' experiences of possession and not seek merely to explain them away as something at once less dramatic and more clinical than they appear.

In what follows, I observe that, as others (for example, Bastide 1958; Crapanzano 1973, 1977, 1980; Lambek 1981, n.d.; Kapferer 1983; Kleinman 1980; Metraux 1959; Nelson 1971; Obeyesekere 1981) who have investigated such cults have found, spirit possession in Sudan is concerned with fundamental questions of identity and selfhood. Further, the preponderance of women among the possessed can be seen to derive from an interplay of factors, salient among them women's reproductive function as it is culturally constructed in Hofriyat. A major issue addressed by the *zar* is, I suggest, a problem of socialization: the cultural overdetermination of women's selves. And, although I agree that possession trance and ritual are legitimate psychotherapy, I would not stop short, as have others who pursue this approach (Bourguignon 1979:290–291; Kennedy 1967:191; Prince 1964:115), of acknowledging their potential to foster insightful reflection in the possessed. The province of *zar* is meaning, and it is best addressed in that light.

---

[1] In 1977: N = 129, 54 possessed and 75 non-possessed; in 1984: N = 135, 63 possessed and 72 non-possessed.

[2] Of the original 129 women whose status was determined in 1977, 66 (51 percent) were acknowledged to have been possessed when I returned in 1984. Several had since died or left the village, hence the discrepancy with note 1.

[3] For further discussion of such perspectives see Boddy, in press.

THE CULTURAL CONTEXT: FEMALE SELVES

Hofriyat is a village of some 500 Arabic-speaking Muslim residents and is similar in size, character, and composition to dozens of other farming settlements that cling to the Nile in the desert north of Khartoum. Hofriyati are loosely organized into a number of patrilineal, variably corporate, and putatively endogamous descent groups. Ideally, marriage takes place between patrilateral parallel cousins but in practice the majority of couples are close cognatic kin whose natal families reside in Hofriyat. The most important criterion of marriageability is that the families of prospective spouses be bound, prior to their wedding, by a thick net of moral obligation, the legacy of past intermarriages and generations of ramifying kinship. In Hofriyat, marriage is informed by an idiom or symbolic orientation I have elsewhere termed "interiority" (1982; in press): an inward focus, a concern for limiting social and physical openings, which constitutes a general organizing paradigm and aesthetic standard of Hofriyat culture. "Interiority" expresses the defensive orientation of the village, an orientation sustained, in part, by a history of invasion, colonization, and exploitation from without, and similar to the stance of other peoples living in precarious social and physical environments (cf. Faris 1972; Isbell 1978).

The idiom of interiority or defense underwrites a range of other customs *(ādāt)*, significant among them the genital operation performed on female children known as pharaonic circumcision (excision of the labia and clitoris followed by almost complete infibulation: intentional occlusion of the vulva entailing obliteration of the vaginal meatus). According to villagers, this operation complements the procedure of removing the penile prepuce for Hofriyati boys and, like it, is performed between the ages of 5 and 10. Prepubescent circumcision accomplishes the social definition of a child's sex by removing physical traits deemed appropriate to his or her opposite: external genitalia in the case of females, the covering or "veil" of the penis in the case of males (cf. also Assaad 1980:4). The socially salient reproductive organ of the male is established as such when exposed, and that of the female—the womb—when covered and enclosed. Genital surgery ritually initiates the process of genderization, and implicitly identifies neophytes with their gender-appropriate spheres of operation as adults: the interiors of house-yards enclosed by high mud walls in the case of females; the outside world of farmlands, markets, other villages, and cities in the case of males. Females are associated with enclosure, with the maintenance of life within the village; males are associated with the precarious outside world, with political and economic life. Following their operations children begin to perform gender-specific tasks and are increasingly segregated from their counterparts.

Male and female in Hofriyat are thus defined, not only as physiological opposites, but as fundamentally different kinds of persons exhibiting complementary qualities, abilities, and dispositions (cf. Wikan 1980:43 for Egypt). To understand what is involved here requires us next to consider Hofriyati conceptualizations of the self. Villagers stipulate that all humans are composed of three vital essences: *rûh,* or breath, identified as the soul; *nafs,* or animal life-force, including lusts, desires, and emotions; and 'aqel, or reason, rationality, the ability to control one's emotions and behave in socially appropriate ways. All living humans have breath or soul: its presence in the body is absolute; but *nafs* and 'aqel are relative qualities, and men and women are thought to differ in the amounts of these that each is capable of developing (cf. Rosen 1978:567–568 for Morocco). Whereas men are thought to develop considerable 'aqel as they mature, the amount that women are able to develop is less. On this point women and men concur. But men go on to propose that women are wholly governed by their carnal natures and unable to exercise conscious restraint. In this lies a masculine explanation for the practice of pharaonic circumcision: the need to curb and socialize a woman's sexuality lest she should, even unwittingly, bring irreparable shame to her family through misbehavior.

To women circumcision has a different significance, for although it restrains their sexuality, this is not, they say, its purpose. The surgery, in that it is "hot" or "painful" (*hārr*), prepares a girl for womanhood; makes her body clean, smooth, and pure; renders her marriageable; confers on her the right to bear children; and invests her with fertility (cf. Boddy 1982).[4] Fertility and sexuality are, of course, two sides of the same coin, yet each sex emphasizes one more than the other. Both point to a fundamental concern in Hofriyat with human reproduction, the responsibility for which rests principally with women. Only when physically transformed and shaped to the image of human morality can they be entrusted to reproduce.

Women's susceptibility to possession is, I submit, closely bound up with the implications of pharaonic circumcision for a female child's developing self-perception and is, I will argue below, indicative of women's problematic, socially overdetermined selfhood. I suggest that through this operation and ancillary procedures[5] involving heat or pain—the two are equated here—appropriate feminine dispositions are being inculcated in young girls, dispositions which, following Bourdieu (1977:15), are embedded in their bodies not only physically, but also cognitively and emotionally, in the form of mental inclinations, "schemes of perception and thought." The trauma of pharaonic circumcision alone is insufficient to cultivate a prescriptively feminine self: such acts must also be meaningful to those who undergo and reproduce them. For villagers, meaning is carefully built up through metaphors and associations that operate implicitly and overtly to establish an identification of circumcised women with morally appropriate fertility, thence to orient them subjectively toward their all-important generative and transformative roles in Hofriyati society.

---

[4] Explanations abound for the practice of pharaonic circumcision. See Abdalla 1982; Assaad 1980; Boddy 1982; El Dareer 1982; Gruenbaum 1982; Hayes 1975; McLean 1980.

[5] Such as smoke-bathing, depilation, the painful plaiting of a woman's hair. For discussion of these, see Boddy 1982 and in press.

For example, in everyday conversations and interactions circumcised females are explicitly linked with certain types of birds because both are considered "pure."[6] Among domestic birds, pigeons are said to be pure *(tāhir)* and chickens dirty *(waskhan)*. One reason the former are pure, I was told, is because they splash around in water that is set out for them. Their meat, referred to as *lahma nazīfa*—"clean flesh"—is a delicacy and pigeon broth a local panacea. By contrast, the flesh of chickens is considered filthy and almost never eaten, except by Hofriyat's nomadic neighbors and the very poor. Yet hens are kept by villagers because they produce eggs, which are, again, "clean food" *(ākil nazīf)*. According to a local variant of the humoral theory of physiology, foods considered "clean" are said to "bring blood," to increase the amount of blood in the body.

Cleanliness, purity, and femininity are therefore linked with birds and certain fluids, notably water and blood. Water is associated with agricultural fertility and generativity, for Hofriyat is located on the Nile at the edge of the desert and food production depends on the river's annual inundation. Blood, on the other hand, is associated with human fertility: a woman's blood is considered the source of her fecundity, hence great care is taken to prevent its loss or misappropriation. The enclosure of her womb through circumcision is but one such procedure.[7]

Associations like these pervade daily life in Hofriyat. They implicitly yet continuously direct villagers' attention to what are culturally appropriate feminine characteristics. And in this process gender images are naturalized: they become part of the taken-for-granted world within which women's gender identities are reproduced and reaffirmed. To remain with the "bird" metaphor, unmarried women who dance at wedding parties are referred to as "pigeons going to market." They regard themselves as on display for prospective husbands, since it is usually at such affairs that arrangements for subsequent marriages are initiated. All women dance at these parties with a mincing, rhythmic forward step, their arms, draped with the cloth of their wraps, forming wing-like extensions to the sides. This, sometimes called the "pigeon dance" (see also Cloudsley 1983:40, 54), involves moving the head to and fro, chin upturned and eyes rolled back, in the controlled manner of a courting pigeon walking along the ground. Also, until recently, people had the cheekbones of their daughters incised with a small scar or tattoo in the shape of a rounded "T," called a "bird track" *(derab at-tăr)*. It is said to resemble the footmarks of water birds on the beach and is considered a mark of beauty, one which enhances a woman's desirability.

The metaphoric connection between circumcised, marriageable women and birds associated with water is strong. Both are *nazīf* or clean and identified with the blood of human fertility. Both domestic water-linked birds (pigeons) and women are pure—*tāhir*. Marriageable women are sometimes referred to as birds and in some cases said to act like birds. Further, the association is repeated by village men, who speak of having amassed

---

[6] The following is summarized from an earlier article (1982).

[7] For others, referred to as *mushahara,* see Kennedy 1978, and Boddy in press.

sufficient funds to wed in terms of being able to "nest" *('aish)* a wife: to provide the materials she requires to remain within the houseyard, in the village, and raise a family.

Links between femininity, blood, purity, birds, and fertility are echoed in a variety of other situations. During my first field trip, Hofriyati sleeping rooms were decorated with ostrich eggshells suspended from the corner rafters. These objects, notable again for their association with birds, are thought to enhance the fertility of women who view them. They are prized for their shape, resistance, enclosedness, smooth rounded surfaces, and creamy white color.

Whiteness and enclosure are qualities normally associated with cleanliness, purity, and value. Foods that are white (for example, milk, sugar, white flour) are generally classed as "clean," hence thought to bring blood. Earlier I noted that in Hofriyat a woman's fertility is related to the quantity of blood she carries within her. Thus foods which "increase" the blood invigorate latent fertility or impart strength during pregnancy. And all must be obtained for women by men through men's involvement in the outside world.

There is another group of foods considered "clean" and purchased for pregnant women. They include tinned fish, tinned jam, oranges, bananas, watermelon, and grapefruit, and are generally associated with Europeans, Egyptians, and Lebanese, that is, with people having light or, as villagers say, "white" complexions. The link to foreign groups is intriguing, since villagers generally consider the outside world to be an important locus of power. It is up to Hofriyati men to contain and harness this power, which, when brought into the household under appropriate conditions, positively contributes to the generative power of women. Such foods associated with the outside world are considered especially potent because they are all contained or enclosed, hence protected from dirt and dryness. The enclosedness, cleanliness, and imperviousness of valued edibles evoke images of the infibulated womb and of fecundity. And all of this is concentrated, if more crudely put, in the popular simile "a Sudanese girl is like a watermelon because there is no way in" (cf. Cloudsley 1983:118).

Objects described as "enclosing," whether oranges, tins, or wombs, are deemed to contain moisture, and we are left once more with a connection between Hofriyati women and fluids. This is negatively expressed by the term for prostitute: *sharmūta,* which in local parlance contains a reference to meat that is cut in strips and hung to dry. The relation of dry to moist sets off the distinction between prostitutes and "brides," hence, between female sexuality (inappropriate fertility) and female fertility (appropriate sexuality).

According to Hofriyati theories of conception, a fetus is formed from the union of a man's semen, spoken of as his seed, with his wife's uterine blood, the source of her fertility. Sexual intercourse causes the woman's blood to thicken or coagulate and she ceases menstruation until after the baby's birth: while pregnant a woman is said to nourish her husband's future "crop" within her. Ideas about conception parallel those concerning parents' respective contributions to the body of their child, who is said to receive its bones from its father and its flesh and blood from its mother.

In several other contexts fluids and moisture figure prominently as markers of femininity and potential fertility. The most obvious of these has to do with the division of labor by sex. While cultivation is thought to be primarily men's work, fetching water from village wells for household consumption is ideally considered the women's task. Hence, through their individual labors, farming grain and getting water, men and women provide the household with materials for its staple food, *kisra,* a type of bread.

Kisra is made by first combining sorghum flour with an almost equal amount of water. The mixing is done by hand in a small rounded pottery container called a *gūlla,* designed to resist seepage. A cupful of batter is then spread thinly over an extremely hot seasoned griddle and left a few moments to bake; when the edges are crisp and dry the moist, crepe-like product is removed.

Now, the process of mixing and baking bread provides an implicit, though conceptually acknowledged metaphor[8] for the complementary roles of women and men in the reproductive domain: in the impervious *gūlla* the fruits of men's and women's labors are combined, but combined asymmetrically, in less than equal measure. The liquid mixture when transformed by heat produces bread, the staple food, that which sustains life. It is important to note that only women mix and bake *kisra.* Similarly, in the impervious womb are mixed a man's seed and a woman's blood: substance and fluid, like grain and water. This mixture, when transformed by the generative "heat" of the womb, reproduces human life, hence also sustains it. And of course only women can gestate and give birth.

Thus, the simple acts of getting water and baking bread, which girls begin to perform following their circumcisions, or even, perhaps, of peeling an orange, or opening a tin of fish, all are resonant with implicit meanings. They are metaphors both in thought and practice which, following Fernandez (1974), when predicated upon the inchoate self contribute to its identity. For in appropriating them, in enacting them, a girl or woman becomes an object to herself (1974:122). Such objectification must occur—by taking the view of the "other"—before she can become a subject to herself (1974:122). The metaphors predicated on female Hofriyati by themselves and others help to shape their dispositions, their orientations toward the world, their selfhood. They are the means by which women's subjective reality, closely governed by the cultural construction of womanhood, is—not merely expressed—but realized and maintained. The painful and traumatic experience of pharaonic circumcision first orients a woman toward a disposition and self-image compelled by her culture's values, and she is invited to relive that experience at various points in her life: vicariously, through participating in younger women's operations; actually, with her reinfibulation after each delivery; and metaphorically, with any procedure involving heat or pain, fluids, or other "feminine" qualities detailed above. Both in ritual

---

[8] The metaphor is explicit in villagers' descriptions of how they dispose of miscarried fetuses and stillbirths (Boddy 1982:692–693).

and in many small moments throughout her working day, informative values are implicitly restated and her disposition reinforced.

Thus, women in Hofriyat are inexorably shaped by themselves and others into quintessential moral beings. Once infibulated and appropriately socialized, they reverse the original feminine situation, for they represent most completely the human triumph of *'aqel* over *nafs,* reason over animal life force, or, inverting Ortner's formulation (1974), of culture over nature. With continuous monitoring, women become the embodiments of morality and local tradition.

This begs consideration of cross-gender contexts. If women are vested with the right and the obligation to reproduce Hofriyati society both physically and morally within the confines of the village, men mediate the power of the outside world to women, protecting them, acting as a buffer, and providing consumables (substances) for women to convert into sustenance and thence into human beings. Sexual complementarity, here and in other contexts, expresses the essential tension in Hofriyati culture: the desire to maintain social, cultural, and physical boundaries, and the practical need to overcome them, albeit selectively. Both are significant, for neither can be ignored if villagers are to heed the lessons of a turbulent history and harsh physical environment. This dialectic is also essential to the possession phenomenon, as we shall see.

Both men's and women's everyday experience is informed by the inward orientation of Hofriyat; yet the surgically altered bodies of women actively symbolize this cultural logic and their society's principal values.[9] In this exist some additional implications for women's identity: (1) Hofriyati women bear the onus of maintaining those values, a responsibility amplified by increasing male labor emigration (cf. Hale 1985); (2) women, who are identified with the inside, are not only protected but also dependent; and (3) intrusions of powerful forces from without are more likely to be registered in female bodies than in male ones.[10]

Taking these points in order, not only does a village woman's self-image rest squarely with her procreative ability, but also her sense of worth and social value. For only by giving birth, legitimately, to sons, might she achieve a position of respect and informal authority and, correspondingly, might her husband fulfill the ideal male role as founder of a lineage section. But more than this, the equation of femininity with socialized fertility and of the female marital role with reproduction means that responsibility for ensuring successful procreation—for giving men fitting, properly raised descendants and continuing society—belongs almost entirely to women. So, in the first stage of this process, if a woman fails to conceive within a year or two of her marriage, if she miscarries, bears a stillborn

---

[9] Following Strathern 1981, female in Hofriyat is constructed figuratively or metaphorically: in same sex contexts femaleness stands for certain things without necessitating reference to maleness.

[10] This pertains as much to the Muslim honor/shame complex in Hofriyat (not discussed here) as to spirit possession.

child, produces a daughter with her first pregnancy, or loses an unweaned infant, it is her ability to procreate that is called into question, not her husband's, and it is she who suffers as a result, through divorce or co-wifery. Such occurrences illuminate a fundamental contradiction for women in Hofriyat: they are collectively indispensable to society while individually dispensable to men. At the very least, fertility problems place intense strain on a woman's self-image and often fragile marital relations.

As noted earlier, the sexes are segregated. Women are expected to spend most of their time within family compounds bounded by high mud-brick walls; men, on the other hand, have considerable mobility. The sexes rarely eat together, and never do so in public or before guests. In traditional households—the majority—they also sleep in separate quarters. In most respects there is a significant rift between men's and women's worlds, which is widened by labor emigration, entailing prolonged separations of husbands from their wives (cf. Kennedy 1978:10 for Egyptian Nubians).

Within this polarized world, the sexes are conceived to be economically and productively interdependent: husbands and adult sons bear primary responsibility for production—they provide for their families through wage labor and/or farming—whereas wives and adult daughters consume and transform materials into items for consumption. Related to this, the essential dialectic between husband and wife, set in motion at their wedding,[11] is that between producer and social reproducer. The dual role of a married woman, that of consumer and reproducer, is aptly expressed in symbols and metaphors that identify her with pigeons and livestock: domestic animals kept within family houseyards, fed on grain and fodder supplied by male labor, and valued—apart from their use as food—for their capacity to beget offspring.[12]

In other matters, asymmetric gender complementarity extends to religion and, until recently,[13] education. Men participate fully in the public rites of Islam and most, having learned the Qu'ran, are functionally literate. They belong with rare exception to one of the two religious fraternities in the area and regularly attend their ceremonies, called *zikrs*. On the other hand, women over the age of 25 are largely illiterate. They perform their daily prayers in private, if at all, and only the elderly among them attend mosque. Women are

---

[11] One of the most important events preceding the wedding feast is presentation of the *shaila* (burden, that which is carried) to the bride by the groom. The main part of the *shaila* is a trousseau consisting of sets of outfits, the greater the number of the sets, the higher the prestige of the donor, and the better the demonstration of his potential to provide for his wife and future children. After the feast the wedding culminates in the symbolic defloration of the bride.

[12] The metaphoric association of women with domestic animals resonates with O'Laughlin's material from Chad (1974); however, unlike the Mbum, Hofriyati women are not subject to sumptuary restrictions that differ from men's.

[13] In the early 1970s a girl's school was opened in the area. Consequently, most of the younger women in the village have some education.

sometimes permitted to watch a *zikr* but are always barred from active participation, and whether at mosque or a *zikr,* they are segregated from men.

As these points demonstrate, neither sexual complementarity nor the symbolic value of femininity implies gender equivalence. A woman's life is subject to notable constraints in Hofriyat: she is forever a jural minor, morally and financially governed by her male kin, subordinate also to her husband. Moreover, since personal integrity, dignity, and emotional control are highly valued in both sexes, and displays of emotion considered vulgar—especially so in mixed company—a woman may be hard pressed to dispute her husband or brothers should she feel wronged.

However constrained their interactions, and however weighted the system would seem in favor of males, it must be remembered that both sexes participate in and reproduce Hofriyati culture. Both are subject to its pressures, though in different ways; for both there are advantages and disadvantages. If men are better able to cope with problems in a marriage by taking a second wife or divorcing the first, they are still under considerable obligation to conform to kinship values, masculine ideals, and the tenets of Islam. If women are more restricted than men in other ways, they are less constrained with regard to religion: they are neither expected to become familiar with matters of liturgy and doctrine, nor to have sufficient moral strength on their own to uphold them. Phrased positively, this means that women are relatively freer to embrace what men consider folk beliefs, those having so-called pagan elements and in whose company they place the *zar.*

To men, possession is a feminine susceptibility. Women's moral frailty, their greater natural proportion of *nafs,* makes them less able to resist incursions of opportunistic spirits. While female Hofriyati are apt to take issue here, both sexes agree that *zairan* are greatly attracted to women[14]—and married women in particular—for it is they who use henna, cologne, scented oils, and soaps, and wear gold jewelry and diaphanous wraps, human finery which spirits are known to covet. The proclivities *of zairan,* though largely alien to villagers' (discussed below), are similar in some respects to those of village women: both are seen as inherently less governed by *'aqel* than men, and regarded as consumers of goods that men provide.

Although men publicly scorn the *zar,* privately they are not so intractable. For they, too, recognize the superior powers of *zairan,* and, feminine associations notwithstanding, a few told me they believe themselves to be possessed but would not openly admit to the affliction for fear of losing face. So, despite appearances of opposition, men tolerate women's involvement in the cult and are generally willing to provide for the spirits' demands. Few are inclined to doubt its efficacy.

---

[14] Kapferer's information on demonic possession in Sri Lanka (1983) is similar to mine in this respect.

ZAIRAN AND ZAR POSSESSION

In order to grasp what is involved in women's possession, we need to know something more about the spirits themselves. *Zairan* belong to a class of beings known as *jinn,* whose existence is substantiated in several verses of the Qu'ran. According to Hofriyati, jinn are the physical complementaries of humans in a holistic, quadripartite creation: where humans are composed of earth and water (Adam, the first human, is said to have been fashioned by Allah from moist clay), jinn are made up of fire and wind, or air. Humans are visible, substantial, and diurnal; jinn are normally invisible (though able to take human shape), formless, and nocturnal. Thus, jinn are natural beings—they are born, eventually they die—but their nature is such that they cannot wholly be confined by physical barriers like those (bodies, walls, and so forth) that contain human beings. They are therefore able to infiltrate humans and take possession of them at will. Once in possession, a jinn can influence the health and behavior of its human host; it does so either from within the body or by taking up a position above the head.

Most jinn are assimilated into three categories, coded by color. White jinn are benign; possession by one is not serious and in fact may go unnoticed. Black jinn or devils *(shawātīn)* bring grave disease and intractable mental illness; possession by one is a dire matter, and curable, if at all, only by violent exorcism. Sickness caused by a black jinn might well result in death. Last, there are red jinn or *zairan,* whose color points to a characteristic association with blood and human fertility. These are pleasure-seeking, capricious, ambivalent beings that bring milder forms of illness which, though initially distressful, never result in death or severe mental dysfunction. Should someone who is *zar* possessed fall critically ill, then natural causes or sentient agents other than *zairan* are implicated. *Zairan* must be placated and do not respond kindly to attempted exorcism.

Zar possession is a lifelong, fundamentally incurable condition that is, however, manageable. Indeed, after its initial stages, it may be transformed out of all resemblance to what we might consider illness. The possessed can hope to gain some control over her symptoms first, by accepting—both subjectively and publicly—the possession diagnosis, then by undergoing a curing ceremony during which she enters, via trance, into a contractual relationship with the spirit(s) responsible for her lapse in health. During the ceremony chants are drummed invoking the schedule of named *zairan.* When the spirit that plagues her is summoned, the patient ideally enters trance; now identified, the intruder manifests itself through her body and makes known its demands, in return for which it should agree to restore, and refrain from further jeopardizing, her well-being (see Figure 1).

Yet the successful conclusion of a woman's curing ceremony by no means ends her association—in or out of trance—with her *zar.* The spirit is said to remain above her, ready to enter her body at will. From a spirit's perspective, contracts with humans are infinitely renegotiate: if the possessed wishes to allay further attack from her *zar* she must mollify it continually. This requires her regular attendance at the *zar* ceremonies of others

Figure 1. *The woman in the foreground smokes a cigarette while going into trance at a zar ritual. The woman standing up manifests a male spirit with gestures and behavior appropriate to him.*

and performance of certain ritual acts on the spirit's behalf (for example, staining her hands or feet with henna in a particular [spirit] design). Should spirit or human neglect to uphold their agreement at any time, the latter may suffer relapse of her former illness. Yet the "cure" has opened communications between the two and any future difficulties can be dealt with expeditiously. If all goes well, what begins as an uneasy truce between a willful spirit and its reluctant host might graduate to positive symbiosis as their relationship stabilizes and matures.

One thing that the hedonistic *zar* hopes to gain by possessing a human being is a venue for access to the human world in ceremonial contexts where it can frolic and be entertained. Thus, when a spirit is ritually summoned by its chant, it simultaneously infiltrates each of its entranced hosts so as to interact with the human assembly through their bodies. Such rituals are always fraught with tension and surprise, for at any moment a woman might be "seized" by a spirit that Hofriyati did not before know existed, or she did not know she had. One by one, throughout an evening's drumming, the spirits "descend" (*nazal*) into their hosts in the order that their chants are played. A spirit enters its host when called upon and, if well behaved, relinquishes her body when its chant is over and the rhythm shifts to that of another *zar*. Since an adept may be possessed by several different spirits at once, a woman might be in and out of trance all night as her various spirits descend and manifest themselves for up to 20 minutes each. When not entranced she participates in the drumming and chanting while observing other women who are.

Thus, in Hofriyat a woman is not considered to be possessed because she becomes entranced; rather, she becomes entranced because she is possessed.[15] According to villagers, since possession trance fulfills their part of a bargain with the spirit world to restore and maintain human health, it is not pathological but therapeutic. Yet just how it might be therapeutic remains unresolved, and is an issue I will shortly address. On leaving trance women say they "see things differently" and they "feel well," statements that might be construed as affirming that the state itself has intrinsic remedial powers. But, even should

---

[15] This point has been cogently argued by Lambek (1981) for possession in Mayotte, Comoro Islands.

this be the case, to limit the therapeutic value of *zar* to that of trance would be artificial and inadequate. The *zar* rite is a cultural therapy; its curative powers derive less from a virtual experience of trance than from the entire possession context that renders it, and countless other experiences, meaningful. Indeed, an individual's experience of trance is largely constructed by its context: in Hofriyat, possession provides her with a model of what trance is and should be like.

Still, if trance is an integral part of possession therapy and relapse prophylaxis, it is only one manifestation of possession, not consistently evinced by the possessed during ceremonies and, when evinced, variable in apparent depth and duration from one individual to the next. Not all who enter trance do so for immediate therapeutic motives; many who manifest their spirits do not feel sick at the time, though they are classed as ill. A *zar* rite is more than just a cure; it is also referred to as a "party" *(hafla)* (cf. Saunders 1977 on *zar* in Egypt). Despite its solemn aim to alleviate suffering, it can be a great deal of fun, mixing comedy, satire, and intellectual challenge in a heady atmosphere where nothing is quite as it seems. Possession trance is, I contend, therapeutic, but its therapeutic potential is broad, not confined to achieving a medical or psychological cure, and lies as much with observing it in others as experiencing it oneself. Even the experience of it is subordinate to an earlier acceptance of a possession diagnosis. In short, the relevant issue in the case of the *zar* is not trance per se, but trance firmly situated in a meaningful cultural context—possession—having medical, social, psychological, and often profound aesthetic implications. Before considering these, the nature of the illness that signals possession remains to be addressed.

POSSESSION AS ILLNESS

Here I will begin to pull together the threads of my argument, indicating how possession is linked to what I consider is Hofriyati women's problematic selfhood. But on this issue, especially, I walk the ethnographer's unsteady line between keeping faith with informants' experience of their world and rendering that experience intelligible in the more familiar parlance of Western culture. In the attempt I must surely transgress realities on either side. For the *zar* in Hofriyat is a holistic phenomenon; it penetrates every facet of human existence. Consequently, it defies analytic reduction to a single constituent dimension: psychological, medical, or social, with which members of Western cultures might feel more at home (cf. Crapanzano 1977:11). I have no doubt that in partially subjecting the possession idiom to an alien culture's constructs, some of its texture, richness, and cultural integrity will be lost. But similarly, in adapting concepts that have accepted meanings in our culture to aspects of another in which they do not exactly apply, the concepts—such as "illness," "person," or "self"—may be altered. The result is a partial distortion from either perspective. Yet, as the *zar* itself proposes, distortions can sometimes be instructive.

By now it is commonplace to say that a sociocultural system provides the stresses that trigger the illnesses to which its members succumb, directs those members' coping responses, and furnishes an interpretive framework which renders their experiences meaningful, enables them to be expressed, and suggests possible therapeutic resolutions. Earlier I described some stresses and constraints to which Hofriyati women are exposed, and noted the strong identification they are implicitly and materially subjected, in the Foucaultian sense, (Foucault 1980:97) to feel with their fertility. When a woman's fertility mandate is impaired—for whatever reason—her self-image, social position, and ultimately general health are threatened. Women undergoing severe marital and/or fertility crises tend to phrase their experiences as illness or, less directly, to co-locate their difficulties with the onset of apparently unrelated physical symptoms. In thus complaining of illness, a woman avails herself of a culturally sanctioned medium for articulating her dysphoria (Constantinides 1977:65; cf. Kleinman 1980 passim; with specific reference to complaints of possession illness, cf. Crapanzano 1977, Firth 1967, Lambek 1981, Obeye-sekere 1970). Once this is done she can act upon her problems, where before she could not, by setting out to find a cure. The woman who claims to be ill but does not appear diseased does not feign sickness; her pain is real and may be attributed to what, from her perspective, are natural agents: *zairan.*

Hofriyati themselves link fertility problems and illness, although more subtly and obliquely than I have just proposed. A woman who is anxious or depressed is considered a prime target for *zairan* seeking entry to the human world; should such a spirit descend upon her it makes her feel "unwell." But, tautologically, *zairan* are able to create the very circumstances that make a woman anxious and prone to spirit assault. Their most common tactic is to "seize," "hold," or "steal" offspring, bringing about miscarriage, stillbirth, amenorrhea, or other problems affecting women's blood. Thus spirits can hold a woman's future and that of her husband for ransom, forcing both to acknowledge their presence and accede to their demands. *Zairan* have considerable leverage over human reproduction, and for this reason also are drawn to married women and unlikely to beset the unwed. However, not all possession incidents can be traced to uncertain fertility,[16] and it must be remembered that such problems are first expressed as "illness" *(aya);* for here possession is the ultimate of several potential etiologies.

Whatever the precipitating context, initial indications of possession are usually physical, ranging from vague somatic complaints—nausea, listlessness, fatigue, unspecified aches and pains—to those resembling symptoms of hysterical conversion disorders in the

---

[16] Still, fertility problems, especially when associated with marital difficulty, are most frequently implicated in cases of possession. In 1977 and 1984 respectively, 53.7 percent (N = 54) and 46 percent (N = 63) of possessed Hofriyati women linked the onset of zar illness to such incidents. By contrast, 21.3 percent (N = 75) and 18 percent *(N = 72)* of non-possessed women reported ever having experienced fertility and marital problems simultaneously.

West—paralysis of one or more limbs without apparent organic cause, aphonia. Certain more obvious affective conditions are also associated with possession, though Hofriyati might just as easily link them to sorcery or the evil eye, both of which increase susceptibility to spirit attack. These symptoms are all located in parts of the body (generally the abdomen or heart), and include apathy and boredom *(zihuj),* insomnia, anorexia, and "inflamed soul" *(harrāg rûh)*—glossed as excessive worry.

Deciding whether a particular incidence of ill health should be ascribed to possession, to some other cause—or, indeed, to both—can be problematic for the sufferer. Because possession is a chronic and irrevocable condition, it is always considered when a woman who knows she is possessed falls sick, whatever her symptoms may be. But even the possessed can be stricken by natural disease or the mystical act of some human antagonist, intended (sorcery) or not (evil eye). Like one who has yet to establish that she is possessed, an adept cannot presume that *zairan* are at fault if she wishes to avoid being thought disingenuous.[17]

Villagers generally approach any illness that is not immediately debilitating by testing various etiologic possibilities, moving from an initial presumption of organic (our "natural") causes and, having eliminated these, through consideration of various nonorganic ones. Someone who is sick first takes advice from family members, trying a selection of home remedies and available patent medicines. Should these prove ineffective, the individual next seeks relief from Western medical practitioners. If doctors can find nothing wrong, or if something is wrong but is perceived by the patient as poorly responsive to treatment (whether medication, diet, hospitalization, and/or surgery), then nonorganic factors are implicated. These may be inhibiting biomedical therapy or prolonging a natural illness beyond its normal course. Without foresaking Western medical treatment, the patient (or a family member) now visits a religious doctor, a *feki Islam,* who performs an astrological divination and consults religious manuals in an effort to diagnose the complaint. The *feki* specifies whether the illness is due to sorcery, the evil eye, or possession by jinn, then prepares health restoring charms and advises the client on how to conduct her life. If a jinn is found to be the trouble, the *feki* may perform an exorcism, to which *zairan* alone among the jinn are wholly immune. Hence, a relative failure of both Western and Islamic medicine reads as a positive indication that one is possessed by a *zar.*

For men, who disparage bargaining with spirits, this is where the diagnostic process stops; except in rare cases they do not seek treatment for apparent possession. But for women whose symptoms persist the next step is to consult a *sheikha*—a female *zar* practitioner—in order to verify the diagnosis and begin to accommodate the spirit responsible. The *sheikha* communes with her own possessive *zairan,* which provide oneiric evidence of the client's condition. Although possession is by now a foregone conclusion, it is only

---

[17] However, knowing that her spirits become more active during periods of vulnerability, an adept will take extra care to placate them at such times.

when a woman has such support for her diagnosis that she will accept it publicly and begin to organize a "cure." The subjective recognition that she is possessed thus emerges as a product of social discourse through which the full context of her affliction is established to be other than that of normally treatable illness. Worth noting is that her public acknowledgment together with her family's promise to mount a spirit ceremony on her behalf are often followed by a notable remission of the patient's symptoms. Indeed, her curing ceremony may be staged, if at all, months or even years after the initial illness has abated. Public acceptance of one's possession is itself therapeutic and takes the urgency out of having to undergo a spirit cure. It has what Tambiah (1977) refers to as a "performative effect"—it shifts her illness to another plane of discourse and, so doing, transforms it. I discuss the import of this transformation later on.

Considering the character of its initial symptoms, their resistance to Western medicine and their apparent self-punitive features, it is tempting to think of possession as an idiom for symptoms that our culture would label as neurotic. But this would be inaccurate; the categories "neurotic" and "possessed" are not coterminous. Not all who become possessed appear to be neurotic, and many who evince so-called neurotic symptoms are never diagnosed as possessed. Further, if possession is an idiom for certain kinds of illness, the reverse is also true: illness is an idiom for possession (cf. Jilek 1974:32; Kapferer 1983:87–89; Lambek 1981:53), a way of articulating the feeling that one might be possessed. Therefore, those who exhibit nondysphoric signs of possession, like having visions of spirits and spirit-related things, are automatically considered ill (*'ayāna, mardāna*) even if they seem perfectly healthy. This is hardly because such visions are abnormal in Hofriyat. Here the existence of spirits is an undisputed fact and seeing one is rare, but not too unusual. (I was occasionally mistaken for a Western *zar* on first meetings with villagers.) Rather, the possessed are ill because they are possessed.

In another vein, a woman will usually consider herself ill should she have witnessed or experienced something untoward or paradoxical, out of keeping with Hofriyat notions of the way things ought to be: for example, smelling the odor of sweat at a wedding, throwing dust on her elaborately braided hair upon hearing news of a death, or taking fright when walking abroad alone at night. These situations, however common, are all in some way cultural contradictions: weddings extol the purity of women; women's braids signify their married fertility, the opposite of death; humans are diurnal and women ought to remain indoors. Here illness, to paraphrase Douglas (1966), is experience out of place, and events that give rise to it may be read as indications that the external spirit world is impinging on the human and subverting its proper order.[18] They threaten most the ideals and constraints of Hofriyati womanhood, and either signify or precipitate possession by *zairan*.

Inversely, the demands of possessive spirits that their hosts eat "clean" foods; abstain from traditional mourning behavior such as sleeping on the ground; bathe with imported

---

[18] See Kapferer (1983:50) for similar observations about possession in Sri Lanka.

(Lux) soap; use henna and cologne; wear gold and clean clothing; and avoid overwork, anger, and frustration with kin, all have to do with the maintenance of feminine ideals. Combined with the link between possession and fertility,[19] the above points suggest that for Hofriyati women, possession is intimately bound up with feminine self-image and standards of conduct.[20] It is a condition perpetrated by capricious external agents, which demand preservation of a woman's ideal self, but may create or seize upon a situation in which these ideals are jeopardized in order to take control of her body, thus transforming it into a vessel of otherness. This they do so as ultimately to enjoy the earthly pleasure that upholding such ideals provides. But, more convoluted still, the spirits that so admire Hofriyati womanhood are themselves exemplars of its antithesis. This is really the crux of the possession phenomenon, and requires further explication.

DISCUSSION: SPIRITS AND FEMALE SELVES

Earlier I pointed out that within the Hofriyati universe, *zairan* are natural beings whose abilities exceed those of humans but are nonetheless subject to limitation. In composition, morality, and proclivity, *zairan* are the counterparts of humans in a holistic creation. But this exhausts neither their obversity nor their correspondence.

Zairan inhabit a world parallel to our own and contiguous with it, yet imperceptible to humans except under certain conditions. Like us, they are divided into ethnic groups, families, occupations, and religions. They are either male or female (principally the former), and children, adults, or elders. They are neither wholly good nor wholly bad but, like humans, something of both. Their salient characteristics are ambivalence, amorality, and caprice, in all of which they differ from humans only by excess. Among their numbers are the spirit analogues of Muslim saints, Turkish administrators, "Europeans" (including North Americans, Hindus, and Chinese), Ethiopians, Syrian gypsies, West Africans, nomadic Arabs, and Southern Sudanese, in short, of all human groups with whom Hofriyati have had contact over the past 150 years or more. Each spirit within these categories is named and has an individual history, typical behaviors when appearing in the human world, and relationships with other *zairan* that crosscut ethnic and religious lines.

Significantly, the spirits that possess Hofriyati belong only to foreign societies: villagers have no *zairan* that match themselves. Indeed, *zairan* epitomize all that is *not* Hofriyati in an integral, sentient universe; they are quintessential "others," at once physically, socially, and culturally alien to human villagers. This is especially true for Hofriyati women, since

---

[19] Also noted by Constantinides (1977:66) and Saunders (1977:179) for *zar* in Sudan and Egypt respectively, and Bourguignon (1976:33) for *vodou* in Haiti.

[20] Crapanzano (1973:224, 1980) argues along the same lines with regard to masculine ideals and men possessed by 'Aisha Qandisha in Morocco.

zairan represent extreme exteriority: they are powerful outsiders par excellence. Even Muslim *zairan,* exhibiting the positive traits of piety and self-control, ultimately subvert local values by being wed exogamously, to non-kin adherents of other faiths. Unlike circumcised, socialized women, who represent a victory of 'aqe/over their naturally dominant *nafs*—of social concerns over self-interest—*zairan* are beings in whom *nafs* is permitted free rein.

Considering the qualities of *zairan* and villagers' cultural logic, it is unsurprising that women should be thought more vulnerable than men to spirit assault. Clearly this has broader implications than for diagnosing individual illness. This is so because for Hofriyati, who have a keen sense of who they are and how they differ from outsiders (cf. also Kennedy 1978), it is not only fertility but cultural identity that is vested in women's selves. In local thought the body is a virtual microcosm of village society (cf. Douglas 1966, 1973). Like village boundaries, body orifices are ambiguous, however necessary and inevitable. They are prone to a litany of dangers—spirit intrusion not least—and regulated by complex ritual procedures. They are considered best, both defensively and aesthetically, if kept as small as possible. The most ambiguous and problematic body opening is the vaginal meatus, for it is through women's bodies and uterine blood that village society can be renewed appropriately, from within itself, or inappropriately opened up to potentially destructive influences from without. So a woman's fertility must be defended, reserved and safeguarded first by pharaonic circumcision, then by endogamous marriage.

This brings us back to the issue of feminine self-image. I have discussed how through circumcision a woman's body is transformed into a living vessel of her culture's moral values, and she is thereafter exorted to conduct herself accordingly. Female circumcision, plus the entire complex of associations and practices that express and realize femininity, strongly support the identification of the individual with her role—both social and symbolic—in Hofriyati culture.[21] This is the point: so tangibly socialized are women to this view of themselves that, for many, to experience the world otherwise is to experience it, quite literally, as a non-Hofriyati.

Thus reformulated, a central problem that possession addresses, in hundreds of idiosyncratic ways, is the cultural overdetermination of women's selfhood. To review the various concepts of "self" and "person" found in the literature is beyond the scope of this paper (see Carrithers, Collins, and Lukes 1985); however, let me clarify my analytical usage of these terms before giving closer consideration to the Hofriyati case. Drawing upon Burridge's argument in Someone, *No One: An Essay on Individuality* (1979), and, in a parallel vein, from Kegan's constructive-developmental psychology (1982), the self as a theoretical construct can be provisionally conceptualized, not as an entity, but as

---

[21] (Cf. Geertz 1973:386 for Bali.) An irony here is that female circumcision has a deleterious effect on fertility from a physiological standpoint. See the *Sudan Fertility Survey* 7979 (Democratic Republic of Sudan 1982:56).

a creative energy or process, which actively engages the world, integrating the human biological organism with its physical and sociocultural environments, continually moving, becoming, maturing, making and organizing meaning (Burridge 1979:5ff., 21; Kegan 1982:2–15; cf. Elster 1986). Burridge writes,

> the fact of integration—some sort of coherence or coordination of the parts or constituents of being—does not detach the integrative energy or self from its constituents, but still makes it more than the sum of the parts and, in that sense, conceptually and empirically distinct [1979:5].

In these terms, a self that is integrating in conformity with others realizes the "person": "[one] who, in reproducing in word and deed the norms of a given traditional order, manifests the relations of that tradition" (1979:5). In Hofriyat, the extreme identification of women with the cultural image of womanhood precipitates such a compression of the subjective self into an objective female person: a normative set of given roles and statuses, an entity in whom experience is continuously subordinated to cultural categories (Burridge 1979:28, passim), a publicly confirmed social representation (La Fontaine 1985:124). The projections of significant others—just as determined, perhaps, by feminine images and ideals—dominate her internal dialogue. She is compelled to personhood.

What the Hofriyati woman does not become or, better, is not at this stage given scope to become, is, in Burridge's terms, an "individual": a "moral critic who envisages another kind of social or moral order" (1979:5).

> Becoming aware of a gap between the person's reproductions and the truth of things by seizing on or being seized by peculiarly significant events, the self is moved to a transcendance of the traditional categories, to a reintegration of the event in a new rationalization assigning new meaning and relevance. In this transcendance and reintegration, manifest in the new rationalization, the self realizes the individual [1979:7].

Burridge suggests that most people oscillate between these two integrative moments (p. 5); yet, given the close identification women are encouraged to feel with their fertility, the quotidian Hofriyati context actively conspires against such movement and the realization of "individuality" in their case. It effectively denies them the possibility to grow in self-awareness, to mature, to reflect on the categories of early socialization in which selfhood is enmeshed. Women's selfhood is, I submit, culturally overdetermined.

Why *over*determined? Because, paradoxically, the moral self-image women are enjoined to assume cannot always be sustained by experience. In this lies an ambiguity inherent to morality—between what is and what ought to be—which their continuous socialization may eventually fail to overcome: the woman who is, by definition, "morally appropriate fertility," may experience infertility or some other significant contravention of her feminine self-image.

The tension that the awareness of such untoward experience creates in her is first construed as a problem of internal disorder and registered as illness: in Hofriyat, body and person are not distinguished; hence, threats to one's sense of self and to the world in which one's self is located automatically jeopardize physical well-being. When this is coupled with the restriction on expressing emotion, the somatization of her dysphoria seems a normal, culturally appropriate response (cf. Kleinman 1980). It has the added effect of directing attention toward the one imperiled and away from a precipitating context likely to involve close superordinate kin, whom women, especially, feel powerless to rebuke or entreat. This leads to an important point: the feminine self in Hofriyat is constituted not only, as I have suggested, ideally, but also (among other ways) relationally. It is a virtual impossibility for a villager to think of himself or herself except in relation to kin.[22] Thus illness, as an idiom for the expression of threatened selfhood, actually defends certain constituents of the self, notably, its formative relationships.

A great many villagers somatize negative affect, but not all go on to consider their illness a symptom of possession. Such admission signals a profound transformation of context, from one narrowly described by idioms of inferiority that govern the commonsense world, to a broader one that places this orientation in relation to its converse: dysphoria for the possessed originates not within the self and its constituents, but outside them, indeed, outside the human world of Hofriyat. This, on the one hand, rationalizes the untoward event in a way which vehemently defends the socialized self, for the self's experience is again subordinated to "natural" categories—*zairan*—however extraordinary they might seem. From an observer's perspective, *zairan* symbolize and render concrete a woman's experiences of the world that conflict with her consensually validated view of what that experience should be like.

Thus, with acceptance of a possession diagnosis comes disassociation of the experience from her self. Yet this not only supports her self-image, but also plants the seeds of its modification. First, by shifting the context of her illness from one of internal contradiction to external confrontation,[23] of self or self-and-village-other to self-plus-alien-spirit, the potential for a negotiated resolution becomes apparent. More than this, *zairan* are representatives of non-Hofriyati cultures and by virtue of their extraordinariness, of their abilities and powers,

---

[22] Societies with a relational definition of self abound. For examples, see Dumont 1970:8–11; Kleinman 1980 passim; Lindenbaum 1979:37–54; Ohnuki-Tierney 1984:67.

[23] Or, from metonomy to negative metaphor or "what-I-am-not." Crapanzano (1977:19) notes that, during possession trance, such negative metaphor is briefly transformed into *positive* metonym: the host "becomes" her possessive spirit. Ohnuki-Tierney (1984:87–88, citing Fernandez 1974:125–126 and Levi-Strauss 1966:150) makes similar observations on the complex transformations between metonym and metaphor with reference to physiomorphism in Japanese illness processes. Such transformations and counter-transformations as both authors note are, I think, crucial to the relationship between illness and identity.

of their failure to conform with local norms and rules even as they intervene in the course of village life, possession as a human condition allows for the possibility of ambiguity and otherness, otherwise lacking in the gender socialization process for women in Hofriyat. The context of the possessed's situation is now widened to incorporate the actions of beings from an alien yet parallel world. Both the entropy of well-being and location of its source in possession open up pathways for self-renewal, permitting a limited and, in this context, functional dissonance between person and self. In such cases illness itself may be therapeutic.

What I am describing is, I think, rather different from what appears to happen in emotional disorders common to Western cultures. If the self is truly a social construct and individual selves are constructed (cf. Berger and Luckmann 1967) or integrated (Burridge 1979) in the course of social interaction, the constituents and parameters of selfhood can be expected to vary from society to society. So, while parallels can be found between hysterical neurosis and Hofriyati possession, in that both conditions involve dissociation and may present initially as somatic complaints, these may be more obvious than real (cf. Ward 1982:416). The two "illnesses" are grounded in disparate cultural contexts, based on rather different conceptualizations of the self. At the risk of simplification, perhaps one could characterize certain neuroses in Western cultures, where "self" is conceived as a bounded, individuated entity (cf. Geertz 1983:59), as an overdetermination of selfhood whose symptoms are excessive subjectivity—a weakening of the ability to take the role of the "other" relative to one's self. In Hofriyat, where the essential feminine self is highly idealized, the problem seems to be one of excessive objectification: self is firmly identified with village "other" and identity emotionally real-ized in cultural symbolism to the point where any event perceived to negate that tenuous equation negates the woman's self. Thus, the most striking similarities occur between the normative process of curing or accommodating possession illness (that is, disengaging the self from its context) and the aberrant one of developing a neurosis—resulting in many an unfortunate lay observation that adepts are chronic hysterics. Despite thorough disassociation[24] of the untoward event from the Hofriyati woman's self, she does not, like the textbook hysteric, unconsciously deny her experiences of otherness so much as

---

[24] Clearly, the use of "dissociation" and "somatization" in referring to symptoms of possession is prob-lematic: these are not culture-free terms. They are borrowed from Western medicine and as such contain an implicit valuation. As Ohnuki-Tierney (1984:76) observes with regard to illness in Japanese culture, "somatization" implies that the origin of certain physical complaints is ultimately psychodynamic. It suggests a causal chain that comes into play independently of ethnographic realities (an individual *first* experiences psychological distress which is *then* translated into physical symptoms), supposing a linear-ity that may not, in fact, exist. Moreover, the term "somatization" would locate etiological factors in the body to the neglect of other material and physiological agents in the universe (Ohnuki-Tierney 1984:76). In Hofriyat, as in Japan, these are questionable assumptions.

embrace them, while consciously recognizing them as aspects of her being over which she has limited if potentially increasing control.

If we see spirits as symbolic of symptoms (cf. Obeyesekere 1981:34–35), and symptoms as idiomatic of spirit intrusion (cf. Kapferer 1983:87; Lambek 1981:53), we do not stray far from Hofriyati logic. But if we view spirits and symptoms as dissociated facets of the possessed woman's self, as our own psychology might direct us to do (cf. LaBarre 1975:41; Bourguignon 1979:286), we violate villagers' reality. We tacitly dismiss *zairan* as facts of Hofriyati existence and mistakenly employ a highly individualistic and compartmentalized concept of the self which has no basis in village culture. This, in turn, leads to an individualistic orientation to illness which, because it rarely addresses social context, misses the point of most illness in Hofriyat, including possession. Moreover, even the assumption that spirits represent projections of intolerable feelings is, as Crapanzano (1977:12) notes, a debatable one: spirits, like the illnesses they cause, originate outside the human self, not within it. Unlike Western psychotherapy, which encourages the patient to accept and integrate previously dissociated feelings as part of herself, *zar* therapy works by convincing her to recognize them as separated from herself in the first place. Clearly, any attempt to merge such feelings and experiences with the Hofriyati woman's self—which I have described as idealized and relational, but is, after all, her self—would be ethnopsychiatrically inappropriate. It could only deny her the validity of that self and potentially do more harm than good.

Again from an observer's perspective, one way to make sense of all this is by reference to the concept of framing. Following Elster (1986:27), the Hofriyati woman's illness is "reframed" by a diagnosis of possession in such a way that the precipitating behavior or event—for example, infertility—becomes compatible with her self-image: she *is* fertile, for spirits have seen fit to usurp this most valuable asset. She generalizes that future untoward experiences do not undermine the equation of womanhood with fertility and all the rest; they signify the actions of *zairan,* who, unlike humans, are capricious and unpredictable. But for this there is a remedy. Thus, although dissociation may be psychologically adaptive for both Western neurotics and Hofriyati possessed, only for the former may it be symptomatic of pathology. For Hofriyati it is therapeutic. Most of those who acknowledge possession are competent, mentally healthy women who have responded in a culturally appropriate way to a stressful situation (cf. Crapanzano 1977:14).

When a village woman who feels unwell but has identified no organic or mystical source for her complaint accepts that she is possessed, she can begin to recover. Her possessive spirit or spirits, soon to be revealed, gradually take shape as a part of her being which is not, so to speak, a part of her person, her Hofriyati self.[25] It is during possession trance that the identity and characteristics of this non-kin, non-Hofriyati, non-human, but above all non-self existent are publicly established, both for the woman and those who

---

[25] See also Crapanzano (1977:19) and Lambek n.d.

observe her. Once established, this veritable non-self is linked, inextricably, to her self; it is not, however, integrated with her person, a situation that possession rituals stress and seek to maintain. Still, though rarely manifest in her body, the spirit constituents of her non-self are in constant attendance, influencing her decisions and perceptions to the point where some of my informants spoke of themselves as if they were pluralities, substituting "we" (*nehna*) for "I" (*ānā*). Furthermore, since a spirit might possess any number of Hofriyati simultaneously, a woman's non-self, like her self, is unlikely to be individualistic: possession by a common spirit binds her to other Hofriyati selves and *zar* non-selves, yet in ways other than those specified by kinship, providing new ways to think about human relationships.

The felt presence of a "non-self" enhances, by opposition, a woman's sense of personhood, continuously affirming the integrity of what once might have been problematic. Though exogenous to her self, the non-self is, and becomes increasingly, essential to the self's comprehension (cf. Young 1975:578). Conversely, however, a woman's sense of self provides a negative ground by which to apprehend the parameters of her spirits. These two aspects of her being are maintained in contraposition throughout her life, neither reducing to its opposite, each becoming enriched in sympathy with the other, shifting, expanding, or contracting as their mutual situation changes over time.

In this way possession enables a woman to evolve, to recontextualize her experiences from a broadened perspective (cf. Kegan 1982). *Zairan* posit alternative sets of moral discriminations that are realized and displayed through her body and others' during trance. As detailed below, the observation and enactment of such episodes provides the possibility, by no means the assurance, that the integrating self will be "seized with a contrary or critical perception" (Burridge 1979:28) and empowered to alter her conditioning, to transcend the categories that have constrained her, to recognize them for what they are—cultural constructs, not immutable truths. The paradox of Hofriyati possession is that it defends the person while also enabling the self: it is at once a self-enhancing and self-maintaining condition.[26]

---

[26] My information about men who have acknowledged possession, undergone curing ceremonies, and/or acquiesced to their spirits' demands (fewer than 15 in my informants' memory, from the entire three-village area with a population of about 2500) indicates an etiology complementary to that for women. Most are said to have been afflicted as very young children or in utero by spirits which plague their mothers. (This is almost never the case for little girls.) Given the emphasis in Hofriyat on males' autonomy and independence from women, possession illness here might express difficulties in the process of forming and maintaining an appropriate masculine gender identity. The species of *zairan* known to afflict men to the point of illness lend support to this view: all belong to one of two categories—Darawish (Islamic holy men), or Arab (Bedouin and other nomadic pastoralists), and are invariably male. Both spirit types represent extreme expressions of Hofriyati masculine ideals. Thus, a man's *zar* "non-self," in contrast to that of a woman, exhibits qualities deemed appropriate to his sex. In such cases it could perhaps be said

TRANCE

It is through possession trance that the existence of her non-self becomes subjectively real to the possessed, or "introjected" (cf. Crapanzano 1977:13), and the culturally overdetermined self may be felicitously repositioned, perhaps transcended. The experience of trance and its observation in others is the locus of possession's creativity, for in trance a woman becomes, legitimately if temporarily, a non-Hofriyati. In doing so she is indirectly cautioned that she and the symbolic constructs that define her sex are separate and distinct, however much the latter inform her image of self. Trance provides her the possibility of insight, of maturing, yet it does so obliquely, in a way that does not demand she take responsibility for her conclusions.

To begin with the notion of introjection, or the patient's subjective realization of a spirit's attachment and influence, the self of the possessed is not merely absent or repressed during trance in deference to that of the spirit, but, according to Hofriyati, actively engaged. Though she may be unaware of what her *zar* is doing while manifest to others, she is, villagers say, still aware, for when she and her spirit coalesce in her body they exchange experiential domains. With this the possessed transcends the visible world and "sees through the eyes of the spirit" into the normally invisible parallel universe. Thus she has, not a mystical experience, but an eminently social one. If possessed by a European spirit she experiences as a "European" would for the duration of its chant. My informants tell me they see and interact with other Europeans in European ways and perceive themselves to be surrounded by the trappings of European culture.[27] For that brief period, they say, a woman forgets who she is, her village, and family; she "knows nothing from her life." In having such a vision or, to use villagers' description, in briefly stepping outside the Hofriyati world and into another, a woman also briefly divests her self of its personhood, of its normative contents and constraints. In proportion to her subjective experience of otherness, her everyday reality is made to appear as one of many—less naturalized, less unquestionable, indeed, less subjectively real.[28] The experience of trance is also, of course, a cultural one. Spirits are recognized entities; their social milieus are known, if incompletely understood. Yet despite this cultural patterning, or, in fact, because of it, trance is a liminal excursion. By the possessed's own admission the experience is one of temporary isolation, of alienation from her Hofriyati world.

There is, I think, a subtle difference between this situation and what Kapferer (1983, 1986) suggests takes place during the complex Sinhalese exorcism ceremony, which it is instructive

---

that *zar* deals with the indetermination of an individual's selfhood, though my data are too scant to be more than suggestive on this point.

[27] As Wallace (1959) has so ably demonstrated, how one experiences an altered state of consciousness is strongly influenced by cultural meanings and expectations.

[28] See also Kapferer 1983:201.

to explore. There the demonic victim comes to the ritual already in "an existential state of solitude in the world" (1986:185) and it is the purpose of the ceremony to reintegrate her with society. This is accomplished in the structure of the performance where "the culturally understood subjective world of the patient finds external form" (1986:199); the demonic, in all its chaos and terror, becomes temporarily manifest and dominant in the human world. Having drawn the victim's family and friends—non-possessed participants—to experience what is construed to be the subjective state of the possessed, and thus linked their perceptions, the ritual then proceeds, via a subsequent comedic episode, to reassert cultural order and bring both patient and audience back into the world of shared understandings (1986:201).

In Hofriyat it is not so much that shared understandings are precipitately undermined by a woman's untoward experience, but that the rigidity of these understandings and her emotional identification with them *prevents* them from being undermined, prevents her from being able to appreciate the distinction between ideals and the exigencies of concrete situations. If anything, she is too firmly grounded in the social world. In the villagers' view, spirits are attempting to subvert the order of that world but she resists their influence—as she is exorted by Islam to do. Yet as curers and adepts rightly observe, it is only when she lets them in, when she loosens her hold on her reality and enters an "existential state of solitude," that she can start to recover.

Recovery entails the experience and observation of trance in others. Like other such ritual moments, the occasion is rife with ambiguities and potential ambivalences.[29] The qualities of spirits when juxtaposed to those of humans give play to the imagination. It is during such episodes that, as Burridge argues, the would-be individual "perceives a hidden message and accepts the invitation to explore" (1979:145). Possession trance encourages reflection, a limited dismantling of the taken-for-granted world, enabling the possessed, in its aftermath, to see her life in a very different light. To take a mundane example: an orange or a piece of bread, when eaten with knife and fork by a Westerner *zar* during trance (which normally Hofriyati would not do), becomes something other than villagers' food, or a metaphor for Hofriyati gender dialectics: interior/exterior, fluid/substance, and so on. Its "natural" associations are stripped away, deconstructed.

A more protracted example further illustrates my point: it relates to the Hofriyati wedding. The climax of that ceremony comes near dawn of the third day when the virgin bride is led out of seclusion. A bridal shawl of red and gold silk, used also to cover girls at their circumcisions and women during childbirth, is draped over her head, concealing all of her body but her legs. She is positioned on a red mat in the center of the courtyard, where she stands, barefoot and immobile, until her husband steps onto the mat and removes the

---

[29] Spirits are ambivalent figures, representing exaggerations of village values (for example, piety, dignity, or fertility), while also demonstrating their opposites: exogamous marriage or promiscuous sexuality. *Zairan* in their biographies are liminal: they "mediate between alternative and opposing contexts and are thus important in bringing about their transformation" (Turner 1982:113). In the case of *zar*, transformation takes place in the consciousness of the possessed.

shawl. Now unveiled, she is seen in all her finery and her family's gold, elaborately hennaed hands covering her face in a gesture of timidity. Gently the groom releases her arms and she begins the exacting bridal dance—eyes tightly shut, arms extended to the sides, back arched, feet moving in mincing rhythmic steps that barely leave the mat. Toward the end of each song she breaks off her dance and shyly recovers her face, then recommences with the groom's signal, as before, repeating the sequence until she has had enough and her kinswomen lead her away. At no time ought the bride to have seen her husband or the gathering for whom her dance was the focus of rapt attention and long anticipation. The wedding dance is a poetic, crystalline demonstration of femininity in Hofriyat.

By contrast, in the *zar* realm, Luliya is a female Ethiopian prostitute spirit which demands that its human host obtain Sudanese wedding incense, jewelry, and a bridal shawl for its use during possession ceremonies. When Luliya appears during a ritual, a bridal mat is spread and the spirit, in the body of its host, dances as a Hofriyati bride. When the silken veil is removed Luliya's host's hands cover her face; when these are pulled away she starts to dance with eyes closed, though in a less inhibited manner than the bride and with obvious pretense at shyness.

What is happening here? On one level, a wanton, uncircumcised, nominally Christian alien presumes to dance as a chaste, circumcised, Muslim village woman. In the attempt the spirit tries to suppress its libertine disposition but overcompensates, exaggerating the controlled steps of a bride to the point where simulated Hofriyati drama becomes a spirit farce. Luliya is not by nature bashful; its timidity must be feigned. The spirit's real personality shows through the facade it erects with the aid of its host, illuminating the enacted Hofriyati behaviors against a background of patently non-Hofriyati traits.

But this is not all. What the audience actually observes is a normally restrained, circumcised Hofriyati woman in the role of a wanton, uncircumcised alien who in turn "plays" a village woman who is the epitome of restraint and self-control. In looking at the "other," Hofriyati see the other looking at them, while in looking at the woman entranced, they see themselves looking at the other looking at them. The multiple reflection is dramatically sustained … then suddenly shatters as Luliya peeks furtively over the hands of its host, giving itself away to the uproarious laughter of its human audience.

These and other densely convoluted episodes constitute more than a comic discourse on the ambiguities of gender and sexuality, for, as such, they raise them as issues in themselves and point to the somewhat subversive observation (in Hofriyat) that gender is not a natural attribute but a cultural construct and thus, perhaps, modifiable. Hence, categories that are largely unquestioned in the course of daily life become problematic in the zar. Through the accumulation of such episodes trance affords the participant an opportunity to mature: to grow, as Turner says, through antistructure (1982:114), to grasp not only her context, but the context of her context (cf. Bateson 1972). Possession is as much an aesthetic, a means to perceive new and rewarding or possibly disturbing significances in what was formerly taken for granted, as it is therapy, a means to correct faulty perceptions, to cure.

Yet many who consider possession trance and ritual legitimate psychotherapy nonetheless disclaim their capacity to promote insightful reflection among the possessed (Bourguignon 1979:290–291; Kennedy 1967:191; Prince 1964:115). Such "folk" therapies are generally considered to be effective in repatterning idiosyncratic conflicts and defenses in culturally appropriate ways, and furnishing a corrective emotional experience, the sanctioned release of negative affect (Bourguignon 1979:274; Devereaux 1980:17–18; Kennedy 1967:189; Kleinman 1980:169–170). Here the patient's condition may be remedied, not cured, though her acknowledged vulnerability to relapse may be mitigated if she is incorporated into a cult providing group support for a healthful reorientation (Bourguignon 1979:291; Kennedy 1967:191–192; Lewis 1971 passim; Messing 1958:1125). Yet, despite the success of "folk" psychotherapies in securing symptom remission, and regardless of how culturally appropriate such techniques may be, they are often dismissed as inadequate when compared to Western psychoanalysis (Kiev 1964; for example, Derret 1979:291 and Ozturk 1964:361). They are judged deficient because apparently unable to provide the patient an opportunity for mature reflection, which constitutes the basis for a psychiatric cure (Devereaux 1980:17–18).

None of these views does justice to the richness of the possession experience. In Hofriyat the context of possession carries within it the potential for insightful self-examination, however differently conceived from that of Western psychoanalysis. For what constitutes insight into the self is surely described by the cultural construction of an individual's self-hood. In cases of neurosis in Western cultures, psychotherapy provides a context in which the patient can learn to objectivate himself through conversation, to gain distance from an exaggerated "I." In Hofriyat, as we have seen, possession trance provides a context in which the patient is encouraged to achieve distance from her cultural context, the source of her over-objectification. Both therapies aim at replenishing the culturally specific constitution of the self by exploring and transcending former pitfalls: as individuals acquire insight into the process of self-construction, healthy, more appropriate dispositions of selfhood are suggested.

In the *zar*, dialogue takes place between a woman and her spirit(s)—her non-self—internally, through visions and dreams, and externally, through the reports of fellow villagers about her spirit's actions during trance (cf. Lambek 1980). Through such oblique discourse the possessed might work through her problems to achieve a greater understanding of herself and her society (Crapanzano 1977:26). She is now given occasion to achieve a degree of detachment from the gender constructs that have so completely shaped her being, thus to establish a basis for the negotiation of her subordination.[30] Possession, like

---

[30] For further examination of women and the *zar* cult, see Boddy in press.

anthropology, is a reflexive discourse: through it Hofriyati women can step outside their everyday world and gain perspective on their lives.

Trance is a significant factor in this process, whether experienced or observed. It has been defined as a temporary, subjectively felt change in an individual's reality orientation accompanied by a fading to abeyance of reflective, critical awareness (Deikman 1969:45; Ludwig 1968; Shor 1969:246; Van der Walde 1968). If we accept this view, the woman who sees into the spirit world during trance is in a state of heightened receptivity; she becomes, like the Ndembu initiand, a virtual tabula rasa (Turner 1969:103). If her trance is deep enough and involving enough, she is thus presented with pure experience, vivid, unedited, emotionally real, and not just once, but several times, as throughout the ritual she takes on a sequence of other selves. It may not be during trance that she deepens her understanding of herself but afterwards, in remembering her trance experiences (cf. Kapferer 1986:198) as she is expected to do. Such insights as are gleaned come indirectly, through witnessing several dimensions of what her self is not. Yet none of this is certain. The therapeutic efficacy of possession trance resists objective measurement, as does any aesthetic experience. For some who say they see things differently, this may signal a real change in outlook, somatic disposition, and emotional balance. For others, it may not.

When discussing the therapeutics of possession trance, its potential effect on an unentranced audience is rarely considered. But possession trance is only part experience; it is also part performance (Leiris 1958). When the spirits manifest themselves in the bodies of their hosts a catalogue of otherness comes to life. The spirits behave in ways appropriate to their respective ethnic groups, social roles, religions, and sex. They may be wanton and undignified, take on superior airs, beg piteously, dance about wildly, speak in brash or coy tones, exhibit any conduct fitting to their type. Spirits may be kings or slaves, prostitutes, nuns, male homosexuals, merchants, Coptic priests, or fierce tribal warriors. When a spirit's chant is sung and all whom it possesses ideally enter trance, it manifests itself in each simultaneously, sometimes presenting different aspects of its character, but always interacting with the audience in strange and sometimes terrifying ways.

To observe possession trance in another is to witness a paradox: a woman who is not who she is—not human, not Hofriyati, not even, in most cases, female. Although the identities of the possessed and her intrusive *zar* are distinct, and it is the aim of the ceremony to cultivate awareness of their distinction in the possessed, for observers this separation of entities is not always easy to maintain. During trance the two are brought into intimate and often perplexing association, and those describing the episode often refer to the woman and her spirit interchangeably. Yet this risk of confusion, this ambiguity, is, I think, key to the aesthetics and therapeutics of *zar* in Hofriyat. Just as when one sees a play, the interpretation of a trance event is never wholly given in the event but must, in part, be constructed anew by each observer, who brings to the moment her own past experiences, present concerns, and critical awareness. But unlike the audience at a play, the

Hofriyati observer of possession trance is utterly committed to the literal reality of what she sees. And what she sees is someone at once essential to her own construction of self and a symbol of it, who is also her own sheer antithesis. This thorough paradox, taken with the various properties of the entranced and her spirit, their individual traits and biographies, and the relations of parody, travesty, and inversion among elements of the episode, makes possible any number of interpretations, destructuring naturalized associations and temporarily freeing ideation from its moorings in the everyday world. In the course of a ceremony the possessed alternately observes and experiences trance; thus, for an entire evening she is given to see herself and those around her as in a hall of mirrors, the proportions of her selfhood shifting from moment to moment, context to context, now familiar, now alien, now frightening, now bizarre. In the course of her long association with the *zar* there are many such occasions, each affording her the possibility of new insights, refined understandings, and continued growth.

Zar (as both possession and performance) is a powerful medium for unchaining thought from the fetters of hegemonic cultural constructs and, to paraphrase Ricoeur (1976), for opening it up in different and possibly illuminating directions. In the possession context, of which trance is an integral part, the self becomes a pure issue, a subject for contemplation, negotiation, and, perhaps, felicitous regeneration.

ACKNOWLEDGMENTS

I am grateful to many people for their comments and criticisms of this manuscript from its earliest stages of development, but especially to Ken Burridge, Michael Lambek, Shuichi Nagata, Ronald Wright, and four anonymous reviewers. Fieldwork in Northern Sudan was conducted between January 1976 and March 1977, and December 1983 through April 1984. I acknowledge with thanks the support of the Canada Council (doctoral research) and the Social Sciences and Humanities Council of Canada (postdoctoral research). And, as ever, I am deeply indebted to my friends and neighbors in "Hofriyat."

REFERENCES CITED

Abdala, Raqiya Haji Dualeh 1982 Sisters in Affliction: Circumcision and Infibulation of Women in Africa. London: Zed.

Assaad, Marie Bassili 1980 Female Circumcision in Egypt. Social Implications, Current Research, and Prospects for Change. Studies in Family Planning 11(1):3–16.

Bastide, Roger 1958 Le Codomble de Bahia. Paris: Mouton.

Bateson, Gregory 1972 Steps to an Ecology of Mind. New York: Ballantine Books.

Berger, Peter L, and Thomas Luckmann 1967 The Social Construction of Reality. Garden City, NY: Doubleday.

Boddy, Janice 1982 Womb as Oasis: The Symbolic Context of Pharaonic Circumcision in Rural Northern Sudan. American Ethnologist 9(4):682–698.

in press Wombs and Alien Spirits: Women, Men, and the *Zar* Cult in Northern Sudan. Madison, Wl: University of Wisconsin Press.

Bourdieu, Pierre 1977 Outline of a Theory of Practice. Richard Nice, trans. London: Cambridge University Press.

Bourguignon, Erika 1976 Possession. San Francisco: Chandler and Sharp.

1979 Psychological Anthropology. New York: Holt, Rinehart and Winston.

Burridge, Kenelm 1979 Someone, No One: An Essay on Individuality. Princeton, NJ: Princeton University Press.

Carrithers, Michael, Steven Collins, and Steven Lukes, eds. 1985 The Category of the Person. Cambridge: Cambridge University Press.

Cloudsley, Ann 1983 Women of Omdurman: Life, Love, and the Cult of Virginity. London: Ethnographica.

Constantinides, Pamela 1977 "Ill at Ease and Sick at Heart." Symbolic Behavior in a Sudanese Healing Cult. *In* Symbols and Sentiments: Cross Cultural Studies in Symbolism. I. M. Lewis, ed. pp. 61–83. New York: Academic Press.

Crapanzano, Vincent 1973 The Hamadsha: A Study in Moroccan Ethnopsychiatry. Berkeley: University of California Press.

1977 Introduction. *In* Case Studies in Spirit Possession. Vincent Crapanzano and Vivian Garrison, eds. pp. 1–39. New York: John Wiley.

1980 Tuhami: Portrait of a Moroccan. Chicago: University of Chicago Press.

Deikman, Arthur J. 1969 Deautomatization and the Mystic Experience. *In* Altered States of Consciousness. Charles T. Tart, ed. pp. 25–46. New York: Anchor Books.

Democratic Republic of Sudan, Ministry of National Planning 1982 The Sudan Fertility Survey, 1979. Vol. 1. Khartoum: Department of Statistics.

Derret, J. Duncan 1979 Spirit Possession and the Gerasene Demoniac. Man 14(2):286–293.

Devereaux, George 1980 Basic Problems of Ethnopsychiatry. Basia Miller Gulati and George Devereaux, trans. Chicago: University of Chicago Press.

Douglas, Mary 1966 Purity and Danger: An Analysis of Concepts of Pollution and Taboo. London: Routledge and Kegan Paul.

1973 Natural Symbols. Harmondsworth, England: Penguin.

Dumont, Louis 1970 Homo Hierarchicus. Chicago: University of Chicago Press.

El Dareer, Asma 1982 Woman, Why Do You Weep? Circumcision and Its Consequences. London: Zed.

Elster, Jon 1986 Introduction. *In* The Multiple Self. Jon Elster, ed. London: Cambridge University Press.

Faris, James 1972 Cat Harbour. Newfoundland Social and Economic Studies No. 3. St. John's: Institute of Social and Economic Research, Memorial University of Newfoundland.

Fernandez, James 1974 The Mission of Metaphor in Expressive Culture. Current Anthropology 15:119–146.

Firth, Raymond 1967 Tikopia Ritual and Belief. Boston: Beacon.

Foucault, Michel 1980 Power/Knowledge. Colin Gordon, ed. Colin Gordon et al., trans. New York: Pantheon.

Geertz, Clifford 1973 The Interpretation of Cultures. New York: Basic Books.
    1983 Local Knowledge: Further Essays in Interpretive Anthropology. New York: Basic Books.

Gruenbaum, Ellen 1982 The Movement against Clitoridectomy and Infibulation in Sudan: Public Health Policy and the Women's Movement. Medical Anthropology Newsletter 1 3(2):4–12.

Hale, Sondra 1985 Women, Work, and Islam: Sudanese Women in Crisis. Paper presented at the Annual Meeting of the American Anthropological Association, 3–8 December. Washington, DC.

Hayes, Rose Oldfield 1975 Female Genital Mutilation, Fertility Control, Women's Roles, and the Patrilineage in Modern Sudan: A Functional Analysis. American Ethnologist 2:617–633.

Isbell, Billie-Jean 1978 To Defend Ourselves: Ecology and Ritual in an Andean Village. Prospect Heights, IL: Waveland.

Jilek, Wolfgang G.1974 Salish Indian Mental Health and Culture Change. Toronto: Holt, Rinehartand Winston.

Kapferer, Bruce 1983 A Celebration of Demons: Exorcism and the Aesthetics of Healing in Sri Lanka. Bloomington: Indiana University Press.
    1986 Performance and the Structure of Meaning and Experience. In The Anthropology of Experience. V. W. Turner and E. M. Bruner, eds. pp. 188–206. Chicago: University of Illinois Press.

Kegan, Robert 1982 The Evolving Self: Problem and Process in Human Development. Cambridge, MA: Harvard University Press.

Kehoe, Alice B., and Dody H. Gilleti 1981 Women's Preponderance in Possession Cults: The Calcium-Deficiency Hypothesis Extended. American Anthropologist 83(3):549–561.

Kennedy, John G. 1967 Nubian Zar Ceremonies as Psychotherapy. Human Organization 26:185–194.

Kennedy, John G., ed. 1978 Nubian Ceremonial Life: Studies in Islamic Syncretism and Culture Change. Los Angeles: University of California Press.

Kiev, Ari 1964 The Study of Folk Psychiatry. In Magic, Faith, and Healing. Ari Kiev, ed. pp. 3–35. New York: Free Press.

Kleinman, Arthur 1980 Patients and Healers in the Context of Culture. Berkeley: University of California Press.

La Barre, Weston 1975 Anthropological Perspectives on Hallucination and Hallucinogens. In Hallucination: Behavior, Experience, and Theory. R. K. Siegel and L. J. West, eds. New York: John Wiley.

La Fontaine, J. S. 1985 Person and Individual: Some Anthropological Reflections. *In* The Category of the Person. M.Carrithers, S. Collins, and S. Lukes, eds. Cambridge: Cambridge University Press.

Lambek, Michael 1980 Spirits and Spouses: Possession as a System of Communication among the Malagasy Speakers of Mayotte. American Ethnologist 7(2):318–331.
1981 Human Spirits: A Cultural Account of Trance in Mayotte. New York: Cambridge University Press. n.d. From Disease to Discourse: Remarks on the Conceptualization of Trance.

Leiris, Michel 1958 La possession es ses aspects theatraux chez les Ethiopiens de Gondar. L'homme: Cahiers d'eth-nologie, de geographie et de linguistique. Paris: Plon.

Levi-Strauss, Claude 1966 The Savage Mind. Chicago: University of Chicago Press. Lewis, I. M.
1971 Ecstatic Religion: An Anthropological Study of Possession and Shamanism. Harmondsworth, England: Penguin.
1986 Religion in Context: Cults and Charisma. Cambridge: Cambridge University Press.

Lindenbaum, Shirley 1979 Kuru Sorcery: Disease and Danger in the New Guinea Highlands. Palo Alto, CA: Mayfield.

Ludwig, Arnold M. 1968 Altered States of Consciousness. *In* Trance and Possession States. Raymond Prince, ed. pp. 69–95. Montreal: R. M. Bucke Memorial Society.

McLean, Scilla, ed. 1980 Female Circumcision, Excision and Infibulation: The Facts and Proposals for Change. London: Minority Rights Group, Report No. 47.

Messing, Simon 1958 Group Therapy and Social Status in the *Zar* Cult of Ethiopia. American Anthropologist 60:1122–1126.

Metraux, Alfred 1959 Voodoo in Haiti. New York: Oxford University Press.

Nelson, Cynthia 1971 Self, Spirit Possession, and World View: An Illustration from Egypt. International Journal of Psychiatry 17:194–209.

Obeyesekere, Gananath 1970 The Idiom of Possession. Social Science and Medicine 4:97–111.
1981 Medusa's Hair. Chicago: University of Chicago Press.

Ohnuki-Tierney, Emiko 1984 Illness and Culture in Contemporary Japan: An Anthropological View. London: Cambridge University Press.

O'Laughlin, Bridget 1974 Mediation of Contradiction: Why Mbum Women Do Not Eat Chicken. *In* Woman, Culture, and Society. Michelle Rosaldoand Louise Lamphere, eds. pp. 310–318. Stanford, CA: Stanford University Press.

Ortner, Sherry 1974 Is Female to Male as Nature Is to Culture? *In* Woman, Culture and Society. Michelle Rosaldo and Louise Lamphere, eds. pp. 67–87. Stanford: Stanford University Press.

Ozturk, Orhan M. 1964 Folk Treatment of Mental Illness in Turkey. *In* Magic, Faith, and Healing. Ari Kiev, ed. pp. 343–363. New York: Free Press.

Prince, Raymond 1964 Indigenous Yoruba Psychiatry. *In* Magic, Faith, and Healing. Ari Kiev, ed. pp. 84–120. New York: Free Press.

Ricoeur, Paul 1976 Interpretation Theory: Discourse and the Surplus of Meaning. Fort Worth: Texas Christian University Press.

Rosen, Lawrence 1978 The Negotiation of Reality: Male-Female Relations in Sefrou, Morocco. *In* Women in the Muslim World. L. Beck and N. Keddie, eds. pp. 561–584. Cambridge, MA: Harvard University Press.

Saunders, Lucy Wood 1977 Variants in *Zar* Experience in an Egyptian Village. *In* Case Studies in Spirit Possession. Vincent Crapanzano and Vivian Garrison, eds. pp. 177–191. New York: John Wiley.

Shor, Ronald E. 1969 Hypnosis and the Concept of Generalized Reality Orientation. *In* Altered States of Consciousness. Charles T. Tart, ed. pp. 239–267. New York: Anchor Books.

Strathern, Marilyn 1981 Culture in a Netbag: The Manufacture of a Subdiscipline in Anthropology. Man (NS) 16:665–688.

Tambiah, S. J. 1977 The Cosmological and Performative Significance of a Thai Cult of Healing through Meditation. Culture, Medicine and Psychiatry 1:97–132.

Turner, Victor 1969 The Ritual Process. Chicago: Aldine.

1982 From Ritual to Theatre: The Human Seriousness of Play. New York: Performing Arts Journal Publications.

VanderWalde, Peter H. 1968 Trance States and Ego Psychology. *In* Trance and Possession States. Raymond Prince, ed. pp. 57–68. Montreal: R. M. Bucke Memorial Society.

Wallace, Anthony 1959 Cultural Determinants of Response to Hallucinatory Experiences. A.M.A. Archives of General Psychiatry 1:58–69.

Ward, Colleen 1982 A Transcultural Perspective on Women and Madness: The Case of the Mystical Affliction. Women's International Journal Forum 5(5):411–418.

Wikan, Unni 1980 Life among the Poor in Cairo. Ann Henning, trans. London: Tavistock.

Young, Allan 1975 Why Amhara Get Kureynya: Sickness and Possession in an Ethiopian Zar Cult. American Ethnologist 2(3):567–584.

Wanderer Between Worlds
Anthropological Perspectives on Healing Rituals and Music

Jörg Fachner

Abstract

Discussions on music therapy theory often focus on the role of music in ethnic healing contexts. This article explores aspects of biomedicine and relational medicine in ethnotherapy approaches involving music, the role of sound, trance, dance, sensory perception and rituals, and the way in which concepts from ethnic traditions—informed by experience and introduction—were traded through performance. This article describes problems that emerge in defining and explaining experiential systems, illustrate the pertinent paradigms with reference to the effects of music—for example in the discussion of trance mechanisms—from the perspectives of biomedicine and relational medicine, and interpret the role of monochromatic and pulsing sounds, of rhythm and movement as a ritual performance that is intended to induce alterations in consciousness, attitude and behaviour. Ethno music opens the theoretical and practical frame of reference for existing knowledge, for a wide anthropological range of thinking and experience, for rituals where contents of significance for the individual situation, according to biography and socialisation, can be coded and decoded.

INTRODUCTION

'World music is a hit now' according to the cashier of the local music store, and music sales reveal that world music as a genre fills concert halls and makes profit. Ethno music therapy? An attempt to sell the music of foreign cultures as a product with healing effects? Many people with a classical western education appear to be disposed towards the traditions and music, healing rituals and life styles of foreign cultures with a fascinated and sometimes uncritical openness that dismisses their own existence and growth in the 'well-known paths of the west' as limited and unsatisfactory, as superficial and short-sighted. Individuals who for whatever reasons are considered therapy resistant here feel 'attracted by shamans'. They project their last hopes onto those who are perceived to be 'completely different', with 'a different view' of persons, whose culture is influenced by a different cosmology. And do their wise shamans and medicine men not always play instruments in their healing rituals? At least a drum or another traditional instrument? Are they not music therapists, too? Their music making does not involve 'technical sophistication', but is rather a symbolic activity, representative, the 'energetic recharging of the instrument through generations of healers' who use 'exactly this type of drum'. Can we hope that this potential will be passed on? Does ethno music therapy require more than just the use of musical instruments and modes of play that are rather unknown in, or untypical of, our own culture? Or the celebration of rites that somewhere else stand for our Sunday church-going tradition which today is not attractive enough to our young people to lure them away from the computer screen?

Timmermann (1996) points out that improvisation and reception of modern western music therapy use a variety of instruments from all over the world, independent of their traditional uses. Monochromatic sounds and pulsation instruments are used with notable frequency in ethnic healing rituals. Drums, wind or string instruments—many of the instruments used have specific functions within the rituals that are rooted in respective traditions, myths, cosmologies and musical practice. There is an ongoing debate among researchers and clinicians which is more significant: the sound qualities of the instruments and their symbolic content on the one hand, or context and procedures on the other (Fachner, Jörg, 2006a; Matussek, 2001; Rittner & Fachner, 2004; Rouget, 1985). The conviction that ethnic healing methods may induce changes in consciousness precisely because of their specific experience, which is marked by analogy, spirit worlds and irrationality, appears firmly established since the 1950s and has interested ethnologists from early colonial times.

PARADIGMS

Looking at the use of ethnic music in healing rituals we find that various systems work with instruments stemming from the respective ethnic context, with altered states of consciousness, rituals and all sensory channels and their combinations in the sense of synestheses.

The first part addresses experiential systems. A purposive therapy approach in the areas of music, consciousness, ritual and synesthesis requires individual training according to established rules. In most ethnic traditions such knowledge is passed on to disciples orally, in specific initiation rituals and in close teacher-disciple relationship (Eliade, 1954). The disciple embarks upon a spiritual shamanistic path of enlightenment where he achieves such knowledge in practical application and in contact with his teacher (Castaneda, 1975). Teaching is marked by systems of terms combined with experiences, the meaning of which is not immediately clear but becomes understood only in the course of training in situational context and becomes perceived reality. According to social scientists, individuals believe situations to be real, and this concept of reality then becomes real in its consequences.

The question how music induces altered states of consciousness, and states of trance and ecstasy in particular, is discussed on many levels (Aldridge, D. & Fachner, J., 2006). The following paradigms may be used in explaining the effects of music in therapeutic settings:

1. *Biomedical* therapy concepts: music has an immediate and physically transmitted effect on consciousness. This effect is produced by certain sounds, instruments and modes of play that are intended to alter consciousness like drugs. Altered states of consciousness are induced by additional factors (drugs, lack of sleep, dancing, fasting, pain stimuli etc.). In such states music is perceived as altered in significance and sound. This approach is mainly based on biomedical therapy concepts.

2. Therapy concepts based on *relational medicine*: Scenic presentation and contextualisation of sound, joint play, symbolism and figuration within rituals that focus on issues from the respective cultural cognitive matrix in lyrics and music produce changes in attention, in cognitive function, and as a consequence induce altered states of consciousness. Music as a relational development shapes intentional information from transmitter and receiver.

3. *Rituals integrate* biomedical functions as well as relational structures into a temporal pattern of performative actions, ordered according to purpose. Music may mark and guide the ritual stages in their temporal sequence and may produce intensities.

There are examples to demonstrate how music, musical instruments and modes of music-making are rooted in cultural traditions, how music in rituals focuses attention, and which role rhythmical body movements play in dancing and drumming with regard to altered states of consciousness. The co-excitation of several senses, so-called 'synesthesia', appears to be an important element in rituals. Interactions of sensory modes like smell, vision, touch, hearing and taste may produce a heightened accord of the content and form of perception and induce ritually evoked stereotype images and feelings (De Rios, 2006).

MUSIC THERAPY AND EXPERIENTIAL SYSTEMS

On his search for the origins of music Walter Freeman (2000) explored ways in which music and dance were related to the cultural evolution of human behaviour and forms of social attachment. He perceives connections in the traded knowledge on altered states of alert consciousness caused by chemical and behavioural forms of induction. Trance states produced in this manner served to break through habits and beliefs about reality, but also to make alert for new and more complex information. What are the preconditions for heightened perceptiveness or the modes for purposive new imprinting? In 1966, in the 'Archives of General Psychiatry, Ludwig described altered states of consciousness as changes in thinking, in time perception, loss of control, changes in emotionality, body scheme, perception, significance, feelings of the inexpressible, of renewal and rebirth and hyper suggestibility (Ludwig 1966). Such purposive changes and the pertinent contents to be traded possibly resulted in the emergence of 'initiated' groups and trust in the passing on of important findings. In times of primarily oral information transfer, memorizing techniques were required that stimulated all senses for storing and processing that information. Musical abilities in particular seemed to be important for an effective transfer of knowledge.

The example of Traditional Oriental Music Therapy training in Rosenau (Austria) shows how difficult it can be to do justice to the traditions and social entwinement (Elias, 1969) of such initiation paths, to organise on this basis an educational programme in music therapy and its application in practice that corresponds to *clinical practice* in modern hospitals, and at the same time to maintain the inherent cosmology of a shamanistic Sufi tradition in music therapy.

> 'People in the middle ages, in orient and occident alike, interpreted music as an objective quality of the self. Individuals were able to make this quality visible but not to produce it. Today, however, we interpret music as a subjective human expression with the potential to find fulfilment in beauty.' (Tucek, 2006, p.624)

As it turned out, the interaction between therapist and patient, the joint experience of music and dance produces something meaningful here, and it is not the knowledge of *cosmic orders*—hidden in scales and interpretation—of a humoral-pathological medical tradition as a bath of sound that necessarily results in healing (Aldridge, D.; Tucek, Fritz & Ferstl, 2006; Tucek, Murg et al., 2006). Until late in the 19th century, the medical paradigms of traditional oriental music therapy were influenced by humoral pathology (Tucek,

Fritz et al., 2006); this paradigm was then replaced by the discovery of microorganisms as disease agents, the technical reproducibility of nerve and brain activities and other developments that led to today's biomedical concepts. The Sufi way into the secrets of microtonal structures of the Makam systems is different from that of the patient (Aldridge, D., 2006). A music therapy education is not intended to produce Sufis therapists who work as such and are capable of accompanying patients on their way through and out of their illness, in the sense of therapeuia.

Even if the music therapy approaches described below are not ethno therapies in the narrower sense, there are similar problems concerning paradigms of biomedicine and relational medicine that characterize the relation between Nordoff/Robbins music therapy and anthroposophy with its specific music therapy (see Fachner, J., 2004). Anthroposophical music therapy strives for an immediate therapeutic integration of Steiner's ideas on the basis of the anthroposophical concept of world and mankind. It is about *harmonical structures* of the world, of man, and of the cosmos which comparable to the ideas of Hans Kayser of a 'harmonical resonalism' are based on nomothetical concepts of musical relations between numbers, spherical harmony and sound isomorphism according to Pythagoras (compare Hamel, 1984, p. 104–105; Koestler, 1980, p.24–39; Möller, 1974, p. 63ff; Pfrogener, 1985, p. 338). Findings from anatomy and physiology are to be compared to musical laws and patterns. 'Music shall be related to these scientific fields as a source of knowledge' (Husemann, 1982, p.7). Sources of art that among others are seen in higher intellectual activity like inspiration, imagination and intuition, are to be used to expand sensory perception and cognitive faculty in the sense of an esoteric (anthroposophical) training.

The concept of self is a core concept (see Kienle & Schily, 1980, p.43) that plays an essential theoretical and practical role in Nordoff/Robbins music therapy as well. A music therapist

> 'must try to reach a patient's inner activity to mobilize it in fighting the disturbance. *He appeals to the patient's self* (italics J. Fachner). The appeal to the patient to become active, the support to his performing and expressive potential are the therapeutic concept. The medium within which all this takes place is music' (Schily 1977 in Eschen, 1982, p.258) because music is 'the art of the self'. (Pfrogener, 1985, p.335).

The *activity of the self* that 'comparable to music must be created into the world in each moment' (Pfrogener, 1985, p.336) is the objective in both therapy approaches. Anthroposophical music therapy has a methodological focus on a specific interpretation of the inner activity of the *sound* as it is heard and actively produced by therapist or patient in the form of receptive music therapy. In contrast, Nordoff/Robbins music therapy stresses the musical activity itself and the situational musical expression of a patient's 'inner world' and physical condition. 'In this application of music the self is grasped immediately and *induced to become active* (italics J. Fachner) within, and despite of, the handicapped or disturbed emotional life' (Nordoff & Robbins, 1975, p.41). 'In musical experience their self may become active without restrictions, they can show their perceptive potential and their intelligence in musical play. This power of music and musical activities is something we can use to strengthen the personalities of handicapped children' (ibid. 125/6). Active therapy thus offers the opportunity to observe and understand the self in action.

The essence of anthroposophical music therapy, on the other hand, is the process of listening and inner resonance or vibration with the music. This is believed to stimulate own activities and 'creative powers'. Creative powers are those forces that originally produce and shape living, mental and spiritual matter (compare Bühler, 1984, p.20). The auditive therapy described here is 'a therapy 'composed' individually for a patient, his illness and biographical situation on the basis of phenomenal studies (anthroposophical studies on the phenomenon of music; annotation by J. Fachner)' (Voigt, 1981, p.61). In anthroposophical music therapy 'the medium generally plays a minor role ... since the idea is mainly to influence him (the patient, annotation J. Fachner) ...' (ibid. 63). Anthroposophical music therapy underlines the *tonal character of instruments*, because the tonal character of an instrument is seen as isomorphic to physical-mental developments.

TRADITION AND RECEPTION

The reception of the traditional and modern significance of instruments, tonal systems, rhythms and melodies—for example the icarus songs in South American healing rituals (compare De Rios, 2006) or the poly-rhythms of African healing ceremonies (compare Maas & Strubelt, 2006)—and their applicability in clinical practice is influenced by the reflection and acceptance potentials of clinicians, depending on their personal social identity and also on the reception by colleagues in the clinic and professional community; ultimately it depends on clients and their concepts of healing. Patients want one thing: relief from suffering. How exactly this happens is not uppermost in the minds of patients who have suffered for a long time. But those with acute problems do not necessarily react with enthusiasm to shamans and strange rituals on their wards.

Which elements of an ethno therapy setting and range of instruments may be used for the figurations of dance and masks of ethnic healing rituals in the clinic or in private practice? In most cases such applications can be realized only in contexts where there is a willingness to accept them. Or, how Even Ruud remarks with regard to the believers in Indian music tradition and supporters of the biomedical effectivity of certain ragas:

'I suppose that a raga without this perceived cosmology does not have much of an (therapeutic) effect upon any listener.' (Ruud, 2001)

The sociologist W. I. Thomas (1927) coined the sentence: 'If people define situations as real, situational definitions are real in their consequences', i.e. a mutually shared system of beliefs and symbols seems to stimulate the activation of healing potentials. 'Music and consciousness are things we do', as David Aldridge writes at the beginning of our book (Aldridge, D. & Fachner, J., 2006), and what we do we do in a temporally and spatially perceptible context where we direct our attention selectively to the contents we perceive and see as significant in the moment. On the role of music I quote the musicologist Rösing from the prologue to his book 'Music as drug? On the theory and practice of consciousness-changing effects of music':

> 'In the framework of reception variables, music can only be of limited significance compared to factors related to the individual or to society. Consequently, music ultimately appears to be only what the recipient as an individual influenced by his social environment makes of it in the moment' (Rösing, 1991, 8).

TRANCE AND THERAPY

TRANCE AND ECSTASY

Witnessing a growing interest in the effects of ethnic music, music therapists started to experiment with the trance-inducing effect of monochromatic and pulsing sounds and formulated concepts on the basis of their experience (Hamel, 1984; Hess, Peter, 1999; Oelmann, 1993; Rittner & Hess, 1996; Strobel, 1999). The function of sound in therapy is to induce, control and withdraw the sound trance as a music therapy specific altered state of alert consciousness (Hess, P. & Rittner, 1996b). In such interventions, music serves not only to induce altered states of alert consciousness but also to keep them up and to structure them in order to make the healing potential of trance states available for the therapy process. Pulsating and monochromatic sounds have their effect through an 'intensive rhythmic charge for the field of perception' and a 'reduction of the field of perception and focussing'; the effects are either physiologically stimulating (ergotropic) or calming and contemplative (trophotropic) (Hess, P. & Rittner, 1996b, p.401).

The terms '*trance*' (from lat. transire, passing over) and '*ecstasy*' (lat. ekstasis—having stepped outside the self) are defined in many and sometimes contradictory terms in the literature (Meszaros, Szabo & Csako, 2002; Pekala & Kumar, 2000; Rouget, 1985). Rouget wrote a standard textbook on music and trance and used ethnographic material to set up a table with opposite states of trance and ecstasy (compare table 1). According to him ecstasy has a trophotropic profile of a calm, contemplative and almost motionless state. Trance, however, is an ergotropic state characterized by dance as a symbolically coded movement with loud music.

TABLE 1.   Opposite states in ecstasy and trance

Ecstasy	Trance
Motionlessness	Motion
Silence	Noise
Without crisis	Crisis
Sensory deprivation	Sensory overstimulation
Memory	Amnesia
Hallucinations	No hallucinations

Gilbert Rouget, from *Music and Trance: A Theory of the Relations Between Music and Possession*, p. 11. Copyright © 1985 by University of Chicago Press.

FUNCTION OF MUSIC IN TRANCE RITUALS

Trance in the course of rituals in ethnic ceremonies was often explained as a function of music, but Rouget (1985) concludes from his analyses that there is no universal law to explain the exact relation between music and trance. *Music creates conditions* that favour the onset of trance, that regulate form and development and make them more predictable and easier to control. Trance depends on its significance in the respective cultural context and finds symbolic expression. Each trance induced in such contexts receives its power from music at the individual stages associated with the function and meaning of trance in rituals and ceremonies. The function of music is here to create a very special emotional atmosphere, to stimulate processes of identification within social groups and to be either trance-inducing (invocation) or trance-accompanying or guiding. This depends on cultural beliefs, and therefore there are as many different combinations of music and trance as there are cultural beliefs. This applies to melody ('motto melodies' or invocatory songs for certain spirits in Rouget, 1985, 94–99) as much as for rhythm: 'no rhythmic system is specifically related to trance' (ibid. p. 90). There are no general musical qualities that have trance as a causal effect. The most general musical characteristics are continuous intensifications, mainly of tempo and volume, the deliberate use of accelerando and crescendo (compare Rouget, 1985: 82–86), but also extreme consistence and monotony in the case of ecstasy, and long duration (hours), simple forms, minimal variations in many repetitions, Bordun or ostinati, no precise motifs, but steps, tonal variations, slow glissandi and a narrow tonal range. Acoustic stimuli of trance are certain transitory developments and accentuations, for example slowly and consistently growing and fading volume.

SOUND TRANCE

Sound trance may be triggered by live music or recorded music, and also by joint free improvisation in a ritual context. 'Set' as the psychosicial context combined with personal condition, memories and beliefs, and 'setting' as the temporal-spatial frame that has a symbolical and physical influence, play an important role in the induction of altered states of consciousness (Hess & Rittner, 1996b). Rituals structure the suggestive context of *set and setting* and 'open the biological door' (Felicitas Goodman in Hess & Rittner, 1996b, p. 402). The therapists aims at 'an extraordinary and healing state of consciousness' (Haerlin, 1998, p. 238) in single and group therapy with sound instruments (sound bowl, gong, monochord etc.) and pulsation instruments (drums, rattles etc.). Timmermann (1996) underlines the monotonous *repetition* of sounds as a core element of trance induction. The duration of sounds having their effect on clients also seems to influence trance induction. According to Angeles Arrien 'most individuals need 13–15 minutes until they are affected or carried away by drums' (in Haerlin, 1998, p. 239). For Haerlin, the dominant effect of trance-inducing instruments is the 'induction of an empty trance matrix that reduces the noise of thought and more or less suspends the normal and pathological framework of belief and reference' (ibid. p. 240). Strobel (1988, p. 121) assumes a psychodynamic perspective:

> 'Strictly speaking it is not only the sound but also the therapist who affects the patient via sound, and the patient in his reaction again affects the therapist.'

PHYSIOLOGICAL PROCESSES IN TRANCE STATES

An EEG experiment demonstrates individual reactions of persons to instruments and sound trance: Rittner & Fachner determined the suggestibility to hypnosis in individuals through corrsponding EEG frequency patterns, caused by the recumbent position of test persons on a monochord. An individual with higher suggestibility to hypnosis showed a slowing of EEG waves in comparison with an uninfluenced state of rest, while a test person with less suggestibility to hypnosis revealed accelerated EEG waves.

Hess and Rittner (1996a) distinguish between *different depths of trance*, and thereby between active trance with high motoric elements, for example the 'Mevlevi Sema' of the Sufi dervishes, and passive trance with minor movement, as in classical hypnosis. Everyday and mini trances, as in day-dreaming, are at the beginning of the whole range of trances that reaches from hypnoid trance in autogenous training, to religious trance of a Tibetian oracle, to forms of obsessional trance where humans for a short while appear to be hosts of other beings like spirits or gods (Oohashi et al., 2002; Rouget, 1985).

Rouget (1985, p. 169–176) criticizes Neher's (1962) thesis that obsessional trance and its epilepsy-like phenomena are causally produced in ceremonial drumming by certain frequency patterns, for example a sound spectrum of drums dominated by bass frequencies, by repetitions and the speed (bpm) of rhythmic patterns of drum beat sequences. Neher performed his laboratory experiment to explore a complex phenomenon that is also called 'entrainment' (a coupling of inner rhythms through external timers): a conformity of body movements, breath, heart beat and nerve activity triggered and synchronized by rhythm. Neher (1962) calculated the number of drum beats and their frequency per second and formed an analogy[1] with the EEG frequency pattern of trance states.

Rouget (1985, p. 167–183) believed such attempts to explain a universal 'trance mechanism' with reference to music alone to be incomplete, since the laboratory situation in Neher's experiment with trance cannot be compared to other settings. Ritual leader and musician do not enter trance states unintentionally. A person must be willing to fall in trance and must know the pertinent cultural techniques of music, singing and trance and be prepared for trance intellectually (Rouget, 1985, p. 315–326). In the case of obsessional trance, the obsessed individual must identify with the respective form of divine being pertinent to his culture and possibly attract the spirit through characteristic movements (Rouget, 1985, p. 35, 103, 105–108). Matussek (2001) writes that the contents of the cultural trance matrix and the physiological effects (in Neher's sense) complement each other functionally, in order to produce a state of amnesia and a willingness to assimilate new information. And this relates to the above-mentioned function of music within experiential systems.

DANCE AND TRANCE

In drumming and also in dancing we can see that rhythmic body movements synchronize with the rhythm of the music. This happens almost automatically in the course of longer activities, effortless and without control. The impression may be created that we 'become one with the rhythm', an experience known to many dancers in a long rave party night (Mitterlehner, 1996). Rhythmical body movements are accompanied by reduced movements in blood circulation. In addition, breathing becomes synchronized with movements, and so-called respiratory sinus arrythmias (of heart frequency) appear in heart rhythms. Blood pressure rises, which again stimulates the baroceptors in the carotid artery. This stimulation

---

[1] Neher hoped to demonstrate an ‚auditory driving' with the same EEG frequency range in his laboratory experiment, analogous to the epilepsy-inducing effect of‚ photic driving' (brain cramps caused by rhythmic light emissions). But he found that the possible drum frequencies are more in the range of theta waves (4–8 Hz), while photic driving is in the range of alpha waves (8–13 Hz) and is difficult to realize on drums because of the extremely quick pulsating sequence (compare Neher, 1962, p.153/154). Computer technology and appropriate music hardware (sampler sequencer, sound modules etc.), however, permit such modes of play. So Neher's ideas were taken up again in the Rave culture in order to explain the trance states occurring in the context of techno music and rave parties through sound (bass frequencies), repetition (loops and sequences), and tempo (bpm) of rhythmic patterns (Hutson, 2000; Weir, 1996).

not only decelerates heart frequencies, it also reduces arousal reactions and cortical excitability (compare Vaitl et al., 2005, p. 207). In studies with a stretcher moving rhythmically up and down Vaitl and colleagues demonstrated that a stimulation of baroceptors through rhythmic movement may induce trance states and an increase in theta waves (3–8 Hz) in the EEG, particularly in persons with high suggestibility to hypnosis according to the Tellegen Absorption Scale. Rhythmic body movements like dancing and (monotonous) drumming may cause altered states of consciousness depending on the subject's personality. Bachner-Melman et al. (2005) compared genetic preconditions for the transport of serotonin (neurotransmitter; regulates blood pressure in vessels) and the arginin vasopressin receptor 1a (regulates vascular dilatation and contraction with specific amino acid activities) in professional dancers, athletes and a control group. Apart from the fact that the decision to become a professional dancer also seems to be dependent upon genetic conditions, dancers had higher scores on the Tellegen Absorption Scale and in Cloniger's Personality Test TCI (this test evaluates empathy and socially learned reward behaviour) compared to athletes and controls. Consequently there seems to be a connection between personality traits and trance phenomena induced by rhythmic movement (Fachner, Jörg, 2006a).

RITUALS AND PERFORMATIVE HEALTH

The term 'ritual' may be used in a wider as well as a narrower sense. Every culture recognizes certain sophisticated procedures explicitly as rituals and frequently associates them with formal religious procedures; but they may also be secular. These are mainly transition rituals like weddings, births or funerals. There are other forms of behaviour which in general are not considered rituals but which psychologists, anthropologists and sociologists identify as ritual forms; the latter determine social relations that determine normal human interaction, for example sitting down for a meal together.

David Aldridge, FRSM, explores issues like spirituality and healing, altered states of consciousness and therapy in complementary medical approaches. In a lecture (see Aldridge, D., Fachner, J. & Schmid, W., 2006) he used video excerpts from music therapy, ethnic healing rituals and examples from blues and rock music to illustrate that all musical activity—in therapy, in everyday life or on a stage—is performance where communication takes place that involves all individual and social elements of the persons concerned (Aldridge, D., 2006).

Rituals that focus attention and structure the symbols and actions influenced by tradition and cultural heritage for each ethnic group—in the Mississippi delta, in tarantella dances in the south of Italy, or in the South American rain forest—according to the ceremonial masters' instructions provide specific experiences for participants and the specific client. The songs, prayers, rhythms, music, theatrical treatment figurations, dancing, visionary rigidity etc. that are used in rituals may be seen as symbolic interactions of the respective ethno-social context and be experienced on traditional and situational-subjective levels of meaning. These are rituals where for example a socially sanctioned behaviour may be indulged (in the tarantella the obsessed individuals are permitted to leave their narrowly defined traditional role as females); where a journey together through the dangerous jungle stands for the fear of physical damage or lack of social recognition after successful hunting; or the expulsion from the African homeland as a collective and almost psychogenetic heritage that defines lyrics and rhythm of the blues which addresses the past as well as the hopeless present on the plantations but at the same time evokes the joy and the culturally uniting and supporting elements of this unique musical heritage.

Music in all its form is part of everyday life; one video example shown was a black mother who talked about her current and rather hopeless plans for her future as a singer in Paris while holding her baby with humming and rhythmical movements and transmitting this rhythmic activity to the other children sitting on the sofa beside her who also swayed with the rhythm. Aldridge presented such examples to illustrate how it is possible to enjoy activity together, to alter our conscious perception of the miserable present and to change life with music.

> 'Achieving consciousness, from the Latin *con* (with) and *scire* (to know), is the central activity of human knowledge. At the heart of the word is a concept of mutuality, knowing with others. Our consciousness is a mutual activity; it is performed. Consciousness is also a means of personal knowing, our self-consciousness. We have interior understandings that are privatized but we also have experiences that are external and socialized. Balancing our internal lives with our social performance is a necessary activity of everyday living. Performing both music and consciousness are potent ways of achieving this balance of unity of the external and the internal.' (Aldridge, D., 2006, p.10)

Maas (2006) describes his initiation to a tribal cult in Gabun and his observations as a physician and musician during an altered state on consciousness induced by a highly potent psychoactive drug (Iboga). His musical analyses, observations and interpretation suggest the possible significance of each seemingly unimportant detail in such traditional healing rituals. The image on the back of an instrument, the pattern of a blanket in the rest room, the feather on the way to the ritual washing, all this achieves importance in an altered state of consciousness. Such details and their significance are known to the entire indigenous population and form part of their daily lives, and all tribe members attended and still attend the rituals and the celebrations afterwards.

SYNESTHESIA, SENSORY EXPERIENCE AND PERCEPTION

Mastnak (1996, p. 236) quotes from the studies of Habib Hassan Touma as follows:

> 'The function of music within a healing ceremony may be analysed only if we
> include the interaction of all levels of communication—auditory, visual, tactile,
> olfactory, gustatory and ultimately psychical. Depending on the occasion, the focus
> is more on one component, either on the visual through gestures, mimics, dance
> of the magician, or on the auditory through sounds, drums, screaming or music.'

The deliberate processual change in the perception of one's own person, the self and the body, through music, meditation, hypnosis, psychoactive substances etc. was and is used for therapy purposes in many forms (see Fachner, Jörg, 2006a, 2006b). Traditionally it has been a therapy objective to change the (habitual) focussing of perception. In 1902 William James already experimented with nitrous oxide (laughing gas) to explore the limits of sensory perception and the socially and culturally determined selective processes of a consciously perceived world. Altered states of consciousness may be perceived voluntarily by searching for and employing psychological and pharmacological triggers (Dittrich, 1996). What is thus experienced and perceived can open up new perspectives and insights, can raise questions about personal growth, provide an intensive experience of togetherness, reveal hidden knowledge, or change an individual's attitude to himself and his life. It is one of the aims of arts as therapy (Aldridge, D., 2004) to transcend the limits and obstacles erected by illness through an aesthetic variation of the perceptive context. I would like to add here that 'Guided Imagery in Music' has its origins in the psychedelic therapy of the early 1960s where psychoactive substances were used under supervision of psychotherapists. The idea was to weaken the defense and selection mechanisms of the psyche for therapy purposes, in combination with a programmatic use of classical and modern music, and thus to produce an unhampered associative flow for psychotherapy purposes (Bonny & Savary, 1973). De Rios (2006) demands a musicological approach for psychotherapy practice with drugs and music, in order to induce altered states of alert consciousness with therapeutic intentions and to guide by way of music. De Rios' ethnological field research and analyses underline that therapy practice might learn from observations of such cultural traditions and that transfer might be possible. The question is still under debate whether there is a trance mechanism that connects the triggering of trance to music and its parameters, that is, whether body rhythms and psycho-physiological states are inevitably influenced by external timers in music and alter consciousness as a consequence.

Changes in attentive focus guided by music and its ritual context, the length of rituals, repetitions, monotonies, growing and fading volume and density of sound and rhythm produce altered levels of intensity, altered perception of time and space, and as a consequence, altered associations of musical parameters in the acoustic field of perception.

Rhythm in particular, in combination with dance, and also altered perception of time and space appear to be essential factors that trigger altered states of consciousness through music. In addition, music in combination with imagery techniques appears to make visual images more vivid through sensory dynamics, particularly where various sensory perceptions come together (synesthesia) (Fachner, Jörg, 2006a).

Music functions and acts like a mental space where significant things may be coded and decoded, depending on an individual's biography and socialization. Music focusses and directs attention and structures temporal occurrence and memories of internally and externally perceived events. It has the potential to support therapeuia, the accompaniment through a professional helper or even to be the accompaniment itself during altered states of consciousness. The musician Lal Shabaz Qalander from the Indus valley says in his ode to music (in Pannke & Friedrichs, 1999, p.88):

> I am the admirer of all wanderers,
> lover of the absolutely enraptured,
> guide to travelling mystics,
> dog in the street where Ali lives, the lion of God,
> drunken Qalander am I,
> serf of Murtaza Ali.

CONCLUSION

In Nepal we can see how western biomedical and traditional shamanistic treatment models can complement each other and coexist (Häußermann, 2006). Classical ethnomedical research approaches distinguish between *disease, illness* and *sickness* (Kleinman, 1981). *Disease* is described as malfunction or maladaptation in the biological or psychological sense (for example an organic change in the patient), that is, an explanation model based on complex mechanisms of generation. *Disease* comprises the opinion of an expert in health and illness and is mostly reduced to the perspective of biomedicine, that is, the scientifically based component. According to Kleinman (compare 1978, p.88) *illness*, in contrast, describes the patient's experience with derivations from a state he himself defines as healthy, and the significance he, his family and environment attach to these derivations, as well as personal explanations of the cause. *Sickness* is the general term covering both components of disease and illness. Sickness therefore stands for technical as well as personal, socially informed explanation models for being ill, as absence of health.

We may conclude that the debate about effects of music and its elements in healing rituals with an ethnic and cultural background resembles debates about music therapy theory. Is the music effective, is the relationship effective, or are both inseparable? The spontaneous answer is, the latter, of course, but if we take a closer look then each approach has a different focus and underlines either one or the other element.

Ethnotherapy interventions use sonorous and pulsating instruments, but in a wider sense also trance induction and synesthesia in rituals. Relating Kleinman's definition of 'disease' to ethno music therapy approaches, we see the influence of music and the physiological exertions caused by the ritual. This is where the ongoing debate on *trance mechanism* as discussed by Neher and Rouget plays a role, i.e. attempts are made to interpret the effects of music mainly from the perspective of biomedicine.

Modern music therapy practice, however, relies heavily on communication between therapist, music and client. Even primarily receptive approaches are directed to the individual and see the music therapy process as a joint, purposeful or open interpretation. Following a biomedical perspective of illness, the interpretation of the effects of music widens to become a joint interactive performance that in ethno music therapy also comprises the respective cultural traditions, their cosmologies and corresponding symbols and social experiences of participants. The ritual, the ceremony with the performative act that is meant to cure a specific problem (sickness) is the treatment that integrates the senses to a wholeness experienced in the act.

Individuals from western industralized nations without personal experience with the cultures from which certain musical styles emerged appear fascinated by the exotic performance in such rituals. Considering that in addition to the triad of therapist, music and client, other transcendent and powerful entities form part of the interaction and exert their situational influence in the sense mentioned above by Thomas (1927), then what we find here is the fundamental search for transcendence, religiosity and spirituality described by C.G. Jung. Such needs will certainly be met by therapeutic approaches that use music, trance and ecstasy in rituals and procedures evoking an experience of sensory wholeness.

Ethnologists confirm that traditions in other cultures may only be truly understood if we experience them in their original environment for longer periods. Maas & Strubelt (2006) underlined the significance of detail in ritual, and how important it is to live on site until such traditions have been absorbed. Well-meant imitations are often rather clumsy and even unwise. We will have to wait and see whether a so-called world music as part of the general global trend and aimed at greatest possible integration will appeal to a majority, and will sell, or whether it will only satisfy a certain section of the public with an open mind for this relatively new but at the same time very old style of music in therapy.

REFERENCES

Aldridge, D. (2004). *Health, the individual and integrated medicine-revisiting an aesthetic of health care*. London: Jessica Kingsley.

Aldridge, D. (2006). Music, consciousness and altered states. In D. Aldridge & J. Fachner (Eds.), *Music and altered states—Consciousnes, transcendence, therapy and addictions* (pp. 9–14). London: Jessica Kingsley.

Aldridge, D. (2006, 31. March). Performative Health—a commentary on Traditional Oriental Music Therapy [Electronic Version]. *Music Therapy Today*, 7, 1: 65–69. Retrieved 1. April 2006 from http://www.musictherapyworld.net/modules/mmmagazine/issues/20060331100549/20060331101924/MTT7_1_Aldridge.pdf.

Aldridge, D., & Fachner, J. (Eds.). (2006). *Music and altered states—Consciousness, transcendence, therapy and addictions*. London: Jessica Kingsley.

Aldridge, D., Fachner, J., & Schmid, W. (2006, 31. März). Music, perception and altered states of consciousness [Electronic Version]. *Music Therapy Today*, 7, 1: 70–76. Retrieved 1. April from http://www.musictherapyworld.net/modules/mmmagazine/issues/20060331100549/20060331101804/MTT7_1_Fachner.pdf.

Bachner-Melman, R., Dina, C., Zohar, A. H., Constantini, N., Lerer, E., Hoch, S., et al. (2005). AVPR1a and SLC6A4 gene polymorphisms are associated with creative dance performance. PLoS Genet, 1(3), e42.

Bonny, H. L., & Savary, L. M. (1973). *Music and your mind. Listening with a new consciousness*. New York: Harper & Row.

Bühler, W. (1984). Anthroposophische Medizin und zeitgemäße Heilmittel. In *Weleda Almanach* (Vol. 16, pp. 20–26). Schwäbisch Gmünd: Weleda AG

Castaneda, C. (1975). *Die Lehren des Don Juan : ein Yaqui-Weg des Wissens* (Ungekürzte u. überarb. Ausg., 26.–32. Tsd. ed.). Frankfurt am Main: Fischer-Taschenbuch-Verl.

De Rios, M. D. (2006). The Role of Music in Healing with Hallucinogens: Tribal and Western Studies. In D. Aldridge & J. Fachner (Eds.), *Music and Altered States—Consciousness, Transcendence, Therapy and Addictions* (pp. 97–101). London: Jessica Kingsley.

Dittrich, A. (1996). *Ätiologie-unabhängige Strukturen veränderter Wachbewusstseinszustände. Ergebnisse empirischer Untersuchun-gen über Halluzinogene I. und II. Ordnung, sensorische Deprivation, hypnagoge Zustände, hypnotische Verfahren sowie Reizüberflutung* (2 ed.). Berlin: Verlag für Wissenschaft und Bildung.

Eliade, M. (1954). *Schamanismus und archaische Ekstasetechnik*. Zürich Stuttgart: Rascher.

Elias, N. (1969). *Über den Prozess der Zivilisation*. Frankfurt a. M.: Suhrkamp.

Eschen, T. J. (1982). Mentorenkurs Musiktherapie Herdecke. *Musikther-apeutische Umschau*, 3 255–282.

Fachner, J. (2004, *Die kunsttherapeutisch orientierte Nordoff/Robbins Musiktherapie in Herdecke*. In D. Aldridge & J. Fachner (Eds.), Music Therapy Info CD-ROM. Vol. V, [PDF].

Fachner, J. (2006a). Music and altered states of consciousness—an overview. In D. Aldridge & J. Fachner (Eds.), *Music and Altered States—Consciousness, Transcendence, Therapy and Addictions* (pp. 15–37). London: Jessica Kingsley.

Fachner, J. (2006b). Music and drug induced altered states. In D. Aldridge & J. Fachner (Eds.), *Music and Altered States—Consciousness, Transcendence, Therapy and Addictions* (pp. 82–98). London: Jessica Kingsley.

Freeman, W. (2000). A neurobiological role of music in social bonding. In N. L. Wallin, B. Merker & S. Brown (Eds.), *The origins of music* (pp. 411–424). Cambridge, Mass.: MIT Press.

Haerlin, P. (1998). The use of music instruments in psychotherapy in order to alter states of consciousness. *Psychotherapeut*, 43(4), 238–242.

Hamel, P. M. (1984). *Durch Musik zum Selbst* (3 ed.). München: DTV-Bärenreiter.

Häußermann, C. (2006, 1. Oktober). Shamanism and biomedical approaches in Nepal—Dualism or Sythesis? [Electronic Version]. *Music Therapy Today*, 7, 3: 514–622. Retrieved 2. Oktober 2006 from http://www.musictherapyworld.net/modules/mmmagazine/issues/20060929134150/20060929134533/MTT7_3_Carolin.pdf.

Hess, P. (1999). Musiktherapie mit archaischen Klangkörpern. *Musik-therapeutische Umschau*, 20(2), 77–92.

Hess, P., & Rittner, S. (1996a). Trance. In H. H. Decker-Voigt, P. Knill & E. Weymann (Eds.), *Lexikon Musiktherapie* (pp. 395–398). Göttingen: Hogrefe.

Hess, P., & Rittner, S. (1996b). Verändertes Wachbewusstsein. In H. H. Decker-Voigt, P. Knill & E. Weymann (Eds.), *Lexikon Musikthera-pie* (pp. 398–403). Göttingen: Hogrefe.

Husemann, A. J. (1982). *Der musikalische Bau des Menschen. Entwurf einer plastisch-musikalischen Menschenkunde*. Stuttgart: Verlag Freies Geistesleben.

Hutson, S. R. (2000). The Rave: spiritual healing in modern western subcultures. *Anthropological Quarterly*, 73, 35–49.

James, W. (1902). *The variety of religous experience*. New York: Modern Library.

Kienle, G., & Schily, K. (1980). Zur gegenwärtigen Diskussion des Krankheitsbegriffes. *Musik-therapeutische Umschau*, 1(1), 37–44.

Kleinman, A. (1978). Concepts and a model for the comparison of medical systems as cultural systems. *Social Science and Medicine*, 12, 85–93.

Kleinman, A. (1981). *Patients and Healers in the Context of Culture —An Exploration of the Borderland between Anthropology, Medicine and Psychiatry*. Berkeley, Los Angeles; London: University of California Press.

Koestler, A. (1980). *Die Nachtwandler* (1 ed.). Frankfurt: Suhrkamp Taschenbuch.

Ludwig, A. M. (1966). Altered States of Consciousness. *Arch Gen Psychiatry*, 15(3), 225–234.

Maas, U., & Strubelt, S. (2006). Polyrhythms supporting a pharmacotherapy: Music in the Iboga initiation ceremony in Gabon. In D. Aldridge & J. Fachner (Eds.), *Music and Altered States—Consciousness, Transcendence, Therapy and Addictions* (pp. 101–124). London: Jessica Kingsley.

Mastnak, W. (1996). Musikethnologie-Schamanismus-Musiktherapie. In H. H. Decker-Voigt, P. Knill & E. Weymann (Eds.), *Lexikon Musiktherapie* (pp. 233–237). Göttingen: Hogrefe.

Matussek, P. (2001). Berauschende Geräusche. Akustische Trancetechni-ken im Medienwechsel. In A. Hiepko & K. Stopka (Eds.), *Rauschen. Seine Phänomenologie zwischen Sinn und Störung* (pp. 225–240). Würzburg: Königshausen & Neumann.

Meszaros, I., Szabo, C., & Csako, R. I. (2002). Hypnotic susceptibility and alterations in subjective experiences. *Acta Biol Hung*, 53(4), 499–514.

Mitterlehner, F. (1996). Lets Fly Together, zur Untersuchung veränderter Bewußtseinszustände während einer Techno-Party. In H. C. Leuner & M. Schlichting (Eds.), *Jahrbuch des Europäischen Collegiums für Bewußtseinsstudien* (pp. 49–62). Berlin: Verlag für Wissenschaft und Bildung.

Möller, H. J. (1974). Psychotherapeutische Aspekte in der Musikanschauung der Jahrtausende. In W. J. Revers, G. Harrer & W. C. M. Simon (Eds.), *Neue Wege der Musiktherapie* (1 ed., pp. 53–160). Düsseldorf: Econ.

Neher, A. (1962). A physiological explanation of unusual behavior in ceremonies involving drums. *Hum Biol*, 34, 151–160.

Nordoff, P., & Robbins, C. (1975). *Musik als Therapie für behinderte Kinder* (1 ed.). Stuttgart: E. Klett.

Oelmann, J. (1993). Klang, Wahrnehmung, Wirkung. Zur therapeutis-chen Arbeit mit Gongs und Tam-Tams in rezeptiver Therapie. *Musiktherapeutische Umschau*, 14(4), 289–305.

Oohashi, T., Kawai, N., Honda, M., Nakamura, S., Morimoto, M., Nishina, E., et al. (2002). Electroencephalographic measurement of possession trance in the field. *Clinical Neurophysiology*, 113(3), 435–445.

Pannke, P., & Friedrichs, H. A. (1999). *Troubadure Allahs—Sufi-Musik im Industal*. München: Frederking & Thaler.

Pekala, R. J., & Kumar, V. K. (2000). Operationalizing 'trance' I: Rationale and research using a psychophenomenological approach. *Am J Clin Hypn*, 43(2), 107–135.

Pfrogener, H. (1985). Rudolf Steiner und die Musik. *Musiktherapeutische Umschau*, 6, 335–340.

Rittner, S., & Fachner, J. (2004). Klang und Trance im EEG—Brainmapping mit dem Ganzkör-per-Monochord im therapeutischen Setting. *Musiktherapeutische Umschau*, 25(1), 70–80.

Rittner, S., & Hess, P. (1996). Klangtrance. Trance. Veränderte Bewußt-seinszustände. In H. H. Decker-Voigt, E. Weymann & P. Knill (Eds.), *Lexikon Musiktherapie* (pp. 169–173). Göttin-gen: Hogrefe.

Rösing, H. (1991). Musik als Droge? In H. Rösing (Ed.), *Musik als Droge? Zu Theorie und Praxis bewußtseinsverändernder Wirkungen von Musik* (Vol. 1, pp. 7–8). Mainz: Villa Musica.

Rouget, G. (1985). *Music and Trance. A Theory of the Relations between Music and Possession*. Chicago: University Press.

Ruud, E. (2001, 1st November). Music Therapy-History and Cultural Contexts [Electronic Ver-sion]. *Voices*, *1*, 3 Retrieved 13. Januar 2007 from http://www.voices.no/mainissues/Voices1(3) Ruud.html.

Strobel, W. (1999). *Reader Musiktherapie. Klanggeleitete Trance u.a. Beiträge*. Wiesbaden: Reichert.

Strobel, W. (1988). Klang-Trance-Heilung. Die archetypische Welt der Klänge in der Psychothera-pie. *Musiktherapeutische Umschau*, 9, 119–139.

Thomas, W. I. (1927). Situational Analysis: The Behavior Pattern and the Situation. *Publications of the American Sociological Society*, 22, 1–13.

Timmermann, T. (1996). Ethnologische Aspekte in der Musiktherapie. In H. H. Decker-Voigt, P. Knill & E. Weymann (Eds.), *Lexikon Musik-therapie* (pp. 87–90). Göttingen: Hogrefe.

Tucek, G. (2006, 1. Oktober). Traditional oriental music therapy–a regulatory and relational approach [Electronic Version]. *Music Therapy Today*, 7, 3: 623–647. Retrieved 2. Oktober 2006 from http://www.musictherapyworld.net/modules/mmmagazine/issues/20060929134150/20060929134747/MTT7_3_Tucek.pdf.

Tucek, G., Fritz, F. M., & Ferstl, E. (2006). Psychophysiologisches Monitoring während einer Alto-rientalischen Musiktherapie-Untersu-chung der Beziehung zwischen Arzt und Patient. *Musik-, Tanz-und Kunsttherapie*, 17(2), 88–95.

Tucek, G., Murg, M., Auer-Pekarsky, A. M., Oder, W., & Stepansky, R. (2006, 31. März). The revival of Traditional Oriental Music Therapy discussed by cross cultural reflections and a pilot scheme of a quantitative EEG-analysis for patients in Minimally Responsive State [Electronic Version]. *Music Therapy Today*, 7, 1: 39–64. Retrieved 1. April 2006 from http://www.musictherapyworld.net/modules/mmmagazine/showarticle.php?articletoshow=168&language=en.

Vaitl, D., Birbaumer, N., Gruzelier, J., Jamieson, G. A., Kotchoubey, B., Kübler, A., et al. (2005). Psychobiology of Altered States of Consciousness. Psychological Bulletin, 131(1), 98–127.

Voigt, A. (1981). *Musiktherapeutische Praxis*. Frankfurt: Paritätisches Bildungswerk, Bundesverband e.V.

Weir, D. (1996). *Trance: from magic to technology*. Ann Arbour: Trans Media.

This article can be cited as:

Fachner, J. (2007) Wanderer between worlds—Anthropological perspectives on healing rituals and music. *Music Therapy Today* (Online 18th July) Vol.VIII (2) 166–195. available at http://musictherapyworld.net

THE VIRGIN OF GUADALUPE
A MEXICAN NATIONAL SYMBOL

Eric R. Wolf

Occasionally, we encounter a symbol which seems to enshrine the major hopes and aspirations of an entire society.[1] Such a master symbol is Virgin represented by the Virgin of Guadalupe, Mexico's patron saint. During the Mexican War of Independence against Spain, her image preceded the insurgents into battle.[2] Emiliano Zapata and his agrarian rebels fought under her emblem in the Great Revolution of 1910.[3] Today, her image adorns house fronts and interiors, churches and home altars, bull rings and gambling dens, taxis and buses, restaurants and houses of ill repute. She is celebrated in popular song and verse. Her shrine at Tepeyac, immediately north of Mexico City, is visited each year by hundreds of thousands of pilgrims, ranging from the inhabitants of far-off Indian villages to the members of socialist trade union locals. "Nothing to be seen in Canada or Europe," says F. S. C. Northrop, "equals it in the volume or the vitality of its moving quality or in the depth of its spirit of religious devotion."[4]

---

[1] Parts of this paper were presented to the Symposium on Ethnic and National Ideologies, Annual Spring Meeting of the American Ethnological Society in conjunction with the Philadelphia Anthropological Society, on 12 May 1956.

[2] Niceto de Zamacois, *Historia de México* (Barcelona-Mexico, 1878–82), VI, 253.

[3] Antonio Pompa y Pompa, *Album del IV centcnario guadalupano* (Mexico, 1938), p. 173.

[4] F. S. C. Northrop, *The Meeting of East and West* (New York, 1946), p. 25.

In this paper, I should like to discuss this Mexican master symbol, and the ideology which surrounds it. In making use of the term "master symbol," I do not wish to imply that belief in the symbol is common to all Mexicans. We are not dealing here with an element of a putative national character, defined as a common denominator of all Mexican nationals. It is no longer legitimate to assume "that any member of the [national] group will exhibit certain regularities of behavior which are common in high degree among the other members of the society."[5] Nations, like other complex societies, must, however, "possess cultural forms or mechanisms which groups involved in the same overall web of relationships can use in their formal and informal dealings with each other."[6] Such forms develop historically, hand in hand with other processes which lead to the formation of nations, and social groups which are caught up in these processes must become "acculturated" to their usage.[7] Only where such forms exist, can communication and coordinated behavior be established among the constituent groups of such a society. They provide the cultural idiom of behavior and ideal representations through which different groups of the same society can pursue and manipulate their different fates within a coordinated framework. This paper, then, deals with one such cultural form, operating on the symbolic level. The study of this symbol seems particularly rewarding, since it is not restricted to one set of social ties, but refers to a very wide range of social relationships.

The image of the Guadalupe and her shrine at Tepeyac are surrounded by an origin myth.[8] According to this myth, the Virgin Mary appeared to Juan Diego, a Christianized Indian of commoner status, and addressed him in Nahuatl. The encounter took place on the Hill of Tepeyac in the year 1531, ten years after the Spanish Conquest of Tenochtitlan. The Virgin commanded Juan Diego to seek out the archbishop of Mexico and to inform him of her desire to see a church built in her honor on Tepeyac Hill. After Juan Diego was twice unsuccessful in his efforts to carry out her order, the Virgin wrought a miracle. She bade Juan Diego pick roses in a sterile spot where normally only desert plants could grow, gathered the roses into the Indian's cloak, and told him to present cloak and roses to the incredulous archbishop. When Juan Diego unfolded his cloak before the bishop, the image of the Virgin was miraculously stamped upon it. The bishop acknowledged the miracle, and ordered a shrine built where Mary had appeared to her humble servant.

The shrine, rebuilt several times in centuries to follow, is today a basilica, the third highest kind of church in Western Christendom. Above the central altar hangs Juan Diego's cloak with the miraculous image. It shows a young woman without child, her head

---

[5] David G. Mandelbaum, "On the Study of National Character," *American Anthropologist*, LV (1953), p. 185.

[6] Eric R. Wolf, "Aspects of Group Relations in a Complex Society: Mexico," *American Anthropologist*, LVII (1956), 1065–1078.

[7] Eric R. Wolf, "La formación de la nación," *Ciencias Sociales*, IV, 50–51.

[8] Ernest Gruening, *Mexico and Its Heritage* (New York, 1928), p. 235.

lowered demurely in her shawl. She wears an open crown and flowing gown, and stands upon a half moon symbolizing the Immaculate Conception.

The shrine of Guadalupe was, however, not the first religious structure built on Tepeyac; nor was Guadalupe the first female supernatural associated with the hill. In pre-Hispanic times, Tepeyac had housed a temple to the earth and fertility goddess Tonantzin, Our Lady Mother, who—like the Guadalupe—was associated with the moon. Temple, like basilica, was the center of large scale pilgrimages. That the veneration accorded the Guadalupe drew inspiration from the earlier worship of Tonantzin is attested by several Spanish friars. F. Bernardino de Sahagiin, writing fifty years after the Conquest, says: "Now that the Church of Our Lady of Guadalupe has been built there, they call her Tonantzin too. ... The term refers ... to that ancient Tonantzin and this state of affairs should be remedied, because the proper name of the Mother of God is not Tonantzin, but Dios and Nantzin. It seems to be a satanic device to mask idolatry ... and they come from far away to visit that Tonantzin, as much as before; a devotion which is also suspect because there are many churches of Our Lady everywhere and they do not go to them; and they come from faraway lands to this Tonantzin as of old."[9] F. Martin de Leon wrote in a similar vein: "On the hill where Our Lady of Guadalupe is they adored the idol of a goddess they called Tonantzin, which means Our Mother, and this is also the name they give Our Lady and they always say they are going to Tonantzin or they are celebrating Tonantzin and many of them understand this in the old way and not in the modern way. ..."[10] The syncretism was still alive in the seventeenth century. F. Jacinto de la Serna, in discussing the pilgrimages to the Guadalupe at Tepeyac, noted: "... it is the purpose of the wicked to [worship] the goddess and not the Most Holy Virgin, or both together."[11]

Increasingly popular during the sixteenth century, the Guadalupe cult gathered emotional impetus during the seventeenth. During this century appear the first known pictorial representations of the Guadalupe, apart from the miraculous original; the first poems are written in her honor; and the first sermons announce the transcendental implications of her supernatural appearance in Mexico and among Mexicans.[12] Historians have long tended to neglect the seventeenth century which seemed "a kind of Dark Age in Mexico." Yet "this quiet time was of the utmost importance in the development of Mexican Society."[13] During this century, the institution of the hacienda comes to dominate Mexican life.[14] During this

[9] Bernardino de Sahagún, *Historia general de las cosas de nueva españa* (Mexico, 1938), I, lib. 6.

[10] Quoted in Carlos A. Echánove Trujillo, *Sociología mexicana* (Mexico, 1948), p. 105.

[11] Quoted in Jesús Amaya, *La madre de Dios: genesis e historia de nuestra señora de Guadalupe* (Mexico, 1931), p. 230.

[12] Francisco de la Maza, *El guadalupismo mexicano* (Mexico, 1953), PP 12–14, 143, 30, 33, 82.

[13] Lesley B. Simpson, "Mexico's Forgotten Century," *Pacific Historical Review*, XXII (1953), 115, 114.

[14] Francois Chevalier, *La formation des grands domaines au Mexique* (Paris, 1952), p. xii.

century, also, "New Spain is ceasing to be 'new' and to be 'Spain.'"[15] These new experiences require a new cultural idiom, and in the Guadalupe cult, the component segments of Mexican colonial society encountered cultural forms in which they could express their parallel interests and longings.

The primary purpose of this paper is not, however, to trace the history of the Guadalupe symbol. It is concerned rather with its functional aspects, its roots and reference to the major social relationships of Mexican society.

The first set of relationships which I would like to single out for consideration are the ties of kinship, and the emotions generated in the play of relationships within families. I want to suggest that some of the meanings of the Virgin symbol in general, and of the Guadalupe symbol in particular, derive from these emotions. I say "some meanings" and I use the term "derive" rather than "originate," because the form and function of the family in any given society are themselves determined by other social factors: technology, economy, residence, political power. The family is but one relay in the circuit within which symbols are generated in complex societies. Also, I used the plural "families" rather than "family," because there are demonstrably more than one kind of family in Mexico.[16] I shall simplify the available information on Mexican family life, and discuss the material in terms of two major types of families.[17] The first kind of family is congruent with the closed and static life of the Indian village. It may be called the Indian family. In this kind of family, the husband is ideally dominant, but in reality labor and authority are shared equally among both marriage partners. Exploitation of one sex by the other is atypical; sexual feats do not add to a person's status in the eyes of others. Physical punishment and authoritarian treatment of children are rare. The second kind of family is congruent with the much more open, mobile, manipulative life in communities which are actively geared to the life of the nation, a life in which power relationships between individuals and groups are of great moment. This kind of family may be called the Mexican family. Here, the father's authority is unquestioned on both the real and the ideal plane. Double sex standards prevail, and male sexuality is charged with a desire to exercise domination. Children are ruled with a heavy hand; physical punishment is frequent.

The Indian family pattern is consistent with the behavior towards the Guadalupe noted by John Bushnell in the Matlazinca speaking community of San Juan Atzingo in the Valley

---

[15] de la Maza, p. 41.

[16] Maria Elvira Bermúdez, *La vida familiar del mexicano* (Mexico, 1955), chapters 2 and 3.

[17] For relevant material, see: Bermúdez; John Gillin, "Ethos and Cultural Aspects of Personality," and Robert Redfield and Sol Tax, "General Characteristics of Present-Day Mesoamerican Indian Society," in Sol Tax, ed., *Heritage of Conquest* (Glencoe, 1952), pp. 193–212, 31–39; Gordon W. Hewes, "Mexicans in Search of the 'Mexican'," *American Journal of Economics and Sociology,* XIII (1954), 209–223; Octavio Paz, *El laberinto de la soledad* (Mexico, 1947), pp. 71–89.

of Toluca.[18] There, the image of the Virgin is addressed in passionate terms as a source of warmth and love, and the *pulque* or century plant beer drunk on ceremonial occasions is identified with her milk. Bushnell postulates that here the Guadalupe is identified with the mother as a source of early satisfactions, never again experienced after separation from the mother and emergence into social adulthood. As such, the Guadalupe embodies a longing to return to the pristine state in which hunger and unsatisfactory social relations are minimized. The second family pattern is also consistent with a symbolic identification of Virgin and mother, yet this time within a context of adult male dominance and sexual assertion, discharged against submissive females and children. In this second context, the Guadalupe symbol is charged with the energy of rebellion against the father. Her image is the embodiment of hope in a victorious outcome of the struggle between generations.

This struggle leads to a further extension of the symbolism. Successful rebellion against power figures is equated with the promise of life; defeat with the promise of death. As John A. Mackay has suggested, there thus takes place a further symbolic identification of the Virgin with life; of defeat and death with the crucified Christ. In Mexican artistic tradition, as in Hispanic artistic tradition in general,[19] Christ is never depicted as an adult man, but always either as a helpless child, or more often as a figure beaten, tortured, defeated and killed. In this symbolic equation we are touching upon some of the roots both of the passionate affirmation of faith in the Virgin, and of the fascination with death which characterizes Baroque Christianity in general, and Mexican Catholicism in particular. The Guadalupe stands for life, for hope, for health; Christ on the cross, for despair and for death.

Supernatural mother and natural mother are thus equated symbolically, as are earthly and otherworldly hopes and desires. These hopes center on the provision of food and emotional warmth in the first case, in the successful waging of the Oedipal struggle in the other.

Family relations are, however, only one element in the formation of the Guadalupe symbol. Their analysis does little to explain the Guadalupe as such. They merely illuminate the female and maternal attributes of the more widespread Virgin symbol. The Guadalupe is important to Mexicans not only because she is a supernatural mother, but also because she embodies their major political and religious aspirations.

To the Indian groups, the symbol is more than an embodiment of life and hope; it restores to them the hopes of salvation. We must not forget that the Spanish Conquest signified not only military defeat, but the defeat also of the old gods and the decline of the old ritual. The apparition of the Guadalupe to an Indian commoner thus represents on one level the return of Tonantzin. As Tannenbaum has well said, "The Church … gave

---

[18] John Bushnell, "La Virgen de Guadalupe as Surrogate Mother in San Juan Atzingo," paper read before the 54th Annual Meeting of the American Anthropological Association, 18 November 1955.

[19] John A. Mackay, *The Other Spanish Christ* (New York, 1933), pp 110–117.

the Indian an opportunity not merely to save his life, but also to save his faith in his own gods."[20] On another level, the myth of the apparition served as a symbolic testimony that the Indian, as much as the Spaniard, was capable of being saved, capable of receiving Christianity. This must be understood against the background of the bitter theological and political argument which followed the Conquest and divided churchmen, officials, and conquerors into those who held that the Indian was incapable of conversion, thus inhuman, and therefore a fit subject of political and economic exploitation; and those who held that the Indian was human, capable of conversion and that this exploitation had to be tempered by the demands of the Catholic faith and of orderly civil processes of government.[21] The myth of the Guadalupe thus validates the Indian's right to legal defense, orderly government, to citizenship; to supernatural salvation, but also to salvation from random oppression.

But if the Guadalupe guaranteed a rightful place to the Indians in the new social system of New Spain, the myth also held appeal to the large group of disinherited who arose in New Spain as illegitimate offspring of Spanish fathers and Indian mothers, or through impoverishment, acculturation or loss of status within the Indian or Spanish group.[22] For such people, there was for a long time no proper place in the social order. Their very right to exist was questioned in their inability to command the full rights of citizenship and legal protection. Where Spaniard and Indian stood squarely within the law, they inhabited the interstices and margins of constituted society. These groups acquired influence and wealth in the seventeenth and eighteenth centuries, but were yet barred from social recognition and power by the prevailing economic, social and political order.[23] To them, the Guadalupe myth came to represent not merely the guarantee of their assured place in heaven, but the guarantee of their place in society here and now. On the political plane, the wish for a return to a paradise of early satisfactions of food and warmth, a life without defeat, sickness or death, gave rise to a political wish for a Mexican paradise, in which the illegitimate sons would possess the country, and the irresponsible Spanish overlords, who never acknowledged the social responsibilities of their paternity, would be driven from the land.

In the writings of seventeenth century ecclesiastics, the Guadalupe becomes the harbinger of this new order. In the book by Miguel Sánchez, published in 1648, the Spanish Conquest of New Spain is justified solely on the grounds that it allowed the

---

[20] Frank Tannenbaum, *Peace by Revolution* (New York, 1933), p. 39.

[21] Silvio Zavala, *La filosofía en la conquista de América* (Mexico, 1947).

[22] Nicolas León, *Las castas del México colonial o Nueva España* (Mexico, 192/-+ C. E. Marshall, "The Birth of the Mestizo in New Spain," *Hispanic American Historical Review,* XIX (1939), 161–184; Wolf, "La formación de la nación," pp. 103–106.

[23] Gregorio Torres Quintero, *México hacía el fin del virreinato español* (Mexico, 1921); Eric R. Wolf, "The Mexican Bajío in the Eighteenth Century," *Middle American Research Institute Publication* XVII (1955), 180–199; Wolf, "Aspects of Group Relations in a Complex Society: Mexico."

Virgin to become manifest in her chosen country, and to found in Mexico a new paradise. Just as Israel had been chosen to produce Christ, so Mexico had been chosen to produce Guadalupe. Sanchez equates her with the apocalyptic woman of the Revelation of John (12: 1), "arrayed with the sun, and the moon under her feet, and upon her head a crown of twelve stars" who is to realize the prophecy of Deuteronomy 8: 7–10 and lead the Mexicans into the Promised Land. Colonial Mexico thus becomes the desert of Sinai; Independent Mexico the land of milk and honey. F. Francisco de Florencia, writing in 1688, coined the slogan which made Mexico not merely another chosen nation, but the Chosen Nation: *non fecit taliter omni nationi*,[24] words which still adorn the portals of the basilica, and shine forth in electric light bulbs at night. And on the eve of Mexican independence, Servando Teresa de Mier elaborates still further the Guadalupan myth by claiming that Mexico had been converted to Christianity long before the Spanish Conquest. The apostle Saint Thomas had brought the image of Guadalupe-Tonantzin to the New World as a symbol of his mission, just as Saint James had converted Spain with the image of the Virgin of the Pillar. The Spanish Conquest was therefore historically unnecessary, and should be erased from the annals of history.[25] In this perspective, the Mexican War of Independence marks the final realization of the apocalyptic promise. The banner of the Guadalupe leads the insurgents; and their cause is referred to as "her law."[26] In this ultimate extension of the symbol, the promise of life held out by the supernatural mother has become the promise of an independent Mexico, liberated from the irrational authority of the Spanish father-oppressors and restored to the Chosen Nation whose election had been manifest in the apparition of the Virgin on Tepeyac. The land of the supernatural mother is finally possessed by her rightful heirs. The symbolic circuit is closed. Mother; food, hope, health, life; supernatural salvation and salvation from oppression; Chosen People and national independence—all find expression in a single master symbol.

The Guadalupe symbol thus links together family, politics and religion; colonial past and independent present; Indian and Mexican. It reflects the salient social relationships of Mexican life, and embodies the emotions which they generate. It provides a cultural idiom through which the tenor and emotions of these relationships can be expressed. It is, ultimately, a way of talking about Mexico: a "collective representation" of Mexican society.

---

[24] Gregorio Torres Quintero, *México hacía el fin del virreinato español* (Mexico, 1921); Eric R. Wolf, "The Mexican Bajío in the Eighteenth Century," *Middle American Research Institute Publication* XVII (1955), 180-199; Wolf, "Aspects of Group Relations in a Complex Society: Mexico."

[25] Luis Villoro, *Los grandes momentos del indigenismo en México* (Mexico, 1950), pp. 131–138.

[26] Luis González y González, "El optimismo nacionalista como factor en la independencia de México," *Estudios de historiografía americana* (Mexico, 1948), p. 194.

Part III

Human Social Identities

When Brothers Share a Wife

Melvyn C. Goldstein

E ager to reach home, Dorje drives his yaks hard over the 17,000-foot mountain pass, stopping only once to rest. He and his two older brothers, Pema and Sonam, are jointly marrying a woman from the next village in a few weeks, and he has to help with the preparations.

Dorje, Pema, and Sonam are Tibetans living in Limi, a 200-square-mile area in the northwest corner of Nepal, across the border from Tibet. The form of marriage they are about to enter—fraternal polyandry in anthropological parlance—is one of the world's rarest forms of marriage but is not uncommon in Tibetan society, where it has been practiced from time immemorial. For many Tibetan social strata, it traditionally represented the ideal form of marriage and family.

The mechanics of fraternal polyandry are simple. Two, three, four, or more brothers jointly take a wife, who leaves her home to come and live with them. Traditionally, marriage was arranged by parents, with children, particularly females, having little or no say. This is changing somewhat nowadays, but it is still unusual for children to marry without their parents' consent. Marriage ceremonies vary by income and region and range from all the brothers sitting together as grooms to only the eldest one formally doing so. The age of the brothers plays an important role in determining this: very young brothers almost never participate in actual marriage ceremonies, although they typically join the marriage when they reach their mid-teens.

The eldest brother is normally dominant in terms of authority, that is, in managing the household, but all the brothers share the work and participate as sexual partners. Tibetan males and females do not find the sexual aspect of sharing a spouse the least bit unusual, repulsive, or scandalous, and the norm is for the wife to treat all the brothers the same.

Offspring are treated similarly. There is no attempt to link children biologically to particular brothers, and a brother shows no favoritism toward his child even if he knows he is the real father because, for example, his other brothers were away at the time the wife became pregnant. The children, in turn, consider all of the brothers as their fathers and treat them equally, even if they also know who is their real father. In some regions children use the term "father" for the eldest brother and "father's brother" for the others, while in other areas they call all the brothers by one term, modifying this by the use of "elder" and "younger."

Unlike our own society, where monogamy is the only form of marriage permitted, Tibetan society allows a variety of marriage types, including monogamy, fraternal polyandry, and polygyny. Fraternal polyandry and monogamy are the most common forms of marriage, while polygyny typically occurs in cases where the first wife is barren. The widespread practice of fraternal polyandry, therefore, is not the outcome of a law requiring brothers to marry jointly. There is choice, and in fact, divorce traditionally was relatively simple in Tibetan society. If a brother in a polyandrous marriage became dissatisfied and wanted to separate, he simply left the main house and set up his own household. In such cases, all the children stayed in the main household with the remaining brother(s), even if the departing brother was known to be the real father of one or more of the children.

The Tibetans' own explanation for choosing fraternal polyandry is materialistic. For example, when I asked Dorje why he decided to marry with his two brothers rather than take his own wife, he thought for a moment, then said it prevented the division of his family's farm (and animals) and thus facilitated all of them achieving a higher standard of living. And when I later asked Dorje's bride whether it wasn't difficult for her to cope with three brothers as husbands, she laughed and echoed the rationale of avoiding fragmentation of the family and land, adding that she expected to be better off economically, since she would have three husbands working for her and her children.

Exotic as it may seem to Westerners, Tibetan fraternal polyandry is thus in many ways analogous to the way primogeniture functioned in nineteenth-century England. Primogeniture dictated that the eldest son inherited the family estate, while younger sons had to leave home and seek their own employment—for example, in the military or the clergy. Primogeniture maintained family estates intact over generations by permitting only one heir per generation. Fraternal polyandry also accomplishes this but does so by keeping all the brothers together with just one wife so that there is only one *set* of heirs per generation.

While Tibetans believe that in this way fraternal polyandry reduces the risk of family fission, monogamous marriages among brothers need not necessarily precipitate the division of the family estate: brothers could continue to live together, and the family land could continue to be worked jointly. When I asked Tibetans about this, however, they invariably responded that such joint families are unstable because each wife is primarily oriented to her own children and interested in their success and well-being over that of the children of the other wives. For example, if the youngest brother's wife had three sons while the eldest brother's wife had only one daughter, the wife of the youngest brother might begin to demand more resources for her children since, as males, they represent the future of the family. Thus, the children from different wives in the same generation are competing sets of heirs, and this makes such families inherently unstable, Tibetans perceive that conflict will spread from the wives to their husbands and consider this likely to cause family fission. Consequently, it is almost never done.

Although Tibetans see an economic advantage to fraternal polyandry, they do not value the sharing of a wife as an end in itself. On the contrary, they articulate a number of problems inherent in the practice. For example, because authority is customarily exercised by the eldest brother, his younger male siblings have to subordinate themselves with little hope of changing their status within the family. When these younger brothers are aggressive and individualistic, tensions and difficulties often occur despite there being only one set of heirs.

In addition, tension and conflict may arise in polyandrous families because of sexual favoritism. The bride normally sleeps with the eldest brother, and the two have the responsibility to see to it that the other males have opportunities for sexual access. Since the Tibetan subsistence economy requires males to travel a lot, the temporary absence of one or more brothers facilitates this, but there are also other rotation practices. The cultural ideal unambiguously calls for the wife to show equal affection and sexuality to each of the brothers (and vice versa), but deviations from this ideal occur, especially when there is a sizable difference in age between the partners in the marriage.

Dorje's family represents just such a potential situation. He is fifteen years old and his two older brothers are twenty-five and twenty-two years old. The new bride is twenty-three years old, eight years Dorje's senior. Sometimes such a bride finds the youngest husband immature and adolescent and does not treat him with equal affection; alternatively, she may find his youth attractive and lavish special attention on him. Apart from that consideration, when a younger male like Dorje grows up, he may consider his wife "ancient" and prefer the company of a woman his own age or younger. Consequently, although men and women do not find the idea of sharing a bride or bridegroom repulsive, individual likes and dislikes can cause familial discord.

Two reasons have commonly been offered for the perpetuation of fraternal polyandry in Tibet: that Tibetans, practice female infanticide and therefore have to marry polyandrously, owing to a shortage of females; and that Tibet, lying at extremely high altitudes, is so barren and bleak that Tibetans would starve without resort to this mechanism. A Jesuit who lived in Tibet during the eighteenth century articulated this second view; "One reason for this most odious custom is the sterility of the soil, and the small amount of land that can be cultivated owing to the lack of water. The crops may suffice if the brothers all live together, but if they form separate families they would be reduced to beggary."

Both explanations are wrong, however. Not only has there never been institutionalized female infanticide in Tibet, but Tibetan society gives females considerable rights, including inheriting the family estate in the absence of brothers. In such cases, the woman takes a bridegroom who comes to live in her family and adopts her family's name and identity. Moreover, there is no demographic evidence of a shortage of females. In Limi, for example, there were (in 1974) sixty females and fifty-three males in the fifteen-to thirty-five-year age category, and many adult females were unmarried.

The second reason is also incorrect. The climate in Tibet is extremely harsh, and ecological factors do play a major role perpetuating polyandry, but polyandry is not a means of preventing starvation. It is characteristic, not of the poorest segments of the society, but rather of the peasant land-owning families.

In the old society, the landless poor could not realistically aspire to prosperity, but they did not fear starvation. There was a persistent labor shortage throughout Tibet, and very poor families with little or no land and few animals could subsist through agricultural labor, tenant farming, craft occupations such as carpentry, or by working as servants. Although the per person family income could increase somewhat if brothers married polyandrously and pooled their wages, in the absence of inheritable land, the advantage of fraternal polyandry was not generally sufficient to prevent them from setting up their own households. A more skilled or energetic younger brother could do as well or better alone, since he would completely control his income and would not have to share it with his siblings. Consequently, while there was and is some polyandry among the poor, it is much less frequent and more prone to result in divorce and family fission.

An alternative reason for the persistence of fraternal polyandry is that it reduces population growth (and thereby reduces the pressure on resources) by relegating some females to lifetime spinsterhood. Fraternal polyandrous marriages in Limi (in 1974) averaged 2.35 men per woman, and not surprisingly, 31 percent of the females of child-bearing age (twenty to forty-nine) were unmarried. These spinsters either continued to live at home, set up their own households, or worked as servants for other families. They could also become Buddhist nuns. Being unmarried is not synonymous with exclusion from the reproductive pool. Discreet extramarital relationships are tolerated, and actually half of the adult unmarried women in Limi had one or more children. They raised these children as single mothers, working for wages or weaving cloth and blankets for sale. As a group, however, the unmarried woman had far fewer offspring than the married women, averaging only 0.7 children per woman, compared with 3.3 for married women, whether polyandrous, monogamous, or polygynous. While polyandry helps regulate population, this function of polyandry is not consciously perceived by Tibetans and is not the reason they consistently choose it.

If neither a shortage of females nor the fear of starvation perpetuates fraternal polyandry, what motivates brothers, particularly younger brothers, to opt for this system of marriage? From the perspective of the younger brother in a land-holding family, the main incentive is the attainment or maintenance of the good life. With polyandry, he can expect a more secure and higher standard of living, with access not only to this family's land and animals but also so its inherited collection of clothes, jewelry, rugs, saddles, and horses. In addition, he will experience less work pressure and much greater security because all responsibility does not fail on one "father." For Tibetan brothers, the question is whether to trade off the greater personal freedom inherent in monogamy for the real or potential economic security, affluence, and social prestige associated with life in a larger, labor-rich polyandrous family.

A brother thinking of separating from his polyandrous marriage and taking his own wife would face various disadvantages. Although in the majority of Tibetan regions all brothers theoretically have rights to their family's estate, in reality Tibetans are reluctant to divide their land into small fragments. Generally, a younger brother who insists on leaving the family will receive only a small plot of land, if that. Because of its power and wealth, the rest of the family usually can block any attempt of the younger brother to increase his share of land through litigation. Moreover, a younger brother may not even get a house and cannot expect to receive much above the minimum in terms of movable possessions, such as furniture, pots, and pans. Thus, a brother contemplating going it on his own must plan on achieving economic security and the good life not through inheritance but through his own work.

The obvious solution for younger brothers—creating new fields from virgin land—is generally not a feasible option. Most Tibetan populations live at high altitudes (above 12,000 feet), where arable land is extremely scarce. For example, in Dorje's village, agriculture ranges only from about 12,900 feet, the lowest point in the area, to 13,300 feet. Above that altitude, early frost and snow destroy the staple barley crop. Furthermore, because of the low rainfall caused by the Himalayan rain shadow, many areas in Tibet and northern Nepal that are within the appropriate altitude range for agriculture have no reliable sources of irrigation. In the end, although there is plenty of unused land in such areas, most of it is either too high or too arid.

Even where unused land capable of being fanned exists, clearing the land and building the substantial terraces necessary for irrigation constitute a great undertaking. Each plot has to be completely dug out to a depth of two to two and half feet so that the large rocks and boulders can be removed. At best, a man might be able to bring a few new fields under cultivation in the first years after separating from his brothers, but he could not expect to acquire substantial amounts of arable land this way.

In addition, because of the limited farmland, the Tibetan subsistence economy characteristically includes a strong emphasis on animal husbandry. Tibetan farmers regularly maintain cattle, yaks, goats, and sheep, grazing them in the areas too high for agriculture.

These herds produce wool, milk, cheese, butter, meat, and skins. To obtain these resources, however, shepherds must accompany the animals on a daily basis. When first setting up a monogamous household, a younger brother like Dorje would find it difficult to both farm and manage animals.

In traditional Tibetan society, there was an even more critical factor that operated to perpetuate fraternal polyandry—a form of hereditary servitude somewhat analogous to serfdom in Europe. Peasants were tied to large estates held by aristocrats, monasteries, and the Lhasa government. They were allowed the use of some farmland to produce their own subsistence but were required to provide taxes in kind and corvée (free labor) to their lords. The corvée was a substantial hardship, since a peasant household was in many cases required to furnish the lord with one laborer daily for most of the year and more on specific occasions such as the harvest. This enforced labor, along with the lack of new land and ecological pressure to pursue both agriculture and animal husbandry, made polyandrous families particularly beneficial. The polyandrous family allowed an internal division of adult labor, maximizing economic advantage. For example, while the wife worked the family fields, one brother could perform the lord's corvée, another could look after the animals, and a third could engage in trade.

Although social scientists often discount other people's explanations of why they do things, in the case of Tibetan fraternal polyandry, such explanations are very close to the truth. The custom, however, is very sensitive to changes in its political and economic milieu and, not surprisingly, is in decline in most Tibetan areas. Made less important by the elimination of the traditional serf-based economy, it is disparaged by the dominant non-Tibetan leaders of India, China, and Nepal. New opportunities for economic and social mobility in these countries, such as the tourist trade and government employment, are also eroding the rationale for polyandry, and so it may vanish within the next generation.

Melvyn C. Goldstein, now a professor of anthropology at Case Western Reserve University in Cleveland, has been interested in the Tibetan practice of fraternal polyandry (several brothers marrying one wife) since he was a graduate student in the 1960s.

African Polygyny
Family Values and Contemporary Changes

Philip L. Kilbride

Marriage is a cultural universal, although particular forms of marriage and family structure vary throughout the world. In the United States, polygamy, or plural marriage, is illegal. People have very strong feelings about what marriage is supposed to be like. The ideal of romantic love and lifelong monogamous marriage between people who are intimate companions—even best friends—is a dominant theme in American culture. Yet in all societies, including our own, there are significant differences between the sociocultural ideals and social realities. Divorce is so common in American society that many anthropologists and sociologists say that we actually practice serial monogamy; that is, we have more than one spouse but not at the same time. The nature of marriage is also being debated in our society in regard to gay and lesbian couples and adoption of children by gay couples.

In this selection, Philip Kilbride argues that marriage has much more to do with children and community than it does with sex. Divorce, he says, has negative effects on children's psychological and economic well-being. Deadbeat dads who fail to pay court-ordered child support are a major cause of the impoverishment of single-parent households and are a national disgrace. Teenage pregnancy is yet another problem to contend with.

From the child's point of view, is it better to have blended families linked through plural marriages? In contemporary Africa, this subject raises lively discussion—in part because it pits traditional culture against Christian morality and in part because marriage structure is a critical factor for understanding gender relations. Kilbride has examined polygyny in Africa and among Mormons and has also studied a phenomenon called "man sharing" in the African American community. It is a controversial topic that has led him to some TV talk shows. But for an anthropologist to stir up controversy—that's nothing new.

As you read this selection, ask yourself the following questions:
- *Why do Americans think that polygamy is immoral?*
- *Is the author correct in saying that American men might be mildly for polygyny but American women are strongly against it? Why would this be so?*
- *Even in societies that allow polygyny, most people live in monogamous marriages. The author says that this is because polygyny is too expensive. What social functions does marriage serve that involve economic resources?*
- *Would the problem of deadbeat dads go away if polygyny were an option?*
- *Why do Africans see the American marriage system, with its high frequency of divorce, as inferior to traditional polygyny? Is this really from the child's perspective?*

The following terms are discussed in this selection:

extended family	*polygyny*
polyandry	*serial monogamy*
polygamy	

RETHINKING POLYGAMY

I
n the Western world today, the term *marriage* is defined as a social institution that legally joins one man and one woman at the same time; that is, it is synonymous with monogamy. Nevertheless, anthropologists define marriage more broadly as to include cultural variation, such as number of mates, at the same time recognizing the universal function of marriage as a public contract that makes socially legitimate any offspring resulting from the marital union or unions. Anthropologists tell us that monogamy is the norm around the world (Fisher 1992). This assertion is correct in the pragmatic sense because even in cultures that permit polygyny, or marriage between one man and more than one woman at a time, the majority of individuals, in actuality, are married monogamously. Nevertheless, in the majority of the world's cultures, polygyny exists along with monogamy as a viable and, in many cases, ideal form of marriage. Ford and Beach (1951), for example, found that in 84 percent of the 185 cultures they studied, men were

permitted to have more than one wire at a time. One common misconception in the west about polygyny is that its function is primarily one of sexual gratification. That this is not the case can be derived from the sociology of polygynous family life, which reveals that in all cultures in which polygyny is practiced, there are a number of commonalities. Ideally, for example, work is divided evenly among wives; the fair practice visiting rule requires the husband to visit each wife equally; wives usually have separate houses and sleeping quarters; and the first wife is given the most respected status of senior wife.

One of the best-known cases of polygyny comes from the Islamic religion. An important ordinance in Islam provides limits on the institution of polygyny: "And if you fear that you cannot act equitably toward orphans, then marry such women as seem good to you, 2, 3, of 4, or if you fear you will not do justice (between them) then marry only one or what your right hand possesses" (the Koran 4:3). Polygyny, in this case, cannot be understood apart from community obligations toward widows and children. The actual practice allows considerable variation, although as set forth as a religious ideology in the Koran, its basis is understood best in a humanitarian, communitarian context.

Polyandry, found in less than 1 percent of the world's cultures, always exists in combination with polygyny. Among the Irigwe of Nigeria (Sangree 1969), there are two basic types of marriage. The first type, the "primary marriage," is arranged by parents prior to the couple's adolescence. "Second marriage" is arranged later by the couple itself. When a woman leaves her primary husband and goes to a secondary husband or later on to still another secondary husband, she leaves behind everything except the clothes and jewelry she is wearing. She may be fetched back by her former husband, or she may decide to stay and take up residence with her new husband, who then provides her with a house and everything she needs for housekeeping. The traditional Irigwe marriage system has no divorce. A woman's prior marriages are not terminated by her switching residence to another spouse. At any point in time, she may return to any of her spouses and resume residence with him. Paternity is settled by consensus, and a husband competes with his wife's other husbands for the paternity of the child she bears.

Advocates for Euro-American polygamy have met with stiff resistance. For example, the great nineteenth-century explorer Captain Richard Francis Burton shocked and angered the Victorians by writing openly about sexual matters. He also angered his wife with his private opinions concerning polygamy. Nevertheless, he believed that polygamy would help keep families stable, lessen the need for prostitutes, and help the single wife with her many household chores. Although Victorians may not have understood Burton's opinion, it is probably fair to say that most Irigwe men and women would have agreed with him.

AFRICAN POLYGYNY AS A CULTURAL VALUE

In her research on family structure among the Yoruba of Nigeria, Sudarkasa (1982) describes the typical situation. Whether or not a husband is polygynous, he has his own room separate from that of his wife or wives who, in turn, have their own rooms and their own household belongings. Although separated physically at times, the polygynous family should be thought of as one family, not as separate families sharing a common husband. Sudarkasa points out that the latter view would rule out the very significant role that the senior wife plays in the polygynous family. The senior wife must be a confidant and a cowife to the other wives, and she sometimes serves as an intermediary between her cowives and their common husband. Wives of the same husband frequently cooperate in economic activities. Distinction is made between children of the same father and children of the same mother by the same father. Sudarkasa emphasizes that for certain purposes, a mother and her children constitute a "*subunit* within the family, but they do not constitute a separate *unit* within the family" (p. 142). After her many years of studying African social organization, it is her opinion that widespread in Africa is the preference for a system of cowives rather than one where women bear children outside of marriage or where women have to live as childless spinsters. In Africa, spinsterhood would be perceived as very much outside the normal range of human behavior.

The anthropological literature frequently reports that African cultures in fact value polygyny; however, some evidence suggests that this may be primarily a male's point of view. At a minimum, this requires us to consider a possible gender bias in this generalization. There is evidence that women, in fact, do traditionally value polygyny. There is also evidence that suggests that men value it even more. There is also strong evidence that modernizing or Westernizing women most likely value it not at all. We will consider some evidence in this direction, since the gender question has occurred over and over again when polygyny is considered in any particular cultural context. Sudarkasa writes that before being bombarded with Western propaganda against polygyny, African women valued the companionship of cowives. In fact, in one study of Nigerian women conducted within the last 15 years, a majority of the women interviewed stated that they would be "pleased" to have a second wife in the home (Ware 1979). The negative bias of some Western-educated African women toward polygyny cannot, Sudarkasa emphasizes, be taken as indicative of the traditional attitude toward it.

On many occasions, female students from Bryn Mawr College have been taken to Uganda and Kenya, where they lived with families in both urban and rural locations. When the subject of polygyny has been introduced into our "theoretical" discussions, these highly educated students who, by their academic training, are sympathetic toward and knowledgeable about cultural variation, uniformly expressed unfavorable comments concerning the practice or even the concept of polygyny in our initial discussions. A conversation that took place in a Nairobi pub one evening is a good illustration of the cultural gap between Western-educated male and female values and East African male values concerning polygyny.

Two female students had been living in the home of one of the married Kenyan men present in the pub with us. They had quickly become attached to his wife and children and sympathized with her when her husband was not present at dinner time because, like many urban Kenyan men, he stopped regularly at a pub after work before going home. Nevertheless, they could see that he was a good father and provider for ids family. Although not meeting their Western ideal of the "husbandly role," they liked him very much and could understand why he might be thought of favor ably by his family, friends, and colleagues. They were therefore somewhat shocked and dismayed when he mentioned to the group that he was thinking about taking a second wife. With such a charming, intelligent, and attractive wife at home, the students especially could not understand why he should be contemplating this. He explained that he was getting a lot of pressure from his mother to do so because she was all alone in the rural area and needed someone to help her farm. His mother also stated that there were many single women in her village who needed husbands, and she wanted grandchildren who would live near or with her rather than far away in the city. This man's wife opposed the idea because she was afraid that there would then not be enough money to pay for her own children's school fees. Besides, the second wife might want to come to the city to live also. He said that he told his wife that he would make sure that she stayed on the farm. One African man who pragmatically supported monogamy stated that there was no way to guarantee that the second wife wouldn't want to come to the city. He stated that he might consider polygyny himself if he could insure that one would stay in the rural area, but he didn't think that was probable.

For the sake of argument (and because one might accept the practice of polygyny under the right circumstances), the professor asked whether a "feminist" perspective shouldn't look favorably on this man being compassionate to the needs of an older woman, his mother, should he decide to marry a second wife. To make more salient to the students the cultural influence on their negative attitudes toward polygyny, another dimension to our cross-cultural discussion of marriage was added. The group was asked their opinion of two men marrying each other and adopting children. While the two students, in conformity with their liberal ideology and anthropological training, felt that this would be perfectly reasonable, the reaction of the African males present was one of stunned silence followed by asking the professor to repeat what their ears could not have heard correctly. When he did so, these men, who had just been divided on the question of polygyny, laughed heartily and stated that this would be impossible because it was not natural. Their disbelief and laughter at what *to them* was such a culturally dissonant idea were still evident on the way home.

POLYGAMY AND GENDER

While there appears to be a female bias against the institution of polygamy among Western-educated women, including those in Africa, there is considerable evidence that traditional African women do value polygyny, at least under certain circumstances. At this time, it may be informative for us to consider some of the evidence for this contention. Those Africans who have written in praise of polygyny have invariably been men, but some African women have noted that polygyny is to be preferred over stigmatized concubinage. In general, little is known about the issue of "women's views of polygyny in the broad context of their perceptions of marriage and women's issues as a whole" (Ware 1979). A survey of over 6,000 Yoruba females, ranging in age from 15 to 59, from the city of Ibadan, Nigeria, found that about one wife in two lives in a polygynous marriage; the proportion for women over 40 rises to about two out of three. About 60 percent of the women in the survey reported that they would be "pleased" if their husbands took another wife. They would then have some companionship and someone with whom they could share housework, husband care, and child care. Only 23 percent expressed anger at the idea of sharing with another wife. More traditionally oriented women without education (67 percent) were more favorable toward polygyny man women with some formal education (54 percent).

Ware (1979) suggests that sharing economic and domestic responsibilities among women might well appeal to modern feminists. She goes on to point out that the sharing of a husband might be viewed as a detriment or an advantage, depending on the extent to which husbands as such are considered to be assets or liabilities. Some Ibadan wives see little value in having a husband except as a "recognized progenitor for their children" (1979:190). When these women, who live in a society where 99 percent of women marry by the age of 40, were asked whether there was a need for a husband apart from his role in begetting children, 47 percent answered that women do not need husbands. They felt that there were many disadvantages in marriage, and since women were equal to men, they often did better on their own. Those women who did consider other roles played by husbands (in addition to progenitor) mentioned companionship most frequently.

Around the time of the Ware study, a survey was undertaken in western Kenya by a Catholic nun and a Kenyan nurse. Lwanga (1976) reports the following concerning their discussions of polygyny with 27 Samia women living in a remote rural area of western Kenya. Many women felt that polygyny can be a happy and beneficial experience if the cowives cooperate with each other. They caution, however, that this is not likely to happen unless the husband allows the senior wife the chance to look for a second wife. Then she may choose a relative or the daughter of another family of which she approves. If he should require a third wife, these two wives would then be informed so that they could help to look for someone with whom they would wish to share their lives and work. Women felt that the most common reason a wife would advise her husband to take another wife was that he was a rich man with lots of cattle and land, too much for one wife to handle alone. Twenty-five out of the 27 women considered polygyny to be better than monogamy. Other studies have also suggested that traditional (usually rural, uneducated) women view polygyny more positively than their educated counterparts.

Susan Whyte (1980) provides information from Marachi, Kenya, on the practice known as *okhwenda eshiebo,* in which a wife could bring her sister's or brother's daughter or occasionally her mother's brother's daughter to be her cowife. She points out that this often happened at the instigation of the husband, but the Mariachi view of it is that "it is the woman who brings herself a cowife" (p. 137). Whyte states that polygyny has become more problematic in today's deteriorating economic climate. Many men still want the respect they can gain by having many wives and children, but women emphasize the difficulties of polygyny due to a shortage of land and labor and an increasing need for money for school fees, clothing, labor, and food. Whyte points out that while polygyny, in her opinion, has never been popular with women, it is even less so at present because the resources of individual men are becoming less adequate; thus, there is an increase in competition for the already scarce resources of the polygynous husband.

Studying another Kenyan society, Monique Mulder (1992) found that married women have strong views concerning polygyny that are generally positive. Seventy-six percent of the women in her survey viewed polygyny favorably. In general, cowife relations are not full of tension, nor do polygynously married women suffer reproductive costs! Neither women nor their parents expressed antipathy toward polygyny (Mulder 1989:179).

Whatever the value orientation is toward polygyny, the reality is that throughout Africa, most men foirn out to be monogamous. A recent study among the Zulu of southern Africa by Moller and Welch (1990) helps explain this male point of view regarding polygyny. Among the Zulus, polygynists account for about 10 percent of rural married men. There continues to be a shift from overt polygyny to covert polygyny or monogamy owing to several factors. Among these are (1) a shortage of agriculturally productive land and other" Monomic changes; (2) social pressures to accept values of politically and socially dominant whites; and (3) the inflexible teachings and policy of Christian mission churches." Prom their research surveys. Moller and Welch (1990) found that a majority of monogamist and polygynist men reported both economic advantages and disadvantages to the practice of polygyny, although most men professed to favor monogamy. In the views of the majority who favored monogamy, the main disadvantage of polygyny, as they saw it was an economic one. They found, for example, that the notion of the large polygynous family as a social security investment is now being replaced by the problems associated with educating children during an extended period of their life cycle. It must be pointed out, however, that these are view of men who are faced with the prospect of polygyny in a modern economy for which many of the advantages of the past are not available to them. One of the frequently mentioned circumstances resulting in polygyny is the practice of labor migration, in which many Africans travel away from their home areas in search of cash income. For these men, polygyny provides a solution to the problem of being required to spend lengthy periods away from their home families. Thus, one wife may visit the husband in town while the other one cares for the rural homestead. Polygynist wives may also share labor and keep each other company in the rural area when the husband is away (Moller and Welch 1990:208).

One serendipitous finding from this study was that polygynist men reported higher-quality work lives than did monogamous men. The former had higher job satisfaction, more voluntary retirement, better health, and higher degrees of social adjustment including a better adjustment to aging and retirement. Very significantly, Moller and Welch discovered that in a mood index analysis, polygynous men overall felt less lonely and neglected than other men in the survey. It may be that part of this positive mood adjustment can be seen by reference to spiritual values in Zulu society as men age. The older cohorts of returned migrants are more likely to be traditionally oriented and therefore more likely to choose polygynous lifestyles, since it may be seen as pleasing to the ancestors. More research needs to be done in this area, however, before one can conclude that the practice of polygyny per se has a directly positive effect on the morale of these men.

There is not much evidence available to consider whether polygyny does cut down on male infidelity, but one recent study conducted in Nigeria by Orubu-loye, Caldwell, and Caldwell (1990) suggests that it might. In this extensive survey done in the Akiki district of Nigeria, the researchers found that for monogamous males in the rural area, 56 percent of their most recent sexual experiences were outside their marriages; this figure rose to 67 percent in the urban area. Contributing to this practice is sexual abstinence during pregnancy and for two years postpartum, but also the belief common in polygynous societies that men need more than one woman. Sexual variety may be achieved by acquiring another wife. Polygynous men are more likely to turn to one of their other wives for gratification while another one is sexually abstaining. Only 38 percent of polygynous men in the rural area had their most recent sexual experience outside of marriage, and in the urban area 44 percent of polygynous men's most recent sexual partners were women other than their wives. These data suggest that, at least in this society, monogamous men are much more likely to have extramarital partners than are polygynous men. However, we see the opposite pattern for female respondents. Thirty-four percent of rural polygynous wives and 47 percent of urban polygynous wives reported that their most recent sexual encounter was an extramarital one. Only 14 percent of monogamous rural women and 36 percent of their urban counterparts reported that their most recent sexual partner was someone other than their spouse (Orubuloye, J. Caldwell, and P. Caldwell 1990:12). Thus, it appears that polygyny allows greater sexual equality, at least in terms of extramarital sexual relations, than does monogamy. Future research on marital relationships within monogamous and polygynous households should attempt a closer examination of de facto male and female balance of power and responsibilities within these two marital forms.

DELOCALIZED POLYGYNY

The fate of polygyny in Africa is very much caught up in the processes of moral and economic change. The churches vary considerably in terms of overt condemnation of polygyny, with the mainstream churches being predominantly opposed and many independent churches being favorable toward polygyny. Community sanctions traditionally at work in regulating polygyny have changed as well, and elders and other traditional moral leaders have lost the authority they had in the past when practices like polygyny were closely monitored. One finds, for example, that today in Kenya, many men who traditionally would not have been considered acceptable as polygynists in terms of their economic resources are practicing polygyny because community sanctions no longer operate with the same degree of salience as in the past. As traditions change and the modern economy and moral order impose themselves more and more into the everyday lives of people, polygyny increasingly takes on a negative ambiance. Much of the current female opposition to polygyny may in fact be related to the Irresponsible practice of this custom by many men in modernizing circumstances throughout the African continent. A few examples drawn from the Kenya media will provide readers with a sense of the tone surrounding what can be thought of as a public discourse concerning doubts over the suitability of polygyny in contemporary times.

Kilbride and Kilbride (1990), in discussing the modernization of tradition in East Africa, present excerpts from newspapers and magazines published in Nairobi, Kenya. The gist of the polygyny debate as seen in mass media discourse will be presented here. Many Western-educated, urban Kenyan women no longer find polygyny acceptable. One prominent female Kenyan politician, in her address at a seminar on "Women and the Church," urged that the churches ban polygyny, which she described as "more dangerous than malaria" (*Daily Nation*, May 18, 1985). She was, however, compassionate with the plight of single women who, because of an imbalance in the sex ratio, found themselves chasing after other women's husbands or settling for second or third wives. As the folio wing "argument from a male Kenyan politician will illustrate, modern educated men tend to be more favorable to polygyny. In his view, foreign influences are responsible for present social ills. To counteract this "moral decline, he suggests returning to their traditions, including polygyny, which he believes would "help reduce the number of unmarried women roaming the streets as prostitutes" (*Daily Nation*, July 9,1985).

Unlike the Roman Catholic Church, which is officially opposed to the practice of polygyny, some Protestant churches are becoming more tolerant of it. A bishop of the Anglican Church in Kenya stated that while monogamy may be ideal "for the expression of love between a husband and wife," the church should consider that in certain cultures polygyny is socially acceptable and that the belief that polygyny is contrary to Christianity was no longer tenable (*The Weekly Review*, August 1, 1987). The Catholic Archbishop of Nairobi, who himself was raised in a polygynous home, expressed the Catholic Church's opposition to it when he spoke to a gathering of young people about the sacrament of marriage. He admonished them to do "the will of God" rather than blindly following their customs. As he put it, "God wanted one Adam and one Eve, not one Adam and three Eves nor five Adams and one Eve" (*Daily Nation,* February 11, 1985). Sometimes differences of opinion regarding polygyny erupt within splinter groups of a particular religion. The Friends Church in Kakamega, Kenya, for example, faced a leadership crisis between its "old and monogamist founders" and its "young and polygamist followers" who formed a splinter group over the parent church's opposition to polygyny (*Sunday Nation,* January 6, 1985).

GROWING UP IN A POLYGYNOUS HOME

In general, our interviews revealed that East Africans have both positive and negative memories about growing up in polygynous homes. Although jealousy and conflict were present, especially between cowives concerning economic injustices, this was less likely to by the case when the polygynous home was a wealthy one. Importantly, in keeping with traditional values, whether talking about the past or the present, more positive impressions about life in a polygynous home as parents or as children were given if the family was rich. Two cases from Kenyan research will illustrate this variation.

The first case deals with the recollections of a Ugandan woman, here called Marjorie, who is 40 years old; she is a high school graduate whose father is a wealthy agricultural officer. He has four wives and 25 children. Her own mother was the senior wife. Before taking a second wife, her father provided her mother with her own home and land near to where two of her other children were attending boarding school. When Marjorie was in sixth grade, she went to live with her father and his second wife and her children so that she could attend school nearby their residence. Interestingly, she states that although her stepmother gave her a lot of chores to do, she didn't mind. She liked her stepmother, whom she described as being good. On school holidays, she went back to her own mother, who was even stricter with her because it was her mother's job to teach Marjorie all her female duties. Marjorie states that although their family was large, everyone always had enough to eat and plenty of land to farm. The children treated each other well. "Myself and the stepsisters, we don't say, 'Who is your mother? We are all like sisters and brothers'" (Kilbride and Kilbride 1990:207). As behooves a good polygynous husband, her father showed no favoritism—at least as could be perceived by Marjorie. She stated that she never knew who her father loved best. The cowives also followed the traditional custom of giving respect and deference to the senior wife. Marjorie also reported that she liked her father very much.

Our next account is a less favorable recollection of growing up in a polygynous home by a man in his mid-20s, here called Robert. His father, like Marjorie's, also has four wives. Unfortunately, this man's economic situation is much less favorable. He has 31 children, thus far, with his youngest being less than one year old. Also, Robert's mother is not in as favorable a position economically or in terms of respect in that she is his father's second wife. In Robert's early childhood, his father had only two wives, both of whom Robert called "mother." It was not until he was seven years old that he began to question his status. When he was eight years old, he recollects going to school for awhile with the sons of the first wife. It was not a pleasant memory in that his stepbrothers beat him, made him carry their books to and from school, and forced him to get money from his mother to give to them for their own lunches. He finally refused to go to that school, which was 10 kilometers away, so he was transferred to a school near his home. After fourth trade, he states that he was forced to go to another primary school near the home of the fourth wife. While living at her house, which is 15 miles from the home of his mother and the other two wives, who all share the same compound, Robert complains that he was forced to do many household chores, including cooking, cleaning, and tending livestock, at times going without food from breakfast until dinner. He also disliked the fact that when he had friends over to visit, his stepmother would say that he wasn't living in the home of his mother. "It made me feel that I was born somewhere else but was now under the control of another person" (Kilbride and Kilbride 1990:208).

As an adult, Robert understands that there are some advantages to polygyny, such as sharing the workload, protection from outsiders, helping to care for other family members when they or their children are sick, and preventing childlessness and thus gaining immortality through one's children. Nevertheless, the disadvantages he has experienced personally, which he sees as being mainly the result of a lack of sufficient economic resources on the part of his father, who married more wives and had more children than he could support, makes him unfavorable to polygyny and what he perceives to be its many problems of jealousy and conflict over insufficient resources for food, clothing, and education. He reports that during times of food shortage, each mother looked after only her own children rather than sharing with the others, while his father tended to "disappear" until the worst was over. In Robert's case, we can see the workings of modernized polygyny in that his father did not fit the traditional ideal of being wealthy enough to be a polygynist, at least on the scale that he practiced it. There are indications that two wives would have been better for all concerned.

MONOGAMY RECONSIDERED

A very different definite pattern is visible in Kenya today: professional women rejecting marriage altogether because many of them feel that men on the whole are unsympathetic to their attempts to have careers, to seek education beyond the B.A., and to practice independent lifestyles frequently associated with modern, professional occupations. At the same time, many women feel that men involve themselves too frequently with other women (mistresses) while they expect their wives to remain at home caring for the children.

There is also the problem of wife beating, which women have traditionally agreed is the "right of the husband if they do not perform their duties or act properly. Although many professional women are opting against marriage, they have not given up on their desire to have children. For this reason, such women frequently find themselves in a position of seeking out a man, married or single, to give them a child or to become a father to that child or to one that they already have.

Perlez (1991) reports the views of a Miss Makuku, who is a postgraduate student in French at Nairobi University and a former schoolteacher. She sees herself ten years from now as a single parent with a male companion, but not a husband. She points out that this is a choice made not only by herself but by many of her over 30 female friends with occupations ranging from television producers to professors. For example, many educated women are delaying marriage; more than half of the 16 female law graduates of Nairobi University in 1980 are still single. Miss Makuku admonishes that traditionally, African men looked after their women, but today the average man contributes to the rent if one is lucky while using the rest for mistresses and beer. According to Perlez, anecdotal evidence from Kenya abounds concerning professional women who have been previously married but have left their husbands because they cannot tolerate the restrictions imposed by these men. Eventually, these women seek a relationship of some kind with a man. Miss Makuku points out that it is difficult to raise a child without the financial help of a man. By the age of 35, however, most of her economically self-sufficient, single, female friends have decided to have children even though they are not married. Some choose to have a child by a younger man because he is less likely to "boss them around" than would an older man. A second choice would be to have a child by a married man, paradoxically choosing to do one of the very things that has turned them against marriage to begin with.

We see here that exclusive monogamy, in Kenya as in the United States, does not appear to be working very well. There seems to be a tendency for polygyny to be reinvented as more and more single women have 'relationships' with married" men. Perhaps these men will involve themselves in the role of father to their outside children. Here we have a situation, similar to that described for man sharing in the African American community, developing in the East African setting where, ironically, polygamy was, until recently, the ideal. Very much present in Kenya at this time is a consciousness of the importance of having fathers for children. For example, the July 18, 1993, issue of the *Sunday Nation*, a prominent Kenyan newspaper, published a cartoon that accompanied a story entitled "Choice: The New Trend." The cartoon shows a woman dressed in fashionable clothing and a young boy, presumably her son, leaning against their car with a man standing beside them looking at them. The woman says, "I have everything I want, a good job, a good house, and a good child. Why should I need a man?" The child, however, is shown to be thinking: "But a daddy, we don't have." The story itself reported that in nearly all their interviews, women stated that they would find it acceptable having children without marriage if they were financially secure. One woman who is a company executive replied that she had reached the age where she was ready for a child, but not a husband, since she wanted to advance in her career and found that men were usually intolerant of ambitious women. Many of the single women interviewed were involved with men who were already married. While encouraging his mistress to have his child, he may promise that he is going to divorce his wife, which ten years later she finally realizes will never happen. At this point, the woman may feel that it is too late for her, given her increasing age, to meet anyone else. The article does not offer any analysis of this situation in terms of whether or not, on balance, quasi-polygyny is more or less desirable than divorce, especially when children are involved.

The interview material with Kenyan men in Kilbride and Kilbride (1990) presents a similar picture of frustration and difficulties associated with the current situation. One man in his late 40s, for example, responded to the AIDS crisis by curtailing his outside girlfriends so that he had a long-standing relationship with a single woman from an ethnic group other than his own. He required secrecy from this woman so that his wife and family would not be offended. The child that resulted from this relationship, who is now a young girl, is presently being raised entirely by her mother, since my informant no longer gives her any support. In spite of this, he seemed to feel that everything would be fine for his daughter. Another informant who spoke openly about polygyny is a wealthy Kenyan who is Roman Catholic and states that although he does not himself favor polygyny, he is not opposed to others practicing it. He believes that it is, in fact, a fairly common practice. He himself has been "offered" a wife when he has gone into rural areas, although he has not involved himself because of his wife's opposition to polygyny. He nevertheless confesses that at present he has numerous girlfriends and would like to know whether his wife would prefer him to be polygynous with a small number of wives or monogamous with the large number of mistresses that he now has. Moreover, each of his mistresses is unaware of the other women in his life and are themselves in search of a permanent relationship. Some of his girlfriends do not even know that he is married.

PLURAL MARRIAGE AS A REINVENTED OPTION

Is it worth considering plural marriage as a morally viable option for American men and women, particularly in light of our national family crisis and increased calls for cultural pluralism? A myriad of legal considerations, including property ownership, inheritance, child disciplinary obligations, and health insurance, to name but a few, will require special study and legal adjustment. In the United States, the monogamous companionate marriage, though viewed as an ideal, is not in the majority. In fact, given our high divorce rate, it can be argued that the United States now has a high rate of informal, unrecognized polygyny, at least as we would infer from Remi Clignet's comment that "Africans argue that remarriage subsequent to a divorce is merely another form of polygyny, one less desirable because it imposes on Westerners succession and discontinuity in married life" (1970:3). Blended families are known to be particularly stressful for children, given the ambiguous status of this rapidly emerging family structure. Once marriage is consistently considered from the perspective of children, perhaps more people will come to see that seemingly radical forms of now improper plurality are actually "smart" opportunities for children to have multiple parents and often access to a better life through foster parents or blended parents who are *added* to their biological family.

REFERENCES

Clignet, R. 1970. *Many Wives, Many Powers: Authority and Power in Polygynous Families.* Evanston, IL: Northwestern University Press.

Fisher, H. E. 1992. *Anatomy of Love: The Natural History of Monogamy, Adultery, and Divorce.* New York: W. W. Norton and Company.

Ford, C, and F. Beach. 1951. *Patterns of Sexual Behavior.* New York: Harper & Row.

Kilbride, P. L., and J. E. Kilbride. 1990. *Changing Family Life in East Africa: Women and Children at Risk.* University Park: Pennsylvania State University Press.

Lwanga, G. 1976. Report on the Health Education of Clan Health Workers. Nangina Hospital, Nangina, Kenya.

Moller, V., and G. J. Welch. 1990, Polygamy, Economic Security, and Well-being of Retired Zulu Migrant Workers. *Journal of Cross-Cultural Gerontology* 5:205–216.

Mulder, M. 1989. Polygyny and the Extent of Women's Contributions to Subsistence: A Reply to White. *American Anthropologist* 91:178–180.

—. 1992. Women's Strategies in Polygynous Marriage. *Human Nature* 3(l):45–70.

Orubuloye, I, O., J, Caldwell, and P. Caldwell, 1990. Experimental Research on Sexual Networking in the Ekti District of Nigeria. Health Transition Working Paper No. 3.

Perlez, J. 1991. Elite Kenyan Women Avoid a Rite: Marriage. *The New York Times,* March 3, p. 14.

Sangree, W, 1969, Going Home to Mother: Traditional Marriage Among the Irigwe of Benue-Plateau State, Nigeria. *Journal of the American Anthropological Association* 71(6); 946–1056.

Sudarkasa, N. 1982. African and Afro-American Family Structure. In *Anthropology for the Eighties,* J. Cole, ed. Pp. 132–161. New York: Free Press.

Ware, H. 1979. Polygyny, Women's Views in a Transitional Sodety, Nigeria 1975. *Journal of Marriage and the Family* 41(1):185–195.

Whyte, S. 1980. Wives and Co-wives in Marachi, Kenya. *Folk,* 21–22; 134–136.

Custer Died for Your Sins

Deloria Vine, Jr.

Into each life, it is said, some rain must fall. Some people have bad horoscopes; others take tips on the stock market. McNamara created the TFX and the Edsel. American politics has George Wallace. But Indians have been cursed above all other people in history. Indians have anthropologists.

Every summer when school is out, a stream of immigrants heads into Indian country. The Oregon Trail was never as heavily populated as Route 66 and Highway 18 in the summertime. From every rock and cranny in the East, *they* emerge, as if responding to some primeval migratory longing, and flock to the reservations. They are the anthropologists—the most prominent members of the scholarly community that infests the land of the free and the homes of the braves. Their origin is a mystery hidden in the historical mists. Indians are certain that all ancient societies of the Near East had anthropologists at one time, because all those societies are now defunct. They are equally certain that Columbus brought anthropologists on his ships when he came to the New World. How else could he have made so many wrong deductions about where he was? While their origins are uncertain, anthropologists can readily be identified on the reservations. Go into any crowd of people. Pick out a tall, gaunt white man wearing Bermuda shorts, a World War Two Army Air Corps flying jacket, an Australian bush hat and tennis shoes and packing a large knapsack incorrectly strapped on his back. He will invariably have a thin, sexy wife with stringy hair, an IQ of 191 and a vocabulary in which even the prepositions have 11 syllables. And he usually has a camera, tape recorder, telescope, and life jacket all hanging from his elongated frame.

This odd creature comes to Indian reservations to make *observations*. During the winter, these observations will become books by which future anthropologists will be trained, so that they can come out to reservations years from now and verify the observations in more books, summaries of which then appear in the scholarly journals and serve as a catalyst to inspire yet other anthropologists to make the great pilgrimage the following summer. And so on.

The summaries, meanwhile, are condensed. Some condensations are sent to Government agencies as reports justifying the previous summer's research. Others are sent to foundations, in an effort to finance the following summer's expedition West. The reports are spread through the Government agencies and foundations all winter. The only problem is that no one has time to read them. So $5000-a-year secretaries are assigned to decode them. Since these secretaries cannot comprehend complex theories, they reduce the reports to the best slogans possible. The slogans become conference themes in the early spring, when the anthropological expeditions are being planned. They then turn into battle cries of opposing groups of anthropologists who chance to meet on the reservations the following summer.

Each summer there is a new battle cry, which inspires new insights into the nature of the "Indian problem." One summer Indians will be greeted with the joyful cry "Indians are bilingual!" The following summer this great truth will be expanded to "Indians are not only bilingual, they are *bicultural*." Biculturality creates great problems for the opposing anthropological camp. For two summers, they have been bested in sloganeering and their funds are running low. So the opposing school of thought breaks into the clear faster than Gale Sayers. "Indians," the losing anthros cry, "are a *folk* people!" The tide of battle turns and a balance, so dearly sought by Mother Nature, is finally achieved. Thus go the anthropological wars, testing whether this school or that school can long endure. The battlefields, unfortunately, are the lives of Indian people.

The anthro is usually devoted to *pure research*. A 1969 thesis restating a proposition of 1773, complete with footnotes to all material published between 1773 and 1969, is pure research. There are, however, anthropologists who are not clever at collecting footnotes. They depend on their field observations and write long, adventurous narratives in which their personal observations are used to verify their suspicions. Their reports, books and articles are called *applied research*. The difference, then, between pure and applied research is primarily one"of footnotes. Pure has many footnotes, applied has few footnotes. Relevancy to subject matter is not discussed in polite company.

Anthropologists came to Indian country only after the tribes had agreed to live on reservations and had given up their warlike ways. Had the tribes been given a choice of fighting the cavalry or the anthropologists, there is little doubt as to who they would have chosen. In a crisis situation, men always attack the biggest threat to their existence. A warrior killed in battle could always go to the happy hunting grounds. But where does an Indian laid low by an anthro go? To the library?

The fundamental thesis of the anthropologist is that people are objects for observation. It then follows that people are considered objects for experimentation, for manipulation, and for eventual extinction. The anthropologist thus furnishes the justification for treating Indian people like so many chessmen, available for anyone to play with-The mass production of useless knowledge by anthropologists attempting to capture real Indians in a network of theories has contributed substantially to the invisibility of Indian people today. After all, who can believe in the actual existence of a food-gathering berrypicking, seminomadic, fire-worshiping, high-plains-and-mountain-dwelling, horse-riding, canoe-toting, bead-using, pottery-making, ribbon-coveting, wickiup-sheltered people who began flourishing when Alfred Frump mentioned them in 1803 in *Our Feathered Friends*?

Not even Indians can see themselves as this type of creature—who, to anthropologists, is the "real" Indian. Indian people begin to feel that they are merely shadows of a mythical super-Indian. Many Indians, in fact, have come to parrot the ideas of anthropologists, because it appears that they know everything about Indian communities. Thus, many ideas that pass for Indian thinking are in reality theories originally advanced by anthropologists and echoed by Indian people in an attempt to communicate the real situation. Many anthros reinforce this sense of inadequacy in order to further influence the Indian people.

Since 1955, there have been a number of workshops conducted in Indian country as a device for training "young Indian leaders." Churches, white Indian-interest groups, colleges, and, finally, poverty programs have each gone the workshop route as the most feasible means for introducing new ideas to younger Indians, so as to create leaders. The tragic nature of the workshops is apparent when one examines their history. One core group of anthropologists has institutionalized the workshop and the courses taught in it. Trudging valiantly from workshop to workshop, from state to state, college to college, tribe to tribe, these noble spirits have served as the catalyst for the creation of workshops that are identical in purpose and content and often in the student-body itself.

The anthropological message to young Indians has not varied a jot or a tittle in ten years. It is the same message these anthros learned as fuzzy-cheeked graduate students in the post-War years—Indians are a folk people, whites are an urban people, and never the twain shall meet. Derived from this basic premise are all the other sterling insights: Indians are between two cultures, Indians are bicultural, Indians have lost their identity, and Indians are warriors. These theories, propounded every year with deadening regularity and an overtone of Sinaitic authority, have become a major mental block in the development of young Indian people. For these slogans have come to be excuses for Indian failures. They are crutches by which young Indians have avoided the arduous task of thinking out the implications of the status of Indian people in the modern world.

If there is one single cause that has importance today for Indian people, it, is tribalism. Against all odds, Indians have retained title to some 53,000,000 acres of land, worth about three and a half billion dollars. Approximately half of the country's 1,000,000 Indians relate meaningfully to this land, either by living and working on it or by frequently visiting it. If Indians fully recaptured the idea that they are tribes communally in possession of this land, they would realize that they are not truly impoverished. But the creation of modern tribalism has been stifled by a ready acceptance of the Indians-are-a-folk-people premise of the anthropologists. This premise implies a drastic split between folk and urban cultures, in which the folk peoples have two prime characteristics: They dance and they are desperately poor. Creative thought in Indian affairs has not, therefore, come from the younger Indians who have grown up reading and talking to anthropologists. Rather, it has come from the older generation that believes in tribalism—and that the youngsters mistakenly insist has been brainwashed by Government schools.

Because other groups have been spurred on by their younger generations, Indians have come to believe that, through education, a new generation of leaders will arise to solve the pressing contemporary problems. Tribal leaders have been taught to accept this thesis by the scholarly community in its annual invasion of the reservations. Bureau of Indian Affairs educators harp continuously on this theme. Wherever authority raises its head in Indian country, this thesis is its message. The facts prove the opposite, however. Relatively untouched by anthropologists, educators, and scholars are the Apache tribes of the Southwest. The Mescalero, San Carlos, White Mountain, and Jicarilla Apaches have very few young people in college, compared with other tribes. They have even fewer people in the annual workshop orgy during the summers. If ever there was a distinction between folk and urban, this group of Indians characterizes it.

The Apaches see themselves, however, as neither folk nor urban but *tribal*. There is little sense of a lost identity. Apaches could not care less about the anthropological dilemmas that worry other tribes. Instead, they continue to work on massive plans for development that they themselves have created. Tribal identity is assumed, not defined, by these reservation people. Freedom to choose from a wide variety of paths of progress is a characteristic of the Apaches; they don't worry about what type of Indianism is real. Above all, they cannot he ego-fed by abstract theories and, hence, unwittingly manipulated.

With many young people from other tribes, the situation is quite different. Some young Indians attend workshops over and over again. Folk theories pronounced by authoritative anthropologists become opportunities to escape responsibility. If, by definition, the Indian is hopelessly caught between two cultures, why struggle? Why not blame all one's lack of success on this tremendous gulf between two opposing cultures? Workshops have become, therefore, summer retreats for non thought rather than strategy sessions for leadership. Therein lies the Indian's sin against the anthropologist. Only those anthropologists who appear to boost Indian ego and expound theories dear to the hearts of workshop Indians are invited to teach at workshops. They become human recordings of social confusion and are played and replayed each summer, to the delight of a people who refuse to move on into the real world.

The workshop anthro is thus a unique creature, partially self-created and partially supported by the refusal of Indian young people to consider their problems in their own context. The normal process of maturing has been confused with cultural difference. So maturation is cast aside in favor of cult recitation of great truths that appear to explain the immaturity of young people.

While the anthro is thus, in a sense, the victim of the Indians, he should, nevertheless, recognize the role he has been asked to play and refuse to play it. Instead, the temptation to appear relevant to a generation of young Indians has clouded his sense of proportion. Workshop anthros often ask Indians of tender age to give their authoritative answers to problems that an entire generation of Indians is just now beginning to solve. Where the answer to reservation health problems may be adequate housing in areas where there has never been adequate housing, young Indians are shaped in their thinking processes to consider vague doctrines on the nature of man and his society.

It is preposterous that a teen-aged Indian should become an instant authority, equal in status to the Ph.D. interrogating him. Yet the very human desire is to play that game every summer, for the status acquired in the game is heady. And since answers can be given only in the vocabulary created by the Ph.D., the entire leadership-training process internalizes itself and has no outlet beyond the immediate group. Real problems, superimposed on the ordinary problems of maturing, thus become insoluble burdens that crush people of great leadership potential.

Let us take some specific examples. One workshop discussed the thesis that Indians were in a terrible crisis. They were, in the words of friendly anthro guides, "between two worlds." People between two worlds, the students were told, "drank." For the anthropologist, it was a valid explanation of drinking on the reservation. For the young Indians, it was an authoritative definition of their role as Indians. Real Indians, they began to think, drank; and their task was to become real Indians, for only in that way could they recreate the glories of the past. So they *drank*. I've lost some good friends who drank too much.

Abstract theories create abstract action. Lumping together the variety of tribal problems and seeking the demonic principle at work that is destroying Indian people may be intellectually satisfying, but it does not change the situation. By concentrating on great abstractions, anthropologists have unintentionally removed many young Indians from the world of real problems to the lands of make-believe.

As an example of a real problem, the Pyramid Lake Paiutes and the Gila River Pima and Maricopa are poor because they have been systematically cheated out of their water rights, and on desert reservations, water is the single most important factor in life. No matter how many worlds Indians straddle, the Plains Indians have an inadequate land base that continues to shrink because of land sales. Straddling worlds is irrelevant to straddling small pieces of land and trying to earn a living.

Along the Missouri River, the Sioux used to live in comparative peace and harmony. Although land allotments were small, families were able to achieve a fair standard of living through a combination of gardening and livestock raising and supplemental work. Little cash income was required, because the basic necessities of food, shelter, and community life were provided. After World War Two, anthropologists came to call. They were horrified that the Indians didn't carry on their old customs, such as dancing, feasts, and giveaways. In fact, the people did keep up a substantial number of customs, but they had been transposed into church gatherings, participation in the county fairs, and tribal celebrations, particularly fairs and rodeos. The people did Indian dances. But they didn't do them all the time.

Suddenly, the Sioux were presented with an authority figure who bemoaned the fact that whenever he visited the reservations, the Sioux were not out dancing in the manner of their ancestors. Today, the summers are taken up with one great orgy of dancing and celebrating, as each small community of Indians sponsors a weekend powwow for the people in the surrounding communities. Gone are the little gardens that used to provide fresh vegetables in the summer and canned goods in the winter. Gone are the chickens that provided eggs and Sunday dinners. In the winter, the situation becomes critical for families who spent the summer dancing. While the poverty programs have done much to counteract the situation, few Indians recognize that the condition was artificial from start to finish. The people were innocently led astray, and even the anthropologists did not realize what had happened.

One example: The Oglala Sioux are perhaps the most well known of the Sioux bands. Among their past leaders were Red Cloud, the only Indian who ever defeated the United States in a war, and Crazy Horse, most revered of the Sioux war chiefs. The Oglala were, and perhaps still are, the meanest group of Indians ever assembled. They would take after a cavalry troop just to see if their bowstrings were taut enough. When they had settled on the reservation, the Oglala made a fairly smooth transition to the new life. They had good herds of cattle, they settled along the numerous creeks that cross the reservation, and they created a very strong community spirit. The Episcopalians and the Roman Catholics had the missionary franchise on the reservation and the tribe was pretty evenly split between the two. In the Episcopal Church, at least, the congregations were fairly self-governing and stable.

But over the years, the Oglala Sioux have had a number of problems. Their population has grown faster than their means of support. The Government allowed white farmers to come into the eastern part of the reservation and create a county, with the best farmlands owned or operated by whites. The reservation was allotted—taken out of the collective hands of the tribe and parceled out to individuals—and when ownership became too complicated, control of the land passed out of Indian hands. The Government displaced a number of families during World War Two by taking a part of the reservation for use as a bombing range to train crews for combat. Only last year was this land returned to tribal and individual use.

The tribe became a favorite subject for anthropological study quite early, because of its romantic past. Theories arose attempting to explain the apparent lack of progress of the Oglala Sioux. The true issue—white control of the reservation—was overlooked completely. Instead, every conceivable intangible cultural distinction was used to explain the lack of economic, social, and educational progress of a people who were, to all intents and purposes, absentee landlords because of the Government policy of leasing their lands to whites.

One study advanced the startling proposition that Indians with many cattle were, on the average, better off than Indians without cattle. Cattle Indians, it seems, had more capital and income than did noncattle Indians. Surprise! The study had innumerable charts and graphs that demonstrated this great truth beyond the doubt of a reasonably prudent man. Studies of this type were common but unexciting. They lacked that certain flair of insight so beloved by anthropologists. Then one day a famous anthropologist advanced the theory, probably valid at the time and in the manner in which he advanced it, that the Oglala were "warriors without weapons."

The chase was on. Before the ink had dried on the scholarly journals, anthropologists from every library stack in the nation converged on the Oglala Sioux to test this new theory. Outfitting anthropological expeditions became the number-one industry of-the small off-reservation Nebraska towns south of Pine Ridge. Surely, supplying the Third Crusade to the Holy Land was a minor feat compared with the task of keeping the anthropologists at Pine Ridge.

Every conceivable difference between the Oglala Sioux and the folks at Bar Harbor was attributed to the quaint warrior tradition of the Oglala Sioux. From lack of roads to unshined shoes, Sioux problems were generated, so the anthros discovered, by the refusal of the white man to recognize the great desire of the Oglala to go to war. Why expect an Oglala to become a small businessman, when he was only waiting for that wagon train to come around the bend? The very real and human problems of the reservation were considered to be merely by-products of the failure of a warrior people to become domesticated. The fairly respectable thesis of past exploits in war, perhaps romanticized for morale purposes, became a' spiritual force all its own. Some Indians, in a tongue-in-cheek manner for which Indians are justly famous, suggested that a subsidized wagon train be run through the reservation each morning at nine o'clock and the reservation people paid a minimum wage for attacking it.

By outlining this problem, I am not deriding the Sioux. I lived on that reservation for 18 years and know many of the problems from which it suffers. How, I ask, can the Oglala Sioux make any headway in education when their lack of education is ascribed to a desire to go to war? Would not, perhaps, an incredibly low per-capita income, virtually nonexistent housing, extremely inadequate roads, and domination by white farmers and ranchers make some difference? If the little Sioux boy or girl had no breakfast, had to walk miles to a small school, and had no decent clothes nor place to study in a one-room log cabin, should the level of education be comparable with that of Scarsdale High?

What use would roads, houses, schools, businesses, and income be to a people who, everyone expected, would soon depart on the warpath? I would submit that a great deal of the lack of progress at Pine Ridge is occasioned by people who believe they are helping the Oglala when they insist on seeing, in the life of the people of that reservation, only those things they want to see. Real problems and real people become invisible before the great romantic and nonsensical notion that the Sioux yearn for the days of Crazy Horse and Red Cloud and will do nothing until those days return.

The question of the Oglala Sioux is one that plagues every Indian tribe in the nation, if it will closely examine itself. Tribes have been defined; the definition has been completely explored; test scores have been advanced promoting and deriding the thesis; and, finally, the conclusion has been reached: Indians must be redefined in terms that white men will accept, even if that means re-Indian-izing them according to the white man's idea of what they were like in the past and should logically become in the future.

What, I ask, would a school board in Moline, Illinois—or Skokie, even—do if the scholarly community tried to reorient its educational system to conform with outmoded ideas of Sweden in the glory days of Gustavus Adolphus? Would they be expected to sing "*Eiri feste Burg*" and charge out of the mists at the Roman Catholics to save the Reformation every morning as school began? Or the Irish—would they submit to a group of Indians coming to Boston and telling them to dress in green and hunt leprechauns?

Consider the implications of theories put forward to solve the problem of poverty among the blacks. Several years ago, the word went forth that black poverty was due to the disintegration of the black family, that the black father no longer had a prominent place in the home. How incredibly shortsighted that thesis was. How typically Anglo-Saxon! How in the world could there have been a black family if people were sold like cattle for 200 years, if there were large plantations that served merely as farms to breed more slaves, if white owners systematically ravaged black women? When did the black family unit ever become integrated? Herein lies a trap into which many Americans have fallen: Once a problem is defined and understood by a significant number of people who have some relation to it, the fallacy goes, the problem ceases to exist. The rest of America had better beware of having quaint mores that attract anthropologists, or it will soon become a victim of the conceptual prison into which blacks and Indians, among others, have been thrown. One day you may find yourself cataloged—perhaps as a credit-card-carrying, turnpike-commuting, condominium-dwelling, fraternity-joining, church-going, sports-watching, time-purchase-buying, television-watching, magazine subscribing, politically inert transmigrated urbanite who, through the phenomenon of the second car and the shopping center, has become a golf-playing, wife-swapping, etc., etc., etc., suburbanite. Or have you already been characterized—and caricatured—in ways that struck you as absurd? If so, you will understand what has been happening to Indians for a long, long time.

In defense of the anthropologists, it must be recognized that those who do not publish perish. Those who do not bring in a substantial sum of research money soon slide down the scale of university approval. What university is not equally balanced between the actual education of its students and a multitude of small bureaus, projects, institutes, and programs that are designed to harvest grants for the university?

The effect of anthropologists on Indians should be clear. Compilation of useless knowledge for knowledge's sake should be utterly rejected by the Indian people. We should not be objects of observation for those who do nothing to help us. During the critical days of 1954, when the Senate was pushing for termination of all Indian rights, not one scholar, anthropologist, sociologist, historian, or economist came forward to support the tribes against the detrimental policy. Why didn't the academic community march to the side of the tribes? Certainly the past few years have shown how much influence academe can exert when it feels compelled to enlist in a cause. Is Vietnam any more crucial to the moral stance of America than the great debt owed to the Indian tribes?

Perhaps we should suspect the motives of members of the academic community. They have the Indian field well defined and under control. Their concern is not the ultimate policy that will affect the Indian people, but merely the creation of new slogans and doctrines by which they can climb the university totem pole. Reduction of people to statistics for purposes of observation appears to be inconsequential to the anthropologist when compared with the immediate benefits he can derive—the acquisition of further prestige and the chance to appear as the high priest of American society, orienting and manipulating to his heart's desire.

Roger Jourdain, chairman of the Red Lake Chippewa tribe of Minnesota, casually had the anthropologists escorted from his reservation a couple of years ago. This was the tip of the ice berg. If only more Indians had the insight of Jourdain. Why should we continue to provide private zoos for anthropologists? Why should tribes have to compete with scholars for funds, when their scholarly productions are so useless and irrelevant to life?

Several years ago, an anthropologist stated that over a period of some 20 years he had spent, from all sources, close to $ 10,000,000 studying a tribe of fewer than 1000 people. Imagine what that amount of money would have meant to that group of people had it been invested in buildings and businesses. There would have been no problems to study.

I sometimes think that Indian tribes could improve relations between themselves and the anthropologists by adopting the following policy; Each anthro desiring to study a tribe should be made to apply to the tribal council for permission to do his study. He would be given such permission only if he raised as a contribution to the tribal budget an amount of money equal to the amount he proposed to spend on his study. Anthropologists would thus become productive members of Indian society, instead of ideological vultures.

This proposal was discussed at one time in Indian circles. It blew no small number of anthro minds. Irrational shrieks of "academic freedom" rose like rockets from launching pads. The very idea of putting a tax on useless information was intolerable to the anthropologists we talked with. But the question is very simple. Are the anthros concerned about freedom—or license? Academic freedom certainly does not imply that one group of people has to become chessmen for another group of people. Why should Indian communities be subjected to prying non-Indians any more than other communities? Should any group have a franchise to stick its nose into someone else's business?

I don't think my proposal ever will be accepted. It contradicts the anthropologists' self-image much too strongly. What is more likely is that Indians will continue to allow their communities to be turned inside out until they come to realize the damage that is being done to them. Then they will seal up the reservations and no further knowledge—useless or otherwise—will be created. This may be the best course. Once, at a Congressional hearing, someone asked Alex Chasing Hawk, a council member of the Cheyenne Sioux for 30 years, "Just what do you Indians want?" Alex replied, "A leave-us-alone law."

The primary goal and need of Indians today is not for someone to study us, feel sorry for us, identify with us, or claim descent from Pocahontas to make us feel better. Nor do we need to be classified as semiwhite and have programs made to bleach us further. Nor do we need further studies to see if we are "feasible." We need, instead, anew policy from Congress that acknowledges our intelligence, and our dignity.

In its simplest form, such a policy would give a tribe the amount of money now being spent in the area on Federal schools and other services. With this block grant, the tribe itself would communally establish and run its own schools and hospitals and police and fire departments—and, in time, its own income-producing endeavors, whether in industry or agriculture. The tribe would not be taxed until enough capital had accumulated so that individual Indians were getting fat dividends.

Many tribes are beginning to acquire the skills necessary for this sort of independence, but the odds are long: An Indian district at Pine Ridge was excited recently about the possibility of running its own schools, and a bond issue was put before them that would have made it possible for them to do so. In the meantime, however, anthropologists visiting the community convinced its people that they were culturally unprepared to assume this sort of responsibility; so the tribe voted down the bond issue. Three universities have sent teams to the area to discover why the issue was defeated. The teams are planning to spend more on their studies than the bond issue would have cost.

I would expect an instant rebuttal by the anthros. They will say that my sentiments do not represent the views of all Indians—and they are right, they have brainwashed many of my brothers. But a new day is coming. Until then, it would be wise for anthropologists to climb down from their thrones of authority and pure research and begin helping Indian tribes instead of preying on them. For the wheel of karma grinds slowly, but it does grind fine. And it make's a complete circle.

AAA Statement on Race

The following statement was adopted by the Executive Board of the American Anthropological Association, acting on a draft prepared by a committee of representative American anthropologists. It does not reflect a consensus of all members of the AAA, as individuals vary in their approaches to the study of "race." We believe that it represents generally the contemporary thinking and scholarly positions of a majority of anthropologists.

In the United States both scholars and the general public have been conditioned to viewing human races as natural and separate divisions within the human species based on visible physical differences. With the vast expansion of scientific knowledge in this century, however, it has become clear that human populations are not unambiguous, clearly demarcated, biologically distinct groups. Evidence from the analysis of genetics (e.g., DNA) indicates that most physical variation, about 94%, lies *within* so-called racial groups. Conventional geographic "racial" groupings differ from one another only in about 6% of their genes. This means that there is greater variation within "racial" groups than between them. In neighboring populations there is much overlapping of genes and their phenotypic (physical) expressions. Throughout history whenever different groups have come into contact, they have interbred. The continued sharing of genetic materials has maintained all of humankind as a single species.

Physical variations in any given trait tend to occur gradually rather than abruptly over geographic areas. And because physical traits are inherited independently of one another, knowing the range of one trait does not predict the presence of others. For example, skin color varies largely from light in the temperate areas in the north to dark in the tropical areas in the south; its intensity is not related to nose shape or hair texture. Dark skin may be associated with frizzy or kinky hair or curly or wavy or straight hair, all of which are found among different indigenous peoples in tropical regions. These facts render any attempt to establish lines of division among biological populations both arbitrary and subjective.

Historical research has shown that the idea of "race" has always carried more meanings than mere physical differences; indeed, physical variations in the human species have no meaning except the social ones that humans put on them. Today scholars in many fields argue that "race" as it is understood in the United States of America was a social mechanism invented during the 18th century to refer to those populations brought together in colonial America: the English and other European settlers, the conquered Indian peoples, and those peoples of Africa brought in to provide slave labor.

From its inception, this modern concept of "race" was modeled after an ancient theorem of the Great Chain of Being, which posited natural categories on a hierarchy established by God or nature. Thus "race" was a mode of classification linked specifically to peoples in the colonial situation. It subsumed a growing ideology of inequality devised to rationalize European attitudes and treatment of the conquered and enslaved peoples. Proponents of slavery in particular during the 19th century used "race" to justify the retention of slavery. The ideology magnified the differences among Europeans, Africans, and Indians, established a rigid hierarchy of socially exclusive categories underscored and bolstered unequal rank and status differences, and provided the rationalization that the inequality was natural or God-given. The different physical traits of African-Americans and Indians became markers or symbols of their status differences.

As they were constructing US society, leaders among European-Americans fabricated the cultural/behavioral characteristics associated with each "race," linking superior traits with Europeans and negative and inferior ones to blacks and Indians. Numerous arbitrary and fictitious beliefs about the different peoples were institutionalized and deeply embedded in American thought.

Early in the 19th century the growing fields of science began to reflect the public consciousness about human differences. Differences among the "racial" categories were projected to their greatest extreme when the argument was posed that Africans, Indians, and Europeans were separate species, with Africans the least human and closer taxonomically to apes.

Ultimately "race" as an ideology about human differences was subsequently spread to other areas of the world. It became a strategy for dividing, ranking, and controlling colonized people used by colonial powers everywhere. But it was not limited to the colonial situation. In the latter part of the 19th century it was employed by Europeans to rank one another and to justify social, economic, and political inequalities among their peoples.

During World War II, the Nazis under Adolf Hitler enjoined the expanded ideology of "race" and "racial" differences and took them to a logical end: the extermination of 11 million people of "inferior races" (e.g., Jews, Gypsies, Africans, homosexuals, and so forth) and other unspeakable brutalities of the Holocaust.

"Race" thus evolved as a worldview, a body of prejudgments that distorts our ideas about human differences and group behavior. Racial beliefs constitute myths about the diversity in the human species and about the abilities and behavior of people homogenized into "racial" categories. The myths fused behavior and physical features together in the public mind, impeding our comprehension of both biological variations and cultural behavior, implying that both are genetically determined. Racial myths bear no relationship to the reality of human capabilities or behavior. Scientists today find that reliance on such folk beliefs about human differences in research has led to countless errors.

At the end of the 20th century, we now understand that human cultural behavior is learned, conditioned into infants beginning at birth, and always subject to modification. No human is born with a built-in culture or language. Our temperaments, dispositions, and personalities, regardless of genetic propensities, are developed within sets of meanings and values that we call "culture." Studies of infant and early childhood learning and behavior attest to the reality of our cultures in forming who we are.

It is a basic tenet of anthropological knowledge that all normal human beings have the capacity to learn any cultural behavior. The American experience with immigrants from hundreds of different language and cultural backgrounds who have acquired some version of American culture traits and behavior is the clearest evidence of this fact. Moreover, people of all physical variations have learned different cultural behaviors and continue to do so as modern transportation moves millions of immigrants around the world.

How people have been accepted and treated within the context of a given society or culture has a direct impact on how they perform in that society. The "racial" worldview was invented to assign some groups to perpetual low status, while others were permitted access to privilege, power, and wealth. The tragedy in the United States has been that the policies and practices stemming from this worldview succeeded all too well in constructing unequal populations among Europeans, Native Americans, and peoples of African descent. Given what we know about the capacity of normal humans to achieve and function within any culture, we conclude that present-day inequalities between so-called "racial" groups are not consequences of their biological inheritance but products of historical and contemporary social, economic, educational, and political circumstances.

AAA POSITION PAPER ON "RACE": COMMENTS?

As a result of public confusion about the meaning of "race," claims as to major biological differences among "races" continue to be advanced. Stemming from past AAA actions designed to address public misconceptions on race and intelligence, the need was apparent for a clear AAA statement on the biology and politics of race that would be educational and informational. Rather than wait for each spurious claim to be raised, the AAA Executive Board determined that the Association should prepare a statement for approval by the Association and elicit member input.

Commissioned by the Executive Board of the American Anthropological Association, a position paper on race was authored by Audrey Smedley (*Race in North America: Origin and Evolution of a Worldview,* 1993) and thrice reviewed by a working group of prominent anthropologists: George Armelagos, Michael Blakey, C. Loring Brace, Alan Goodman, Faye Harrison, Jonathan Marks, Yolanda Moses, and Carol Mukhopadhyay. A draft of the current paper was published in the September 1997 *Anthropology Newsletter* and posted on the AAA website http://www.aaanet.org for a number of months, and member comments were requested. While Smedley assumed authorship of the final draft, she received comments not only from the working group but also from the AAA membership and other interested readers. The paper above was adopted by the AAA Executive Board on May 17, 1998, as an official statement of AAA's position on "race."

[*Note: For further information on human biological variations, see the statement prepared and issued by the American Association of Physical Anthropologists, 1996 (AJPA 101:569-570).*]

Multiple Genders Among North American Indians

Serena Nanda

The early encounters between Europeans and Indian societies in the New World, in the fifteenth through the seventeenth centuries, brought together cultures with very different sex/gender systems. The Spanish explorers, coming from a society where sodomy was a heinous crime, were filled with contempt and outrage when they recorded the presence of men in American Indian societies who performed the work of women, dressed like women, and had sexual relations with men (Lang 1996; Roscoe in 1995).

Europeans labelled these men "berdache," a term originally derived from an Arabic word meaning male prostitute. As such, this term is inappropriate and insulting, and I use it here only to indicate the history of European (mis)understanding of American Indian sex/gender diversity. The term berdache focused attention on the sexuality associated with mixed gender roles, which the Europeans identified, incorrectly, with the "unnatural" and sinful practice of sodomy in their own societies. In their ethnocentrism, the early European explorers and colonists were unable to see beyond their own sex/gender systems and thus did not understand the multiple sex/gender systems they encountered in the Americas. They also largely overlooked the specialized and spiritual functions of many of these alternative sex/gender roles and the positive value attached to them in many American Indian societies.

By the late-nineteenth and early-twentieth centuries, some anthropologists included accounts of North American Indian sex/gender diversity in their ethnographies. They attempted to explain the berdache from various functional perspectives, that is, in terms of the contributions these sex/gender roles made to social structure or culture. These accounts, though less contemptuous than earlier ones, nevertheless largely retained the emphasis on berdache sexuality. The berdache was defined as a form of "institutionalized homosexuality," which served as a social niche for individuals whose personality and sexual orientation did not match the definition of masculinity in their societies, or as a "way out" of the masculine or warrior role for "cowardly" or "failed" men (see Callender and Kochems 1983).

Anthropological accounts increasingly paid more attention to the association of the berdache with shamanism and spiritual powers and also noted that mixed gender roles were often central and highly valued in American Indian cultures, rather than marginal and deviant. These accounts were, nevertheless, also ethnocentric in misidentifying indigenous gender diversity with European concepts of homosexuality transvestism, or hermaphroditism, which continued to distort their indigenous meanings.

In American Indian societies, the European homosexual/heterosexual dichotomy was not culturally relevant and the European labeling of the berdache as homosexuals resulted from their own cultural emphasis on sexuality as a central, even defining, aspect of gender and on sodomy as an abnormal practice and/or a sin. While berdache in many American Indian societies did engage in sexual relations and even married persons of the same sex, this was not central to their alternative gender role. Another overemphasis resulting from European ethnocentrism was the identification of berdache as **transvestites.** Although berdache often cross-dressed, transvestism was not consistent within or across societies. European descriptions of berdache as **hermaphrodites** were also inaccurate. Considering the variation in alternative sex/gender roles in native North America, a working definition may be useful: the berdache in the anthropological literature refers to people who partly or completely take on aspects of the culturally defined role of the other sex and who are classified neither as women nor men, but as genders of their own (see Callender and Kochems 1983:443). It is important to note here that berdache thus refers to variant gender roles, rather than a complete crossing over to an opposite gender role.

In the past twenty-five years there have been important shifts in perspectives on sex/gender diversity among American Indians and anthropologists, both Indian and non-Indian (Jacobs, Thomas, and Lang 1997:Introduction). Most current research rejects institutionalized homosexuality as an adequate explanation of American Indian gender diversity, emphasizing the importance of occupation rather than sexuality as its central feature. Contemporary ethnography views multiple sex/gender roles as a normative part of American Indian sex/gender systems, rather than as a marginal or deviant part (Albers 1989:134; Jacobs et al. 1997; Lang 1998). A new emphasis on the variety of alternative sex/gender roles in North America undercuts the earlier treatment of the berdache as a unitary phenomenon across North (and South) America (Callender and Kochems 1983; Jacobs et al. 1997; Lang 1998; Roscoe 1998).

Current research also emphasizes the integrated and often highly valued position of gender variant persons and the association of sex/gender diversity with spiritual power (Roscoe 1996; Williams 1992).

A change in terminology has also taken place. Berdache generally has been rejected, but there is no unanimous agreement on what should replace it. One widely accepted suggestion is the term ***two-spirit*** (Jacobs et al. 1997; Lang 1998), a term coined in 1990 by urban American Indian gays and lesbians. Two-spirit has the advantage of conveying the spiritual nature of gender variance as viewed by gay, lesbian, and transgendered American Indians and also the spirituality associated with traditional American Indian gender variance, but the cultural continuity suggested by two-spirit is in fact a subject of debate. Another problem is that two-spirit emphasizes the Euro-American gender construction of only two genders. Thus, I use the more culturally neutral term, variant genders (or gender variants) and specific indigenous terms wherever possible.

DISTRIBUTION AND CHARACTERISTICS OF VARIANT SEX/GENDER ROLES

Multiple sex/gender systems were found in many, though not all, American Indian societies. Male gender variant roles (variant gender roles assumed by biological males) are documented for 110 to 150 societies. These roles occurred most frequently in the region extending from California to the Mississippi Valley and upper-Great Lakes, the Plains and the Prairies, the Southwest, and to a lesser extent along the Northwest Coast tribes. With few exceptions, gender variance is not historically documented for eastern North America, though it may have existed prior to European invasion and disappeared before it could be recorded historically (Callender and Kochems 1983; Fulton and Anderson 1992).

There were many variations in North American Indian gender diversity. American Indian cultures included three or four genders: men, women, male variants, and female variants (biological females who by engaging in male activities were reclassified as to gender). Gender variant roles differed in the criteria by which they were defined; the degree of their integration into the society; the norms governing their behavior; the way the role was acknowledged publicly or sanctioned; how others were expected to behave toward gender variant persons; the degree to which a gender changer was expected to adopt the role of the opposite sex or was limited in doing so; the power, sacred or secular, that was attributed to them; and the path to recruitment.

In spite of this variety, however, there were also some common or widespread features: transvestism, cross-gender occupation, same sex (but different gender) sexuality, some culturally normative and acknowledged process for recruitment to the role, special language and ritual roles, and associations with spiritual power.

A Native American artist's rendition of the mixed gender qualities of the berdache. (After Joe Lawrence Lembo 1987. Rendition by Sue Ellen Jacobs 1997. Reprinted from *Two-Spirit People* © 1997 by the Board of Trustees University of Illinois Press.) Reprinted with permission.

TRANSVESTISM

The degree to which male and female gender variants were permitted to wear the clothing of the other sex varied. Transvestism was often associated with gender variance but was not equally important in all societies. Male gender variants frequently adopted women's dress and hairstyles partially or completely, and female gender variants partially adopted the clothing of men; sometimes, however, transvestism was prohibited. The choice of clothing was sometimes an individual matter and gender variants might mix their clothing and their accoutrements. For example, a female gender variant might wear a woman's dress but carry (male) weapons. Dress was also sometimes situationally determined: a male gender variant would have to wear men's clothing while engaging in warfare but might wear women's clothes at other times. Similarly, female gender variants might wear women's clothing when gathering (women's work), but male clothing when hunting (men's work) (Callender and Kochems 1983:447). Among the Navajo, a male gender variant, **nádleeh,** would adopt almost all aspects of a woman's dress, work, language and behavior; the Mohave male gender variant, called **alyha,** was at the extreme end of the cross-gender continuum in imitating female physiology as well as transvestism (the transvestite ceremony is discussed later in this chapter). Repression of visible forms of gender diversity, and ultimately the almost total decline of transvestism, were a direct result of American prohibitions against it.

Finds Them and Kills Them, a Crow Indian gender variant, widely known as a superior warrior (National Anthropological Archives, Smithsonian Institution, photo no. 88–135.) Reprinted with permission.

OCCUPATION

Contemporary analysis emphasizes occupational aspects of American Indian gender variance as a central feature. Most frequently a boy's interest in the implements and activities of women and a girl's interest in the tools of male occupations signaled an individual's wish to undertake a gender variant role (Callender and Kochems 1983:447; Whitehead 1981). In hunting societies, for example, female gender variance was signaled by a girl rejecting the domestic activities associated with women and participating in playing and hunting with boys. In the arctic and subarctic, particularly, this was sometimes encouraged by a girl's parents if there were not enough boys to provide the family with food (Lang 1998). Male gender variants were frequently considered especially skilled and industrious in women's crafts and domestic work (though not in agriculture, where this was a man's task) (Roscoe 1991; 1996). Female gender crossers sometimes won reputations as superior hunters and warriors.

Male gender variants' households were often more prosperous than others, sometimes because they were hired by whites. In their own societies the excellence of male gender variants' craftwork was sometimes ascribed to a supernatural sanction for their gender transformation (Callender and Kochems 1983:448). Female gender variants opted out of motherhood, so were not encumbered by caring for children, which may explain their success as hunters or warriors. In some societies, gender variants could engage in both men's and women's work, and this, too, accounted for their increased wealth. Another source of income was payment for the special social activities of gender variants due to their intermediate gender status, such as acting as go-betweens in marriage. Through their diverse occupations, then, gender variants were often central rather than marginal in their societies.

Early anthropological explanations of male gender variant roles as a niche for a "failed" or cowardly man who wished to avoid warfare or other aspects of the masculine role are no longer widely accepted. To begin with, masculinity was not associated with warrior status in all American Indian cultures. In some societies, male gender variants were warriors and in many others, men who rejected the warrior role did not become gender variants. Sometimes male gender variants did not go to war because of cultural prohibitions against their using symbols of maleness, for example, the prohibition against their using the bow among the Illinois. Where male gender variants did not fight, they sometimes had other important roles in warfare, like treating the wounded, carrying supplies for the war party, or directing postbattle ceremonials (Callender and Kochems 1983:449). In a few societies male gender variants became outstanding warriors, such as Finds Them and Kills Them, a Crow Indian who performed daring feats of bravery while fighting with the United States Army against the Crow's traditional enemies, the Lakota Sioux (Roscoe 1998:23),

GENDER VARIANCE AND SEXUALITY

Generally, sexuality was not central in defining gender status among American Indians. But in any case, the assumption by European observers that gender variants were homosexuals meant they did not take much trouble to investigate or record information on this topic. In some American Indian societies same-sex sexual desire/practice did figure significantly in the definition of gender variant roles; in others it did not (Callender and Kochems 1983:449). Some early reports noted specifically that male gender variants lived with and/or had sexual relations with women as well as men; in other societies they were reported as having sexual relations only with men, and in still other societies, of having no sexual relationships at all (Lang 1998:189–95).

The bisexual orientation of some gender variant persons may have been a culturally accepted expression of their gender variance. It may have resulted from an individual's life experiences, such as the age at which he or she entered the gender variant role, and/or it may have been one aspect of the general freedom of sexual expression in many American Indian societies. While male and female gender variants most frequently had sexual relations with, or married, persons of the same biological sex as themselves, these relationships were not considered homosexual in the contemporary Western understanding of that term. In a multiple gender system the partners would be of the same sex but different genders, and homogender, rather than homosexual, practices bore the brunt of negative cultural sanctions. The sexual partners of gender variants were never considered gender variants themselves.

The Navajo are a good example (Thomas 1997). The Navajo have four genders; in addition to man and woman there are two gender variants: masculine female-bodied nádleeh and feminine male-bodied nádleeh. A sexual relationship between a female nadleeh and a woman or a sexual relationship between a male-bodied nádleeh and a man were not stigmatized because these persons were of different genders, although of the same biological sex. However, a sexual relationship between two women, two men, two female-bodied nádleeh or two male-bodied nádleeh, was considered homosexual, and even incestual, and was strongly disapproved of.

The relation of sexuality to variant sex/gender roles across North America suggests that sexual relations between gender variants and persons of the same biological sex were a result rather than a cause of gender variance. Sexual relationships between a man and a male gender variant were accepted in most American Indian societies, though not in all, and appear to have been negatively sanctioned only when it interfered with child-producing heterosexual marriages. Gender variants' sexual relationships varied from casual and wide-ranging (Europeans used the term promiscuous), to stable, and sometimes even involved life-long marriages. In some societies, however, male gender variants were not permitted to engage in long-term relationships with men, either in or out of wedlock. In many cases, gender variants were reported as living alone.

There are some practical reasons why a man might desire sexual relations with a (male) gender variant: in some societies taboos on sexual relations with menstruating or pregnant women restricted opportunities for sexual intercourse; in other societies, sexual relations with a gender variant person were exempt from punishment for extramarital affairs; in still other societies, for example, among the Navajo, some gender variants were considered especially lucky and a man might hope to vicariously partake of this quality by having sexual relations with them (Lang 1998:349).

BIOLOGICAL SEX AND GENDER TRANSFORMATIONS

European observers often confused gender variants with hermaphrodites. Some American Indian societies explicitly distinguished hermaphrodites from gender variants and treated them differently; others assigned gender variant persons and hermaphrodites to the same alternative gender status. With the exception of the Navajo, in most American Indian societies biological sex (or the intersexedness of the hermaphrodite) was not the criterion for a gender variant role, nor were the individuals who occupied gender variant roles anatomically abnormal. The Navajo distinguished between the intersexed and the alternatively gendered, but treated them similarly, though not exactly the same (Thomas 1997; Hill 1935).

And even as the traditional Navajo sex/gender system had biological sex as its starting point, it was only a starting point, and Navajo nádleeh were distinguished by sex-linked behaviors, such as body language, clothing, ceremonial roles, speech style, and work. Feminine, male bodied nádleeh might engage in women's activities such as cooking, weaving, household tasks, and making pottery. Masculine, female-bodied nádleeh, unlike other female-bodied persons, avoided childbirth; today they are associated with male occupational roles such as construction or firefighting (although ordinary women also sometimes engage in these occupations). Traditionally, female-bodied nádleeh had specific roles in Navajo ceremonials.

Thus, even where hermaphrodites occupied a special gender variant role, American Indian gender variance was defined more by cultural than biological criteria. In one recorded case of an interview with and physical examination of a gender variant male, the previously mentioned Finds Them and Kills Them, his genitals were found to be completely normal (Roscoe 1998).

If American Indian gender variants were not generally hermaphrodites, or conceptualized as such, neither were they conceptualized as transsexuals. Gender transformations among gender variants were recognized as only a partial transformation, and the gender variant was not thought of as having become a person of the opposite sex/gender. Rather, gender variant roles were autonomous gender roles that combined the characteristics of men and women and had some unique features of their own. This was sometimes symbolically recognized: among the Zuni a male gender variant was buried in women's dress but men's trousers on the men's side of the graveyard (Parsons quoted in Callender and Kochems 1983:454; Boscoe 1991:124, 145). Male gender variants were neither men—by virtue of their chosen occupations, dress, demeanor, and possibly sexuality—nor women, because of their anatomy and their inability to bear children. Only among the Mohave do we find the extreme imitation of women's physiological processes related to reproduction and the claims to have female sexual organs—both of which were ridiculed within Mohave society. But even here, where informants reported that female gender variants did not menstruate, this did not make them culturally men. Rather it was the mixed quality of gender variant status that was culturally elaborated in native North America, and this was the source of supernatural powers sometimes attributed to them.

SACRED POWER

The association between the spiritual power and gender variance occurred in most, if not all, Native American societies. Even where, as previously noted, recruitment to the role was occasioned by a child's interest in occupational activities of the opposite sex, supernatural sanction, frequently appearing in visions or dreams, was also involved. Where this occurred, as it did mainly in the Prairie and Plains societies, the visions involved female supernatural figures, often the moon. Among the Omaha, for example, the moon appeared in a dream holding a burden strap—a symbol of female work—in one hand,

and a bow—a symbol of male work—in the other. When the male dreamer reached for the bow, the moon forced him to take the burden strap (Whitehead 1981). Among the Mohave, a child's choice of male or female implements heralding gender variant status was sometimes prefigured by a dream that was believed to come to an embryo in the womb (Devereux 1937).

Sometimes, by virtue of the power associated with their gender ambiguity, gender variants were ritual adepts and curers, or had special ritual functions (Callender and Kochems 1983:453, Lang 1998), Gender variants did not always have important sacred roles in native North America, however. Where feminine qualities were associated with these roles, male gender variants might become spiritual leaders or healers, but where these roles were associated with male qualities they were not entered into by male gender variants. Among the Plains Indians, with their emphasis on the vision as a source of supernatural power, male gender variants were regarded as holy persons, but in California Indian societies, this was not the case and in some American Indian societies gender variants were specifically excluded from religious roles (Lang 1998:167). Sometimes it was the individual personality of the gender variant rather than his/her gender variance itself, that resulted in occupying sacred roles (see Commentary following Callender and Kochems 1983). Nevertheless, the importance of sacred power was so widely associated with sex/gender diversity in native North America that it is generally agreed to be an important explanation of the frequency of gender diversity in this region of the world.

In spite of cultural differences, some significant similarities among American Indian societies are particularly consistent with multigender systems and the positive value placed on sex/gender diversity (Lang 1996). One of these similarities is a cosmology (system of religious beliefs and way of seeing the world) in which transformation and ambiguity are recurring themes. Thus a person who contains both masculine and feminine qualities or one who is transformed from the sex/gender assigned at birth into a different gender in later life manifests some of the many kinds of transformations and ambiguities that are possible, not only for humans, but for animals and objects in the natural environment, Indeed, in many American Indian cultures, sex/gender ambiguity, lack of sexual differentiation, and sex/gender transformations play an important part in the story of creation. American Indian cosmology may not be "the cause" of sex/gender diversity but it certainly (as in India) provides a hospitable context for it (Lang 1996:187).

THE ALYHA: A MALE GENDER VARIANT ROLE AMONG THE MOHAVE

One of the most complete classic anthropological descriptions of a gender variant role is from the Mohave, a society that lives in the southwest desert area of the Nevada/California border. The following description, based on interviews by anthropologist George Devereux (1937) with some old informants who remembered the transvestite ceremony and had heard stories about gender variant individuals from their elders, indicates some of the ways in which gender variance functioned in native North America.

The Mohave had two gender variant roles: a male role called alyha and a female role called **hwame**. In this society, pregnant women had dreams forecasting the anatomic sex of their children. Mothers of a future alyha dreamt of male characteristics, such as arrow feathers, indicating the birth of a boy, but their dreams also included hints of their child's future gender variant status. A boy indicated he might become an alyha by "acting strangely" around the age of 10 or 11, before he had participated in the boys' puberty ceremonies. At this age, young people began to engage seriously in the activities that would characterize their adult lives as men and women; boys, for example, learned to hunt, ride horses, make bows and arrows, and they developed sexual feelings for girls. The future alyha avoided these masculine activities. Instead he played with dolls, imitated the domestic work of women, tried to participate in the women's gambling games, and demanded to wear the female bark skirt rather than the male breechclout.

The alyha's parents and relatives were ambivalent about this behavior. At first his parents would try to dissuade him, but if the behavior persisted his relatives would resign themselves and begin preparations for the transvestite ceremony. The ceremony was meant to take the boy by surprise; it was considered both a test of his inclination and an initiation. Word was sent out to various settlements so that people could watch the ceremony and get accustomed to the boy in female clothing. At the ceremony, the boy was led into a circle of onlookers by two women, and the crowd began singing the transvestite songs. If the boy began to dance as women did, he was confirmed as an alyha. He was then taken to the river to bathe and given a girl's skirt to wear. This initiation ceremony confirmed his changed gender status, which was considered permanent.

After this ceremony the alyha assumed a female name (though he did not take the lineage name that all females assumed) and would resent being called by his former, male name. In the frequent and bawdy sexual joking characteristic of Mohave culture, an alyha resented male nomenclature being applied to his genitals. He insisted that his penis be called a clitoris, his testes, labia majora, and anus a vagina. Alyha were also particularly sensitive to sexual joking, and if they were teased in the same way as women they responded with assaults on those who teased them. Because they were very strong, people usually avoided angering them.

Alyha were considered highly industrious and much better housewives than were young girls. It is partly for this reason that they had no difficulty finding spouses, and alyha generally had husbands. Alyha were not courted like ordinary girls, however (where the prospective husband would sleep chastely beside the girl for several nights and then lead her out of her parents' house), but rather courted like widows, divorcees, or "wanton" women. Intercourse with an alyha was surrounded by special etiquette. Like Mohave heterosexual couples, the alyha and her husband practiced both anal and oral intercourse, with the alyha taking the female role. Alyha were reported to be embarrassed by an erection and would not allow their sexual partners to touch or even comment on their erect penis.

When an alyha found a husband, she would begin to imitate menstruation by scratching herself between the legs with a stick until blood appeared. The alyha then submitted to puberty observations as a girl would, and her husband also observed the requirements of the husband of a girl who menstruated for the first time. Alyha also imitated pregnancy, particularly if their husbands threatened them with divorce on the grounds of barrenness. At this time they would cease faking menstruation and follow the pregnancy taboos, with even more attention than ordinary women, except that they publicly proclaimed their pregnancy, which ordinary Mohave women never did. In imitating pregnancy, an alyha would stuff rags in her skirts, and near the time of the birth, drank a decoction to cause constipation. After a day or two of stomach pains, she would go into the bushes and sit over a hole, defecating in the position of childbirth. The feces would be treated as a stillbirth and buried, and the alyha would weep and wail as a woman does for a stillborn child. The alyha and her husband would then clip their hair as in mourning.

Alyha were said to be generally peaceful persons, except when teased, and were also considered to be cowards. They did not have to participate in the frequent and harsh military raids of Mohave men. Alyha did participate in the welcoming home feast for the warriors, where, like old women, they might make a bark penis and go through the crowd poking the men who had stayed home, saying, "You are not a man, but an alyha."

In general, alyha were not teased or ridiculed for being alyha (though their husbands were teased for marrying them), because it was believed that they could not help it and that a child's inclinations in this direction could not be resisted. It was believed that a future alyha's desire for a gender change was such that he could not resist dancing the women's dance at the initiation ceremony. Once his desires were demonstrated in this manner, people would not thwart him. It was partly the belief that becoming an alyha was a result of a "temperamental compulsion" or predestined (as forecast in his mother's pregnancy dream) that inhibited ordinary Mohave from ridiculing alyha. In addition, alyha were considered powerful healers, especially effective in curing sexually transmitted diseases (also called alyha) like syphilis.

The alyha demonstrates some of the ways in which gender variant roles were constructed as autonomous genders in North America. In many ways the alyha crossed genders, but the role had a distinct, alternative status to that of both man and woman (as did the hwame). Although the alyha imitated many aspects of a woman's role—dress, sexual behavior, menstruation, pregnancy, childbirth, and domestic occupations—they were also recognized as being different from women. Alyha did not take women's lineage names; they were not courted like ordinary women; they publicly proclaimed their pregnancies; and they were considered more industrious than other women in women's domestic tasks.

In spite of the alyha's sexual relations with men, the alyha was not considered primarily a homosexual (in Western terms). In fact, among ordinary Mohave, if a person dreamed of having homosexual relationships, that person would be expected to die soon, but this was not true of the alyha. Most significantly, the alyha were believed to have special supernatural powers, which they used in curing illness.

FEMALE GENDER VARIANTS

Female gender variants probably occurred more frequently among American Indians than in other cultures, although this has been largely overlooked in the historic and ethnographic record (But see Blackwood 1984; Jacobs et al. 1997; Lang 1998; Medicine 1983).

Although the generally egalitarian social structures of many American Indian societies provided a hospitable context for female gender variance, it occurred in perhaps only one-quarter to one-half of the societies with male variant roles (Callender and Kochems 1983:446; see also Lang 1998:262-65). This may be explained partly by the fact that in many American Indian societies women could—and did—adopt aspects of the male gender role, such as warfare or hunting, and sometimes dressed in male clothing, without being reclassified into a different gender (Blackwood 1984; Lang 1998:261ff; Medicine 1983).

As with men, the primary criteria of changed gender status for females was an affinity for the occupations of the other gender. While this inclination for male occupations was often displayed in childhood, female gender variants entered these roles later in life than did males (Lang 1998:303). Among some Inuit, "men pretenders" would refuse to learn women's tasks and were taught male occupations when they were children, by their fathers. They played with boys and participated in the hunt. Among the Kaska, a family who had only daughters might select one to "be like a man;" by engaging in the male activity of hunting, she would help provide the family with food. Among the Mohave, too, hwame refused to learn women's work, played with boys, and were considered excellent providers, as well as particularly efficient healers (Blackwood 1984:30; Lang 1998:286). Among the Cheyenne, the *hetaneman* (defined as a hermaphrodite having more of the female element) were great female warriors who accompanied the male warrior societies into battle. In all other groups, however, even outstanding women warriors were not recast into a different gender role (Roscoe 1998:75). Female gender variants also sometimes entered specialized occupations, becoming traders, guides for whites, or healers. The female preference for male occupations might be motivated by a female's desire to be independent, or might be initiated or encouraged by a child's parents, and in some societies was sanctioned through supernatural omens or in dreams.

In addition to occupation, female gender variants might assume other characteristics of men. Cocopa *warrhameh* wore a masculine hairstyle and had their noses pierced, like boys (Lang 1998:283). Among the Maidu, the female *suku* also had her nose pierced on the occasion of her initiation into the men's secret society. Mohave hwame were tattooed like men instead of women. Transvestism was commonly though not universally practiced: it occurred, for example, among the Kaska, Paiute, Ute, and Mohave.

Like male gender variants, female gender variants exhibited a wide range of sexual relationships. Some had relationships with other females, who were generally regarded as ordinary women. Only rarely, as among a southern Apache group, was the female gender variant (like her male counterpart) defined in terms of her sexual desire for women. Mohave hwame engaged in sexual and marriage relationships with women, although they courted them in a special way, different from heterosexual courtships If a hwame married a pregnant woman, she could claim paternity of the child, although the child belonged to the descent group of its biological father (Devereux 1937:514). Like an alyha's husband, a hwame's wife was often teased, and hwame marriages were generally unstable. Masahai Amatkwisai, the most well known hwame, married women three times and was also known to have sexual relationships with many men. Masahai's wives were all aggressively teased by male Mohave who viewed "real" sexual relations only in terms of penetration by a penis. At dances Masahai sat with the men, described her wife's genitals, and flirted with girls, all typical male behavior. Masahai's masculine behavior was ridiculed, and the men gravely insulted her (though never to her face), by referring to her by an obscene nickname meaning the female genitals. The harassment of Masahai's wives apparently led to the eventual breakup of her marriages.

Sexual relationships between women in American Indian societies were rarely historically documented, but in any case, were generally downplayed in female gender variant roles, even when this involved marriage. One female gender variant, for example, Woman Chief, a famous Crow warrior and hunter, took four wives, but this appeared to be primarily an economic strategy: processing animal hides among the Crow was women's work, so that Woman Chief's polygyny (multiple spouses) complemented her hunting skills.

While most often American Indian women who crossed genders occupationally, such as Woman Chief, were not reclassified into a gender variant role, several isolated cases of female gender transformations have been documented historically. One of these is Ququnak Patke, a "manlike woman" from the Kutenai (Schaeffer 1965). Ququnak Patke had married a white fur trader and when she returned to her tribe, claimed that her husband had transformed her into a man. She wore men's clothes, lived as a man, married a woman and claimed supernatural sanction for her role change and her supernatural powers. Although whites often mistook her for a man in her various roles as warrior, explorer's guide, and trader, such transformations were not considered a possibility among the Kutenai, and many thought Ququnak Patke was mad. She died attempting to mediate a quarrel between two hostile Indian groups.

It is difficult to know how far we can generalize about the relation of sexuality to female gender variance in precontact American Indian cultures from the lives of the few documented female gender variants. These descriptions (and those for males, as well) are mainly based on ethnographic accounts that relied on twentieth-century informants whose memories were already shaped by white hostility toward gender diversity and same-sex sexuality. Nevertheless, it seems clear that although American Indian female gender variants clearly had sexual relationships with women, sexual object choice was not their defining characteristic. In some cases, female gender variants were described "as women who never marry," which does not say anything definitive about their sexuality; it may well be that the sexuality of female gender variants was more variable than that of men.

Occasionally, as with Masahai and Ququnak Patke, and also for some male gender variants, contact with whites opened up opportunities for gender divergent individuals (see Roscoe 1988; 1991). On the whole, however, as a result of Euro-American repression and the growing assimilation of Euro-American sex/gender ideologies, both female and male gender variant roles among American Indians largely disappeared by the 1930s, as the reservation system was well under way. And yet, its echoes may remain. The current academic interest in American Indian multigender roles, and particularly the testimony of contemporary two-spirits, remind us that alternatives are possible and that understanding American Indian sex/gender diversity in the past and present makes a significant contribution to understandings of sex/gender diversity in the larger society.

A Pacific Culture Among Wild Baboons

Its Emergence and Transmission

Robert M. Sapolsky[1,2], Lisa J. Share[1]

Reports exist of transmission of culture in nonhuman primates. We examine this in a troop of savanna baboons studied since 1978. During the mid-1980s, half of the males died from tuberculosis; because of circumstances of the outbreak, it was more aggressive males who died, leaving a cohort of atypically unaggressive survivors. A decade later, these behavioral patterns persisted. Males leave their natal troops at adolescence; by the mid-1990s, no males remained who had resided in the troop a decade before. Thus, critically, the troop's unique culture was being adopted by new males joining the troop. We describe (a) features of this culture in the behavior of males, including high rates of grooming and affiliation with females and a "relaxed" dominance hierarchy; (b) physiological measures suggesting less stress among low-ranking males; (c) models explaining transmission of this culture; and (d) data testing these models, centered around treatment of transfer males by resident females.

1 Department of Biological Sciences and Department of Neurology and Neurological Sciences, Stanford University, Stanford, California, United States of America.

2 Institute of Primate Research, National Museums of Kenya Karen, Nairobi, Kenya

INTRODUCTION

A goal of primatology is to understand the enormous variability in primate social behavior. Early investigators examined interspecies differences, e.g., that pair-bonding is more common among arboreal than terrestrial primates (Crook and Gartlan 1966). Attention has also focused on geographical differences in behavior within species (Whiten et al. 1999). Often, such differences reflect environmental factors (e.g., a correlation between quantities of rainfall and foraging time) or, in theory, could reflect genetic drift. However, increasing evidence suggests that group-specific traits can also represent "traditions" or "cultures" (the latter term will be used, commensurate with the near consensus among primatologists that the term can be appropriately applied to nonhuman primates).

As traditionally applied to humans, such "culture" can be defined as behaviors shared by a population, but not necessarily other species members, that are independent of genetics or ecological factors and that persist past their originators (Kroeber and Kluckhohn 1966; Cavalli-Sforza 2000; de Waal 2000; de Waal 2001). Thus defined, transmission of culture occurs in apes (McGrew 1998; Whiten et al. 1999; van Schaik et al. 2003), monkeys (Kawai 1965; Cambefort 1981; Perry et al. 2003), cetaceans (Noad et al. 2000; Rendell and Whitehead 2001), and fish and birds (Laland and Reader 1999; Laland and Hoppitt 2003). As particularly striking examples, chimpanzees (*Pan troglodytes*) across Africa demonstrate variability in 39 behaviors related to tool use, grooming, and courtship (Whiten et al. 1999), and the excavation of near-millenium-old chimpanzee tools has been reported (Mercader et al. 2002).

Nearly all such cases of nonhuman culture involve either technology (for example, the use of hammers for nut cracking by chimpanzees), food acquisition, or communication. In this paper, we document the emergence of a unique culture in a troop of olive baboons (Papio anubis) related to the overall structure and social atmosphere of the troop. We also document physiological correlates of this troop atmosphere, the transmission of relevant behaviors past their originators, and possible mechanisms of transmission.

RESULTS/DISCUSSION

Circumstances Leading to the Emergence of a Unique Culture

In the early 1980s, Forest Troop slept in trees 1 km from a tourist lodge. During that period, an open garbage pit was greatly expanded at the lodge. This attracted an adjacent baboon troop, Garbage Dump Troop, which slept near the pit and foraged almost exclusively there.

By 1982, many Forest Troop males went to the garbage pit at dawn for food. While such refuse eaters did not differ in age distribution (data not shown) or average dominance rank from non-refuse eaters, they were more aggressive (Table 1); such aggressiveness

Table 1. *Characteristics of Forest Troop Males As a Function of Whether They Competed for Refuse with the Garbage Dump Troop*

Trait or Behavior	Refuse Eaters	Remaining Males	Statistical Significance
Rank	6.5 ± 6 1.5	9.5 ± 1.5	n.s.
Rate of male–male aggression	15.1 ± 4.6	4.0 ± 1.3	< 0.05,
Rate of male–male approach– avoid interactions	199 ± 46	73 ± 20	< 0.05
Rate of aggression directed at females	10.6 ± 6.0	0± 0	n.s.,< 0.10
Seconds of grooming of non- estrous females	3.6 ± 1.5	6 7 ± 3.1	n.s.,< 0.15

Statistical comparisons by unpaired t-test, $n = 7$ and $n = 8$ for refuse eaters and remaining males, respectively. Dominance rank based on approach–avoidance criteria (Altmann 1974). Data concerning refuse eaters were derived solely from their time in the troop, rather than including time spent with the Garbage Dump Troop. Rate of male–male aggression consisted of aggression with any other adult or subadult male in the troop. Rate of aggression directed at females included all adult and subadult females. Rates of behaviors are per 100 h of focal observation, except for grooming, which is per 10 h. Data are mean 6 standard error of the mean (SEM). DOI: 10.1371/journal.pbio.0020106.t001

could be viewed as a prerequisite in order to compete with Garbage Dump males for access to refuse. Refuse eaters were also involved in more dominance interactions within Forest Troop than were non-refuse eaters (note that frequency of dominance interactions is independent of outcome, and thus of rank).

In 1983, an outbreak of bovine tuberculosis occurred, originating from infected meat in the dump. From 1983 to 1986, most Garbage Dump animals died, as did all refuse-eating Forest Troop males (46% of adult males); no other Forest Troop animals died (Tarara et al. 1985; Sapolsky and Else 1987).

These deaths greatly altered Forest Troop composition, such that there were fewer adult males and more adult females; this more than doubled the female:male ratio (Table 2). By 1986, troop behavior had changed markedly, because only less aggressive males had survived.

Because of these events, observations of the troop were stopped, and only censusing was done until 1993. Research was begun on Talek Troop, approximately 50 km away.

In 1993, informal observation of Forest Troop indicated that the behavioral features seen by 1986 had persisted. Critically, by 1993, no adult males remained from 1983–1986; all current adult males had joined the troop following 1986. Thus, the distinctive behaviors that emerged during the mid-1980s because of the selective deaths were being carried out by the next cohort of adult males that had transferred into the troop. Focal sampling on

Table 2. *Troop Composition Before and After the Tuberculosis Outbreak*

Troop	Years	Total	Males	Females	Female : Male
Forest	1979–1982	62 ± 2	15.2 ± 0.3	15.6 ± 0.3	1.0 ± 0.2
	1987–1996	54 ± 5	7.5 ± 0.6	19.1 ± 1.0	2.6 ± 0.2
Talek	1993–1998	68 ± 7	16.2 ± 1.3	17.8 ± 0.7	1.1 ± .03

Data from annual troop censuses. Census numbers include both "subadult" animals (undergoing the emergence of secondary sexual characteristics) and "fully adult" (fully emerged secondary sexual characteristics). DOI: 10.1371/journal.pbio.0020106.t002

Forest Troop recommenced in 1993, in order to document this phenomenon. Data from Forest Troop 1993–1996 (henceforth, F93–96) were compared with two other data sets that served as controls: observations from 1993–1998 on the Talek Troop (henceforth T93–98), and observations of Forest Troop itself prior to the deaths (1979, 1980, 1982; henceforth F79–82). These two control data sets did not differ significantly from each other and were combined, henceforth T93–98/F79–82.

ATYPICAL FEATURES OF THE BEHAVIOR OF FOREST TROOP MALES

Male–male dominance interactions

Males of F93–96 and T93–98/F79–82 had similar rates of approach–avoidance dominance interactions (data not shown). Moreover, dominance stability did not differ, as measured by the percentage of approach–avoidance interactions which represented a reversal of the direction of dominance within a dyad of males of adjacent rank (16% 6 5% and 20% 6 5% for F93– 96 and T93–98/F79–82, respectively, n.s.). There was also no difference in the average tenure length of the highest-ranking male (approximately a year).

Despite those similarities, dominance behavior in F93–96 differed from the two control cases in ways that, arguably, made for less stress for low-ranking males. A first example concerns approach–avoidance dominance interactions between males more than two ranks apart in the hierarchy. The overwhelming majority of such interactions were won by the higher-ranking individual. Because a male is rarely seriously threatened by an individual more than two ranks lower in the hierarchy, interactions between individuals that far apart typically represent harassment of or displacement of the subordinate by the higher-ranking male, rather than true competition. In T93–98 and F79–82, approximately 80% of approach–avoidance interactions were between males more than two ranks apart in the hierarchy. In contrast, a significantly smaller percentage of approach–avoidance interactions were soin F93–96 (Figure 1A). Instead, a disproportionate percentage of F93–96 dominance interactions occurred among males of adjacent ranks (with, as

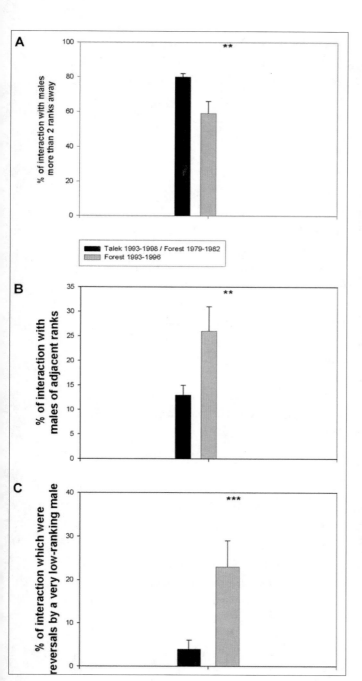

Figure 1. Quality of Male–Male Dominance Interactions

(A) Percentage of male approach–avoidance dominance interactions occurring between males more than two ranks apart.

(B) Percentage of male approach–avoidance interactions occurring between males of adjacent ranks.

(C) Percentage of approach–avoidance interactions representing a reversal of the direction of dominance within a dyad by a male more than two steps lower ranking. Mean ± SEM, ** and *** indicate $p < 0.02$ and $p < 0.01$, respectively, by t-test, treating each male/year as a data point. Data were derived from a total of ten different males in F93–96, 31 different males in T93–98, and 19 different males in F79–82. Potentially, the result in (B) could have arisen from different numbers of males in F93–96 versus the other two troops (a smaller group size does not change the number of adjacent animals available to any given subject, but decreases the number of nonadjacent animals available). However, the same results were found if the numbers of males in the three troops were artificially made equal by excluding excess males from either the top or the bottom of the hierarchy (data not shown).

DOI: 10.1371/journal.pbio.0020106.g001

noted, no difference in dominance stability)(Figure 1B). Moreover, high-ranking males in F93–96 were more "tolerant" of very low-ranking males, as there was a disproportionately high number of reversals with males more than two steps lower in the hierarchy (Figure 1C). Thus, in F93–96, with a typical level of dominance stability, approach–avoidance dominance interactions were concentrated among closely ranking animals, with low-ranking males being more tolerated and less subject to harassment and/or displacement by high-ranking males.

Aggression

Patterns of aggression also differed between F93–96 and T93–98/F79–82 in a way that suggested a less stressful environment for subordinates in F93–96. The troops had similar overall rates of aggressive interactions (Table 3). However, aggression in F93–96 was more likely than in the control troops to occur between closely ranked animals (i.e., within two rank steps), rather than to reflect high-ranking males directing aggression at extremely low-ranking ones; the latter type of interaction is particularly stressful for a subordinate, because of its typical unpredictability. Moreover, F93–96 males were less likely than T93–98/F79–82 males to direct aggression at females.

We examined the data for reconciliative behavior (i.e., affiliative behaviors between pairs following aggressive interactions [de Waal and van Roosmalen 1979]) in F93–96 and T93–98/F79–82. However, we saw no male–male reconciliation in any troop, in agreement with prior reports (Cheney et al. 1995).

Affiliative behaviors

Quantitative data on affiliative behaviors were not available for F79–82. However, F93–96 males socially groomed more often than did control T93–98 males (Figure 2A) this difference was due to more grooming between males and females. F93–96 males were also in close proximity to other animals more often than were T93–98 males (Figure 2B). While males did not differ between troops in the average number of adult male neighbors (i.e., within 3 m), F93–96 males were more likely than T93–98 males to have adult females, infants, adolescents, and juveniles as neighbors.

Sexual behavior

Sexual behavior did not differ between F93–96 and T93–98/F79–82. The percentages of nonpregnant, nonlactating females in estrus per day did not differ (27% ± 7% and 30% ± 4%, respectively, n.s.). Moreover, the relationship between male rank and reproductive success did not differ (R^2 of correlation between rank and reproductive success: 0.25 ± 0.25 and 0.54 ± 0.10, respectively, n.s.).

Table 3. *Patterns of Aggression in Forest Troop 1993–1996 versus Talek Troop 1993–1998 and Forest Troop 1979–1982*

Behavior	F93–96	T93–98/F79–82	Statistical Significance
Rate of escalated aggression between males (per 100 h)	6.8 ± 1.1	8.3 ± 2.3	n.s.
Observed/expected ratio, fights between males of adjacent ranks	1.9 ± 0.1	0.8 ± 0.2	**
Observed/expected ratio, fights between males ± 2 ranks apart	1.3 ± 0.4	0.7 ± 0.6	n.s.
Rate of aggression directed at females (per 100 h)	1.1 ± 0.3	6.1 ± 0.9	***

** and *** indicate $p < 0.025$ and $p < 0.01$ by unpaired t-test, respectively. Observed/expected ratios were derived by comparing observed frequencies of behavior with the frequencies expected with even distribution of aggressive interactions across all dyads; a ratio of 1.0 indicates the behavior occurring at the expected rate. Data from T93–98 and F79–82 did not differ significantly, and thus were pooled. Data were derived from a total of ten different males in F93–96, 31 different males in T93–98, and 19 different males in F79–82. DOI: 10.1371/journal.pbio.0020106.t003

PHYSIOLOGICAL CORRELATES OF BEHAVIORAL FEATURES OF FOREST TROOP

Thus, F93–96 males had high rates of affiliative behaviors, and low-ranking males were subject to low rates of aggressive attack and subordination by high-ranking males. In a stable hierarchy, low-ranking baboon males show physiological indications of being stressed, including elevated basal levels of glucocorticoids (the adrenal hormones secreted in response to stress), hypertension, and decreased levels of high density lipoprotein cholesterol, growth factors, and circulating lymphocytes (Sapolsky 1993; Sapolsky and Share 1994; Sapolsky and Spencer 1997). We tested whether subordinate males in F93–96 were spared the stress-related physiology of subordination seen in other troops.

This was the case (Figure 3A). In F79–82, i.e., prior to the tuberculosis outbreak, subordination was associated with elevated basal levels of glucocorticoids, as in other species in which subordination entails extensive stressors and low rates of coping outlets (Sapolsky 2001). While glucocorticoids aid in surviving an acute physical stressor, chronic overexposure increases the risk of glucose intolerance, hypertension, ulcers, and reproductive and immune suppression (Sapolsky et al. 2000). In contrast to this picture in F79–82, in which subordination was associated with a physiology suggesting a chronic state of stress, subordinate F93–96 males did not have elevated basal glucocorticoid levels (levels were unavailable for T93–98).

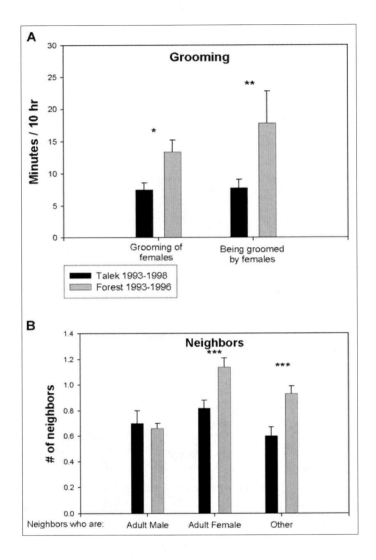

Figure 2. Quality of Affiliative Behaviors

(A) Amount of grooming involving adult males in Forest Troop 1993–1996 and Talek Troop 1993–1996. The first pair of columns represents mean time adult males spent grooming adult females; the second pair, mean time adult males were groomed by adult females.

(B) Comparison of average number of neighbors (i.e., within 3 m) of adult males in the two troops. Mean ± SEM. *, **, and *** indicate p < 0.05, 0.02, and 0.01, respectively, by unpaired t-test. Data were derived from a total of ten different males and 17 different females in F93–96, 31 different males and 21 different females in T93–98, and 19 different males and 23 different females in F79–82.

DOI: 10.1371/journal.pbio.0020106.g002

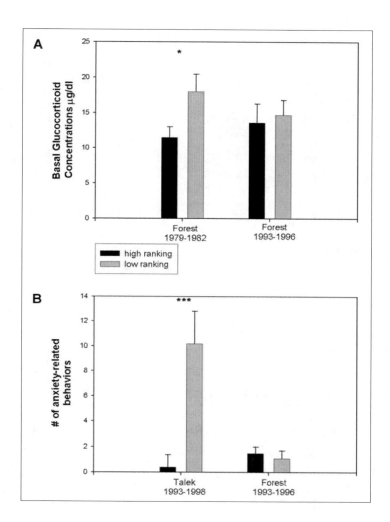

Figure 3. Stress-Related Physiological Profiles

(A) Basal glucocorticoid levels (ug/100 ml). Males were split into higher-and lower-ranking 50%, by approach–avoidance criteria. The primate glucocorticoid, cortisol, was measured by radioimmunoassay.

*(B) Number of anxiety-related behaviors observed 10–20 min after ß-carboline-3-carboxylic acid administration (M-156, Research Bio-chemicals International, Natick, Massachusetts, United States), after subtracting the number observed 10–20 min after vehicle administration (dextrin in 1 ml saline); 0.5 g of the drug in 1ml saline was delivered intramuscularly by dart syringe (Pneu-Dart, Inc., Williamsport, Pennsylvania, United States) fired from a blowgun at 5 m. Mean ± SEM. * and *** indicate* p < 0.05 *and* p < 0.01, *respectively, by unpaired t-test. Data were derived from a total of ten different males in F93–96, 31 different males in T93–98, and 18 different males in F79–82.*

DOI: 10.1371/journal.pbio.0020106.g003

Subordinate F93–96 males were spared another stress-related physiological marker. Experimental anxiety was induced by darting males, intramuscularly, with b-carboline-3-carboxylic acid, a benzodiazepine receptor antagonist which induces behavioral and physiological indices of anxiety in primates (benzodiazepine receptors bind tranquilizers such as valium and librium and mediate their anxiolytic effects)(Ninan et al. 1982). Males were darted on days when they had not had a fight, injury or mating. As a control, they were darted on separate days with vehicle alone (order of dartings randomized). Males were then monitored by an observer unaware of treatment.

ß-carboline-3-carboxylic acid had no effect on behavior in high-ranking males in T93–98 or F93–96 (Figure 3B).The drug increased anxiety-related behaviors in low-ranking males in T93–98 but not in F93–96 (the recorded anxiety-related behaviors were self-scratching, rhythmic head shaking, assuming a vigilant stance, repeated wiping of nose, and jaw grinding in a solitary male [Ninan et al. 1982; Aureli and van Schaik 1991; Castles et al. 1999]).

Thus, in the more typical F79–82 and T93–98 troops, subordination had distinctive stress-related physiological correlates. In contrast, F93–96 males lacked these rank-related differences.

POTENTIAL MECHANISMS UNDERLYING TRANSMISSION OF THIS CULTURE

A decade after the deaths of the more aggressive males in the troop, Forest Troop preserved a distinct social milieu accompanied by distinct physiological correlates. Critically, as noted, no adult males in F93-96 had been troop members at the end of the tuberculosis outbreak. Instead, these males had subsequently transferred in as adolescents, adopting the local social style. A number of investigators have emphasized how a tolerant and gregarious social setting facilitates social transmission (e.g., van Schaik et al. 1999), exactly the conditions in F93-96.

The present case of social transmission is reminiscent of some prior cases. For example, juvenile rhesus monkeys (*Macaca mulatta*) housed with stumptail macaques (*M. artoides*) assume the latter's more conciliatory style (de Waal and Johanowicz 1993). Moreover, anubis baboons (*Papio anubis*) and hamadryas baboons (*P. hamadryas*) differ in social structure, and females of either species experimentally transferred into a group of the other adopt the novel social structure within hours (Kummer 1971).

Several models have been hypothesized to explain transmission of cultures (Whiten et al. 1999; de Waal 2001; Galef 1990). For clarity, it is useful to first consider their application to an established example of transmission of a "technology" before then applying them to the transmission of the social milieu of F93-96. An example of the former is the nut cracking with stone hammers by West African chimpanzees (Boesch and Boesch 1983; Boesch 2003), a trait transmitted transgenerationally.

In "instructional models" of chimpanzee tool use, young are actively taught hammer use. In the case of F93-96, instructional models would involve new transfer males being subject to socially rewarding interactions (e.g., grooming) or aversive ones (e.g., supplantation or attack) contingent upon their assimilating the troop tradition. In such models, a key question is who "instructs." Much as with the term "culture" being used with respect to animal behavior, the use of the term "instruction" has also generated some controversy, with some preferring the concept of "active behavioral modification" by others bringing about the change. As a striking example of that, when young male cowbirds learn to produce their local song, they initially produce an undifferentiated repertoire of songs, and females react to the production of appropriate dialect with copulation solicitation displays, thus providing positive reinforcement and shaping those behaviors (Smith et al. 2000).

In "observational models" applied to chimpanzee tool use, young learn nut cracking by observing and copying adults. As applied to F93–96, transfer males would model behavior upon that of resident males.

In "facilitation models" of the chimpanzee example, proximity to adults and their hammers increases the likelihood of the young experimenting with hammers and deriving the skill themselves. As applied to the baboons, male F93–96 behaviors would be an implicit default state where, in the absence of the more typical rates of male aggression (either male–male or male–female), females broadly tend to become more affiliative, and in the context of more affiliative female behavior, transfer males broadly tend to become less aggressive. As perhaps a way of stating the same, the default state may emerge because of the atmosphere of a troop with a high female:male ratio (with less need for male competition for access to estrus females).

Finally, a "self-selection model" may apply to the baboons, in which particular kinds of males were more prone to transfer into such a troop (note that the fact that males transferred in from an array of surrounding troops rules out the possibility of an additional model, in which the culture was continued by genetic means).

We assessed these models by analyzing cases where adolescent males transferred on known dates and were observed for at least 2–6 mo afterward. Thus, we searched for behavioral patterns involving new transfer males that might differ between F93–96 (five such transfers) and T93–98/F79–82 (12 transfers).

Many interactions involving new transfer males did not differ (Table 4). Transfer males in F93–96, T93–98, and F79– 82 all attacked and supplanted females from feeding or resting sites at equal rates. Moreover, despite the different dominance structure among resident F93–96 males, resident males in F93–96, T93–98, and F79–82 all treated new transfer males similarly. There were similar latencies until transfer males were first lunged at by residents, and transfer males were involved in dominance and aggressive interactions at similar rates in all three troops (note that because there were half as many resident males in F93–96 as in T93–98 or F79–82, the rate of such interactions within any given resident/transfer male dyad would differ). We examined instances where resident males

Table 4. *Behaviors of Newly Transferred Males*

Behavior	F93–96	T93–98/F79–82	Statistical Significance
Rate of aggressive displacements by transfer males onto females (per 100 h)	7 ± 5	15 ± 6	n.s.
Rate of supplantations of females by transfer males (per 100 h)	26 ± 17	18 ± 7	n.s.
Latency (in days) until transfer male first lunged at by resident male	34 ± 20	52 ± 25	n.s.
Rate of dominance interactions between a transfer male and resident males (per 100 h)	142 ± 17	133 ± 36	n.s.
Rate of aggressive interactions between a transfer male and resident males (per 100 h)	5 ± 3	9 ± 4	n.s.

Subjects consisted of the five transfer males in F93–96 and the 12 in T93–98/F79–82. DOI: 10.1371/journal.pbio.0020106.t004

acted aggressively towards transfer males, determining whether such behaviors were more prevalent during the 20 min after aggressive behavior by the transfer male than at other, randomly selected times (de Waal and Yoshihara 1983; de Waal and Johanowicz 1993). We found no evidence for such contingent behavior (data not shown).

We then examined affiliative interactions between females and new transfer males, and found striking differences between F93–96 and T93–98/F79–82, in that F93–96 females treated new transfer males in the same affiliative manner that they treated resident males. F93–96 transfer males had a shorter latency until first being groomed by or presented to by a female than did T93–98/F79–82 transfer males (Figure 4A). (The differences between F93–96 and T93–98 did not arise from a single F93–96 female accounting for the much shorter latencies until presentation and grooming: three different females accounted for the first interactions with the five F93–96 transfer males). Moreover, F93–96 transfers sat in closer proximity to and had more grooming bouts with females than did T93–98/F79–82 transfers (Figure 4B). While estrous females are more likely than nonestrous females to interact with transfer males (Smuts 1999), the percentage of females in estrus did not differ among the troops (see above). In addition, F93–96 females did not seem to treat transfer males in a contingent manner (de Waal and Yoshihara 1983; de Waal and Johanowicz 1993). To test for this, we first examined instances where resident females were affiliative towards transfer males, determining whether this was more likely during the 20 min following an affiliative behavior on the part of the transfer male than at other, randomly selected times. Second, we determined whether females were less likely to be

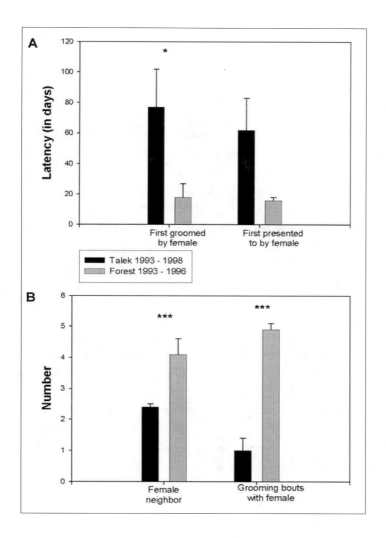

Figure 4. Quality of Interactions Between Resident Females and Transfer Males

(A) Latency, in days, until a newly transferred male is first groomed by a female (left) or presented to by a female (right).

(B) Average number of adult female neighbors per scan (i.e., within 3 m; left) and average number of grooming bouts with females per 100 h of observation (right) for transfer males. Mean ± SEM. * and *** indicate $p < 0.05$ and $p < 0.01$, respectively, by unpaired t-test. Latency until first presented to by a female approached significance ($p < 0.08$). Data were derived from a total of ten different males and 17 different females in F93–96, and 31 different males and 21 different females in T93–98.

DOI: 10.1371/journal.pbio.0020106.g004

affiliative during the 20 min following an aggressive behavior on the part of a transfer male. We found no evidence for either pattern (data not shown).

These data allow some insight as to the mechanisms of social transmission in F93–96 (without remotely allowing an analysis fine-grained enough to see whether these mechanisms were equally relevant to the transmission of all the components of the F93–96 culture, namely the low rates of male aggression, the high rates of female affiliation, and the relaxed dominance structure). The lack of contingency in the treatment of transfer males by residents argues against instruction; commensurate with this, there is relatively little evidence for "instruction" in nonhuman primate cultural transmission (de Waal 2001; for an exception, see Boesch 1991). The similar rates of displacement behaviors by transfer males onto females in all three troops argue against self-selection (i.e., the possibility that F93–96 transfer males already behaved differently than transfer males elsewhere).

This is not surprising. While adolescent male baboons may transfer repeatedly before choosing a troop (Pusey and Packer 1986), as well as later in life (Sapolsky 1996), we have seen little evidence among these animals of the systematic sampling of different troops required by a self-selection model.

The data instead support either observational or facilitative/default models. Insofar as resident males in all troops interacted with transfer males similarly, transmission in F93–96 could have involved observation only if such observations were of how resident males interacted with females or each other. Some, but not all, studies support observational models of social transmission in other primates (Visalberghi and Fragaszy 1990; Whiten 1998; Boesch 2003; Whiten et al. 2003); there are few data at present from baboons concerning this issue. As shown, F93–96 transfer males were had high rates of affiliative interactions with females. The preponderance of females in F93–96 is a plausible explanation for their unconditional (or, at least, less conditional) increase in tolerance of and affiliation with males (including transfer males), insofar as males in the troop had less numeric means to be aggressive to females. (Note that this skewed sex ratio continues in this troop to the present, for unknown reasons.) Thus, affilative data support a facilitative/default model only if it involves preferential sensitivity to the quality of interactions with females.

This analysis raises the possibility that there is no social transmission, but that the F93–96 pattern is merely the emergent outcome of the 2:1 female:male ratio. To test this, we analyzed the five available studies of baboon troops with adult female:male ratios of 2 or more which contained quantitative data comparable to the present data (Seyfarth 1976, 1978; Strum 1982; Bercovitch 1985; Noe 1994). The key question was whether those prior data more closely resembled those of F93–96 or the control troops. Previous data more closely resembled, and did not differ significantly from, data from the control troops for the percentage of time males groomed females (based on Seyfarth 1978), the percentage of time females groomed males (Seyfarth 1978), the rate of intersexual aggression (Seyfarth 1976, 1978), the structure of male–male dominance (Noe 1995), or the structure of male–male aggression (Strum 1982; Bercovitch 1985). In contrast, no quantitative measures more closely resembled F93–96. This strongly suggests that the F93–96 pattern is unique and is being uniquely maintained, rather than being the social structure that automatically emerges whenever a female-skewed female:male ratio occurs. Thus, insofar as a facilitative/default model is operating in this troop, it cannot be a relative paucity of males which "activates" a default state; instead, it would likely be the paucity of aggressive males.

The unconditional (or less conditional) nature of the default model is puzzling, in that it requires that females be relatively affiliative to recent transfer males who, nonetheless, are initially aggressive to them. This seems counter to the long-standing emphasis in primatology on individual relations (i.e., females are unlikely to be unable to distinguish between relatively unaggressive resident males and relatively aggressive newly transferred males). Precedent for this unexpected implication comes from the social epidemiology literature concerning "social capital," in which health and life expectancy increase in a community as a function of community wide attributes that transcend the level of the individual or individual social networks (Kawachi et al 1997).

In summary, we have observed circumstances that produced a distinctive set of behaviors and physiological correlates in a troop of wild baboons. Moreover, these behaviors were taken on by new troop members; while obviously not conclusive, the data suggest that this most likely occurs through observational or facilitative/default models. Finally, somewhat uniquely in nonhuman primate studies, these findings concern the intergenerational transfer of social, rather than material culture.

These findings raise some issues. There appear to be adverse health consequences of the stress-related physiological profile of subordination in typical baboon troops (Sapolsky 1993; Sapolsky and Share 1994; Sapolsky and Spencer 1997). The distinctive rank-related patterns of physiology in F93–96 suggest that subordinate males in that troop may be spared those pathologies. Another issue concerns the consequences of the culture of F93–96 remaining stable over some time. A hallmark of human culture is that it is cumulative (i.e., innovations are built upon each other), and there is only scant evidence, at best, for the same in nonhuman primates (Boesch 2003). It would thus be interesting to see if additional features of the F93–96 social tradition emerge with time.

A converse issue concerns circumstances that might destroy the F93–96 culture. The culture might be destroyed if numerous males transfer into the troop simultaneously, or if a male transfers in who, rather than assuming the F93–96 culture, instead takes advantage of it. Game theory suggests that F93–96 would be vulnerable to such "cheating." Another issue concerns the fate of natal males from F93–96 when they transfer elsewhere. Reciprocal altruism models (Axelrod and Hamilton, 1981) suggest that if one F93–96 male transfers elsewhere and continues his natal behavioral style, he will be at a competitive disadvantage. However, should two F93–96 males simultaneously join another troop and maintain F93– 96–typical interactions between them, they might be at a competitive advantage. This might represent a means to transmit this social style between troops.

Finally, these findings raise the issue of their applicability to understanding human social behavior and its transmission. Human history is filled with examples of the selective loss of demographic subsets of societies (e.g., the relative paucity of adult men following the American Civil War or the relative paucity of girls in contemporary China due to male-biased reproductive technology practices and female-biased infanticide). The present data suggest that demographic skews may have long-term, even multigenerational consequences, including significant changes in the quality of life in a social group.

MATERIALS AND METHODS

Subjects were a troop, Forest Troop, of olive baboons (*Papio anubis*) living in the Masai Mara Reserve of Kenya. Olive baboons live in multimale troops of 30–150 animals, with polygamy and considerable male–male aggression. Males change troops at puberty and, as adults, achieve ranks in somewhat fluid dominance hierarchies. In contrast, females remain in their natal troop, inheriting a rank one below that of their mother.

Subjects were observed each summer from 1978–1986, and continuously since 1993. An additional troop, Talek Troop, was observed continuously since 1984. Behavioral data were collected as 20-min focal samples (Altmann 1974). During years of only summer observation (Forest Troop, 1978–1986), 45 samples were collected per subject per season; otherwise, an average of three samples per subject per week were collected throughout the year. Sampling was distributed throughout the day in the same fashion for each individual. During samples, social behavior, feeding, and grooming were recorded. Rankings were derived from approach–avoidance interactions, which included avoidances, supplants, and presentations, in the absence of aggression. Escalated aggression included open-mouthed lunges, chases, and bites. Nearest neighbor scans were done before and after each sample.

Reproductive success was indirectly estimated from frequencies of matings and consortships (maintenance of exclusive mating with and proximity to an estrous female for at least one sample). The value of any given consortship or mating was adjusted by the probability of a fertile mating occurring that day (Hendrickx and Kraemer 1969).

Endocrine data were collected under circumstances allowing for measures of basal steroid hormone levels (Sapolsky and Share 1997). Subjects were darted unaware with anesthetic from a blowgun syringe between 7 A.M. and 10 A.M., and only on days on which they were not sick, injured, in a consortship, or had not recently had a fight. Blood samples were collected within 3 min of anesthetization.

REFERENCES

Altmann J (1974) Observational study of behavior: Sampling methods. Behaviour 48: 1–33.

Aureli F, van Schaik C (1991) Post-conflict behaviour in long-tailed macaques (*Macaca fascicularis*). I. The social events. Ethology 89: 89–100.

Axelrod R, Hamilton W (1981) The evolution of cooperation. Science 211:1390–1396.

Bercovitch F (1985) Reproductive tactics in adult female and adult male olive baboons [dissertation]. Los Angeles: University of California, Los Angeles. p. 235.

Boesch C (1991) Teaching in wild chimpanzees. Anim Behav 41: 530–532.

Boesch C (2003) Is culture a golden barrier between human and chimpanzee? Evol Anthropol 12: 82–91.

Boesch C, Boesch H (1983) Optimization of nut-cracking with natural hammers by wild chimpanzees [*Pan troglodytes verus*]. Behaviour 83: 265–286.

Cambefort J (1981) A comparative study of culturally transmitted patterns of feeding habits in the chacma baboon *Papio ursinus* and the vervet monkey *Cercopithecus aethiops*. Folia Primatol 36: 243–263.

Castles D, Whiten A, Aureli F (1999) Social anxiety, relationships and self-directed behaviour among wild female olive baboons. Anim Behav 58: 1207–1215.

Cavalli-Sforza L (2000) Genes, peoples and languages. New York: North Point Press. p. 224.

Cheney D, Seyfarth R, Silk J (1995) The role of grunts in reconciling opponents and facilitating interactions among adult female baboons. Anim Behav 50: 249–257.

Crook J, Gartlan J (1966) Evolution of primate societies. Nature 210: 1200–1203. de Waal F (1983) Chimpanzee politics: Power and sex among apes. Baltimore (Maryland): Johns Hopkins University Press. p. 223.

de Waal F (2000) Primates: A natural heritage of conflict resolution. Science 289: 586–590.

de Waal F (2001) The ape and the sushi master: Cultural reflections of a primatologist. New York: Basic Books. p. 256

de Waal F, Johanowicz D (1993) Modification of reconciliation behavior through social experience: An experiment with two macaque species. Child Dev 64: 897–908.

de Waal F, van Roosmalen A (1979) Reconciliation and consolidation among chimpanzees. Behav Ecol Sociobiol 5: 55–71.

de Waal F, Yoshihara D (1983) Reconciliation and redirected affection in rhesus monkeys. Behaviour 85: 224–241.

Galef B (1990) The question of animal culture. Hum Nature 3: 157–178.

Hendrickx I, Kraemer D (1969) Observations on the menstrual cycle, optimal mating time and pre-implantation embryos of the baboon, Papio anubis and Papio cynocephalus. J Reprod Fertil (Suppl.) 6: 119–131.

Kawachi I, Kennedy B, Lochner K, Prothrow-Stith D (1997) Social capital, income inequality, and mortality. Am J Public Health 87: 1491–1498.

Kawai M (1965) Newly acquired precultural behavior of the natural troop of Japanese monkeys on Kishima Islet. Primates 6: 1–30.

Kroeber A, Kluckhohn C (1966) Culture: A critical review of concepts and definitions. New York: Random House. p. 223

Kummer H (1971) Primate societies: Group techniques of ecological adaptation. Wheeling (Illinois): Harlan Davidson, Inc. 160 p. Laland K, Hoppitt W (2003) Do animals have culture? Evol Anthropol 12: 150–159.

Laland K, Reader S (1999) Foraging innovation in the guppy. Anim Behav 52:331–340.

McGrew W (1998) Culture in non-human primates? Annu Rev Anthropol 27: 301–328.

Mercader J, Panger M, Boesch C (2002) Excavation of a chimpanzee stone tool site in the African rainforest. Science 296: 1452–1455.

Ninan P, Insel T, Cohen R, Cook J, Skolnick P, et al. (1982) Benzodiazepine receptor-mediated experimental "anxiety" in primates. Science 218: 1332–1334.

Noad M, Cato D, Bryden M, Jenner M, Jenner K (2000) Cultural revolution in whale songs. Nature 408: 537–538.

Noe R (1994) A model of coalition formation among male baboons with fighting ability as the crucial parameter. Anim Behav 47: 211–224.

Perry S, Baker M, Fedigan L, Gros-Louis J, Jack K, et al. (2003) Social conventions in wild white-faced capuchin monkeys: Evidence for traditions in a neotropical primate. Curr Anthropol 44: 241–268.

Pusey A, Packer C (1986) Dispersal and philopatry. In: Smuts B, Cheney D, Seyfarth R, Wrangham R, Struhsaker T, editors. Primate societies. Chicago: University of Chicago Press. pp. 250–266.

Rendell L, Whitehead H (2001) Culture in whales and dolphins. Brain Behav Sci 24: 309–382.

Sapolsky R (1993) Endocrinology alfresco: Psychoendocrine studies of wild baboons. Recent Prog Horm Res 48: 437.

Sapolsky R (1996) Why should an aged male baboon transfer troops? Am J Primatol 39: 149–155.

Sapolsky R (2001) The physiological and pathophysiological implications of social stress in mammals. In: McEwen B, editor. Coping with the environment: Neural and endocrine mechanisms. Volume 4, Section 7, Handbook of physiology. Oxford: Oxford University Press. p. 517.

Sapolsky R, Else J (1987) Bovine tuberculosis in a wild baboon population: Epidemiological aspects. J Med Primatol 16: 229–234.

Sapolsky R, Share L (1994) Rank-related differences in cardiovascular function among wild baboons: Role of sensitivity to glucocorticoids. Am J Primatol 32: 261–270.

Sapolsky R, Share L (1997) Darting terrestrial primates in the wild: A primer. Am J Primatol 44: 155–163.

Sapolsky R, Spencer E (1997) Social subordinance is associated with suppression of insulin-like growth factor I (IGF-I) in a population of wild primates. Am J Physiol 273: R1346.

Sapolsky R, Romero L, Munck A (2000) How do glucocorticoids influence the stress-response? Integrating permissive, suppressive, stimulatory, and preparative actions. Endocr Rev 21: 55–78.

Seyfarth R (1976) Social relationships among adult female baboons. Anim Behav 24: 917–938.

Seyfarth R (1978) Social relationships among adult male and female baboons. II. Behaviour throughout the female reproductive cycle. Behaviour 64: 227–247.

Smith V, King A, West J (2000) A role of her own: Female cowbirds, Molothrus ater, influence the development and outcome of song learning. Anim Behav 60: 599–609.

Smuts B (1999) Sex and friendship in baboons, 2nd ed. Cambridge (Massachusetts): Harvard University Press. 336 p.

Strum S (1982) Agonistic dominance in male baboons: An alternative view. Int J Primatol 3: 175–188.

Tarara R, Suleman M, Sapolsky R, Wabomba M, Else J (1985) Tuberculosis in wild olive baboons, Papio cynocephalus anubis (Lesson), in Kenya. J Wildlife Dis 21: 137–144.

van Schaik C, Deaner R, Merrill M (1999) The conditions for tool use in primates: Implications for the evolution of material culture. J Hum Evol 36: 719–741.

van Schaik C, Ancrenaz M, Borgen G, Galdikas B, Knott C, et al. (2003) Orangutan cultures and the evolution of material culture. Science 299: 102–105.

Visalberghi E, Fragaszy D (1990) Food-washing behaviour in tufted capuchin monkeys, Cebus apella, and crab-eating macaques, Macaca fascicularis. Anim Behav 40: 829–836.

Whiten A (1998) Imitation of the sequential structure of actions by chimpanzees (Pan troglodytes) J Comp Psychol 112: 270–281.

Whiten A, Goodall J, McGrew W, Nishida T, Reynolds V, et al. (1999) Culture in chimpanzees. Nature 399: 682–685.

Whiten A, Horner V, Marshall-Pescini S (2003) Cultural panthropology. Evol Anthropol 12: 92–105.

ACKNOWLEDGMENTS

We thank the Office of the President, Republic of Kenya, for permission to carry out this work, and the John Templeton Foundation and Harry Frank Guggenheim Foundation for generous funding. Field assistance was provided by David Brooks, Denise Costich, Richard Kones, Francis Onchiri, Hudson Oyaro, and Reed Sutherland. Assistance with data analysis was provided by Milena Banjevic, Elle Behrstock, Margaret Crofoot, and Elizabeth Gordon. Helpful discussions were had with Geoffrey Miller and Frank Sulloway, and manuscript assistance was provided by Frans de Waal, Barbara Smuts, and Joan Silk.

Conflicts of interest. The authors have declared that no conflicts of interest exist.

Author contributions. RMS and LJS conceived, designed, and performed the experiments. RMS analyzed the data and contributed reagents/materials/analysis tools. RMS and LJS wrote the paper.

PART IV

HUMANITY IN ECOLOGICAL AND ECONOMIC PERSPECTIVE

THE CULTURAL ECOLOGY OF INDIA'S SACRED CATTLE

Marvin Harris

In this paper I attempt to indicate certain puzzling inconsistencies in prevailing interpretations of the ecological role of bovine cattle in India. My argument is based upon intensive reading—I have never seen a sacred cow, nor been to India. As a non-specialist, no doubt I have committed blunders an Indianist would have avoided. I hope these errors will not deprive me of that expert advice and informed criticism which alone can justify so rude an invasion of unfamiliar territory.

I have written this paper because I believe the irrational, non-economic, and exotic aspects of the Indian cattle complex are greatly overemphasized at the expense of rational, economic, and mundane interpretations.

My intent is not to substitute one dogma for another, but to urge that explanation of taboos, customs, and rituals associated with management of Indian cattle be sought in "positive-functioned" and probably "adaptive" processes of the ecological system of which they are a part,[1] rather than in the influence of Hindu theology.

---

[1] The author (1960) suggested that the term "adaptive" be restricted to traits, biological or cultural, established and diffused in conformity with the principle of natural selection. Clearly, not all "positive-functioned," i.e., useful, cultural traits are so established.

Marvin Harris, Nirmal K. Bose, Morton Klass, Joan P. Mencher, Kalervo Oberg, Marvin K. Opler, Wayne Suttles, and Andrew P. Vayda, "The Cultural Ecology of India's Sacred Cattle," from *Current Anthropology*, Vol. 7, No. 1; February 1966, pp. 51–66. Copyright © 1966 by University of Chicago Press–Journals. Permission to reprint granted by the publisher.

Mismanagement of India's agricultural resources as a result of the Hindu doctrine of *ahimsa*[2] especially as it applies to beef cattle, is frequently noted by Indianists and others concerned with the relation between values and behavior. Although different anti-rational, dysfunctional, and inutile aspects of the cattle complex are stressed by different authors, many agree that *ahimsa* is a prime example of how men will diminish their material welfare to obtain spiritual satisfaction in obedience to nonrational or frankly irrational beliefs.

A sample opinion on this subject is here summarized: According to Simoons (1961:3), "irrational ideologies" frequently compel men "to overlook foods that are abundant locally and are of high nutritive value, and to utilize other scarcer foods of less value." The Hindu beef-eating taboo is one of Simoons' most important cases. Venkatraman (1938:706) claims, "India is unique in possessing an enormous amount of cattle without making profit from its slaughter." The Ford Foundation (1959:64) reports "widespread recognition not only among animal husbandry officials, but among citizens generally, that India's cattle population is far in excess of the available supplies of fodder and feed … At least 1/3, and possibly as many as 1/2, of the Indian cattle population may be regarded. as surplus in relation to feed supply." Matson (1933:227) writes it is a commonplace of the "cattle question that vast numbers of Indian cattle are so helplessly inefficient as to have no commercial value beyond that of their hides." Srinivas (1952:222) believes "Orthodox Hindu opinion regards the killing of cattle with abhorrence, even though the refusal to kill the vast number of useless cattle which exist in India today is detrimental to the nation."

According to the Indian Ministry of Information (1957:243), "The large animal population is more a liability than an asset in view of our land resources." Chatterjee (1960) calculates that Indian production of cow and buffalo milk involves a "heavy recurring loss of Rs 774 crores. This is equivalent to 6.7 times the amount we are annually spending on importing food grains." Knight (1954:141) observes that because the Hindu religion teaches great reverence for the cow, "there existed a large number of cattle whose utility to the community did not justify economically the fodder which they consumed." Das and Chatterji (1962:120) concur: "A large number of cattle in India are old and decrepit and constitute a great burden on an already impoverished land. This is due to the prejudice among the Hindus against cow killing." Mishra (1962) approvingly quotes Lewis (1955:106): "It is not true that if economic and religious doctrines conflict the economic interest will always win. The Hindu cow has remained sacred for centuries, although this is plainly contrary to economic interest." Darling (1934:158) asserts, "By its attitude to slaughter Hinduism makes any planned improvement of cattle-breeding almost impossible." According to Desai (1959:36), "The cattle population is far in excess of the available fodder and feeds."

---

[2] *Ahimsa* is the Hindu principle of unity of life, of which sacredness of cattle is principal sub-case and symbol.

In the *Report of the Expert Committee on the Prevention of Slaughter of Cattle in India* (Nandra, *et al.* 1955:62), the Cattle Preservation and Development Committee estimated "20 million uneconomic cattle in India." Speaking specifically of Madras, Randhawa (1961:118) insists, "Far too many useless animals which breed indiscriminately are kept and many of them are allowed to lead a miserable existence for the sake of the dung they produce. Sterility and prolonged dry periods among cows due to neglect add to the number of superfluous cattle ..." Mamoria (1953:268–69) quotes with approval the report of the Royal Commission on Agriculture: "... religious susceptibilities lie in the way of slaughter of decrepit and useless cattle and hence the cattle, however weak and poor are allowed to live ... bulls wander about the fields consuming or damaging three times as much fodder as they need ... Unless the Hindu sentiment is abjured altogether the Indian cultivators cannot take a practical view of animal keeping and will continue to preserve animals many of which are quite useless from birth to death." Despite his own implicit arguments to the contrary, Mohan (1962:54) concludes, "We have a large number of surplus animals." The National Council of Applied Economic Research (1963:51) notes in Rajasthan: "The scarcity of fodder is aggravated by a large population of old and useless cattle which share scant feed resources with working and useful cattle."

The Food and Agriculture Organization (1953:109) reports, "In India, as is well-known, cattle numbers exceed economic requirements by any standard and a reduction in the number of uneconomic animals would contribute greatly to the possibilities of improving the quality and condition of those that remain." Kardel (1956:19) reported to the International Cooperation Administration, "Actually, India's 180 million cattle and 87 million sheep and goats are competing with 360 million people for a scant existence." According to Mosher (1946:124), "There are thousands of barren heifers in the Central Doab consuming as much feed as productive cows, whose only economic produce will be their hides, after they have died of a natural cause." Mayadas (1954:28) insists "Large herds of emaciated and completely useless cattle stray about trying to eke out an existence on wholly inadequate grazing." Finally, to complete the picture of how, in India, spirit triumphs over flesh, there is the assertion by Williamson and Payne (1959:137): "The ... Hindu would rather starve to death than eat his cow."

In spite of the sometimes final and unqualified fashion in which "surplus," "useless," "uneconomic," and "superfluous" are applied to part or all of India's cattle, contrary conclusions seem admissible when the cattle complex is viewed as part of an *ecosystem* rather than as a sector of a national price market. Ecologically, it is doubtful that any component of the cattle complex is "useless," i.e., the number, type, and condition of Indian bovines do not per se impair the ability of the human population to survive and reproduce. Much more likely the relationship between bovines and humans is symbiotic[3] instead of competitive. It probably represents the outcome of intense Darwinian pressures acting upon human and bovine population, cultigens, wild flora and fauna, and social structure and ideology. Moreover presumably the degree of observance of taboos against bovine slaughter and beef-eating reflect the power of these ecological pressures rather than *ahimsa;* in other words, *ahimsa* itself derives power and sustenance from the material rewards it confers upon both men and animals. To support these hypotheses, the major aspects of the Indian cattle complex will be reviewed under the following heading: (1) Milk Production, (2) Traction, (3) Dung, (4) Beef and Hides, (5) Pasture, (6) Useful and Useless Animals, (7) Slaughter, (8) Anti-Slaughter Legislation, (9) Old-Age Homes, and (10) Natural Selection.

MILK PRODUCTION

In India the average yield of whole milk per Zebu cow is 413 pounds, compared with the 5,000-pound average in Europe and the U.S.[4] (Kartha 1936:607; Spate 1954:231). In Madhya Pradesh yield is as low as 65 pounds, while in no state does it rise higher than the barely respectable 1,445 pounds of the Punjab (Chatterjee 1960:1347). According to the 9th Quinquennial Livestock Census (1961) among the 47,200,000 cows over 3 years old, 27,200,000 were dry and/or not calved (Chaudri and Giri 1963:598).

These figures, however should not be used to prove that the cows are useless or uneconomic, since milk production is a minor aspect of the sacred cow's contribution to the *ecosystem.* Indeed, most Indianists agree that it is the buffalo, not the Zebu, whose economic worth must be judged primarily by milk production. Thus, Kartha (1959:225) writes, "the buffalo, and not the Zebu, is the dairy cow." This distinction is elaborated by Mamoria (1953:255):

> Cows in the rural areas are maintained for producing bullocks rather than for milk. She-buffaloes, on the other hand, are considered to be better dairy animals than cows. The male buffaloes are neglected and many of them die or are sold for slaughter before they attain maturity.

---

[3] According to Zeuner (1954:328), "Symbiosis includes all conditions of the living-together of two different species, provided both derive advantages therefrom. Cases in which both partners benefit equally are rare." In the symbiosis under consideration, *men* benefit more than cattle.

[4] The U.S. Census of Agriculture (1954) showed milk production averaging from a low of 3,929 pounds per cow in the Nashville Basin sub-region to 11,112 pounds per cow in the Southern California sub-region.

Mohan (1962:47) makes the same point:

> For agricultural purposes bullocks are generally preferred, and, therefore, cows in rural areas are primarily maintained for the production of male progeny and incidentally only for milk.

It is not relevant to my thesis to establish whether milk production is a primary or secondary objective or purpose of the Indian farmer. Failure to separate emics from etics (Harris 1964) contributes greatly to confusion surrounding the Indian cattle question. The significance of the preceding quotations lies in the agreement that cows contribute to human material welfare in more important ways than milk production. In this new context, the fact that U.S. cows produce 20 times more milk than Indian cows loses much of its significance. Instead, it is more relevant to note that, despite the marginal status of milking in the symbiotic syndrome, 46.7% of India's dairy products come from cow's milk (Chatterjee 1960: 1347). How far this production is balanced by expenditures detrimental to human welfare will be discussed later.

TRACTION

The principal positive ecological effect of India's bovine cattle is in their contribution to production of grain crops, from which about 80% of the human calorie ration comes. Some form of animal traction is required to initiate the agricultural cycle, dependent upon plowing in both rainfall and irrigation areas. Additional traction for hauling, transport, and irrigation is provided by animals, but by far their most critical kinetic contribution is plowing.

Although many authorities believe there is an overall surplus of cattle in India, others point to a serious shortage of draught animals. According to Kothavala (1934:122), "Even with ... overstocking, the draught power available for land operations at the busiest season of the-year is inadequate ..." For West Bengal, the National Council of Applied Economic Research (1962:56) reports:

> However, despite the large number of draught animals, agriculture in the State suffers from a shortage of draught power. There are large numbers of small landholders entirely dependent on hired animal labour.

Spate (1954:36) makes the same point, "There are too many cattle in the gross, but most individual farmers have too few to carry on with." Gupta (1959:42) and Lewis and Barnouw (1958:102) say a pair of bullocks is the minimum technical unit for cultivation, but in a survey by Diskalkar (1960:87), 18% of the cultivators had only 1 bullock or none. Nationally, if we accept a low estimate of 60,000,000 rural households (Mitra 1963:298) and a high estimate of 80,000,000 working cattle and buffaloes (Government of India 1962:76), we see at once that the allegedly excess number of cattle in India is insufficient to permit a large portion, perhaps as many as 1/3, of India's farmers to begin the agricultural cycle under conditions appropriate to their techno-environmental system.

Much has been made of India's having 115 head of cattle per square mile, compared with *28* per square mile for the U.S. and 3 per square mile for Canada. But what actually may be most characteristic of the size of India's herd is the low ratio of cattle to people. Thus, India has 44 cattle per 100 persons, while in the U.S. the ratio is 58 per 100 and in Canada, 90 (Mamoria 1953:256). Yet, in India cattle are employed as a basic instrument of agricultural production.

Sharing of draught animals on a cooperative basis might reduce the need for additional animals. Chaudhri and Giri point out that the "big farmer manages to cultivate with a pair of bullock a much larger area than the small cultivators" (1963:596). But, the failure to develop cooperative forms of plowing can scarcely be traced to *ahimsa*. If anything, emphasis upon independent, family-sized farm units follows intensification of individual land tenure patterns and other property innovations deliberately encouraged by the British (Bhatia 1963:18 on). Under existing property arrangements, there is a perfectly good economic explanation of why bullocks are not shared among adjacent households. Plowing cannot take place at any time of the year, but must be accomplished within a few daylight hours in conformity with seasonal conditions. These are set largely by summer monsoons, responsible for about 90% of the total rainfall (Bhatia 1963:4). Writing about Orissa, Bailey (1957:74) notes:

> As a temporary measure, an ox might be borrowed from a relative, or a yoke of cattle and a ploughman might be hired … but during the planting season, when the need is the greatest, most people are too busy to hire out or lend cattle.

According to Desai (1948:86):

> … over vast areas, sowing and harvesting operations, by the very nature of things, begin simultaneously with the outbreak of the first showers and the maturing of crops respectively, and especially the former has got to be put through quickly daring the first phase of the monsoon. Under these circumstances, reliance by a farmer on another for bullocks is highly risky and he has got, therefore, to maintain his own pair.

Dube (1955:84) is equally specific:

The cultivators who depend on hired cattle or who practice cooperative lending and borrowing of cattle cannot take the best advantage of the first rains, and this enforced wait results in untimely sowing and poor crops.

Wiser and Wiser (1963:62) describe the plight of the bullock-short farmer as follows, "When he needs the help of bullocks most, his neighbors are all using theirs." And Shastri (1960:1592) points out, "Uncertainty of Indian farming due to dependence on rains is the main factor creating obstacles in the way of improvements in bullock labor."

It would seem, therefore, that this aspect of the cattle complex is not an expression of spirit and ritual, but of rain and energy.

DUNG

In India cattle dung is the main source of domestic cooking fuel. Since grain crops cannot be digested unless boiled or baked, cooking is indispensable. Considerable disagreement exists about the total amount of cattle excrement and its uses, but even the lowest estimates are impressive. An early estimate by Lupton (1922:60) gave the BTU equivalent of dung consumed in domestic cooking as 35,000,000 tons of coal or 68,000,000 tons of wood. Most detailed appraisal is by National Council of Applied Economic Research (1959:3), which rejects H. J. Bhabha's estimate of 131,000,000 tons of coal and the Ministry of Food and Agriculture's 112,000,000 tons. The figure preferred by the NCAER is 35,000,000 tons anthracite or 40,000,000 tons bituminous, but with a possible range of between 35–45,000,000 of anthracite dung-coal equivalent. This calculation depends upon indications that only 36% of the total wet dung is utilized as fuel (p. 14), a lower estimate than any reviewed by Saha (1956:923). These vary from 40% (Imperial Council on Agricultural Research) to 50% (Ministry of Food and Agriculture) to 66.6% (Department of Education, Health and Lands). The NCAER estimate of a dung-coal equivalent of 35,000,000 tons is therefore quite conservative; it is nonetheless an impressive amount of BTU's to be plugged into an energy system.

Kapp (1963:144 on), who discusses at length the importance of substituting tractors for bullocks, does not give adequate attention to finding cooking fuel after the bullocks are replaced. The NCAER (1959: 20) conclusion that dung is cheaper than coke seems an understatement. Although it is claimed that wood resources are potentially adequate to replace dung the measures advocated do not involve *ahimsa* but are again an indictment of a land tenure system not inspired by Hindu tradition (NCAER 1959:20 on; Bansil 1958:97 on). Finally, it should be noted that many observers stress the slow burning qualities of dung and its special appropriateness for preparation of *ghi* and deployment of woman-power in the household (Lewis and Barnouw 1958:40; Mosher 1946: 153).

As manure, dung enters the energy system in another vital fashion. According to Mujumdar (1960:743), 300,000,000 tons are used as fuel, 340,000,000 tons as manure, and 160,000,000 tons "wasted on hillsides and roads." Spate (1954:238) believes that 40% of dung production is spread on fields, 40% burned, and 20% "lost." Possibly estimates of the amount of dung lost are grossly inflated in view of the importance of "roads and hillsides" in the grazing pattern (see Pasture). (Similarly artificial and culture or even class-bound judgments refer to utilization of India's night soil. It is usually assumed that Chinese and Indian treatment of this resource are radically different, and that vast quantities of nitrogen go unused in agriculture because of Hindu-inspired definitions of modesty and cleanliness. However, most human excrement from Indian villages is deposited in surrounding fields; the absence of latrines helps explain why such fields raise 2 and 3 successive crops each year (Mosher 1946:154, 33; Bansil 1958: 104.) More than usual caution, therefore, is needed before concluding that a significant amount of cattle dung is wasted. Given the conscious premium set on dung for fuel and fertilizer, thoughtful control maintained over grazing patterns (see Pasture), and occurrence of specialized sweeper and gleaner castes, much more detailed evidence of wastage is needed than is now available. Since cattle graze on "hillsides and roads," dung dropped there would scarcely be totally lost to the *ecosystem,* even with allowance for loss of nitrogen by exposure to air and sunlight. Also, if any animal dung is wasted on roads and hillsides it is not because of *ahimsa* but of inadequate pasturage suitable for collecting and processing animal droppings. The sedentary, intensive rainfall agriculture of most of the subcontinent is heavily dependent upon manuring. So vital is this that Spate (1954:239) says substitutes for manure consumed as fuel "must be supplied, and lavishly, even at a financial loss to government." If this is the case, then old, decrepit, and dry animals might have a use after all, especially when, as we shall see, the dung they manufacture employs raw materials lost to the culture-energy system unless processed by cattle, and especially when many apparently moribund animals revive at the next monsoon and provide their owners with a male calf.

BEEF AND HIDES

Positive contributions of India's sacred cattle do not cease with milk-grazing, bullock-producing, traction, and dung-dropping. There remains the direct protein contribution of 25,000,000 cattle and buffalo which die each year (Mohan 1962:54). This feature of the *ecosystem* is reminiscent of the East African cattle area where, despite the normal taboo on slaughter, natural deaths and ceremonial occasions are probably frequent enough to maintain beef consumption near the ecological limit with dairying as the primary function (Schneider 1957:278 on). Although most Hinclus probably do not consume beef, the *ecosystem* under consideration is not confined to Hindus. The human population includes some 55,000,000 "scheduled" exterior or untouchable groups (Hutton 1961:VII), many of whom will consume beef if given the opportunity (Dube 1955:68–69), plus several million more Moslems and Christians. Much of the flesh on the 25,000,000 dead cattle and buffalo probably gets consumed by human beings whether or not the cattle die naturally. Indeed, could it be that without the orthodox Hindu beef-eating taboo, many marginal and depressed castes would be deprived of an occasional, but nutritionally critical, source of animal protein?

It remains to note that the slaughter taboo does not prevent depressed castes from utilizing skin, horns and hoofs of dead beasts. In 1956 16,000,000 cattle hides were produced (Randhawa 1962:322). The quality of India's huge leather industry—the world's largest—leaves much to be desired, but the problem is primarily outmoded tanning techniques and lack of capital, not *ahimsa*.

PASTURE

The principal postive-functioned or useful contributions of India's sacred cattle to human survival and well-being have been described. Final evaluation of their utility must involve assessment of energy costs in terms of resources and human labor input which might be more efficiently expended in other activities.

Direct and indirect evidence suggests that in India men and bovine cattle do not compete for existence. According to Mohan (1962:43on):

> … the bulk of the food on which the animals subsist … is not the food that is required for human consumption, i.e., fibrous fodders produced as incidental to crop production, and a large part of the crop residues or byproducts of seeds and waste grazing.

On the contrary, "the bulk of foods (straws and crop residues) that are ploughed into the soil in other countries are converted into milk" (p. 45).

> The majority of the Indian cattle obtain their requirements from whatever grazing is available from straw and stalk and other residues from human food-stuffs, and are starved seasonally in the dry months when grasses wither.

> In Bengal the banks and slopes of the embankments of public roads are the only grazing grounds and the cattle subsist mainly on paddy straw, paddy husks and … coarse grass … (Mamoria 1953:263–64).

According to Dube (1955:84, "… the cattle roam about the shrubs and rocks and eat whatever fodder is available there." This is confirmed by Moomaw (1949:96): "Cows subsist on the pasture and any coarse fodder they can find. Grain is fed for only a day or two following parturition." The character of the environmental niche reserved for cattle nourishment is described by Gourou (1963:123), based on data furnished by Dupuis (1960) for Madras:

> If faut voir clairement que le faible rendement du bétail indien n'est pas un gaspillage: ce bétail n'entre pas en concurrence avec la consommation de produits agricoles … ils ne leur sacrifient pas des surfaces agricoles, ou ayant un potential agricole.

NCAER (1961: 57) confines this pattern for Tripura: "There is a general practice of feeding livestock on agricultural by-products such as straw, grain wastes and husks;" for West Bengal (NCAER 1962:59): "The state has practically no pasture or grazing fields, and the farmers are not in the habit of growing green fodders … livestock feeds are mostly agricultural by-products;" and for Andhra Pradesh (NCAER 1962:52): "Cattle are stallfed, but the bulk of the feed consists of paddy straw. …"

The only exceptions to the rural pattern of feeding cattle on waste products and grazing them on marginal or unproductive lands involve working bullocks and nursing cows:

> The working bullocks, on whose efficiency cultivation entirely depends, are usually fed with chopped bananas at the time of fodder scarcity. But the milch cows have to live in a semi-starved condition, getting what nutrition they can from grazing on the fields after their rice harvest (Gangulee 1935:17).

> At present cattle are fed largely according to the season. During the rainy period they feed upon the grass which springs up on the *uncultivated* hillsides. … But in the dry season there is hardly any grass, and cattle wander on the *cropless* lands in an often halfstarved condition. True there is some fodder at these times in the shape of rice-straw and dried copra, but it is not generally sufficient, and is furthermore given mainly to the animals actually *working* at the time (Mayer 1952:70, italics added).

There is much evidence that Hindu farmers calculate carefully which animals deserve more food and attention. In Madras, Randhawa, et al. (1961:117) report: "The cultivators pay more attention to the male stock used for ploughing and for draft. There is a general neglect of the cow and the female calf even from birth …"

Similar discrimination is described by Mamoria (1953: 263 on):

Many plough bullocks are sold off in winter or their rations are ruthlessly decreased whenever they are not worked in full, while milch cattle are kept on after lactation on poor and inadequate grazing ... The cultivator feeds his bullocks better than his cow because it pays him. He feeds his bullocks better during the busy season, when they work, than during the slack season, when they remain idle. Further, he feeds his more valuable bullocks better than those less valuable ... Although the draught animals and buffaloes are properly fed, the cow gets next to nothing of stall feeding. She is expected to pick up her living on the bare fields after harvest and on the village wasteland. ...

The previously cited NCAER report on Andhra Pradesh notes that "Bullocks and milking cows during the working season get more concentrates ..." (1962:52). Wiser and Wiser (1963:71) sum up the situation in a fashion supporting Srinivas' (1958:4) observation that the Indian peasant is "nothing if he is not practical":

Farmers have become skillful in reckoning the minimum of food necessary for maintaining animal service. Cows are fed just enough to assure their calving and giving a little milk. They are grazed during the day on lands which yield very little vegetation, and are given a very sparse meal at night.

Many devout Hindus believe the bovine cattle of India are exploited without mercy by greedy Hindu owners. *Ahimsa* obviously has little to do with economizing which produces the famous *phooka* and *doom dev* techniques for dealing with dry cows. Not to Protestants but to Hindus did Gandhi (1954:7) address lamentations concerning the cow:

How we bleed her to take the last drop of milk from her, how we starve her to emaciation, how we ill-treat the calves, how we deprive them of their portion of milk, how cruelly we treat the oxen, how we castrate them, how we beat them, how we overload them ... I do not know that the condition of the cattle in any other part of the world is as bad as in unhappy India.

USEFUL AND USELESS ANIMALS

How then, if careful rationing is characteristic of livestock management, do peasants tolerate the widely reported herds of useless animals? Perhaps "useless" means 1 thing to the peasant and quite another to* the price-market-oriented agronomist. It is impossible at a distance to judge which point of view is ecologically more valid, but the peasants could be right more than the agronomists are willing to admit.

Since non-working and non-lactating animals are thermal and chemical factories which depend on waste lands and products for raw materials, judgment that a particular animal is useless cannot be supported without careful examination of its owner's household budget. Estimates from the cattle census which equate useless with dry or non-working animals are not convincing. But even if a given animal in a particular household is of less-than-marginal utility, there is an additional factor whose evaluation would involve long-range bovine biographies. The utility of a particular animal to its owner cannot be established simply by its performance during season or an animal cycle. Perhaps the whole system of Indian bovine management is alien to costing procedures of the West. There may be a kind of low-risk sweepstakes which drags on for 10 or 12 years before the losers and winners are separated.

As previously observed, the principal function of bovine cows is not their milk-producing but their bullock-producing abilities. Also established is the fact that many farmers are short of bullocks. Cows have the function primarily to produce male offspring, but when? In Europe and America, cows become pregnant under well-controlled, hence predictable, circumstances and a farmer with many animals, can count on male offspring in half the births. In India, cows become pregnant under quite different circumstances. Since cows suffer from malnutrition through restriction to marginal pasture, they conceive and deliver in unpredictable fashion. The chronic starvation of the inter-monsoon period makes the cow, in the words of Mamoria (1953:263), "an irregular breeder." Moreover, with few animals, the farmer may suffer many disappointments before a male is born. To the agriculture specialist with knowledge of what healthy dairy stock look like, the hot weather herds of walking skeletons "roaming over the bare fields and dried up wastes" (Leake 1923:267) must indeed seem without economic potential. Many of them, in fact, will not make it through to the next monsoon. However, among the survivors are an unknown number still physically capable of having progeny. Evidently neither the farmer nor the specialist knows which will conceive, nor when. To judge from Bombay city, even when relatively good care is bestowed on a dry cow, no one knows the outcome: "If an attempt is made to salvage them, they have to be kept and fed for a long time. Even then, it is not known whether they will conceive or not" (Nandra, et al. 1955:9).

In rural areas, to judge a given animal useless may be to ignore the recuperative power of these breeds under conditions of erratic rainfall and unpredictable grazing opportunities. The difference of viewpoint between the farmer and the expert is apparent in Moomaw's (1949) incomplete attempt to describe the life history of an informant's cattle. The farmer in question had 3 oxen, 2 female buffaloes, 4 head of young cattle and 3 "worthless" cows (p. 23). In Moomaw's opinion, "The three cows … are a liability to him, providing no income, yet consuming feed which might be placed to better use." Yet we learn, "The larger one had a calf about once in three years;" moreover 2 of the 3 oxen were "raised" by the farmer himself. (Does this mean that they were the progeny of the farmer's cows?) The farmer tells Moomaw, "The young stock get some fodder, but for the most part they pasture with the village herd. The cows give nothing and I cannot afford to feed them." Whereupon Moomaw's *non sequitur:* "We spoke no more of his cows, for like many a farmer he just keeps them, without inquiring whether it is profitable or not" (p. 25).

The difficulties in identifying animals that are definitely uneconomic for a given farmer are reflected in the varying estimates of the total of such animals. The Expert Committee on the Prevention of Slaughter of Cattle estimated 20,000,000 uneconomic cattle in India (Nandra, *et al.* 1953:62). Roy (1955:14) settles for 5,500,000, or about 3.5%. Mamoria (1953:257), who gives the still lower estimate of 2,900,000, or 2.1%, claims most of these are males. A similarly low percentage—2.5%—is suggested for West Bengal (NCAER 1962:56). None of these estimates appears based on bovine life histories in relation to household budgets; none appears to involve estimates of economic significance of dung contributions of older animals.

Before a peasant is judged a victim of Oriental mysticism, might it not be well to indicate the devastating material consequences which befall a poor farmer unable to replace a bullock lost through disease, old age, jar accident? Bailey (1957:73) makes it clear that in the economic life of the marginal peasantry, "Much the most devastating single event is the loss of an ox (or a plough buffalo)." If the farmer is unable to replace the animal with one from his own herd, he must borrow money at usurious rates. Defaults on such loans are the principal causes of transfer of land titles from peasants to landlords. Could this explain why the peasant is not overly perturbed that some of his animals might turn out to be only dung-providers? After all, the real threat to his existence does not arise from animals but from people ready to swoop down on him as soon as one of his beasts falters. Chapekar's (1960:27) claim that the peasant's "stock serve as a great security for him to fall back on whenever he is in need" would seem to be appropriate only in reference to the unusually well-established minority. In a land where life expectancy at birth has only recently risen to 30 years (Black 1959:2), it is not altogether appropriate to speak of security. The poorest farmers own insufficient stock. Farm management studies show that holdings below 2/3 of average area account for 2/5 of all farms, but maintain only 1/4 of the total cattle on farms. "This is so, chiefly because of their limited resources to maintain cattle" (Chaudhri and Giri 1963:598).

SLAUGHTER

Few, if any, Hindu farmers kill their cattle by beating them over the head, severing their jugular veins or shooting them. But to assert that they do not kill their animals when it is economically important for them to do so may be equally false. This interpretation escapes the notice of so many observers because the slaughtering process receives recognition only in euphemisms. People will admit that they "neglect" their animals, but will not openly accept responsibility for the *etic* effects, i.e., the more or less rapid death which ensues. The strange result of this euphemistic pattern is evidenced in the following statement by Moomaw (1949:96): "All calves born, however inferior, are allowed to live until they die of neglect." In the light of many similar but, by Hindu standards, more vulgar observations, it is clear that this kind of statement should read, "Most calves born are not allowed to live, but are starved to death."

This is roughly the testimony of Gourou (1963: 125), "Le paysan conserve seulement les veaux qui deviendront boeufs de labour ou vaches laitières; les autres sont écartés … et meurent d'epuisement." Wiser and Wiser (1963:70) are even more direct:

> Cows and buffaloes too old to furnish milk are not treated cruelly, but simply allowed to starve. The same happens to young male buffaloes. … The males are unwanted and little effort is made to keep them alive.

Obviously, when an animal, undernourished to begin with, receives neither food nor care, it will not enjoy a long life (compare Gourou 1963:124). Despite claims that an aged and decrepit cow "must be supported like an unproductive relative, until it dies a natural death" (Mosher 1946:124), ample evidence justifies belief that "few cattle die of old age"[5] (Bailey 1957: 75). Dandekar (1964:352) makes the same point: "In other words, because the cows cannot be fed nor can they be killed, they are neglected, starved and left to die a 'natural' death."

The farmer culls his stock by starving unwanted animals and also, under duress, sells them directly or indirectly to butchers. With economic pressure, many Indians who will not kill or eat cows themselves:

> are likely to compromise their principles and sell to butchers who slaughter cows, thereby tacitly supporting the practice for other people. Selling aged cows to butchers has over the centuries become an accepted practice alongside the *mos* that a Hindu must not kill cattle (Roy 1955:15).

---

[5] Srinivas (1962:126) declared himself properly skeptical in this matter: "It is commonly believed that the peasant's religious attitude to cattle comes in the way of the disposal of useless cattle. Here again, my experience of Rampura makes me skeptical of the general belief. I am not denying that cattle are regarded as in some sense sacred, but I doubt whether the belief is as powerful as it is claimed to be. I have already mentioned that bull-buffaloes are sacrificed to village goddesses. And in the case of the cow, while the peasant does not want to kill the cow or bull himself he does not seem to mind very much if someone else does the dirty job out of his sight."

Determining the number of cattle slaughtered by butchers is almost as difficult as determining the number killed by starvation. According to Dandekar (1964:351), "Generally it is the useless animals that find their way to the slaughter house." Lahiry (n.d.: 140) says only 126,900 or .9% of the total cattle population is slaughtered per year. Darling (1934: 158) claims:

> All Hindus object to the slaughter and even to the sale of unfit cows and keep them indefinitely. ... rather than sell them to a cattle dealer, who would buy only for the slaughter house, they send them to a *gowshala* or let them loose to die. Some no doubt sell secretly, but this has its risks in an area where public opinion can find strong expression through the *panchayat*.

Such views would seem to be contradicted by Sinha (1961:95): "A large number of animals are slaughtered privately and it is very difficult to ascertain their numbers." The difficulty of obtaining accurate estimates is also implied by the comment of the Committee on the Prevention of Slaughter that "90% of animals not approved for slaughter are slaughtered stealthily outside of municipal limits" (Nandra, *et al.* 1955:11).

An indication of the propensity to slaughter cattle under duress is found in connection with the food crisis of World War II. With rice imports cut off by Japanese occupation of Burma (Thirumalai 1954:38; Bhatia 1963:309 on), increased consumption of beef by the armed forces, higher prices for meat and foodstuffs generally, and famine conditions in Bengal, the doctrine of *ahimsa* proved to be alarmingly ineffectual. Direct military intervention was required to avoid destruction of animals needed for plowing, milking, and bullock-production:

> During the war there was an urgent need to reduce or to avoid the slaughter for food of animals useful for breeding or for agricultural work. For the summer of 1944 the slaughter was prohibited of: 1) Cattle below three years of age; 2) Male cattle between two and ten years of age which were being used or were likely to be used as working cattle; 3) All cows between three and ten years of age, other than cows which were unsuitable for bearing offspring; 4) All cows which were pregnant or in milk (Knight 1954:141).

Gourou (1963:124–25), aware that starvation and neglect are systematically employed to cull Indian herds, nonetheless insists that destruction of animals through starvation amounts to an important loss of capital. This loss is attributed to the low price of beef caused by the beef-eating taboo, making it economically infeasible to send animals to slaughter. Gourou's appraisal, however, neglects deleterious consequences to the rural tanning and carrion-eating castes if increased numbers of animals went to the butchers. Since the least efficient way to convert solar energy into comestibles is to impose an animal converter between plant and man (Cottrell 1955), it should be obvious that without major technical and environmental innovations or drastic population cuts, India could not tolerate a large beef-producing industry. This suggests that insofar as the beef-eating taboo helps discourage growth of beef-producing industries, it is part of an ecological adjustment which maximizes rather than minimizes the calorie and protein output of the productive process.

ANTI-SLAUGHTER LEGISLATION AND GOWSHALAS

It is evident from the history of anti-slaughter agitation and legislation in India that more than *ahimsa* has been required to protect Indian cattle from premature demise. Unfortunately, this legislation is misinterpreted and frequently cited as evidence of the anti-economic effect of Hinduism. I am unable to unravel all the tangled economic and political interests served by the recent anti-slaughter laws of the Indian states. Regardless of the ultimate ecological consequences of these laws, however, several points deserve emphasis. First it should be recalled that cow protection was a major political weapon in Ghandi's campaign against both British and Moslems. The sacred cow was the ideological focus of a successful struggle against English colonialism; hence the enactment of total anti-slaughter legislation obviously had a rational base, at least among politicians who seized and retained power on anti-English and anti-Moslem platforms. It is possible that the legislation will now backfire and upset the delicate ecological balance which now exists. The Committee on the Prevention of Slaughter claimed that it

> actually saw in Pepsu (where slaughter is banned completely) what a menace wild cattle can be. Conditions have become so desperate there, that the State Government have got to spend a considerable sum for catching and re-domesticating wild animals to save the crops (Nandra, *et al.* 1955:11).

According to Mayadas (1954:29):

> The situation has become so serious that it is impossible in some parts of the country to protect growing crops from grazing by wandering cattle. Years ago it was one or two stray animals which could either be driven off or sent to the nearest cattle pound. Today it is a question of constantly being harassed day and night by herds which must either feed on one's green crops, or starve. How long can this state of affairs be allowed to continue?

Before the deleterious effects of slaughter laws can be properly evaluated, certain additional evolutionary and functional possibilities must be examined. For example, given the increasing growth rate of India's human population, the critical importance of cattle in the *ecosystem,* and the absence of fundamental technical and environmental changes, a substantial increase in cattle seems necessary and predictable, regardless of slaughter legislation. Furthermore, there is some indication, admittedly incomplete but certainly worthy of careful inquiry, that many who protest most against destructiveness of marauding herds of useless beasts may perceive the situation from very special vantage points in the social hierarchy. The implications of the following newspaper editorial are clear:

> The alarming increase of stray and wild cattle over wide areas of Northern India is fast becoming a major disincentive to crop cultivation. … Popular sentiment against cow slaughter no doubt lies at the back of the problem. People prefer to let their aged, diseased, and otherwise useless cattle live at the expense of *other people's crops* (Indian Express, New Delhi, 7 February 1959, italics added).

Evidently we need to know something about whose crops are threatened by these marauders. Despite post-Independence attempts at land reform, 10% of the Indian agricultural population still owns more than % the total cultivated area and 15,000,000, or 22%, of rural households own no land at all (Mitra 1963: 298). Thorner and Thorner (1962:3) call the land reform program a failure, and point out how "the grip of the larger holder serves to prevent the lesser folk from developing the land… ." Quite possibly, in other words, the anti-slaughter laws, insofar as they are effective, should be viewed as devices which, contrary to original political intent, bring pressure to bear upon those whose lands are devoted to cash crops of benefit only to narrow commercial, urban, and landed sectors of the population. To have one's cows eat other people's crops may be a very fine solution to the subsistence problem of those with no crops of their own. Apparently, in the days when animals could be driven off or sent to the pound with impunity, this could not happen, even though *ahimsa* reigned supreme then as now.

Some form of anti-slaughter legislation was required and actually argued for, on unambiguously rational, economic, and material grounds. About 4% of India's cattle are in the cities (Mohan 1962:48). These have always represented the best dairy stock, since the high cost of feeding animals in a city could be offset only by good milking qualities. A noxious consequence of this dairy pattern was the slaughter of the cow at the end of its first urban lactation period because it was too expensive to maintain while awaiting another pregnancy. Similarly, and by methods previously discussed, the author calf was killed after it had stimulated the cow to "let down." With the growth of urban milk consumption, the best of India's dairy cattle were thus systematically prevented from breeding, while animals with progressively poorer milking qualities were preserved in the countryside (Mohan 1962:48; Mayadas 1954: 29; Gandhi 1954:13 on). The Committee on the Prevention of Slaughter of Cattle (Nandra, *et al.* 1955:2) claimed at least 50,000 high-yielding cows and she-buffaloes from Madras, Bombay, and Calcutta were "annually sent to premature slaughter" and were "lost to the country." Given such evidence of waste and the political potential of Moslems being identified as cow-butchers and Englishmen as cow-eaters (Gandhi 1954:16), the political importance of *ahimsa* becomes more intelligible. Indeed, it could be that the strength of Gandhi's *charisma* lay in his superior understanding of the ecological significance of the cow, especially in relation to the underprivileged masses, marginal low caste and out caste farmers. Gandhi (p. 3) may have been closer to the truth than many a foreign expert when he said:

> Why the cow was selected for apotheosis is obvious to me. The cow was in India the best companion. She was the giver of plenty. Not only did she give milk but she also made agriculture possible.

OLD-AGE HOMES

Among the more obscure aspects of the cattle complex are bovine old-age homes, variously identified as *gowshalas*, *pinjrapoles*, and, under the Five-Year Plans, as *gosadans*. Undoubtedly some of these are "homes for cows, which are supported by public charity, which maintain the old and derelict animals till natural death occurs" (Kothavala 1934:123). According to Gourou (1963:125), however, owners of cows sent to these religious institutions pay rent with the understanding that if the cows begin to lactate they will be returned. The economics of at least some of these "charitable" institutions is, therefore, perhaps not as quaint as usually implied. It is also significant that, although the 1st Five-Year Plan called for establishment of 160 *gosadans* to serve 320,000 cattle, only 22 *gosadans* servicing 8,000 cattle were reported by 1955 (Government of India Planning Commission 1956:283).

NATURAL SELECTION

Expert appraisers of India's cattle usually show little enthusiasm for the typical undersized breeds. Much has been made of the fact that 1 large animal is a more efficient dung, milk, and traction machine than 2 small ones. "Weight for weight, a small animal consumes a much larger quantity of food than a bigger animal" (Marmoria 1953:268). "More dung is produced when a given quantity of food is consumed by one animal than when it is shared by two animals" (Ford Foundation 1959:64). Thus it would seem that India's smaller breeds should be replaced by larger, more powerful, and better milking breeds. But once again, there is another way of looking at the evidence. It might very well be that if all of India's scrub cattle were suddenly replaced by an equivalent number of large, high-quality European or American dairy and traction animals, famines of noteworthy magnitude would immediately ensue. Is it not possible that India's cattle are undersized precisely because other breeds never could survive the atrocious conditions they experience most of the year? I find it difficult to believe that breeds better adapted to the present Indian *ecosystem* exist elsewhere.

> By nature and religious training, the villager is unwilling to inflict pain or to take animal life. But the immemorial grind for existence has hardened him to an acceptance of survival of the fittest (Wiser and Wiser 1963).

Not only are scrub animals well adapted to the regular seasonal crises of water and forage and general year-round neglect, but long-range selective pressures may be even more significant. The high frequency of drought-induced famines in India (Bhatia 1963) places a premium upon drought-resistance plus a more subtle factor: A herd of smaller animals, dangerously thinned by famine or pestilence, reproduces faster than an equivalent group of larger animals, despite the fact that the larger animal consumes less per pound than 2 smaller animals. This is because there are 2 cows in the smaller herd per equivalent large cow. Mohan (1962:45) is one of the few authorities to have grasped this principle, including it in defense of the small breeds:

> Calculations of the comparative food conversion efficiency of various species of Indian domestic livestock by the writer has revealed, that much greater attention should be paid to small livestock than at present, not only because of their better conversion efficiency for protein but also because of the possibilities of bringing about a rapid increase in their numbers.

CONCLUSION

The probability that India's cattle complex is a positive-functioned part of a naturally selected *ecosystem* is at least as good as that it is a negative-functioned expression of an irrational ideology. This should not be interpreted to mean that no "improvements" can be made in the system, nor that different systems may not eventually evolve. The issue is not whether oxen are more efficient than tractors. I suggest simply that many features of the cattle complex have been erroneously reported or interpreted. That Indian cattle are weak and inefficient is not denied, but there is doubt that this situation arises from and is mainly perpetuated by Hindu ideology. Given the techno-environmental base, Indian property relationships, and political organization, one need not involve the doctrine of *ahimsa* to understand fundamental features of the cattle complex. Although the cattle population of India has risen by 38,000,000 head since 1940, during the same period, the human population has risen by 120,000,000. Despite the anti-slaughter legislation, the ratio of cattle to humans actually declined from 44: 100 in 1941 to 40:100 in 1961

(Government of India 1962:74; 1963:6). In the absence of major changes in environment, technology or property relations, it seems unlikely that the cattle population will cease to accompany the rise in the human population. If *ahimsa* is negative-functioned, then we must be prepared to admit the possibility that all other factors contributing to the rapid growth of the Indian human and cattle populations, including the germ theory of disease, are also negative-functioned.

Marvin Harris, born in 1927, received his doctorate from Columbia University in 1953. He has practiced ethnography in Ecuador, Brazil and Mozambique. Since 1963, he has been Professor and Chairman of the Department of Anthropology at Columbia.

Harris is the author of a community study, 2 books on comparative race relations, and several articles focussing on economic aspects of anthropological theory. His most recent book, *The Nature of Cultural Things*, is concerned with the identification of cross-culturally valid ethnographic units. He is currently at work on a history of theories of cultural anthropology.

The present article, submitted to CURRENT ANTHROPOLOGY 2 iii 64, was sent for CA* treatment to 49 scholars of whom the following responded with written comments: Nirmal K. Bose, Morton Klass, Joan P. Mencher, Kalervo Oberg, Marvin K. Opler, Wayne Suttles, and Andrew P. Vayda. The comments written for publication are printed in full after the author's text and are followed by a reply from the author.

ABSTRACT

The relationship between human and bovine population in India has hitherto been widely regarded as an important example of resource mismanagement under the influence of religious doctrine. It is suggested that insufficient attention has been paid to such positive-functioned features of the Hindu cattle complex as traction power and milk, dung, beef and hide production in relationship to the costs of ecologically viable alternatives. In general, the exploitation of cattle resources proceeds in such a way as not to impair the survival and economic well-being of the human population. The relationship between the human and bovine population is symbiotic rather than competitive; more traction animals than are presently available are needed for carrying out essential agricultural tasks. Under existing techno-environmental conditions, a relatively high ratio of cattle to humans is ecologically unavoidable. This does not mean, that with altered techno-environmental conditions, new and more efficient food energy systems cannot be evolved.

COMMENTS

By NIRMAL K. BOSE*
Calcutta, India. 30 *iii* 65

I find myself very much in agreement with Professor Harris' thesis. Cattle serve many purposes for the Indian peasant, and the sacredness ascribed to the cow springs from its utility rather than from the tradition of *ahimsa.* According to Rájendralála Mitra (1881:354–88), beef-eating was common in ancient India. It was only in later times that a firm tabu was established against this as food and cattle began to be regarded as extraordinarily sacred.

There is perhaps 1 point at which I can possibly make a useful comment. On p. 58, Harris says: "… it should be recalled that cow protection was a major political weapon in Gandhi's campaign against both the British and the Moslems." This is perhaps not quite correct.

Cow protection was as much a part of Gandhi's "constructive programme" as, say/the removal of untouchability. This was not a political demand. There was much to be done for the improvement of the cow; and if it had to be protected against useless slaughter, it had to be made once more a real part of our economic wealth, so that those who slaughtered cattle for meat would also find * it reasonable to "protect" the cow. This was a call for internal reform, rather than a political demand directed either against the British or Moslems.

But this is no more than a minor slip. Harris breaks substantially new ground, and I congratulate him on that account.

By MORTON KLASS*
New York, NY., U.S.A. 1 iv 65

Many Indianists may find it necessary to correct or amend some of Harris' interpretations. I would doubt, for example, whether the concept of *ahimsa*—in either its traditional religious or contemporary political usage—can adequately account for the Indian ecosystem provides, in prinpresentatives of the subfamily *Bovinae.* Such questions, however, have no bearing on Harris' thesis, with which I find myself in agreement, that the Indian ecosystem provides, in principle and in fact, for adaptive and efficient utilization of cattle power and products.

Implicit, of course, is a question of considerable importance to contemporary anthropological theorists. Is it possible for a culture to exist and perpetuate itself with a dysfunctional ecosystem—in which beliefs and practices directly inhibit an efficient and economic utilization of resources? Those who would argue for such a possibility have now been deprived, by Harris, of their Indian "sacred cow" example. And if the utilization of the cow is indeed eufunctional, then it would be difficult not to conclude that the Indian ecosystem *in toto* is inherently eufunctional: it must provide for maximal utilization of resources available in the given cultural context, in all aspects of production, distribution, and consumption. How could it be otherwise, indeed, given the duration of the culture, the extent of the civilization, and the density of the population?

On the other hand, can we reject all the expert testimony of Indianists (many of them in fact Indians) to the effect that the contemporary Indian ecosystem exhibits a high degree of inefficiency and even economic "irrationality?" I believe that Harris is correct in his analysis and others in their observations, but that there is no necessary paradox. The observers are concerned with present-day, India, with an ecosystem that reflects a millenium or more of massive culture contact, including conquest' and the forcible imposition of alien principles of sociopolitical and economic organization, as well as the more subtle infiltration of alien values and alternatives. Harris, however, is analyzing the classic ecosystem, the socioeconomic practices as they once were—and, perhaps, still are, if we could but see beyond the contemporary trauma and dislocation.

Thus, for example, protein deficiency is a very real problem in India today, and it would be easy to argue that Indian dietary beliefs and practices only aggravate the problem. But Harris directs our attention, by implication, to the classic ecosystem wherein protein was provided for all, in the form of milk for those at the very top and in the form of carrion beef for those at the very bottom. Many factors may have contributed to the present condition of economic inefficiency; not the least of the factors, however, was the acculturation of new values. In the past, high caste Hindus may have found the eating of carrion at least as repugnant as the eating of beef per se, but such repugnance would not normally lead to actual interference with the beliefs and practices of lower-caste people. It would seem, therefore, that some of the current under-utilization of available beef in India reflects the imposition of European-derived beliefs and values: specifically, the belief that if a practice (e.g., carrion-eating) is wrong, then it is wrong for *all*. Similarly, Harris notes the importance of human excrement—traditionally deposited, by village-folk, in the fields—for agriculture in India. Today, community development workers, who claim to be concerned primarily with the improvement of agricultural production, make enormous efforts to introduce latrines into reluctant villages. The impetus—a feeling that all human excrement must be decently interred—would appear to be of European derivation. As in the case of the Northwest Coast Amerindian potlatch, the intrinsic eufunctionalism of the Indian ecosystem has become obscured by the dislocations of massive contact, and the appearance presented is one of uneconomic inefficiency.

Is it, however, also an "irrational" ecosystem? The concept "rational ecosystem" is an unrewarding one to work with: the underlying criteria are often vague or culture-bound. It would appear to be true, however, that most of the processual interrelationships within the Indian ecosystem are unrecognized—frequently even evaded or rejected—by those who participate directly in the system. Harris, for example, notes that "the slaughtering process receives recognition only in euphemism," and that some Indian writers appear to avoid the obvious implication of "neglect": i.e., that in this ecosystem unwanted cattle are disposed of by starving them to death. I noted instances of similar "euphemistic" avoidance of process during my own field-work in Bengal. A dead cow or bullock is delivered by the farmer to a low-caste scavenger with instructions to "bury it." The farmer is perfectly aware that the scavenger sells hides and eats carrion beef, but still he can report, in all honesty, that he "buries" his dead cattle. Press him, and the farmer will declare plaintively that he does not associate with low-caste people and is not responsible for their misdeeds.

The same farmer explains that he would never castrate a bull calf or permit any of his employees to perform the act. He buys bullocks in the market when he requires them for agriculture. Of course, he sells his unwanted bull calves in the same market! He cannot see—does not want to see—that farmers such as himself provide the bullocks that farmers such as himself require. Thus, if the Indian ecosystem is eufunctional in its utilization of cattle, as Harris argues, its functioning must be termed *latent* rather than *manifest*.

All of the foregoing arise out of reflections on Harris' paper, for I find his argument not only cogent but stimulating. I expect it will lead to much meaningful discussion and research.

By Joan P. Mencher*
Ithaca, N.Y., U.S.A. 29 iii 65

This article by Dr. Harris makes a most important contribution to the study of the interrelationship between ecological and socioreligious systems in complex societies, as well as to Indian studies in general. In the course of my 3 1/2 years of work in India, I have always been struck by the common sense and practicality of the Indian farmer despite the tendency on the part of many educated city dwellers to deplore the "rule of religion over economics."

I would certainly agree that the cattle complex in India has been adaptive to the ecological system of which it is a part, and that "the degree of observance of taboos against bovine slaughter and beef-eating reflect the power of ecological pressures." I should like to Confine my discussion to 2 points. I should like, on the one hand, to present certain data in sup port of Harris' main argument and, on the other hand, to comment on certain of the difficulties arising today in relation to the cattle complex because of the changes in the ecosystem during the past 200 years.

In his discussion of milk production and traction, Harris notes that there is often a shortage of draught animals. He also discusses what happens to useless cattle and how laws about slaughter operate. The following data, admittedly limited, from Chingleput District, in the northern part of Madras State, which is said to have a larger amount of cattle than other parts of the State (National Council of Applied Economic Research 1962 1:35–36) seems to support many of his contentions. For 1 Firka in this District in 1946, of 6,171 oxen over the age of 3 years, 95% worked in the fields as draught animals, .7% were used primarily as stud animals, and an additional 4% worked in the fields as well as being used as stud animals. Only .3% of the males were not used for either purpose. On the other hand, among the cows, 68% had calves, and an additional 31% had had calves during the previous 3 or 4 years. Of those which had calves more than half were still giving milk. It is striking chat the ratio of males to females under the age of 3 years was 945:856, whereas among the total cattle population the ratio of males to females was 7,116:4,362. Clearly, something must have happened to the females who stopped having calves and yet were unfit for agricultural work. It is interesting that for buffaloes, whose economic worth is judged primarily by milk production, though males are occasionally used to draw a plow if a farmer has no bullocks, the total proportion of males to females was 1,436:1,766. Obviously, excess males must have somehow been eliminated.

For 1 village in this Firka for which more data is available, in 1946 and also in 1963 there was not a single male ox over 3 years of age which did not work in the fields. In this village, In 1946 there were 298 working oxen and 49 working male buffaloes. This was exactly 9 more than had been in the same village in 1912. The number of cows increased by 10 during this 33-year period, but the number of female buffaloes decreased by 30. In 1912, there were 187 plows in the village for 1,103 acres of paddy land. If each man owning a plow also owned 2 bullocks, then there would have been 374 bullocks in the village. According to the 1895 *Statistical Atlas for the Madras Presidency,* the number of acres tilled by 1 team of cattle in the relatively flat Conjeevaram Taluk to which this village then belonged was 8 acres. It is striking that the number of bullocks and male buffaloes came to 338, or only 38 more than the optimum that would have been employed if a team of bullocks was used for no less than 8 acres. Obviously, at least in this village, many small cultivators who owned plows had to borrow someone else's bullocks for plowing or else had to join with other men in some sort of informal cooperative endeavor if they were to get their plowing done. It is significant that in this village, despite the increase in partition of property and, therefore, in the number of small landowners, there was only an increase of 9 in the number of working animals. Even today, during the plowing season as well as during the harvest when they are needed to pull the carts from the fields, there is a clearly expressed shortage of draught cattle. (There is some indication that this is not the case throughout the District, because the 1962 Atlas lists 45 draught animals per 100 acres for Chingleput District; however, this includes the rockier areas as well as the suburbs of Madras City, where a larger number of draught animals are used for bullock carts.)

It has been stated by 1 historian that the increase during the past 200 years in the amount of land under cultivation has been accompanied by a decrease in the cattle herds. Thus Habib says in his discussion of the agrarian system of Mughal India 1963: (53–57)

> Where the 17th century peasant enjoyed a distinctly superior position to his descendent of today was in respect to cattle and draught animals. From what we know about the extent of cultivation during that period, it is obvious that

the land available for grazing … was far greater in extent than now. … The larger number of working cattle per head of population is better demonstrated by the obvious plentitude of … ghi … the reckless encroachments on grazing and forest lands, in the environment of a moribund economy, have caused a dangerous crisis in animal husbandry, which in a country, where cattle power is used to drag the plough and work the waterlift, must be regarded pre-eminently as a pillar of agriculture.

In this connection, I would hasten to say that plow bullocks are not underemployed; during the periods when plowing can be done, they may often be overworked. I have seen farmers try to vary the time of plowing slightly by taking as much advantage as possible of slight differences in the soil, in the slope of the land, and the type of seed to be sown.

During the past 200 years, and particularly during the past 50 years, the traditional ecosystem has started to change radically. Public health practices have greatly altered the demographic picture. Settlement on former "waste" and forest lands and DDT spraying have made changes in the system. However, they still have not been sufficient to cause any basic changes in the human-bovine symbiotic relationship. True, the large increase in the human population and decrease in grazing lands might be 1 cause of the greater malnutrition among present-day cattle, but still, cattle remain essential for modern Indian agriculture. I remember 1 middle-class farmer who had bought a tractor for paddy cultivation. He used it 1 season, but found that it was less reliable on many accounts and, significantly, cost him more to operate and maintain than bullocks. Still, he tried it out for 1 more year. Now the tractor sits in splendor in his courtyard while his fields are cultivated by traditional means. It is clear that other changes in the agricultural system must precede any change in the basic ecological adaptation, if they are to be successful.

From this point of view, one might say that the religious concept of *ahimsa* plus the veneration of the cow as a sacred animal is functionally interrelated with the traditional ecological system. The parts are certainly interwoven into a complex texture, but it belies common sense to expect a change in the ideology as long as the traditional ecosystem remains functional.

By KALERVO OBERG
Ithaca, N.Y., U.S.A. 29 iii 65

Professor Marvin Harris has presented an important paper, not only by analysing the pertinent pragmatic aspects of the traditional Hindu cattle complex as an integrated ecological system, but also by indicating the significance of this approach for the interpretation of certain aspects of culture. Not being an Indianist nor an expert concerning Hindu cattle-keeping, I have to accept his factual data as correct.

First, he shows the inappropriateness of judging Hindu cattle-keeping in terms of the commercialized cattle industry of the West, where cattle are raised to produce dairy products and beef, enterprises in which input or cost is for the purpose of maximizing productivity in terms of pounds of milk or pounds of beef per animal. When the yield in milk begins to decline or when the beef animal has reached maximum weight with a given feed input, the animals are disposed of at a maximum profit. To the Hindu peasant, in contrast, the cow plays a central role in his household economy, crop production being well-nigh impossible without the cow and its products.

Harris then goes on to show that in Hindu peasant economy, a cow is a multipurpose animal. Among its positive contributions he lists milk, traction power in the form of bullocks, fuel, fertilizer, hides, and beef. Milk, although important, is secondary to traction power upon which cereal production depends. Instead of cattle being surplus and useless, there is actually a shortage of bullocks. His most telling point is in stressing the ecological relationship between cattle and man. The relationship is symbiotic instead of competitive. Cattle live on the by-products of cereal production, such as straw, hulls, and stubble, and graze on non-arable hills and along roadsides. American livestock specialists call this kind of low cost or practically no cost cattle-keeping a "scavenger operation." Just like the Western cattle-keeper, the Hindu peasant maximizes output in relation to input, but he does it in a different way; for the longer a cow lives, the more bullocks, fuel, and fertilizer it will produce, and when the cow ultimately dies the owner gets the hide and the untouchables eat the meat. To the Westerner, short-lived cattle are high cost consumer goods produced for maximum money profit; to the Hindu peasant, a cow is more of a capital asset which, once acquired, continues to pay necessary material dividends to the end of its life at a very low maintenance cost.

If this is true, the ban on killing and eating cattle is an ideological device to protect a capital asset, a measure which can be understood in ecological and economic terms. This measure, sanctioned by religion, can be considered as emphasizing the great value of cattle in Hindu life and the manner in which they must be used. The Bahima cattle-keepers of western Uganda, while having no taboo against eating beef, have an injunction against killing cows. This can readily be understood as a device to protect the calf-producing capacity of cows in a pastoral economy where, in the past, diseases and animal and human raiders took a heavy toll of cattle herds.

In every traditional society, religion sanctions the age-old ways. In India, religion sanctifies the family and the caste system as well as agricultural and cattle-keeping practices. But religion does not explain their form as adaptive mechanisms to living conditions. The Hindu philosophical concept of the unity of life and the proscription against killing any animal or eating any kind of meat belong, I think, to a different level of human adjustment to the external world. By personally diminishing struggle, pain, and death, the devout Hindu strives to make peace with his environment, tries to break the tension between self and non-self with the ultimate aim of reaching complete unity in the absolute. This is a commendable aspiration, but in its ultimate form it takes man away from society and makes a devout Hindu a holy man, a holy beggar divorced from economic and political activities.

I think Harris has opened up a new and rewarding approach to the study of economic and social relations by stressing the need for an intensive study of the concrete measurable factors of positive adaptive processes. In his *Patterns of Race in the Americas* (1964) I think he was successful in showing that the different forms in which race relations in the Western world have developed relate to the central problem of labor supply which faced the European settlers of the New World rather than to the Iberic soul or the inherent racism of the Anglo-Saxon. Similarly he has been able to explain the Indian cattle complex without deriving it from *ahimsa*.

By MARVIN K. OPLER*
Buffalo, N.Y., U.S.A. 27 ii 65

My comment might be titled "Cultural Ecology Reflects Cultural Evolution," because Harris links this specific study of cultural ecology with his brilliantly perceptive paper of 1959, *The Economy Has No Surplus?* with one the year following on biological and cultural adaptations (1960), and with his recent book analyzing the "emic" and "etic" considerations (1964a). I happen to have a personal preference for avoiding such terms as "ecosystem," or "emic" and "etic" controversy, or even the term, "cultural ecology," when the latter is used without evolutionary modifiers, because to my mind the evolutionary modifiers are the whole point of the theoretical discussion. Besides this, I find that ecology has unfortunate spatial and geophysical connotations, and as Harris himself concludes: "… with altered techno-environmental conditions, new and more efficient food energy systems" would be *evolved*.

In short, I am profoundly grateful for each of the previous 3 contributions of Harris, and for the present one in particular. Were he commenting on land use, rather than Indian cattle usage, I imagine he would find as does Kusum Nair's *Blossoms in the Dust* (1961) that land development projects in this country do not usually find people thinking in terms of expanded acreage in anything resembling the extent of Western technicians. Nair subtitles her book "The Human Factor in Indian Development" which more correctly might be the cultural factor. Like Harris I wish area specialists and anthropological theoreticians would more often base economic analyses on human energy computations (considering technology), on biophysical realities, on assessments of the social organization of production, or in sum, on knowledge of the conditions under which technological and economic factors operate, with due regard for these *cultural conditions of existence*. Harris is to be commended for his efforts in this direction, for his quantitative and realistic documentation of economics cross-culturally as essentially "cultural things."

Having paid homage to the tough-minded and discerning scholarship in Harris' economic anthropology, let me point out that this paper, and that on surplus 6 years earlier, add to energy utilization theory the idea that *how* items in economy are used depends on interplay between 1 item, in this instance cattle, and other aspects. Just as technology and its efficiency varies, so also do agriculture and animal husbandry. I recall, as a student, hearing that Kwakiutl were merely fishing and hunting level, yet had chiefs, commoners, and slaves; and then noting in Diamond Jenness that the salmon spawning was like a seasonal crop rising in the waters to be gathered by clubs. To accounts of fierce rivalry between chiefs was added, even in Boas' account of the *numaym* of chiefs, commoners, and slaves, a picture of economic and social in-group co-operativeness; and Boas himself indicated that rivalry in potlatching had been historically preceded by actual warfare between chiefs for favorite coastal and riverine fishing sites. Not merely a crop, but relatively stable methods of preservation (smoking) were involved in this fishing industry, plus occasional surpluses of candlefish oil and sea mammals. By the time the quantities of yams rotting in Trobriand yam-houses were added to the "conspicuous waste" version of Kwakiutl economics, I reacted not only as Harris did in the paper on surplus, but added the search through Malinowski's many-volume prose which netted the information that richer districts of Kiriwina not only had greater activity in the coastal and inland trade, not only related to overseas *kula* trade more vigorously, but had chiefly lines which varied clanship and mother's brother authority to frankly patrilineal descent.

These are instances of micro-evolution, for which Paiute-Ute, Hopi, and Aztec; or Eastern Apache, Western Apache, Navajo, etc., stand as historically attested evolutionary series on a more macroscopic level. As in the example of India, technology is important and with it the relationship of 1 item in the economy to others. Similarly, social control of productive resources must be considered, along with degrees of development of total forces of production. What Harris specifies as degrees of control over climatic, seasonal, and other ecological forces I should prefer to trace through into a system of socioeconomic control, removing ecology from the usual geophysical or crudely environmental connotations which play so limited a role. In view of his rich socioeconomic and cultural documentation, I should recommend he drop the word "ecology" or add the cultural modifier, best labeled "evolutionary."

For Harris' central criticism of the claim that India's animal or agricultural resources have been "mismanaged" for doctrinal or philosophico-religious reasons, no anthropologist, in this day and age, could have reasonable objection. We hasten to add that Henry Zimmer's studies of the sensuous and wordly in Hindu art (see Opler 1956), the philosopher Dale Riepe's more recent work on the materialistic and rational concerns in India's traditional philosophies (1961), or the historical mathematician's genuine respect for Indian contributions and sophistication suffice to place art and ideology in a more correct perspective. Ideology is a part of cultural adaptation and is, therefore, responsive to socioeconomic factors. "Mismanagement" is an individually aimed, pejorative term. My own statement (1960) is: "However, the approach through the individual is not, statistically, the study of normative culture or necessarily a study of its characteristic ranges of behavior. Even more important, in anthropology, the material conditions under which a culture operates constitute the setting and the *binding conditions* affecting this *range* of behavior."

By WAYNE SUTTLES*
Reno, Nev., U.S.A. 30 iii 65

Harris' paper may surely stand as a model for the balanced ecological approach, which seeks to examine all activities and all their consequences—advantageous and disadvantageous—for all participants in the eco-system. It is also commendable in that it clearly rejects the implication that if a practice is "positive-functional" (or "adaptive") then it must be perfect—the best possible solution to the problem. As Mayr (1959:3–4) has pointed out, natural selection is not an "all-or-none phenomenon." The positive functions (adaptive consequences) of *ahimsa* need only slightly outweigh the negative ones for *ahimsa* to be favored by natural selection. Harris has shown that they very likely do. He has not; of course, asserted flatly that *ahimsa* must have been diffused and established throughout the Hindu population by the process of natural selection, though this does seem likely. Perhaps present and future experiments in Indian agriculture will eventually give us the data we need to make such an assertion. Finally, I do not see any claim in Harris' paper that environment or economy *produced* the doctrine of *ahimsa*. Thus he is not, in any sense that I can see, taking a position of environmental determinism or economic determinism. Presumably the doctrine arose, as all do, out of human speculation and human emotion, and presumably it has always been in competition with other doctrines. What Harris has shown is how in the Indian setting the doctrine may have won out in that competition because behaviors motivated by it have more often than not had consequences promoting human survival.

By ANDREW P. VAYDA*
New York, N.Y., U.S.A. 26 iii 65

Harris provides us with good grounds for questioning conventional judgments of the management of food resources in India, and I am very much in sympathy with his attempt to view the Indian use of cattle as a product of "Darwinian pressures." It seems unfortunate to me, however, that Harris is at pains to dismiss the influence of *ahimsa* instead of inquiring whether the doctrine itself has adaptive value. It is, at the very least, a reasonable hypothesis that part of the selective process in human evolution is the emergence of beliefs and moral valuations conducive to behavior that helps populations to survive and, at times, to expand. In line with such a hypothesis, anthropological research can be directed to ascertaining whether beliefs that are irrational by the ethnocentric standards used by market-price-oriented agronomists are less so by the biological standards of survival and differential reproduction.

I add 1 small point: there does not seem to be much warrant for the adjective "cultural" in Harris' title. His paper discusses organisms (human, bovine, etc.) in interaction with one another and with their non-living environments. This is just plain ecology, and the general concepts and principles to which Harris has recourse are for the most part as applicable to other species as they are to culture-bearing man.

REPLY

By MARVIN HARRIS

Although Klass appears to support the view that the Indian cattle system is "eufunctional," he nonetheless remains unconvinced that existing dietary beliefs and practices do not aggravate the protein deficiency which all would agree is one of India's major problems. To resolve this contradiction, Klass suggests that in former times, milk and meat utilizations were more nearly optimal than at present. Diffusion, especially of new values, has diminished the economic efficiency of the system, bringing about an "under-utilization" of available beef. I cannot readily accept this explanation of the inconsistencies exposed by my paper, since the arguments presented all add up to a denial of the proposition that cattle are in general under-utilized. I should want to examine Klass's evidence for the under-utilization of cattle as a source of meat protein, keeping in view the many additional and sometimes contradictory functions which must also be fulfilled by the bovine population. It would also be interesting in this respect to compare the patterns of utilization of beef cattle in other under-developed countries. Brazil for example, has no taboo against beef-eating (not even on Fridays) and has one of the world's largest cattle populations, but there is a protein deficiency in the lower classes which is as bad as that suffered by lower caste Indians. This suggests to me that mere removal of the negative values surrounding beef-eating might not make much of an improvement in the Indian diet. Indeed, it is explicit in my argument that if beef-eating were to be encouraged, a decrease rather than an increase in the overall efficiency of protein utilization should be expected.

It is most interesting that Mencher also points out that in former times—possible as recently as 50 years ago—the ecological balance in India was more favorable to the welfare of both men and cattle. Unlike Klass, however, Mencher explains the changes without appealing to an "acculturation of new values." Instead, she emphasizes the changing demographic picture brought about by the filling up of former waste and grazing lands and the consequent failure of the cattle population to keep pace with the growth in the human population. Her opportune data help to support my hunch that cow protection is the ideological issue it is today precisely because the human population has increased faster than the cattle population. Going back in time, we should expect less and less overt concern with cow protection until finally we reach the situation alluded to by Bose, when a higher ratio of cattle per capita made beef-eating a commonplace.

I should like to make it clear that the ecologically positive contribution of the beef-eating taboo is not emphasized in the text under discussion, because in the larger issue before us, namely the role of ideology in socio-cultural evolution, the majority of anthropologists need no convincing that values are important for understanding economic systems. Indeed, many appear to be firmly convinced that the crucial differences between Northern European and Indian agriculture are mainly under the control of differences embodied in the contrast between Hinduism and Protestantism. It has not hitherto seemed feasible to offer explanations of the Indian cattle complex which would relegate Hindu theology to an importance consistent with neo-materialist premises. In arguing for the positive-functioned and possibly adaptive significance of the Indian cattle complex, my ultimate concern was to show how the material conditions of technology and habitat possibly suffice to explain the principal features of the productive processes characteristic of contemporary Indian agriculture. Klass, judging from his appeal to the possible effect of diffused values, remains unimpressed by the analytic advantages of neo-materialism.

More difficult to comprehend is the reaction of Vayda who, despite a predilection for stressing techno-environmental phenomena, asserts that I have "dismissed the influence of *ahimsa*" instead of enquiring about its "adaptive" value. This opinion cannot derive from careful reading of my paper since it is obvious therein that *ahimsa* or related values make positive-functioned, if not "adaptive" contributions in at least 5 respects: (1) safeguarding milking and traction breeds; (2) preservation of temporaily dry or barren but still useful animals; (3) prevention of growth of energy-expensive beef industry; (4) protection of cattle which fatten in public domain or at landlord's expense; (5) protection of herd's recovery potential during famines. Although I did fail to suggest explicitly that these positive effects are to some extent products of *ahimsa,* it is self-evident that in so far as one regards cattle protection as useful, one must also regard as useful the ideology which supports cattle protection. Oberg experienced none of Vayda's difficulties as evidenced by his clearly stated conclusion that "the ban on killing cattle is an ideological device to protect a capital asset."

To claim that *ahimsa* makes positive contributions to the ecosystem is not to be confused with the claim that this doctrine in all of its unique Hindu elaboration is an essential feature of the basic productive system. On the contrary, I have tried to show that the major features of the ecosystem are derived from the interaction of a given type of technology with a given type of habitat. In my opinion there were and are relatively few viable alternatives to the observed ratio of men to cattle; on the other hand, it would appear that an ideology appropriate to the maintenance of such a ratio need not be restricted to the content furnished by the ritual and belief of Hinduism.

It is perhaps this picture of a rather loose relationship between the basic techno-environmental formula and the specific creeds known as *ahimsa* which provides the basis for Suttles' observation that my position is not that of "environmental determinism or economic determinism." In so far as I propose that culture, (especially technological equipment and productive processes) is as important as habitat, I clearly wish not to be associated with any strictly geographical environmentalists On the other hand, I would definitely prefer not to be removed from the ranks of economic determinism. The notion of socio-cultural causality which I believe both Suttles and I would recommend is epistemologically more sophisticated than the old, perfectly predictable causality of the Laplacian world view. It is in vulgar terms, a matter of probabilities whether a given techno-environmental base will "cause" or determine a given type of ideology. Naturally, this probability diminishes in proportion to the degree of detail with which the content of the ideology is specified. One may cease on this account to be a determinist in the old sense, perhaps to become a "probabilist." If so, then it is economic probabilism which first and foremost appears to me worthwhile. That is, I share with all economic determinists the conviction that in the long run and in most cases, ideology is swung into line by material conditions—by the evolution of techno-environmental and production relationships. The recent history of the social sciences demonstrates that to reverse this relationship, or to loose sight of it in the forest of positivistic ecclecticism is, in effect, to abandon the search for the lawful processes which govern socio-cultural evolution.

Vayda's 2nd suggestion, namely that I dispense with the word "cultural" in "cultural ecology," does not necessarily deserve a fuller response than space permits. I agree that the understanding of a given ecosystem involves anthropological and non-anthropological ecologists in an examination of the same set of factors and relationships. However, man does not play an important role in all ecosystems. Perhaps the phrase should be "human ecology;" but it still seems useful to emphasize for the benefit of non-anthropologists that as man interacts with his environment, his cultural conditioning constitutes an immensely more significant parameter than is true of other organisms. Vayda, however, must surely be more puzzled than I am over Opler's suggestion that we drop the word "ecology" rather than "cultural." Opler's point made with what I take to be courteous indirection, is that there is little new in the method which I advocate, since the conditions emphasized in the name of cultural, ecology have always been important in cultural-evolutionary studies. To this I would rejoin, "Yes, but not enough."

Finally, a comment on Bose's proposal for removing Gandhi's interest in cow protection from the political realm, where I had suggested it played a role in anti-British and anti-Moslem activities. If necessary, Gandhi may thus be protected from irreverence, without, however, diminishing the exploitation of the cow theme for political purposes by many other Hindu politicians. This, of course, does not deny the element of purely technological and economic "reform" which both Bose and I would emphasize in cow protection.

REFERENCES CITED

ANSTEY, VERA. 1952. *The economic development of India.* New York: Longmans, Green.

BAILEY, F. G. 1957. *Caste and the economic frontier.* Manchester: University of Manchester Press.

BANSIL, P. C. 1958. *India's food resources and population,* p. 104. Bombay: Vora. p. 97 (if 1959).

BHATIA, B. M. 1963. *Famines in India.* New York: Asia Publishing House.

BLACK, JOHN D. 1959. Supplementary to the Ford Foundation team's report: India's food crisis and steps to meet it. *The Indian Journal of Agricultural Economics* 14:1–6.

CHAPEKAR, L. N. 1960. *Thakurs of the Sahyadri.* Oxford: Oxford University Press.

CHATTERJEE, I. 1960. Milk production in India. *Economic Weekly* 12:1347–48.

CHAUDHRI, S. C, and R. GIRI. 1963. Role of cattle in India's economy. *Agricultural situation in India* 18:591–99.

COTTRELL, FRED. 1955. *Energy and society.* New York: McGraw-Hill.

DANDEKAR, U.M. 1964. Problem of numbers in cattle development. *Economic Weekly* 16:351–355.

DARLING, M. L. 1934. *Wisdom and waste in a Punjab village.* London: Oxford University Press.

DAS, A. B., and M. N. CHATTERJI. 1962. *The Indian economy.* Calcutta: Bookland Private.

DESAI, M. B. 1948. *The rural economy of Gujarat.* Bombay: Oxford University Press.

—. 1959. India's food crisis. *The Indian Journal of Agricultural Economics* 14: 27–37.

DISKAEKAR, P. D. 1960. *Re survey of a Deccan village Pimple Sandagar.* Bombay: The Indian Society of Agricultural Economics.

DUBE, S. C. 1955. *Indian village.* Ithaca: Cornell University Press.

DUPUIS, J. 1960. *Madras et le nord du Coromandel; etude des conditions de la vie indienne dans un cadre geografique.* Paris: Maisonneuve.

FOOD AND AGRICULTURE ORGANIZATION. 1953. *Agriculture in Asia and the Far East: Development and outlook.* Rome: FAO.

FORD FOUNDATION. 1959. *Report on India's food crisis and steps to meet it.* New Delhi: Government of India, Ministry of Food and Agriculture and Ministry of Community Development and Cooperation.

GANDHI, M. K. 1954. *How to serve the cow.* Edited by Bharaton Kumarappa. Ahmedabad: Navajivan Publishing House.

GANGULEE, N. 1935. *The Indian peasant and his environment.* London: Oxford University Press.

GOUROU, PIERRE. 1963. Civilization et economic pastorale. *L'Homme* 123–29.

GOVERNMENT OF INDIA. 1956. *Second five-year plan.* Planning Commission. New Delhi.

. 1957. *India.* Ministry of Information and Broadcasting. New Delhi.

. 1962. *Statistical Abstract of the Indian Union* 11. Cabinet Secretariat. New Delhi.

. 1963. *India.* Ministry of Information and Broadcasting. New Delhi.

GUPTA, S. C. 1959. *An economic survey of Shamaspur village.* New York: Asia Publishing House.

HABIB, IRFAN. 1963. *The agrarian system of Mughal India: 1556–1707.* New York: Asia Publishing House.   [J.M.]

Harris, Marvin. 1959. The economy has no surplus? *American Anthropologist* 61: 185–99.

—. 1960. Adaptation in biological and cultural science. *Transactions of the New York Academy of Sciences* 23:59–65.

—. *1964a. The nature of cultural things.* New York: Random House.

—. 1964 *b. Patterns of race in the Americas.* New York: Walker.   [KO]

Hopper, W. David. 1955. Seasonal labour cycles in an eastern Uttar Pradesh village. *Eastern Anthropologist* 8:141–50.

Hutton, J. H. 1961. *Caste in India,* p. VII. London: Oxford University Press.

Kapp, K. W. 1963. *Hindu culture, economic development and economic planning in India.* New York: Asia Publishing House.

Kardel, Hans. 1956. *Community development in agriculture: Mysore State, India,* Washington, D.C.: International Cooperation Administration.

Kartha, K. P. R. 1936. A note on the comparative economic efficiency of the Indian cow, the half breed cow, and the buffalo as producers of milk and butter fat. *Agriculture and Livestock in India* 4: 605–23.

—. 1959. "Buffalo," in *An introduction to animal husbandry in, the Tropics.* Edited by G. Williamson and W. J. A. Payne. London: Longmans, Green.

Knight, Henry. 1954. *Food administration in India 1939–47.* Stanford: Stanford University Press.

Kothavala, Zal R. 1934. Milk production in India. *Agriculture and Livestock in India* 2:122–29.

Lahiry, N. L. n.d. "Conservation and utilization of animal food resources," in Proceedings of symposium on food needs and resources. *Bulletin of the National Institute of Sciences of India* 20:140–44.

Leake, H. Martin. 1923. *The foundations of Indian agriculture.* Cambridge: W. Heffer.

Lewis, Oscar, and Victor Barnouw. 1958. *Village life in northern India.* Urbana: University of Illinois Press.

Lewis, W. A. 1955. *The theory of economic growth.* Homewood, 111.: R. D. Irwin.

Lupton, Arnold. 1922. *Happy India.* London: G. Allen & Unwin.

Mamoria, C. B. 1953. *Agricultural problems of India.* Allahabad: Kitab Mahal.

Matson, J. 1933. Inefficiency of cattle in India through disease. *Agriculture and Livestock in India* 1:227—28.

Mayadas, C. 1954. *Between us and hunger.* London: Oxford University Press.

Mayer, Adrian. 1952. *Land and society in Malabar.* Bombay: Oxford University Press.

Mayr, Ernst. 1959. "Darwin and the evo lutionary theory in biology," in *Evolution and anthropology: A centennial appraisal.* Edited by Betty Meggers. Washington, D.C.: The Anthropological Society of Washington. {W.S.]

Mishra, Vikas. 1962. *Hinduism and economic growth.* London: Oxford University Press.

MITRA, ASHOK. 1963. "Tax burden for Indian agriculture," in *Traditions, values, and socio-economic development.* Edited by R. Braibanti and J. J. Spengler, pp. 281–303. Durham: Duke University Press.

MITRA, RAJENDRALALA. 1881. *Indo-Aryans.* London: Edw. Stanford. [NKB]

MOHAN, S. N. 1962. Animal husbandry in the Third Plan. *Bulletin of the National Institute of Sciences of India* 20: 41–54.

MOOMAW, I. W. 1949. *The farmer speaks.* London: Oxford University Press.

MOSHER, ARTHUR T. 1946. *The economic effect of Hindu religion and social traditions on agricultural production by Christians in North India.* Unpublished Ph.D. dissertation, University of Chicago. (Also microfilms T 566.)

MUJUMDAR, N. A. 1960. Cow dung as manure. *Economic Weekly* 12:743–44.

NAIR, K. 1961. *Blossoms in the dust: The human factor in Indian development* New York: F. A. Praeger.   [MKO]

NANDRA, P. N., *et at.* 1955. Report of the expert committee on the prevention of *slaughter of cattle in India.* New Delhi: Government of India Press.

NATIONAL COUNCIL OF APPLIED ECONOMIC RESEARCH. 1959. *Domestic fuels in India.* New York: Asia Publishing House.

. 1960. *Techno-economic survey of Madhya Pradesh.* New Delhi.

. 1961. *Techno-economic survey of Tripura.* New Delhi.

. 1962b. *Techno-economic survey of Andhra Pradesh.* New Delhi.

. 1962b. *Techno-economic survey of Punjab.* New Delhi.

. 1962c. *Techno-economic survey of West Bengal.* New Delhi.

. 1962d. *Economic atlas of Madras State.* New Delhi. [JM]

. 1963. *Techno-economic survey of Raj as than.* New Delhi.

OPLER, MARVIN K. 1956. Review of: *The art of Indian Asia,* by H. Zimmer, as edited by J. Campbell (New York: Pantheon Books, 1955). *Philosophy and Phenomenological Research* 17:269–71.

—. 1960. "Cultural evolution and the psychology of peoples," in *Essays in the science of culture.* Edited by G. Dole and R. Carneiro, pp. 354–79. New York: Thomas Y. Crowell.   {MKO]

RAM, L. 1927. *Cow-protection in India.* Madras: South Indian Humanitarian League.

RANDHAWA, M. S. 1962. *Agriculture and animal husbandry in India.* New Delhi. Indian Council of Agricultural Research.

RANDHAWA, M. S., *et al.* 1961. *Farmers of India. 2* vols. New Delhi: Indian Council of Agricultural Research.

RIEPE, DALE M. 1961. *The naturalistic animal husbandry in India.* New Delhi: University of Washington Press. [MKO]

ROY, PRODIPTO. 1955. The sacred cow in India. *Rural sociology* 20:8–15.

SAHA, M. N. 1956. Fuel in India. *Nature* 177:923–24.

SCHNEIDER, HAROLD. 1957. The subsistence role of cattle among the Pakot and in East Africa. *American Anthropologist* 59:278—300.

SHAHANI, K. M. 1957. Dairying in India. *Journal of Dairying Science* 40:867–73.

SHASTRI, C. P. 1960. Bullock labour utilization in agriculture. *Economic Weekly* 12:1585–92.

Simoons, E. J. 1961. *Eat not this flesh.* Madison: University of Wisconsin Press.

SINHA, R. P. 1961. *Food in India.* London: Oxford University Press.

Spate, Oskar Hermann. 1954. *India and Pakistan: A general and regional geography.* London: Methuen:

SRINIVAS, M. N. 1952. *Religion and society among the Coorgs of South India.* Oxford: Oxford University Press.

—. 1958. India's cultural values and economic development. *Economic Development and cultural change* 7:3—6.

—. 1962. *Caste in modern India.* New York: Asia Publishing House.

Statistical atlas for the Madras Presidency. 1895. Madras Government Press. [JM]

THIRUMALAI, SHRI. 1954. *Post-war agricultural problems and policies in India,* p. 38. New York: Institute of Pacific Relations.

Thorner, Daniel, and Alice Thorner. 1962. *Land and labour in India.* New York: Asia Publishing House.

U.S. Census of Agriculture. 1954. "Dairy producers and dairy production." in *Farmers and farm production in the United States* 3, part 9, chap. V.

VENKATRAMAN, R. B. 1938. The Indian village, its past, present, future. *Agriculture and Livestock in India* 7:702–10).

Williamson, G., and W. J. A. Payne. 1959. *An introduction to animal husbandry in the Tropics.'* London: Longmans, Green.

Wiser, William H., and C. V. Wiser. 1963. *Behind mud walls: 1930–1960.* Berkeley: University of California Press.

Zeuner, F. E. 1954. "Domestication of animals," in *A history of technology.* Edited by C. Singer, *et al,* pp. 327–52. New York: Oxford University Press.

Hallucinogenic Plants and Their Use in Traditional Societies

An Overview

Wade Davis

In Western society, drugs are used for either medicinal purposes or pleasure. Our culture sometimes defines those who use drugs for nonmedicinal purposes as deviant and we have begun to view the use of drugs as a pathological condition unique in the annals of human history. The illegal use of drugs is considered a major social problem.

The use of drugs is widespread in traditional cultures around the world. However, in traditional societies hallucinogenic plants are used for religious purposes and in ritual settings. Throughout history, people have sought ways to see beyond the normal reality of everyday life. They have endured the risk of poison in experimenting with ways to prepare mind-altering substances. These substances may be smoked, chewed, eaten, sniffed, drunk, rubbed onto the skin or into cuts, or even taken as intoxicating enemas. They have taken these risks, not for pleasure or kicks, but for curing illnesses through magic, divining truth, peering into the future, and making contact with the spirit world. This is serious and important for the people involved.

Another difference highlighted by the comparative study of drug use is the important effect of culture and context on the drug experience. Used in different settings, under different sets of expectations, the same drug may cause very different reactions, from nausea on the one hand to a religious experience on the other. Today we may find it odd that

Native Americans (Amerindians) smoked tobacco to cause giddiness (one of the universal symptoms of ecstasy) and to open the pathways through which shamans disassociated themselves from the normal state of awareness.

In light of America's drug problem, getting a broader historical and comparative vision of the role of drugs in society makes sense.

As you read this selection, ask yourself the following questions:

- Were hallucinogenic plants discovered by chance?
- What is the relationship between medicinal drugs, psychotropic drugs, and poisons?
- What factors influence what an individual sees under the influence of hallucinogens?
- How do ritual and the role of the shamanistic leader create a different context for the use of hallucinogenic drugs in traditional and modern societies?
- Do drug users in our society have their own secular rituals?

The following terms are discussed in this selection:

Amerindian	*psychoactive drugs*
decoction	*rite of passage*
hallucinogen	*ritual*
indigenous	*sorcery*

The passionate desire which leads man to flee, from the monotony of everyday life has made him instinctively discover strange substances. He has done so, even where nature has been most niggardly in producing them and where, the products seem very far from, possessing the properties which would enable him to satisfy this desire.

T hus early in this century did Lewis Lewin, perhaps the preeminent pioneer in the study of psychoactive drugs, describe the primal search that led to man's discovery of hallucinogens. Strictly speaking, a hallucinogen is any chemical substance that distorts the senses and produces hallucinations—perceptions or experiences that depart dramatically from ordinary reality. Today we know these substances variously as psychotomimetics (psychosis mimickers), psycho-taraxics (mind disturbers) and psychedelics (mind manifesters); dry terms which quite inadequately describe the remarkable effects they have on the human mind. These effects are varied but they frequently include a dreamlike state marked by dramatic alterations "in the sphere of experience, in the perception of reality, changes even of space and time and in consciousness of self. They invariably induce a series of visual hallucinations, often in kaleidoscopic movement, and usually in indescribably brilliant and rich colours, frequently accompanied by auditory and other hallucinations"—tactile, olfactory, and temporal. Indeed the effects are so unearthly, so unreal that most hallucinogenic plants early acquired a sacred place in indigenous cultures. In rare cases, they were worshipped as gods incarnate.

The pharmacological activity of the hallucinogens is due to a relatively small number of types of chemical compounds. While modern chemistry has been able in most cases successfully to duplicate these substances, or even manipulate their chemical structures to create novel synthetic forms, virtually all hallucinogens have their origins in plants. (One immediate exception that comes to mind is the New World toad, *Bufo marinus,* but the evidence that this animal was used for its psychoactive properties is far from complete.)

Within the plant kingdom the hallucinogens occur only among the evolutionarily advanced flowering plants and in one division—the fungi—of the more primitive spore bearers. Most hallucinogens are alkaloids, a family of perhaps 5,000 complex organic molecules that also account for the biological activity of most toxic and medicinal plants. These active compounds may be found in the various concentrations in different parts of the plant—roots, leaves, seeds, bark and/or flowers—and they may be absorbed by the human body in a number of ways, as is evident in the wide variety of folk preparations. Hallucinogens may be smoked or snuffed, swallowed fresh or dried, drunk in decoctions and infusions, absorbed directly through the skin, placed in wounds or administered as enemas.

To date about 120 hallucinogenic plants have been identified worldwide. On first glance, given that estimates of the total number of plant species range as high as 800,000, this appears to be a relatively small number. However, it grows in significance when compared to the total number of species used as food. Perhaps 3,000 species of plants have been regularly consumed by some people at some period of history, but today only 150 remain important enough to enter world commerce. Of these a mere 12–15, mostly domesticated cereals, keep us alive.

In exploring his ambient vegetation for hallucinogenic plants, man has shown extraordinary ingenuity, and in experimenting with them all the signs of pharmacological genius. He has also quite evidently taken great personal risks. Peyote *(Lophophora williamsii),* for example, has as many as 30 active constituents, mostly alkaloids, and is exceedingly bitter, not unlike most deadly poisonous plants. Yet the Huichol, Tamhumara and numerous other peoples of Mexico and the American Southwest discovered that sun-dried and eaten whole the cactus produces spectacular psychoactive effects.

With similar tenacity, the Mazatec of Oaxaca discovered amongst a mushroom flora that contained many deadly species as many as 10 that were hallucinogenic. These they believed had ridden to earth upon thunderbolts, and were reverently gathered at the time of the new moon. Elsewhere in Oaxaca, the seeds of the morning glory *(Rivea corymbosa)* were crushed and prepared as a decoction known at one time as ololiuqui—the sacred preparation of the Aztec, and one that we now realize contained alkaloids closely related to LSD, a potent synthetic hallucinogen. In Peru, the bitter mescaline-rich cactus *Trichocere.*

us pachanoi became the basis of the San Pedro curative cults of the northern Andes. Here the preferred form of administration is the decoction, a tea served up at the Jong nocturnal ceremonies during which time the patients' problems were diagnosed. At dawn they would be sent on the long pilgrimages high into the mountains to bathe in the healing waters of a number of sacred lakes.

Lowland South America has provided several exceedingly important and chemically fascinating hallucinogenic preparations, notably the intoxicating yopo (*Anadenanthera peregrina*) and ebene (*Virola calophylla, V. calophylloidea, V. theiodora*) snuffs of the upper Orinoco of Venezuela and adjacent Brazil and the ayahuasca-caapi-yagé complex (*Banisteriopsis caapi*) found commonly among the rainforest peoples of the Northwest Amazon. Yopo is prepared from the seeds of a tall forest tree which are roasted gently and then ground into a fine powder, which is then mixed with some alkaline substance, often the ashes of certain leaves. Ebene is prepared from the blood red resin of certain trees in the nutmeg family. Preparations vary but frequently the bark is stripped from the tree and slowly heated to allow the resin to collect in a small earthenware pot where it is boiled down into a thick paste, which in turn is sun dried and powdered along with the leaves of other plants. Ayahuasca comes from the rasped bark of a forest liana which is carefully heated in water, again with a number of admixture plants, until a thick decoction is obtained. All three products are violently hallucinogenic and it is of some significance that they all contain a number of subsidiary plants that, in ways not yet fully understood, intensify or lengthen the psychoactive effects of the principal ingredients. This is an important feature of many folk preparations and it is due in part to the fact that different chemical compounds in relatively small concentrations may effectively potentiate each other, producing powerful synergistic effects—a biochemical version of the whole being greater than the sum of its parts. The awareness of these properties is evidence of the impressive chemical and botanical knowledge of the traditional peoples.

In the Old World may be found some of the most novel means of administering hallucinogens. In southern Africa, the Bushmen of Dobe, Botswana, absorb the active constituents of the plant kwashi (*Pancratium trianthum*) by incising the scalp and rubbing the juice of an onion-like bulb into the open wound. The fly agaric (*Amanita muscaria*), a psychoactive mushroom used in Siberia, may be toasted on a fire or made into a decoction with reindeer milk and wild blueberries. In this rare instance the active principals pass through the body unaltered, and the psychoactive urine of the intoxicated individual may be consumed by the others. Certain European hallucinogens—notably the solanaceous belladonna (*Atropa belladonna*), henbane (*Hyoscyamus niger*), mandrake (*Mandmgora officinarum*) and datura (*Datura metel*)—axe topically active; that is the active principals are absorbed through the skin. We now know, for example, that much of the behavior associated with the medieval witches is as readily attributable to these drugs as to any spiritual communion with the diabolic. The witches commonly nabbed their bodies with hallucinogenic ointments. A particularly efficient means of self-administering the drug for women is through the moist tissue of the vagina; the witches broomstick or staff was considered the most effective applicator. Our own popular image of the haggard woman on a broomstick comes from the medieval belief that the witches rode their staffs each midnight to the sabbat, the orgiastic assembly of demons and sorcerers. In fact, it now appears that their journey was not through space but across the hallucinatory landscape of their minds.

There is in the worldwide distribution of the hallucinogenic plants a pronounced and significant discrepancy that has only inadequately been accounted for but which serves to illustrate a critical feature of their role in traditional societies. Of the 120 or more such plants found to date, over 100 are native to the Americas; the Old World has contributed a mere 15–20 species. How might this be explained? To be sure it is in part an artifact of the emphasis of academic research. A good many of these plants have entered the literature due to the efforts of Professor R. E. Schultes and his colleagues at the Harvard Botanical Museum and elsewhere, and their interest has predominantly been in the New World. Yet were the hallucinogenic plants a dominant feature of traditional cultures in Africa and Eurasia, surely they would have shown up in the extensive ethnographic literature and in the journals of traders and missionaries. With few notable exceptions, they don't. Nor is this discrepancy due to floristic peculiarities. The rainforests of West Africa and Southeast Asia, in particular, are exceedingly rich and diverse. Moreover, the peoples of these regions have most successfully explored them for pharmacologically active compounds for use both as medicines and poisons. In fact, as much as any other material trait the manipulation of toxic plants remains a consistent theme throughout sub-Saharan African cultures. The Amerindians, for their part, were certainly no strangers to plant toxins which they commonly exploited as fish, arrow and dart poisons. Yet it is a singular fact that while the peoples of Africa consistently used these toxic preparations on each other, the Amerindian almost never did. And while the Amerindian successfully explored his forest for hallucinogens, the African did not. This suggests the critical fact that the use of any pharmacologically active plant—remembering that the difference between hallucinogen, medicine and poison is often a matter of dosage—is firmly rooted in culture. If the peoples of Africa did not explore their environment for psychoactive drugs, surely it is because they felt no need to. In many Amerindian societies the use of plant hallucinogens lies at the very heart of traditional life.

To begin to understand the role that these powerful plants play in these societies, however, it is essential to place the drugs themselves in proper context. For one, the pharmacologically active components do not produce uniform effects. On the contrary, any psychoactive drug has within it a completely ambivalent potential for good or evil, order or chaos. Pharmacologically it induces a certain condition, but that condition is mere raw material to be worked by particular cultural or psychological forces and expectations. This is what our own medical experts call the "set and setting" of any drug experience. *Set* in these terms is the individual's expectation of what the drug will do to him;.*setting* is the environment—both physical and social—in which the drug is taken. This may be illustrated by an example from our own country. In the northwest rainforests of Oregon are a native species of hallucinogenic mushrooms. Those who go out into the forest deliberately intending to ingest these mushrooms generally experience a pleasant intoxication. Those who inadvertently consume them while foraging for edible mushrooms invariably end up in the poison unit of the nearest hospital. The mushroom itself has not changed.

Similarly the hallucinogenic plants consumed by the Amerindian induce a powerful but neutral stimulation of the imagination; they create a template, as it were, upon which cultural beliefs and forces may be amplified a thousand times. What the individual sees in the visions is dependent not on the drug but on other factors—the mood and setting of the group, the physical and mental states of the participants, his own expectations based on a rich repository of tribal hare and, above all in Indian societies, the authority, knowledge and experience of the leader of the ceremony. The role of this figure—be it man or woman, shaman, curandero, paye, maestro or brujo—is pivotal. It is he who places the protective cloak of ritual about the participants. It is he who tackles the bombardment of visual and auditory stimuli and gives them order. It is he who must interpret a complex body of belief, reading the power in leaves and the meaning in stones, who must skillfully balance the forces of the universe and guide the play of the winds. The ceremonial use of hallucinogenic plants by the Amerindian is (most often) a collective journey into the unconscious. It is not necessarily, and in fact rarely is, a pleasant or an easy journey. It is wondrous and it may be terrifying. But above all it is purposeful.

The Amerindian enters the realm of the hallucinogenic visions not out of boredom, or to relieve an individual's restless anxiety but rather to fulfill some collective need of the group. In the Amazon, for example, hallucinogens are taken to divine the future, track the paths of enemies, ensure the fidelity of women, diagnose and treat diseases. The Huichol in Mexico eat their peyote at the completion of long arduous pilgrimages in order that they may experience in life the journey of the soul of the dead to the underworld. The Amahuaca Indians of Peru drink yage that the nature of the forest animals and plants may be revealed to their apprentices. In eastern North America during puberty rites, the Algonquin confined adolescents to a longhouse for two weeks and fed them a beverage based in part on datura. During the extended intoxication and subsequent amnesia—a pharmacological feature of this drug—the young boys forgot what it was to be a child so that they might learn what it meant to be a man. But whatever the ostensible purpose of the hallucinogenic journey, the Amerindian imbibes his plants in a highly structured manner that places a ritualistic framework of order around their use. Moreover the experience is explicitly sought for positive ends. It is not a means of escaping from an uncertain existence; rather it is perceived as a means of contribution to the welfare of all one's people.

Is Human Culture Carcinogenic for Uncontrolled Population Growth and Ecological Destruction?

Warren M. Hern

Numerous observers have described the human species as a kind of planetary disease, even comparing it to cancer (Eisley 1961, Forrester 1991, Gregg 1955). In a previous article (Hern 1990), I described the species as a "malignant epiecopathologic process" that is destroying the global ecosystem. I stated that the sum of human activities, viewed over the past tens of thousands of years, exhibits all four major characteristics of a malignant process: rapid, uncontrolled growth; invasion and destruction of adjacent tissues (ecosystems, in this case); metastasis (colonization and urbanization, in this case); and dedifferentiation (loss of distinctiveness in individual components). In this case, dedifferentiation implies that through the invention of culture, humans have developed the ability to adapt to and survive in all ecosystems. We are no longer bound, as are most other organisms, to the specific ecosystems in which we originally evolved. Human culture gives us a unique relationship with all ecosystems as well as with each other.

What are the implications of these characteristics? In an organism, a malignant process continues until the supporting organism ceases to function—it dies. In the case of human populations, parallels to cancer raise the most fundamental questions about our relationship with the planetary ecosystem.

The purpose of this article is to discuss the process by which human culture has brought about this malignant transformation in our relationship with the ecosystem, to show why it

Warren M. Hern, "Is Human Culture Carcinogenic for Uncontrolled Population Growth and Ecological Destruction?" from *BioScience*, Vol. 43, No. 11; December 1993, pp. 768–773. Published by American Institute of Biological Sciences. Copyright © 1993 by University of California Press—Journals. Permission to reprint granted by the rights holder.

is important to examine and test the hypothesis that human activities have become malignant for the planet, and to discuss some of the implications of this hypothesis for the future.

The need for such a hypothesis arises because, in addition to the four basic characteristics of a malignant process mentioned before, we are confronted with a wide variety of apparently disparate phenomena that cannot be ignored and are directly related to human activities. One of these phenomena is the increasing relative uniformity in the appearance and structure of human communities, especially large ones, throughout the planet. Another is the regional and global environmental changes, such as severe pollution of air, water, and earth; global warming (anticipated); increased atmospheric carbon-dioxide concentrations; decreased polar ozone concentrations; universal oceanic dispersion of human trash; rapid global deforestation and desertification; and rapid decline worldwide in biodiversity with increased species extinction rates.

At present, there is no other overall theory or hypothesis that provides a satisfactory explanation for these various well-documented phenomena. Linear mathematical models such as those used in a general circulation model (Stern et al. 1992) or in systems dynamics models (Meadows et al. 1992) are inadequate to describe complex ecological relationships, particularly when they include biological and human sociocultural and political systems. A biocultural model that includes these factors is needed.

CULTURAL COMPONENTS OF THE ECOPATHOLOGIC PROCESS

An essential component of the ecopathological hypothesis is the role of culture in human survival. The principal role of culture is to provide adaptations that promote survival of the species. Over the last two million years of human evolution, cultural adaptations have varied enormously as a function of time and among societies. Cultural adaptations have contributed to and resulted from population growth (Polgar 1969, Tinker et al. 1976). The origin of agriculture in the Middle East was accompanied by large increases in population, and the elaboration of culture permitted the increasingly intensive exploitation of the environment (Hassan 1981). Similar changes have been described in other parts of the world.

Environmental changes resulting from cultural adaptations have been dramatic and frequently permanent (Angel 1975). Europe lost most of its native forests from 900 to 1900 A.D. (Darby 1956), and North America lost most of its forests from 1620 to 1920 (Williams 1989). Current rates of tropical deforestation are alarming, but they are a recent phenomenon compared with the length of human occupation of, for example, the Amazon basin (Martin 1973, Woodwell 1990).

Different societies have varying rates of population growth; these change over time and they have different relationships to the natural environment. Tribal societies have had means of regulating fertility for thousands of years, but some have regulated population more strictly than have others (Hern 1992, Nag 1962). Western culture, especially as exemplified by the European expansion into the Western Hemisphere, has shown a much more aggressive attitude toward the exploitation of natural resources than have many indigenous American societies (Crosby 1986).

Are there real differences in cultural attitudes toward population growth and environmental exploitation, or do the variations simply reflect differential access to technology? Martin (1973,1984) has claimed that the North American megafauna were extinguished by early American hunters, and evidence abounds that rapid species extinction accompanied the human colonization of Pacific islands and other settlement points (Cassels 1984, Diamond 1984). Denevan (1992) demonstrates that the North American landscape was also highly altered by precolonial indigenous people.

A common theme in the expansion of human populations around the world is that culture has permitted human beings, who are biologically almost identical, to occupy a wide variety of ecological niches. Most species are highly restricted in their distributions because of adaptations to specific ecosystems, and they usually do not drive other species to extinction in the process of becoming so adapted. By comparison, human domination of local and regional ecosystems has been accompanied by virtually instantaneous extinction of numerous species during the past 10,000 years. The elaboration or evolution of cultures has permitted humans to become undifferentiated exploiters of the entire planet.

Whereas the life span of early humans was relatively short and comparable to that of other primates, cultural adaptations such as agriculture, weapons for hunting and defense against other animals, and modern medical care have resulted in increasingly long survival times for human beings. In fact, increasing survival times have become a principal problem for industrial societies.

A primary feature of cancer cells is that the genetic regulatory mechanisms fail in several ways. One of the consequences is that cancer cells are immortal: they do not die after the normal lifespan (Prescott and Flexer 1986, Ruddon 1987). Human culture, rather than a genetic change, is the altering factor among populations that permits human survival long beyond our previous term in the ecosystem.

At the community or aggregate level, human communities have had, even before modern times, important similarities and even identities, which is what permits archaeologists to make sense out of the artifacts of very different cultures. As the twentieth century has progressed, however, the easily apparent differences between the Yanomamö village, the Italian hill town, the Dogon village, and the Yoruba compound have become blurred as urbanization compels uniformity in housing. One growing village begins to look much like another, and São Paulo looks more like Chicago every day.

All large cities now essentially perform the same functions and have many of the same economic, environmental, transportation, and communication problems. The morphology of urban settlements, seen in outline, is startlingly similar everywhere and throughout time, having the ragged, aggressive, invasive appearance of a malignant process (Figures 1 and 2). There has been a loss of differentiation in human activities at the aggregate level.

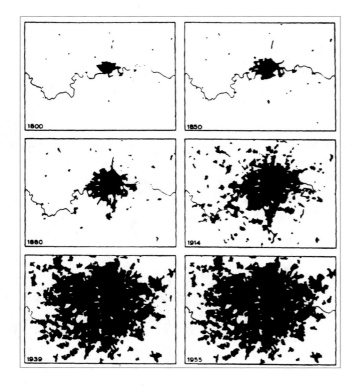

Figure 1. The growth of London, 1800–1955.
James H. Johnson, from *Urban Geography: An Introductory Analysis*, second edition. Copyright © 1972 by James Harmon Johnson. Permission to reprint granted by the author.

Notwithstanding ethnic rivalries, which are increasingly settled by the same violent means (Homer-Dixon et al. 1993), loss of differentiation has accompanied, if not signaled, the loss of important cultural differences (Reining 1991).

MODELS OF POPULATION GROWTH

Demographers have tracked, described, analyzed, and quantified human population growth beyond the capacity of most citizens to understand the results, but demographers cannot necessarily say why that growth is happening. However, it is apparent that population growth and cultural change interact in a positive feedback loop (Dumond 1975, Margalef 1968, Nag 1980).

Population growth and cultural change have been accompanied by increasingly effective technology that permits intensive exploitation of all ecosystems and, indeed, the lithosphere itself. Virtually all modern societies depend on fossil fuels for survival and on extracting a wide variety of inorganic materials from the earth. Evidence is accumulating that the use of fossil fuels and the accompanying destruction of forest ecosystems is altering Earth's atmosphere to the point of affecting all life forms (Firor 1990, Woodwell 1990).

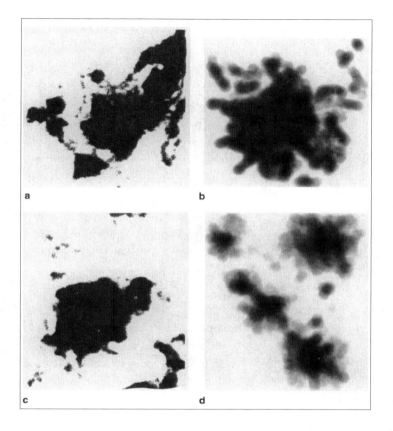

Figure 2. *(a) and (c) Metastatic malignant melanoma of the human brain.* Courtesy William Robinson, Division of Medical Oncology, University of Colorado Health Sciences Center, Denver. Copyright © by William Robinson. Permission to reprint granted by the rights holder.

Demographers almost universally adhere to the logistic model of human population growth, which assumes that human population growth will stabilize at some point in the future, with the projected plateau reached at 11–12 billion individuals near the end of the twenty-first century (Demeny 1991). These projections result from, according to Demeny, "the informal insertion of unspecified assumptions." One of the reasons Demeny gives for this projected stabilization is that higher projected numbers seem "implausible."

Much of the attraction of the logistic curve seems to derive from studies by Raymond Pearl, whose research on fruit flies showed this pattern in a density-dependent population (Pearl 1922,1925, Peterson 1969). Classical demographic transition theory incorporates this idea into its formulation of human population stabilization, after modernization induces the reduction in both mortality and fertility (Notestein 1945). Unfortunately, much experience since World War II has not conformed to these expectations, because fertility has increased in many newly modernizing countries before it has begun to fall. The result has been steady growth of the global human population, notwithstanding falling rates of growth in some populations.

There are several basic problems with the belief that human population growth will eventually stabilize. First, there is no convincing empirical evidence that the global human population as a whole will stop growing in the foreseeable future. Although there are examples of modern societies, such as China, that have made decisions to stop population growth, these decisions have not proven to be highly effective. A few tribal societies have successfully limited growth, and precolonial Japan showed zero growth for more than a century (Peterson 1969), but these phenomena were modified when the societies became less isolated. And although some European nations have recently exhibited a negative intrinsic population growth rate, also losing population from emigration, others have gained from immigration. The US population is growing at the rate of approximately 1% per year (PRB 1992).

A second problem with the proposed population stabilization is that the Pearl-Reed logistic curve, still applied to project population stabilization even though it has been discredited as a predictor of population change, assumes a density-dependent population (Peterson 1969). But the human population has often shown itself historically to be density independent owing to new cultural adaptations. An example is the European population explosion that followed the introduction of New World cultigens and colonial expansion (Crosby 1972).

Third, the belief that population must stabilize in the imaginable range of 11–12 billion because other larger projections seem improbable or incredible is similar to beliefs earlier in the century that the population would stabilize at levels much lower than the current count. Fourth, this belief assumes free access to safe and effective fertility control—including contraception, abortion, and sterilization—for everyone on the planet, whereas this access has not been realized and will not be in the foreseeable future. Fifth, it assumes effective use of all fertility control methods, and this assumption is similarly unwarranted.

The belief that population numbers will stabilize seems warranted only if, as in animal populations, the death rate goes up to exceed the birth rate, or if birth rates plummet due to crowding, social disruption, or other kinds of social pathology (Calhoun 1962, Homer-Dixon et al. 1993). But human population growth is not necessarily diminished by greater density. Growth rates increase with sedentism, aggregation, and modernization (Binford and Chasko 1976, Nag 1980). The response to density is increasingly intense exploitation of the ecosystem (Boserup 1965, Geertz 1963). Humans communicate through culture and form coalitions that defeat limitations posed by ecosystems (Harms 1987). In this respect, humans and their systems are behaving similarly to the cells described by von Foerster in his mathematical analysis leading to the equations for density-independent growth (von Foerster et al. 1960).

Von Foerster's equations, originally describing the behavior of cell coalitions, have proved to be stunningly accurate, if perhaps conservative, in their estimates of human population growth over the last 30 years (Umpleby 1990). This correlation should at least cast doubt on the logistic curve/density-dependent school of thought that predicts stabilization of the human population numbers with the next century. Von Foerster has also shown that the growth rates of the human population that appear to be declining overall are more likely to be tangents to a hyperbolic curve on a semilog scale that describes not a declining growth rate of the human population but one that is actually increasing (Umpleby 1990, von Foerster 1966). This increase is caused by the steady decline in length of doubling times of the human population since A.D. 0 (von Foerster et al. 1960).

There is a choice of perspectives in viewing the ecological changes and species extinctions that have accompanied human population expansion. One may adopt a neo-Darwinian perspective that this progression of events is natural, but that perspective has the potential hazard of being both ideological and anthropocentric. If human activities cause collapse of the global ecosystem, the neo-Darwinian perspective could also prove to be maladaptive. Wilson (1992) estimates that most mammalian species survive up to 5 million years. Humans have been wandering the planet for approximately 2 million years starting with our *Homo erectus* ancestors. But *Homo sapiens* has only been around for 100,000 years or so; current trends indicate the likelihood of population overshoot, collapse, and extinction within the next four centuries. We appear to be accelerating the process somewhat and inventing a new evolutionary experience: auto-extinction.

There is no evidence that other species have caused as many species extinctions as has ours, so the current extinction rate is not merely a reflection of Darwinian competition. Something more relentless is at work. Human beings, almost without exception (and there are some), have tended to simplify ecosystems and exclude other species from their territories. As global biodiversity declines, it is apparent that a principal effect of human activity and population growth, accompanied by increasing cultural sophistication, is a reduction in the total number of species, ecosystem complexity, and the introduction of serious if not irreversible instability into all ecosystems (Allen and Flecker 1993, Skole and Tucker 1993, Stanley and Warne 1993). If we posit a healthy ecosystem that is as complex as possible, relatively stable, with high species diversity and competition, the effect of human activity is almost universally to make ecosystems less healthy.

That being the case, what are we to make of a species that makes ecosystems unhealthy or even destroys them? One strategy is to look at the effects in terms of a disease model (Hern 1990). Although that model has been applied until now only to individual organisms, it can be useful in larger systems. The model, however, must take into account the intangible and perhaps unmeasurable capacity of culture to modify both ecosystems and survival probabilities for human beings.

The previous analysis shows how cultural adaptations, as distinguished from biological adaptations, provide the means by which humans have not only survived, but by which they have become the dominant species on the planet. Cultural adaptations are key components of population growth, colonization of distant sites as original resources are exhausted, and destruction of adjacent ecosystems, which are always replaced by human communities or corporate activities. The fourth component of malignant process, dedifferentiation, is shown by the examples given previously of loss of biological and cultural differentiation at the individual level and loss of aggregate differentiation at the community level.

In making a diagnosis of malignant neoplasm at the organismic level, the pathologist requires only two of the four characteristics of malignancy. Cultural adaptations permit the human species to have all four characteristics of a malignant process. Stopping population growth, even if it were possible to do so tomorrow, does not, by itself, change the diagnosis.

VALUE OF THE ECOPATHOLOGY HYPOTHESIS

It is apparent that, in general, human culture plays the principal role in the transformation of human activities from noninvasive subsistence of a skinny primate in the late Pleistocene to a truly malignant process disrupting the planetary ecosystem. This hypothesis does explain the widespread phenomena that concern us. It can be studied and tested in these ways:

- By examining the many examples of deliberate control of human fertility already cited, including the fact that human governments can change their policies concerning fertility limitation, as President Bill Clinton began doing on 21 January 1993 by lifting the Reagan-Bush administration restrictions on abortion.
- By exploring how various organizations, activities, and official governmental actions are working to save environments and species, reversing the effects of pollution, and slowing the pace of ecological destruction.
- By comparing what the human species has wrought on the planet in the last few thousand years, particularly since the beginning of the Industrial Revolution, with what it may be possible for us to do if we were to decide to stop being a cancer on the planet.
- By examining how humans around the globe convert as much plant, animal, organic, and inorganic matter as possible to human biomass or its adaptive adjuncts.

The testing of epidemiologic hypotheses must often be performed as observational experiments by comparing historical with currently evolving data or in a natural experiment. In this case, the planetary experiment may proceed to its conclusion without a control, as we are doing; we may choose two or more areas for study, leaving control areas with no regulation of fertility or ecologic destruction, and highly regulating other areas with respect to intrinsic population growth and environmental modification; or we may use the past as an uncontrolled control and make decisions now that stop the malignant process everywhere.

The first option may bring extinction not only to us but to many other species. The second option, although theoretically possible, is unworkable and unacceptable for both ethical and political reasons, just as it is unacceptable to let a cancer patient die when you know of a remedy that has a strong likelihood of cure. Another problem is that the forces we address are global, not local, and no locality may escape their consequences. The third option is both ethically acceptable and politically feasible (Ludwig et al. 1993). Whether it is possible remains a question that is not technical but political. We know what to do. Can we do it? Can we do it in ways that are acceptable to enough of us to permit it to happen?

The principal difference between the human species and organismic cancer is that we can think, and we can decide not to be a cancer. Without such a collective decision, taken and expressed globally through our cultural and political institutions, we face the implications of this hypothesis, or diagnosis: the characteristic of a malignant process is to continue until the supportive organism has ceased to function. For us, this lack of a decision could result in the terminal derangement of the global ecosystem to such an extent that it would no longer support human life or activity. It is the ultimate bad news, at least as far as human beings are concerned.

Scientists may honestly debate whether it is useful to consider such a dreadful hypothesis. The hypothesis at least has the value of helping us to understand not only what is happening to us and to the planet but why it is happening. If we conclude that there is more to support the hypothesis than to refute it, but that we can counter it by our decisions and actions, the conclusion gives a compelling new urgency to our task.

Warren M. Hern is an associate adjunct professor at the Institute of Behavioral Science and Department of Anthropology, University of Colorado, Boulder, CO.

ACKNOWLEDGMENTS

This article is based on a presentation at a symposium entitled "Demography and the Environment" at the annual meeting of the Population Association of America, 1 May 1992, in Denver, Colorado.

REFERENCES CITED

Allan, J. D., and A. S. Flecker. 1993. Biodiversity conservation in running waters. *Bio-Science* 43: 32–43.

Angel, J. L. 1975. Paleoecology, paleodemography, and health. Pages 167–190 in S. Polgar, ed. *Population, Ecology, and Social Evolution.* Mouton, The Hague, The Netherlands.

Binford, L. R., and W. J. Chasko Jr. 1976 Nunamiut demographic history: a provocative case. Pages 63–143 in E. B. W. Zubrow, ed. *Demographic Archeology: Quantitative Approaches.* University of New Mexico Press, Albuquerque.

Boserup, E. 1965. *The Conditions of Agricultural Growth*. Aldine, Chicago.

Calhoun, J. B. 1962. Population density and social pathology. *Sci. Am.* 206: 139–148.

Cassels, R. 1984. Faunal extinction and prehistoric man in New Zealand and the Pacific Islands. Pages 741–767 in P. S. Martin and R. G. Klein, eds. *Quarternary Extinctions: A Prehistoric Revolution*. University of Arizona Press, Tucson.

Chapin, F. S. Jr., and S. F. Weiss, eds. 1962. *Urban Growth Dynamics in a Regional Cluster of Cities*. John Wiley & Sons, New York.

Crosby, A. W. 1972. *The Columbian Exchange: Biological and Cultural Consequences of 1492*. Greenwood Press, Westport, CT.

—. 1986. *Ecological Imperialism: The Biological Expansion of Europe, 900–1900*. Cambridge University Press, New York.

Darby, H. C. 1956. The clearing of the woodland in Europe. Pages 183–216 in W. L. Thomas Jr., ed. *Man's Role in Changing the Face of the Earth*. University of Chicago Press, Chicago, IL.

Demeny, P. 1991. Population trends and models. Paper presented at Humankind in Global Change: Indicators and Prospects—Population Change: Present Indicators and Future Trends, a symposium at the annual meeting of the American Association for the Advancement of Science, Washington, DC, 17 February 1991.

Denevan, W. 1992. The pristine myth: the landscape of the Americas in 1492. *Annals of the Association of American Geographers* 82: 369–385.

Diamond, J. 1984. Historic extinction: a Rosetta Stone for understanding prehistoric extinctions. Pages 824–862 in P. S. Martin and R. G. Klein, eds. *Quarternary Extinctions: A Prehistoric Revolution*. University of Arizona Press, Tucson.

Dumond, D. E. 1975. The limitation of human population: a natural history. *Science* 187: 713–721.

Eisley, L. 1961. Lecture in the series "The House We Live In," WCAU-TV, 5 February. Quoted in I. McHarg. *Design With Nature*. Doubleday/Natural History Press, Garden City, NY, 1969.

Firor, J. 1990. *The Changing Atmosphere*. Yale University Press, New Haven, CT.

Forrester, J. 1991. Radio interview quoted in A. Gordon and D. Suzuki. *It's A Matter of Survival*. Harvard University Press, Cambridge, MA.

Geertz, C. 1963. *Agricultural Involution: The Process of Ecological Change in Indonesia*. University of California Press, Berkeley.

Gregg, A. 1955. A medical aspect of the population problem. *Science* 121: 681–682.

Harms, R. 1987. *Games Against Nature*. Cambridge University Press, New York.

Hassan, F. A. 1981. *Demographic Archeology*. Academic, New York.

Hern, W. M. 1990. Why are there so many of us? Description and diagnosis of a planetary eco-pathological process. *Popul. Environ.* 12: 9–39.

—. 1992. Polygyny and fertility among the Shipibo of the Peruvian Amazon. *Popul. Stud.* 46: 53–64.

Homer-Dixon, T. F., J. H. Boutwell, and G. W. Rathjens. 1993. Environmental change and violent conflict. *Sci. Am.* 268: 38–43.

Johnson, J. H. 1972. *Urban Geography: An Introductory Analysis*. Pergamon Press, Oxford, UK.

Ludwig, D., R. Hilborn, and C. Walters. 1993. Uncertainty, resource exploitation, and conservation: lessons from history. *Science 260:* 17,36.

Margalef, R. 1968. *Perspectives in Ecological Theory.* University of Chicago Press, Chicago, IL.

Martin, P. S. 1973. The discovery of America. *Science* 197: 969–974.

—. 1984. Prehistoric overkill: the global model. Pages 354–403 in P.S. Martin and R. G. Klein, eds. *Quarternary Extinctions: A Prehistoric Revolution.* University of Arizona Press, Tucson.

McHarg, I. 1969. *Design With Nature.* Doubleday, Garden City, NY.

Meadows, D. H., D. C. Meadows, and J. Randers. 1992. *Beyond The Limits: Confronting Global Collapse and Envisioning a Sustainable Future.* Chelsea Green Publ., Post Mills, VT.

Nag, M. 1962. *Factors Affecting Human Fertility in Nonindustrial Societies: A Cross-Cultural Study.* HRAF Press, New Haven, CT.

—. 1980. How modernization can also increase fertility. *Curr. Anthropol.* 21: 571–587.

Notestein, F. 1945. Population: the long view. Pages 36–57 in T. W. Schultz, ed. *Food for the World.* University of Chicago Press, Chicago, IL.

Pearl, R. 1922. *The Biology of Death.* Lippin-cott, Philadelphia, PA.

—. 1925. *The Biology of Population Growth.* Knopf, New York.

Peterson, W. 1969. *Population.* Macmillan, New York.

Polgar, S. 1969. Cultural aspects of natality regulation techniques. *Proceedings of the VIII International Congress of Anthropological and Ethnological Sciences* 3: 232–234.

Population Reference Bureau (PRB). 1992. *The United States Population Data Sheet of the Population Reference Bureau.* PRB, Washington, DC.

Prescott, D. M., and A. S. Flexer. 1986. *Cancer: The Misguided Cell.* Sinauer, Sunderland, MA.

Reining, P. 1991. Commentary presented at the symposium, What Are the Effects of Human Activity on the Planetary Ecosystem? at the annual meeting of the American Association for the Advancement of Science, Washington, DC, 8 February 1991.

Ruddon, R. W. 1987. *Cancer Biology.* Oxford University Press, New York.

Skole, D., and C. Tucker. 1993. Tropical deforestation and habitat fragmentation in the Amazon: satellite data from 1978 to 1988. *Science* 260: 1905–1910.

Stanley, D. J., and A. G. Warne. 1993. Nile delta: recent geological evolution and human impact. *Science* 260: 628–634.

Stern, P. C, O. R. Young, and D. Druckman, eds. 1992. *Global Environmental Change: Understanding the Human Dimension.* National Academy Press, Washington, DC.

Tinker, I., P. Reining, W. Swidler, and W. Cousins. 1976. *Culture and Population Change.* American Association for the Advancement of Science, Washington, DC.

Umpleby, S. 1990. The scientific revolution in demography. *Popul. Environ.* 11:159–174.

Von Foerster, H. 1960. Doomsday: Friday, 13 November, A.D. 2026. *Science* 132: 1291–1295.

—. 1966. The numbers of man, past and future. Biological Computer Laboratory Report 13.0. Electrical Engineering Research Laboratory, Department of Electrical Engineering, University of Illinois, Urbana.

Williams, M. 1989. Deforestation: past and present. *Progress in Human Geography* 13: 176–207.

Wilson, E. O. 1992. *The Diversity of Life.* Harvard University Press, Cambridge, MA.

Woodwell, G. M., ed. 1990. *The Earth in Transition: Patterns and Processes of Biotic Impoverishment.* Cambridge University Press, New York.

The Original Affluent Society

Marshall David Sahlins

Hunter-gatherers consume less energy per capita per year than any other group of human beings. Yet when you come to examine it the original affluent society was none other than the hunter's—in which all the people's material wants were easily satisfied. To accept that hunters are affluent is therefore to recognise that the present human condition of man slaving to bridge the gap between his unlimited wants and his insufficient means is a tragedy of modern times.

There are two possible courses to affluence. Wants may be "easily satisfied" either by producing much or desiring little. The familiar conception, the Galbraithean way—based on the concept of market economies states that man's wants are great, not to say infinite, whereas his means are limited, although they can be improved. Thus, the gap between means and ends can be narrowed by industrial productivity, at least to the point that "urgent goods" become plentiful. But there is also a Zen road to affluence, which states that human material wants are finite and few, and technical means unchanging but on the whole adequate. Adopting the Zen strategy, a people can enjoy an unparalleled material plenty with a low standard of living. That, I think, describes the hunters. And it helps explain some of their more curious economic behaviour: their "prodigality" for example— the inclination to consume at once all stocks on hand, as if they had it made. Free from market obsessions of scarcity, hunters' economic propensities may be more consistently predicated on abundance than our own.

Destutt de Tracy, "fish-blooded bourgeois doctrinaire" though he might have been, at least forced Marx to agree that "in poor nations the people are comfortable," whereas in rich nations, "they are generally poor."

SOURCES OF THE MISCONCEPTION

"Mere subsistence economy," "limited leisure save in exceptional circumstances," incessant quest for food," "meagre and relatively unreliable" natural resources, "absence of an economic surplus," "maximum energy from a maximum number of people" so runs the fair average anthropological opinion of hunting and gathering.

The traditional dismal view of the hunters' fix goes back to the time Adam Smith was writing, and probably to a time before anyone was writing. Probably it was one of the first distinctly neolithic prejudices, an ideological appreciation of the hunter's capacity to exploit the earth's resources most congenial to the historic task of depriving him of the same. We must have inherited it with the seed of Jacob, which "spread abroad to the west, and to the east, and to the north," to the disadvantage of Esau who was the elder son and cunning hunter, but in a famous scene deprived of his birthright.

Current low opinions of the hunting-gathering economy need not be laid to neolithic ethnocentrism. Bourgeois ethnocentrism will do as well. The existing business economy will promote the same dim conclusions about the hunting life. Is it so paradoxical to contend that hunters have affluent economies, their absolute poverty notwithstanding? Modern capitalist societies, however richly endowed, dedicate themselves to the proposition of scarcity. Inadequacy of economic means is the first principle of the world's wealthiest peoples.

The market-industrial system institutes scarcity, in a manner completely without parallel. Where production and distribution are arranged through the behaviour of prices, and all livelihoods depend on getting and spending, insufficiency of material means becomes the explicit, calculable starting point of all economic activity.

The entrepreneur is confronted with alternative investments of a finite capital, the worker (hopefully) with alternative choices of remunerative employ, and the consumer … Consumption is a double tragedy: what begins in inadequacy will end in deprivation. Bringing together an international division of labour, the market makes available a dazzling array of products: all these Good Things within a man's reach—but never all within his grasp. Worse, in this game of consumer free choice, every acquisition is simultaneously a deprivation for every purchase of something is a foregoing of something else, in general only marginally less desirable, and in some particulars more desirable, that could have been had instead. That sentence of "life at hard labour" was passed uniquely upon us. Scarcity is the judgment decreed by our economy. And it is precisely from this anxious vantage that we look back upon hunters. But if modern man, with all his technological advantages, still lacks the wherewithal, what chance has the naked savage with his puny bow and arrow? Having equipped the hunter with bourgeois impulses and palaeolithic tools, we judge his situation hopeless in advance.

Yet scarcity is not an intrinsic property of technical means. It is a relation between means and ends. We should entertain the empirical possibility that hunters are in business for their health, a finite objective, and that bow and arrow are adequate to that end.

The anthropological disposition to exaggerate the economic inefficiency of hunters appears notably by way of invidious comparison with neolithic economies. Hunters, as Lowie (1) put it blankly, "must work much harder in order to live than tillers and breeders" (p. 13). On this point evolutionary anthropology in particular found it congenial, even necessary theoretically, to adopt the usual tone of reproach. Ethnologists and archaeologists had become neolithic revolutionaries, and in their enthusiasm for the Revolution spared nothing in denouncing the Old (Stone Age) Regime. It was not the first time philosophers would relegate the earliest stage of humanity rather to nature than to culture. ("A man who spends his whole life following animals just to kill them to eat, or moving from one berry patch to another, is really living just like an animal himself"(2) (p. 122). The hunters thus downgraded, anthropology was freer to extol the Neolithic Great Leap Forward: a main technological advance that brought about a "general availability of leisure through release from purely food-getting pursuits."(3) In an influential essay on "Energy and the Evolution of Culture," Leslie White (5, 6) explained that the neolithic generated a "great advance in cultural development ... as a consequence of the great increase in the amount of energy harnessed and controlled per capita per year by means of the agricultural and pastoral arts." White further heightened the evolutionary contrast by specifying human effort as the principal energy source of palaeolithic culture, as opposed to the domesticated plant and animal resources of neolithic culture. This determination of the energy sources at once permitted a precise low estimate of hunters' thermodynamic potential that developed by the human body: "average power resources" of one twentieth horse power per capita—even as, by eliminating human effort from the cultural enterprise of the neolithic, it appeared that people had been liberated by some labour-saving device (domesticated plants and animals). But White's problematic is obviously misconceived. The principal mechanical energy available to both palaeolithic and neolithic culture is that supplied by human beings, as transformed in both cases from plant and animal source, so that, with negligible exceptions (the occasional direct use of non-human power), the amount of energy harnessed per capita per year is the same in palaeolithic and neolithic economies and fairly constant in human history until the advent of the industrial revolution.(5)

MARVELOUSLY VARIED DIET

Marginal as the Australian or Kalahari desert is to agriculture, or to everyday European experience, it is a source of wonder to the untutored observer "how anybody could live in a place like this." The inference that the natives manage only to eke out a bare existence is apt to be reinforced by their marvelously varied diets. Ordinarily including objects deemed repulsive and inedible by Europeans, the local cuisine lends itself to the supposition that the people are starving to death.

It is a mistake, Sir George Grey (7) wrote, to suppose that the native Australians "have small means of subsistence, or are at times greatly pressed for want of food." Many and "almost ludicrous" are the errors travellers have fallen into in this regard: "They lament in their journals that the unfortunate Aborigines should be reduced by famine to the miserable necessity of subsisting on certain sorts of food, which they have found near their huts; whereas, in many instances, the articles thus quoted by them are those which the natives most prize, and are really neither deficient in flavour nor nutritious qualities." To render palpable "the ignorance that has prevailed with regard to the habits and customs of this people when in their wild state," Grey provides one remarkable example, a citation from his fellow explorer, Captain Stuart, who, upon encountering a group of Aboriginals engaged in gathering large quantities of mimosa gum, deduced that the "unfortunate creatures were reduced to the last extremity, and, being unable to procure any other nourishment, had been obliged to collect this mucilaginous." But, Sir George observes, the gum in question is a favourite article of food in the area, and when in season it affords the opportunity for large numbers of people to assemble and camp together, which otherwise they are unable to do. He concludes:

> "Generally speaking, the natives live well; in some districts there may be at particular seasons of the year a deficiency of food, but if such is the case, these tracts are, at those times, deserted.

> It is, however, utterly impossible for a traveller or even for a strange native to judge whether a district affords an abundance Of food, or the contrary ... But in his own district a native is very differently situated; he knows exactly what it produces, the proper time at which the several articles are in season, and the readiest means of procuring them. According to these circumstances he regulates his visits to different portions of his hunting ground; and I can only say that l have always found the greatest abundance in their huts."(8)

In making this happy assessment, Sir George took special care to exclude the lumpen-proletariat aboriginals living in and about European towns—the exception instructive. It evokes a second source of ethnographic misconceptions: the anthropology of hunters is largely an anachronistic study of ex-savages an inquest into the corpse of one society, Grey once said, presided over by members of another.

"A KIND OF MATERIAL PLENTY"

Considering the poverty in which hunters and gatherers live in theory, it comes as a surprise that Bushmen who live in the Kalahari enjoy "a kind of material plenty," at least in the realm of everyday useful things, apart from food and water:

> "As the !Kung come into more contact with Europeans and this is already happening—they will feel sharply the lack of our things and will need and want more. It makes them feel inferior to be without clothes when they stand among strangers who are clothed. But in their own life and with their own artifacts they were comparatively free from material pressures. Except for food and water (important exceptions!) of which the Nyae Nyae Kung have a sufficiency—but barely so, judging from the fact that all are thin though not emaciated—they all had what they needed or could make what they needed, for every man can and does make the things that men make and every woman the things that women make ... They lived in a kind of material plenty because they adapted the tools of their living to materials which lay in abundance around them and which were free for anyone to take (wood, reeds, bone for weapons and implements, fibres for cordage, grass for shelters), or to materials which were at least sufficient for the needs of the population. ... The !Kung could always use more ostrich egg shells for beads to wear or trade with, but, as it is, enough are found for every woman to have a dozen or more shells for water containers all she can carry and a goodly number of bead ornaments. In their nomadic hunting-gathering life, travelling from one source of food to another through the seasons, always going back and forth between food and water, they carry their young children and their belongings. With plenty of most materials at hand to replace artifacts as required, the !Kung have not developed means of permanent storage and have not needed or wanted to encumber themselves with surpluses or duplicates. They do not even want to carry one of everything. They borrow what they do not own. With this ease, they have not hoarded, and the accumulation of objects has not become associated with status ..."(9)

In the non subsistence sphere, the people's wants are generally easily satisfied. Such "material plenty" depends partly upon the simplicity of technology and democracy of property. Products are homespun: of stone, bone, wood, skin-materials such as "lay in abundance around them." As a rule, neither extraction of the raw material nor its working up take strenuous effort. Access to natural resources is typically direct—"free for anyone to take"—even as possession of the necessary tools is general and knowledge of the required skills common. The division of labour is likewise simple, predominantly a division of labour by sex. Add in the liberal customs of sharing, for which hunters are properly famous, and all the people can usually participate in the going prosperity, such as it is.

For most hunters, such affluence without abundance in the non-subsistence sphere need not be long debated. A more interesting question is why they are content with so few possessions for it is with them a policy, a "matter of principle" as Gusinde (10) says, and not a misfortune.

But are hunters so undemanding of material goods because they are themselves enslaved by a food quest "demanding maximum energy from a maximum number of people," so that no time or effort remains for the provision of other comforts? Some ethnographers testify to the contrary that the food quest is so successful that half the time the people seem not to know what to do with themselves. On the other hand, movement is a condition of this success, more movement in some cases than others, but always enough to rapidly depreciate the satisfactions of property. Of the hunter it is truly said that his wealth is a burden. In his condition of life, goods can become "grievously oppressive," as Gusinde observes, and the more so the longer they are carried around. Certain food collectors do have canoes and a few have dog sleds, but most must carry themselves all the comforts they possess, and so only possess what they can comfortably carry themselves. Or perhaps only what the women can carry: the men are often left free to reach to the sudden opportunity of the chase or the sudden necessity of defence. As Owen Lattimore wrote in a not too different context, "the pure nomad is the poor nomad." Mobility and property are in contradiction. That wealth quickly becomes more of an encumbrance than a good thing is apparent even to the outsider. Laurens van der Post (11) was caught in the contradiction as he prepared to make farewells to his wild Bushmen friends:

> "This matter of presents gave us many an anxious moment. We were humiliated by the realisation of how little there was we could give to the Bushmen. Almost everything seemed likely to make life more difficult for them by adding to the litter and weight of their daily round. They themselves had practically no possessions: a loin strap, a skin blanket and a leather satchel. There was nothing that they could not assemble in one minute, wrap up in their blankets and carry on their shoulders for a journey of a thousand miles. They had no sense of possession."

Here then is another economic "peculiarity"—some hunters at least, display a notable tendency to be sloppy about their possessions. They have the kind of nonchalance that would be appropriate to a people who have mastered the problems of production.

"They do not know how to take care of their belongings. No one dreams of putting them in order, folding them, drying or cleaning them, hanging them up, or putting them in a neat pile. If they are looking for some particular thing, they rummage carelessly through the hodgepodge of trifles in the little baskets. Larger objects that are piled up in a heap in the hut are dragged hither and thither with no regard for the damage that might be done them.

The European observer has the impression that these (Yahgan) Indians place no value whatever on their utensils and that they have completely forgotten the effort it took to make them. Actually, no one clings to his few goods and chattels which, as it is, are often and easily lost, but just as easily replaced. ... The Indian does not even exercise care when he could conveniently do so. A European is likely to shake his head at the boundless indifference of these people who drag brand-new objects, precious clothing, fresh provisions and valuable items through thick mud, or abandon them to their swift destruction by children and dogs. ... Expensive things that are given them are treasured for a few hours, out of curiosity; after that they thoughtlessly let everything deteriorate in the mud and wet. The less they own, the more comfortable they can travel, and what is ruined they occasionally replace. Hence, they are completely indifferent to any material possessions."(10)

The hunter, one is tempted to say, is "uneconomic man." At least as concerns non subsistence goods, he is the reverse of that standard caricature immortalised in any *General Principles of Economics*, page one. His wants are scarce and his means (in relation) plentiful. Consequently he is "comparatively free of material pressures," has "no sense of possession," shows "an undeveloped sense of property," is "completely indifferent to any material pressures," manifests a "lack of interest" in developing his technological equipment.

In this relation of hunters to worldly goods there is a neat and important point. From the internal perspective of the economy, it seems wrong to say that wants are "restricted," desires "restrained," or even that the notion of wealth is "limited." Such phrasings imply in advance an Economic Man and a struggle of the hunter against his own worse nature, which is finally then subdued by a cultural vow of poverty. The words imply the renunciation of an acquisitiveness that in reality was never developed, a suppression of desires that were never broached. Economic Man is a bourgeois construction—as Marcel Mauss said, "not behind us, but before, like the moral man." It is not that hunters and gatherers have curbed their materialistic "impulses;" they simply never made an institution of them. "Moreover, if it is a great blessing to be free from a great evil, our (Montagnais) Savages are happy; for the two tyrants who provide hell and torture for many of our Europeans, do not reign in their great forests, I mean ambition and avarice ... as they are contented with a mere living, not one of them gives himself to the Devil to acquire wealth."(12)

SUBSISTENCE

When Herskovits (13) was writing his Economic Anthropology (1958), it was common anthropological practice to take the Bushmen or the native Australians as "a classic illustration; of a people whose economic resources are of the scantiest," so precariously situated that "only the most intense application makes survival possible." Today the "classic" understanding can be fairly reversed on evidence largely from these two groups. A good case can be made that hunters and gatherers work less than we do; and, rather than a continuous travail, the food quest is intermittent, leisure abundant, and there is a greater amount of sleep in the daytime per capita per year than in any other condition of society.

The most obvious, immediate conclusion is that the people do not work hard. The average length of time per person per day put into the appropriation and preparation of food was four or five hours. Moreover, they do not work continuously. The subsistence quest was highly intermittent. It would stop for the time being when the people had procured enough for the time being which left them plenty of time to spare. Clearly in subsistence as in other sectors of production, we have to do with an economy of specific, limited objectives. By hunting and gathering these objectives are apt to be irregularly accomplished, so the work pattern becomes correspondingly erratic.

As for the Bushmen, economically likened to Australian hunters by Herskovits, two excellent recent reports by Richard Lee show their condition to be indeed the same (14, 16). Lee's research merits a special hearing not only because it concerns Bushmen, but specifically the Dobe section of Kung Bushmen, adjacent to the Nyae about whose subsistence—in a context otherwise of "material plenty"—Mrs. Marshall expressed important reservations. The Dobe occupy an area of Botswana where !Kung Bushmen have been living for at least a hundred years, but have only just begun to suffer dislocation pressures.

ABUNDANCE

Despite a low annual rainfall (6 to 10 inches), Lee found in the Dobe area a "surprising abundance of vegetation." Food resources were "both varied and abundant," particularly the energy rich mangetti nut—"so abundant that millions of the nuts rotted on the ground each year for want of picking." The Bushman figures imply that one man's labour in hunting and gathering will support four or five people. Taken at face value, Bushman food collecting is more efficient than French farming in the period up to World War II, when more than 20 per cent of the population were engaged in feeding the rest. Confessedly, the comparison is misleading, but not as misleading as it is astonishing. In the total population of free-ranging Bushmen contacted by Lee, 61.3 per cent (152 of 248) were effective food producers; the remainder were too young or too old to contribute importantly. In the particular camp under scrutiny, 65 per cent were "effectives." Thus the ratio of food producers to the general population is actually 3:5 or 2:3. But, these 65 per cent of the people "worked 36 per cent of the time, and 35 per cent of the people did not work at all!" (15)

For each adult worker, this comes to about two and one-half days labour per week. (In other words, each productive individual supported herself or himself and dependents and still had 3 to 5 days available for other activities.) A "day's work" was about six hours; hence the Dobe work week is approximately 15 hours, or an average of 2 hours 9 minutes per day. All things considered, Bushmen subsistence labours are probably very close to those of native Australians.

Also like the Australians, the time Bushmen do not work in subsistence they pass in leisure or leisurely activity. One detects again that characteristic palaeolithic rhythm of a day or two on, a day or two off—the latter passed desultorily in camp. Although food collecting is the primary productive activity, Lee writes, "the majority of the people's time (four to five days per week) is spent in other pursuits, such as resting in camp or visiting other camps" (15):

> "A woman gathers on one day enough food to feed her family for three days, and spends the rest of her time resting in camp, doing embroidery, visiting other camps, or entertaining visitors from other camps. For each day at home, kitchen routines, such as cooking, nut cracking, collecting firewood, and fetching water, occupy one to three hours of her time. This rhythm of steady work and steady leisure maintained throughout the year. The hunters tend to work more frequently than the women, but their schedule uneven. It 'not unusual' for a man to hunt avidly for a week and then do no hunting at all for two or three weeks. Since hunting is an unpredictable business and subject to magical control, hunters sometimes experience a run of bad luck and stop hunting for a month or longer. During these periods, visiting, entertaining, and especially dancing are the primary activities of men." (16)

The daily per-capita subsistence yield for the Dobe Bushmen was 2,140 calories. However, taking into account body weight, normal activities, and the age-sex composition of the Dobe population, Lee estimates the people require only 1,975 calories per capita. Some of the surplus food probably went to the dogs, who ate what the people left over. "The conclusion can be drawn that the Bushmen do not lead a substandard existence on the edge of starvation as has been commonly supposed."(15)

Meanwhile, back in Africa the Hadza have been long enjoying a comparable ease, with a burden of subsistence occupations no more strenuous in hours per day than the Bushmen or the Australian Aboriginals. (16) Living in an area of "exceptional abundance" of animals and regular supplies of vegetables (the vicinity of Lake Eyasi), Hadza men seem much more concerned with games of chance than with chances of game. During the long dry season especially, they pass the greater part of days on end in gambling, perhaps only to lose the metal-tipped arrows they need for big game hunting at other times. In any case, many men are "quite unprepared or unable to hunt big game even when they possess the necessary arrows." Only a small minority, Woodburn writes, are active hunters of large animals, and if women are generally more assiduous at their vegetable collecting, still it is at a leisurely pace and without prolonged labour. (17) Despite this nonchalance, and an only limited economic cooperation, Hadza "nonetheless obtain sufficient food without undue effort." Woodburn offers this "very rough approximation" of subsistence-labour requirements: "Over the year as a whole probably an average of less than two hours a day spent obtaining food." (Woodburn, 16)

Interesting that the Hazda, tutored by life and not by anthropology, reject the neo-lithic revolution in order to keep their leisure. Although surrounded by cultivators, they have until recently refused to take up agriculture themselves, "mainly on the grounds that this would involve too much hard work." In this they are like the Bushmen, who respond to the neolithic question with another: "Why should we plant, when there are so many mongomongo nuts in the world?" (14) Woodburn moreover did form the impression, although as yet unsubstantiated, that Hadza actually expend less energy, and probably less time, obtaining subsistence than do neighbouring cultivators of East Africa. (16) To change continents but not contents, the fitful economic commitment of the South American hunter, too, could seem to the European outsider an incurable "natural disposition":

> … the Yamana are not capable of continuous, daily hard labour, much to the chagrin of European farmers and employers for whom they often work. Their work is more a matter of fits and starts, and in these occasional efforts they can develop considerable energy for a certain time. After that, however, they show a desire for an incalculably long rest period during which they lie about doing nothing, without showing great fatigue. … It is obvious that repeated irregulari-ties of this kind make the European employer despair, but the Indian cannot help it. It is his natural disposition." (10)

The hunter's attitude towards farming introduces us, lastly, to a few particulars of the way they relate to the food quest. Once again we venture here into the internal realm of the economy, a realm sometimes subjective and always difficult to understand; where, moreover, hunters seem deliberately inclined to overtax our comprehension by customs so odd as to invite the extreme interpretation that either these people are fools or they really have nothing to worry about. The former would be a true logical deduction from the hunter's nonchalance, on the premise that his economic condition is truly exigent. On the other hand, if a livelihood is usually easily procured, if one can usually expect to succeed, then the people's seeming imprudence can no longer appear as such. Speaking to unique developments of the market economy, to its institutionalisation of scarcity, Karl Polanyi (18) said that our "animal dependence upon food has been bared and the naked fear of starvation permitted to run loose. Our humiliating enslavement to the material, which all human culture is designed to mitigate, was deliberately made more rigorous."

But our problems are not theirs.

Rather, a pristine affluence colours their economic arrangements, a trust in the abundance of nature's resources rather than despair at the inadequacy of human means. My point is that otherwise curious heathen devices become understandable by the people's confidence, a confidence which is the reasonable human attribute of a generally successful economy.

A more serious issue is presented by the frequent and exasperated observation of a certain "lack of foresight" among hunters and gatherers. Orientated forever in the present, without "the slightest thought of, or care for, what the morrow may bring," (19) the hunter seems unwilling to husband supplies, incapable of a planned response to the doom surely awaiting him. He adopts instead a studied unconcern, which expresses itself in two complementary economic inclinations.

The first, prodigality: the propensity to eat right through all the food in the camp, even during objectively difficult times, "as if," Lillian said of the Montagnais, "the game they were to hunt was shut up in a stable." Basedow (20) wrote of native Australians, their motto "might be interpreted in words to the effect that while there is plenty for today never care about tomorrow. On this account an Aboriginal inclined to make one feast of his supplies, in preference to a modest meal now and another by and by." Le Jeune even saw his Montagnais carry such extravagance to the edge of disaster.

> "In the famine through which we passed, if my host took two, three, or four Beavers, immediately, whether it was day or night, they had a feast for all neighbouring Savages. And if those People had captured something, they had one also at the same time; so that, on emerging from one feast, you went to another, and sometimes even to a third and a fourth. I told them that they did not manage well, and that it would be better to reserve these feasts for future days, and in doing this they would not be so pressed with hunger. They laughed at me. 'Tomorrow' (they said) 'we shall make another feast with what we shall capture.' Yes, but more often they capture only cold and wind." (12)

A second and complementary inclination is merely prodigality's negative side: the failure to put by food surpluses, to develop food storage. For many hunters and gatherers, it appears, food storage cannot be proved technically impossible, nor is it certain that the people are unaware of the possibility. (18) One must investigate instead what in the situation precludes the attempt. Gusinde asked this question, and for the Yahgan found the answer in the self same justifiable optimism. Storage would be "superfluous," "because through the entire year and with almost limitless generosity the she puts all kinds of animals at the disposal of the man who hunts and the woman who gathers. Storm or accident will deprive a family of these things for no more than a few days. Generally no one need reckon with the danger of hunger, and everyone almost any where finds an abundance of what he needs. Why then should anyone worry about food for the future ... Basically our Fuegians know that they need not fear for the future, hence they do not pile up supplies. Year in and year out they can look forward to the next day, free of care. ..." (12)

Gusinde's explanation is probably good as far as it goes, but probably incomplete. A more complex and subtle economic calculus seems in play. In fact one must consider the advantages of food storage against the diminishing returns to collection within a confined locale. An uncontrollable tendency to lower the local carrying capacity is for hunters au fond des choses: a basic condition of their production and main cause of their movement. The potential drawback of storage is exactly that it engages the contradiction between wealth and mobility. It would anchor the camp to an area soon depleted of natural food supplies. Thus immobilised by their accumulated stocks, the people may suffer by comparison with a little hunting and gathering elsewhere, where nature has, so to speak, done considerable storage of her own-of foods possibly more desirable in diversity as well as amount than men can put by. As it works out, an attempt to stock up food may only reduce the overall output of a hunting band, for the havenots will content themselves with staying in camp and living off !he wherewithal amassed by the more prudent. Food storage, then, may be technically feasible, yet economically undesirable, and socially unachievable.

What are the real handicaps of the hunting-gathering praxis? Not "low productivity of labour," if existing examples mean anything. But the economy is seriously" afflicted by the imminence of diminishing returns. Beginning in subsistence and spreading from there to every sector, an initial success seems only to develop the probability that further efforts will yield smaller benefits. This describes the typical curve of food-getting within a particular locale. A modest number of people usually sooner than later reduce the food resources within convenient range of camp. Thereafter, they may stay on only by absorbing an increase in real costs or a decline in real returns: rise in costs if the people choose to search farther and farther afield, decline in returns if they are satisfied to live on the shorter supply or inferior foods in easier reach. The solution, of course, is to go somewhere else. Thus the first and decisive contingency of hunting-gathering: it requires movement to maintain production on advantageous terms.

But this movement, more or less frequent in different circumstances, more or less distant, merely transposes to other spheres of production the same diminishing returns of which it is born. The manufacture of tools, clothing, utensils, or ornaments, however easily done, becomes senseless when these begin to be more of a burden than a comfort Utility falls quickly at the margin of portability. The construction of substantial houses likewise becomes absurd if they must soon be abandoned. Hence the hunter's very ascetic conceptions of material welfare: an interest only in minimal equipment, "if that; a valuation of smaller things over bigger; a disinterest in acquiring two or more of most goods; and the like. Ecological pressure assumes a rare form of concreteness when it has to be shouldered. If the gross product is trimmed down in comparison with other economies, it is not the hunter's productivity that is at fault, but his mobility.

DEMOGRAPHIC CONSTRAINTS

Almost the same thing can be said of the demographic constraints of hunting-gathering. The same policy of debarassment is in play on the level of people, describable in similar terms and ascribable to similar causes. The terms are, cold-bloodedly: diminishing returns at the margin of portability, minimum necessary equipment, elimination of duplicates, and so forth—that is to say, infanticide, senilicide, sexual continence for the duration of the nursing period, etc., practices for which many food-collecting peoples are well known. The presumption that such devices are due to an inability to support more people is probably true—if "support" is understood in the sense of carrying them rather than feeding them. The people eliminated, as hunters sometimes sadly tell, are precisely those who cannot effectively transport themselves, who would I hinder the movement of family and camp. Hunters may be obliged to handle people and goods in parallel ways, the draconic population policy an expression of the same ecology as the ascetic economy.

Hunting and gathering has all the strengths of its weaknesses. Periodic movement and restraint in wealth and adaptations, the kinds of necessities of the economic practice and creative adaptations the kinds of necessities of which virtues are made. Precisely in such a framework, affluence becomes possible. Mobility and moderation put hunters' ends within range of their technical means. An undeveloped mode of production is thus rendered highly effective. The hunter's life is not as difficult as it looks from the outside. In some ways the economy reflects dire ecology, but it is also a complete inversion.

THREE TO FIVE HOUR WORKING DAY

Reports on hunters and gatherers of the ethnological present-specifically on those in marginal environments suggest a mean of three to five hours per adult worker per day in food production. Hunters keep banker's hours, notably less than modern industrial workers (unionised), who would surely settle for a 21–35 hour week. An interesting comparison is also posed by recent studies of labour costs among agriculturalists of neolithic type. For example, the average adult Hanunoo, man or woman, spends 1,200 hours per year in swidden cultivation; (21) which is to say, a mean of three hours twenty minutes per day. Yet this figure does not include food gathering, animal raising, cooking and other direct subsistence efforts of these Philippine tribesmen. Comparable data are beginning to appear in reports on other primitive agriculturalists from many parts of the world.

There is nothing either to the convention that hunters and gatherers can enjoy little leisure from tasks of sheer survival. By this, the evolutionary inadequacies of the palaeolithic are customarily explained, while for the provision of leisure the neolithic is roundly congratulated. But the traditional formulas might be truer if reversed: the amount of work (per capita) increases with the evolution of culture, and the amount of leisure decreases. Hunter's subsistence labours are characteristically intermittent, a day on and a day off, and modern hunters at least tend to employ their time off in such activities as daytime sleep. In the tropical habitats occupied by many of these existing hunters, plant collecting is more reliable than hunting itself. Therefore, the women, who do the collecting, work rather more regularly than the men, and provide the greater part of the food supply.

In alleging this is an affluent economy, therefore, I do not deny that certain hunters have moments of difficulty. Some do find it "almost inconceivable" for a man to die of hunger, or even to fail to satisfy his hunger for more than a day or two. (16) But others, especially certain very peripheral hunters spread out in small groups across an environment of extremes, are exposed periodically to the kind of inclemency that interdicts travel or access to game. They suffer although perhaps only fractionally, the shortage affecting particular immobilised families rather than the society as a whole. (10)

Still, granting this vulnerability, and allowing the most poorly situated modern hunters into comparison, it would be difficult to prove that privation is distinctly characteristic of the hunter-gatherers. Food shortage is not the indicative property of this mode of production as opposed to others; it does not mark off hunters and gatherers as a class or a general evolutionary stage. Lowie (22) asks:

> "But what of the herders on a simple plane whose maintenance is periodically jeopardised by plagues-who, like some Lapp bands of the nineteenth century were obliged to fall back on fishing? What of the primitive peasants who clear and till without compensation of the soil, exhaust one plot and pass on to the next, and are threatened with famine at every drought? Are they any more in control of misfortune caused by natural conditions than the hunter-gatherer?"

Above all, what about the world today? One-third to one-half of humanity are said to go to bed hungry every night. In the Old Stone Age the fraction must have been much smaller. This is the era of hunger unprecedented. Now, in the time of the greatest technical power, is starvation an in situation. Reverse another venerable formula: the amount of hunger increases relatively and absolutely with the evolution of culture. This paradox is my whole point. Hunters and gatherers have by force of circumstances an objectively low standard of living. But taken as their objective, and given their adequate means of production, all the people's material wants usually can be easily satisfied.

The world's most primitive people have few possessions but they are not poor. Poverty is not a certain small amount of goods, nor is it just a relation between means and ends; above all it is a relation between people. Poverty is a social status. As such it is the invention of civilisation. It has grown with civilisation, at once as an invidious distinction between classes and more importantly as a tributary relation that can render agrarian peasants more susceptible to natural catastrophes than any winter camp of Alaskan Eskimo.

REFERENCES

1. Lowie, Robert H; 1946 An introduction to Cultural Anthropology (2nd ed.) New York. Rinehart.

2. Braidwood, Robert J. 1957. Prehistoric Men. 3rd ed. Chicago Natural History Museum Popular Series, Anthropology, Number 37.

3. Braidwood; Robert J. 1952. The Near East and the Foundations for Civilisation. Eugene: Oregon State System of Higher Education.

4. Boas, Franz. 1884–85. "The Central Eskimo," Smithsonian Institution, Bureau of American Ethnology, Anthropological Reports 6: 399–699.

5. White, Leslie A. 1949. The Science of Culture. New York: Farrar, Strauss.

6. White, Leslie A. 1959. The Evolution of Culture. New York: McGraw-Hill.

7. Grey, Sir George. 1841. Journals of Two Expeditions of Discovery in North-West and Western Australia, During the Years 1837, 38, and 39... 2 vols. London: Boone.

8. Eyre, Edward John. 1845. Journals of Expeditions of Discovery into Central Australia, and Overland from Adelalde to King George's Sound, in the Years 184041.2 vols. London: Boone.

9. Marshall, Lorna. 1961. "Sharing, Talking, and Giving: Relief of Social Tensions Among "Kung Bushmen," Africa 31:23149.

10. Gusinde, Martin. 1961. The Yamana 5 vols. New Haven, Conn.: Human Relations Area Files. (German edition 1931).

11. Laurens van der Post: The Heart of the Hunter.

12. Le Jeune, le Pere Paul. 1897. "Relation of What Occurred in New France in the Year 1634," in R. G. Thwaites (ed.), The Jesuit Relations and Allied Documents. Vol. 6. Cleveland: Burrows. (First French edition, 1635).

13. Herskovits, Melville J. 1952. Economic Anthropology. New York: Knopf.

14. Lee, Richard. 1968. "What Hunters Do for a Living, or, How to Make Out on Scarce Resources," in R. Lee and I. DeVore (eds.), Man the Hunter. Chicago: Aldine.

15. Lee, Richard. 1969. "Kung Bushmen Subsistence: An Input-Output Analysis," in A. Vayda (ed.), Environment and Cultural Behaviour. Garden City, N.Y.: Natural History Press.

16. Woodburn, James. 1968. "An introduction to Hadza Ecology," in Lee and I. DeVore (eds.), Man the Hunter. Chicago: Aldine.

17. Woodburn, James (director). 1966: "The Hadza" (film available from the anthropological director, department of Anthropology, London School of Economics).

18. Polanyi, Karl. 1974. "Our Obsolete Market Mentality," Commentary 3:109–17.

19. Spencer, Baldwin, and F. J. Gillen, 1899. The Native Tribes of Central Australia London: Macmillan.

20. Basedow, Herbert. 1925. The Australian Aboriginal. Adelaide, Australia: Preece.

21. Conklin, Harold C. 1957. Hanunoo Agriculture. Rome: Food and Agricultural Organisation of the United Nations.

22. Lowie, Robert H. 1938. "Subsistence," in F. Boas (ed.), General Anthropology. (2nd ed.) New York: Rinehart.

Extract from *Stone-Age Economics* by Marshall Sahlins.

EATING CHRISTMAS IN THE KALAHARI

Richard Borshay Lee

T he !Kung Bushmen's knowledge of Christmas is thirdhand. The London Missionary Society brought the holiday to the southern Tswana tribes in the early nineteenth century. Later, native catechists spread the idea far and wide among the Bantu-speaking pastoralists, even in the remotest corners of the Kalahari Desert. The Bushmen's idea of the Christmas story, stripped to its essentials, is "praise the birth of white man's god-chief;" what keeps their interest in the holiday high is the Tswana-Herero custom of slaughtering an ox for his Bushmen neighbors as an annual goodwill gesture. Since the 1930's, part of the Bushmen's annual round of activities has included a December congregation at the cattle posts for trading, marriage brokering, and several days of trance-dance feasting at which the local Tswana headman is host.

As a social anthropologist working with !Kung Bushmen, I found that the Christmas ox custom suited my purposes. I had come to the Kalahari to study the hunting and gathering subsistence economy of the !Kung, and to accomplish this it was essential not to provide them with food, share my own food, or interfere in any way with their food-gathering activities. While liberal handouts of tobacco and medical supplies were appreciated, they were scarcely adequate to erase the glaring disparity in wealth between the anthropologist, who maintained a two-month inventory of canned goods, and the Bushmen, who rarely had a day's supply of food on hand. My approach, while paying off in terms of data, left me open to frequent accusations of stinginess and hard-heartedness. By their lights, I was a miser.

The Christmas ox was to be my way of saying thank you for the cooperation of the past year; and since it was to be our last Christmas in the field, I determined to slaughter the largest, meatiest ox that money could buy, insuring that the feast and trance-dance would be a success.

Through December I kept my eyes open at the wells as the cattle were brought down for watering. Several animals were offered, but none had quite the grossness that I had in mind. Then, ten days before the holiday, a Herero friend led an ox of astonishing size and mass up to our camp. It was solid black, stood five feet high at the shoulder, had a five-foot span of horns, and must have weighed 1,200 pounds on the hoof. Food consumption calculations are my specialty, and I quickly figured that bones and viscera aside, there was enough meat—at least four pounds—for every man, woman, and child of the 150 Bushmen in the vicinity of /ai/ai who were expected at the feast.

Having found the right animal at last, I paid the Herero £20 ($56) and asked him to keep the beast with his herd until Christmas day. The next morning word spread among the people that the big solid black one was the ox chosen by /ontah (my Bushman name; it means, roughly, "whitey") for the Christmas feast. That afternoon I received the first delegation. Ben!a, an outspoken sixty-year-old mother of five, came to the point slowly.

"Where were you planning to eat Christmas?"

"Right here at /ai/ai," I replied.

"Alone or with others?"

"I expect to invite all the people to eat Christmas with me."

"Eat what?"

"I have purchased Yehave's black ox, and I am going to slaughter and cook it."

"That's what we were told at the well but refused to believe it until we heard it from yourself."

"Well, it's the black one," I replied expansively, although wondering what she was driving at.

"Oh, no!" Ben!a groaned, turning to her group. "They were right." Turning back to me she asked, "Do you expect us to eat that bag of bones?"

"Bag of bones! It's the biggest ox at /ai/ai."

"Big, yes, but old. And thin. Everybody knows there's no meat on that old ox. What did you expect us to eat off it, the horns?"

Everybody chuckled at Ben!a's one-liner as they walked away, but all I could manage was a weak grin.

That evening it was the turn of the young men. They came to sit at our evening fire. /gaugo, about my age, spoke to me man-to-man.

"/ontah, you have always been square with us," he lied. "What has happened to change your heart? That sack of guts and bones of Yehave's will hardly feed one camp, let alone all the Bushmen around ai/ai." And he proceeded to enumerate the seven camps in the /ai/ai vicinity, family by family. "Perhaps you have forgotten that we are not few, but many. Or are you too blind to tell the difference between a proper cow and an old wreck? That ox is thin to the point of death."

"Look, you guys," I retorted, "that is a beautiful animal, and I'm sure you will eat it with pleasure at Christmas."

"Of course we will eat it; it's food. But it won't fill us up to the point where we will have enough strength to dance. We will eat and go home to bed with stomachs rumbling."

That night as we turned in, I asked my wife, Nancy: "What did you think of the black ox?"

"It looked enormous to me. Why?"

"Well, about eight different people have told me I got gypped; that the ox is nothing but bones."

"What's the angle?" Nancy asked. "Did they have a better one to sell?"

"No, they just said that it was going to be a grim Christmas because there won't be enough meat to go around. Maybe I'll get an independent judge to look at the beast in the morning."

Bright and early, Halingisi, a Tswana cattle owner, appeared at our camp. But before I could ask him to give me his opinion on Yehave's black ox, he gave me the eye signal that indicated a confidential chat. We left the camp and sat down.

"/ontah, I'm surprised at you: you've lived here for three years and still haven't learned anything about cattle."

"But what else can a person do but choose the biggest, strongest animal one can find?" I retorted.

"Look, just because an animal is big doesn't mean that it has plenty of meat on it. The black one was a beauty when it was younger, but now it is thin to the point of death."

"Well I've already bought it. What can I do at this stage?"

"Bought it already? I thought you were just considering it. Well, you'll have to kill it and serve it, I suppose. But don't expect much of a dance to follow."

My spirits dropped rapidly. I could believe that Ben!a and /gaugo just might be putting me on about the black ox, but Halingisi seemed to be an impartial critic. I went around that day feeling as though I had bought a lemon of a used car.

In the afternoon it was Tomazo's turn. Tomazo is a fine hunter, a top trance performer… and one of my most reliable informants. He approached the subject of the Christmas cow as part of my continuing Bushman education.

"My friend, the way it is with us Bushmen," he began, "is that we love meat. And even more than that, we love fat. When we hunt we always search for the fat ones, the ones dripping with layers of white fat: fat that turns into a clear, thick oil in the cooking pot, fat that slides down your gullet, fills your stomach and gives you a roaring diarrhea," he rhapsodized.

"So, feeling as we do," he continued, "it gives us pain to be served such a scrawny thing as Yehave's black ox. It is big, yes, and no doubt its giant bones are good for soup, but fat is what we really crave and so we will eat Christmas this year with a heavy heart."

The prospect of a gloomy Christmas now had me worried, so I asked Tomazo what I could do about it.

"Look for a fat one, a young one … smaller, but fat. Fat enough to make us //gom ('evacuate the bowels'), then we will be happy."

My suspicions were aroused when Tomazo said that he happened to know of a young, fat, barren cow that the owner was willing to part with. Was Tomazo working on commission, I wondered? But I dispelled this unworthy thought when we approached the Herero owner of the cow in question and found that he had decided not to sell.

The scrawny wreck of a Christmas ox now became the talk of the /ai/ai water hole and was the first news told to the outlying groups as they began to come in from the bush for the feast. What finally convinced me that real trouble might be brewing was the visit from u!au, an old conservative with a reputation for fierceness. His nickname meant spear and referred to an incident thirty years ago in which he had speared a man to death. He had an intense manner; fixing me with his eyes, he said in clipped tones:

> "I have only just heard about the black ox today, or else I would have come here earlier. /ontah, do you honestly think you can serve meat like that to people and avoid a fight?" He paused, letting the implications sink in. "I don't mean fight you, /ontah; you are a white man. I mean a fight between Bushmen. There are many fierce ones here, and with such a small quantity of meat to distribute, how can you give everybody a fair share? Someone is sure to accuse another of taking too much or hogging all the choice pieces. Then you will see what happens when some go hungry while others eat."

The possibility of at least a serious argument struck me as all too real. I had witnessed the tension that surrounds the distribution of meat from a kudu or gemsbok kill, and had documented many arguments that sprang up from a real or imagined slight in meat distribution. The owners of a kill may spend up to two hours arranging and rearranging the piles of meat under the gaze of a circle of recipients before handing them out. And I also knew that the Christmas feast at /ai/ai would be bringing together groups that had feuded in the past.

Convinced now of the gravity of the situation, I went in earnest to search for a second cow; but all my inquiries failed to turn one up.

The Christmas feast was evidently going to be a disaster, and the incessant complaints about the meagerness of the ox had already taken the fun out of it for me. Moreover, I was getting bored with the wisecracks, and after losing my temper a few times, I resolved to serve the beast anyway. If the meat fell short, the hell with it. In the Bushmen idiom, I announced to all who would listen:

"I am a poor man and blind. If I have chosen one that is too old and too thin, we will eat it anyway and see if there is enough meat there to quiet the rumbling of our stomachs."

On hearing this speech, Ben!a offered me a rare word of comfort. "It's thin," she said philosophically, "but the bones will make a good soup."

At dawn Christmas morning, instinct told me to turn over the butchering and cooking to a friend and take off with Nancy to spend Christmas alone in the bush. But curiosity kept me from retreating. I wanted to see what such a scrawny ox looked like on butchering and if there *was* going to be a fight, I wanted to catch every word of it. Anthropologists are incurable that way.

The great beast was driven up to our dancing ground, and a shot in the forehead dropped it in its tracks. Then, freshly cut branches were heaped around the fallen carcass to receive the meat. Ten men volunteered to help with the cutting. I asked /gaugo to make the breast bone cut. This cut, which begins the butchering process for most large game, offers easy access for removal of the viscera. But it also allows the hunter to spot-check the amount of fat on the animal. A fat game animal carries a white layer up to an inch thick on the chest, while in a thin one, the knife will quickly cut to bone. All eyes fixed on his hand as /gaugo, dwarfed by the great carcass, knelt to the breast. The first cut opened a pool of solid white in the black skin. The second and third cut widened and deepened the creamy white. Still no bone. It was pure fat; it must have been two inches thick.

"Hey /gau," I burst out, "that ox is loaded with fat. What's this about the ox being too thin to bother eating? Are you out of your mind?"

"Fat?" /gau shot back, "You call that fat? This wreck is thin, sick, dead!" And he broke out laughing. So did everyone else. They rolled on the ground, paralyzed with laughter. Everybody laughed except me; I was thinking.

I ran back to the tent and burst in just as Nancy was getting up. "Hey, the black ox. It's fat as hell! They were kidding about it being too thin to eat. It was a joke or something. A put-on. Everyone is really delighted with it!"

"Some joke," my wife replied. "It was so funny that you were ready to pack up and leave /ai/ai."

If it had indeed been a joke, it had been an extraordinarily convincing one, and tinged, I thought, with more than a touch of malice as many jokes are. Nevertheless, that it was a joke lifted my spirits considerably, and I returned to the butchering site where the shape of the ox was rapidly disappearing under the axes and knives of the butchers. The atmosphere had become festive. Grinning broadly, their arms covered with blood well past the elbow, men packed chunks of meat into the big cast-iron cooking pots, fifty pounds to the load, and muttered and chuckled all the while about the thinness and worthlessness of the animal and /ontah's poor judgment.

We danced and ate that ox two days and two nights; we cooked and distributed fourteen potfuls of meat and no one went home hungry and no fights broke out.

But the "joke" stayed in my mind. I had a growing feeling that something important had happened in my relationship with the Bushmen and that the clue lay in the meaning of the joke. Several days later, when most of the people had dispersed back to the bush camps, I raised the question with Hakekgose, a Tswana man who had grown up among the !Kung, married a !Kung girl, and who probably knew their culture better than any other non-Bushman.

"With us whites," I began, "Christmas is supposed to be the day of friendship and brotherly love. What I can't figure out is why the Bushmen went to such lengths to criticize and belittle the ox I had bought for the feast. The animal was perfectly good and their jokes and wisecracks practically ruined the holiday for me."

"So it really did bother you," said Hakekgose. "Well, that's the way they always talk. When I take my rifle and go hunting with them, if I miss, they laugh at me for the rest of the day. But even if I hit and bring one down, it's no better. To them, the kill is always too small or too old or too thin; and as we sit down on the kill site to cook and eat the liver, they keep grumbling, even with their mouths full of meat. They say things like, 'Oh this is awful! What a worthless animal! Whatever made me think that this Tswana rascal could hunt!'"

"Is this the way outsiders are treated?" I asked.

"No, it is their custom; they talk that way to each other too. Go and ask them."

/gaugo had been one of the most enthusiastic in making me feel bad about the merit of the Christmas ox. I sought him out first.

"Why did you tell me the black ox was worthless, when you could see that it was loaded with fat and meat?"

"It is our way," he said smiling. "We always like to fool people about that. Say there is a Bushman who has been hunting. He must not come home and announce like a braggard, 'I have killed a big one in the bush!' He must first sit down in silence until I or someone else comes up to his fire and asks, 'What did you see today?' He replies quietly, 'Ah, I'm no good for hunting. I saw nothing at all [pause] just a little tiny one.' Then I smile to myself," /gaugo continued, "because I know he has killed something big."

"In the morning we make up a party of four or five people to cut up and carry the meat back to the camp. When we arrive at the kill we examine it and cry out, 'You mean to say you have dragged us all the way out here in order to make us cart home your pile of bones? Oh, if I had known it was this thin I wouldn't have come.' Another one pipes up, 'People, to think I gave up a nice day in the shade for this. At home we may be hungry but at least we have nice cool water to drink.' If the horns are big, someone says, 'Did you think that somehow you were going to boil down the horns for soup?'

"To all this you must respond in kind. 'I agree,' you say, 'this one is not worth the effort; let's just cook the liver for strength and leave the rest for the hyenas. It is not too late to hunt today and even a duiker or a steenbok would be better than this mess.'

"Then you set to work nevertheless; butcher the animal, carry the meat back to the camp and everyone eats," /gaugo concluded.

Things were beginning to make sense. Next, I went to Tomazo. He corroborated /gaugo's story of the obligatory insults over a kill and added a few details of his own.

"But," I asked, "why insult a man after he has gone to all that trouble to track and kill an animal and when he is going to share the meat with you so that your children will have something to eat?"

"Arrogance," was his cryptic answer.

"Arrogance?"

"Yes, when a young man kills much meat he comes to think of himself as a chief or a big man, and he thinks of the rest of us as his servants or inferiors. We can't accept this. We refuse one who boasts, for someday his pride will make him kill somebody. So we always speak of his meat as worthless. This way we cool his heart and make him gentle."

"But why didn't you tell me this before?" I asked Tomazo with some heat.

"Because you never asked me," said Tomazo, echoing the refrain that has come to haunt every field ethnographer.

The pieces now fell into place. I had known for a long time that in situations of social conflict with Bushmen I held all the cards. I was the only source of tobacco in a thousand square miles, and I was not incapable of cutting an individual off for non-cooperation. Though my boycott never lasted longer than a few days, it was an indication of my strength. People resented my presence at the water hole, yet simultaneously dreaded my leaving. In short I was a perfect target for the charge of arrogance and for the Bushmen tactic of enforcing humility.

I had been taught an object lesson by the Bushmen; it had come from an unexpected corner and had hurt me in a vulnerable area. For the big black ox was to be the one totally generous, unstinting act of my year at /ai/ai, and I was quite unprepared for the reaction I received.

As I read it, their message was this: There are no totally generous acts. All "acts" have an element of calculation. One black ox slaughtered at Christmas does not wipe out a year of careful manipulation of gifts given to serve your own ends. After all, to kill an animal and share the meat with people is really no more than Bushmen do for each other every day and with far less fanfare.

In the end, I had to admire how the Bushmen had played out the farce—collectively straight-faced to the end. Curiously the episode reminded me of the *Good Soldier Schweik* and his marvelous encounters with authority. Like Schweik, the Bushmen had retained a thorough-going skepticism of good intentions. Was it this independence of spirit, I wondered, that had kept them culturally viable in the face of generations of contact with more powerful societies, both black and white? The thought that the Bushmen were alive and well in the Kalahari was strangely comforting. Perhaps, armed with that independence and with their superb knowledge of their environment, they might yet survive the future.

Richard Borshay Lee is a full professor of anthropology at the University of Toronto. He has done extensive fieldwork in southern Africa, is coeditor of *Man the Hunter* (1968) and *Kalahari Hunter-Gatherers* (1976), and author of *The !Kung San: Men, Women, and Work in a Foraging Society.*

From Jíbaro to Crack Dealer

Confronting the Restructuring of Capitalism in El Barrio

Philippe Bourgois

F ollowing his year and a half of fieldwork in a rural coffee-growing county in the central highlands of Puerto Rico from 1948 through 1949, Eric R. Wolf warned that even the small farmers and coffee pickers in the most isolated and traditional rural barrio that he was studying "in the future will supply many hundreds of hands to the coast, to the towns, and to the United States" (Wolf 1956b, 231). Macroeconomic and political forces proved Wolf's warning to be an understatement. American industrial capital was provided with extraordinary incentives and local agricultural development in Puerto Rico atrophied at the same time that emigration to the factories of New York City was actively promoted. The ensuing exodus over the next three and a half decades of almost a third of Puerto Rico's total population resulted proportionally in one of the larger labor migrations in modern history.

STRUCTURAL CONSTRAINTS OF THE NUYORICAN EXPERIENCE

The majority of the immigrants found employment in New York City's most vulnerable subsector of light manufacturing. They arrived precisely on the eve of the structural decimation of factory production in urban North America. Indeed, the post-World War II

Puerto Rican experience provides almost a textbook illustration of what Wolf in his later work refers to as "the growth of ever more diverse proletarian diasporas" that "capitalist accumulation … continues to engender" as it spreads across the globe (1982a, 383). Perhaps most interesting and relevant for understanding Nuyorican ethnicity—that is, the experience of New York City-bom and raised Puerto Ricans—are the contradictory ways that the "changing needs of capital … continuously produce and recreate symbolically marked 'cultural' distinctions" among "the new working classes" who have crisscrossed oceans and continents in their struggle for survival and dignity (Wolf 1982a, 379–380).

Depending upon one's formal definition, over the past three or four generations, the Puerto Rican people—especially those living in New York—have passed through almost a half dozen distinct modes of production: (1) from small landowning semisubsistence peasantry or hacienda peons; (2) to export agricultural laborers on foreign-owned, capital-intensive plantations; (3) to factory workers in urban shantytowns; (4) to sweatshop workers in ghetto tenements; (5) to service sector employees in high-rise inner-city housing projects; (6) to underground economy entrepreneurs homeless on the street.

This marathon sprint through economic history onto New York City's streets has been compounded ideologically by an overtly racist "cultural assault." Literally overnight the new immigrants—many of whom were enveloped in a *jibaro* (hillbilly) dominated culture emphasizing interpersonal webs of patriarchal *respeto*—found themselves transformed into "racially" inferior cultural pariahs. Ever since their arrival they have been despised and humiliated with that virulence so characteristic of America's history of polarized race relations in the context of massive labor migrations. Even though the Puerto Rican experience is extreme, it is by no means unique. On the contrary, peoples all through the world and throughout history have been forced to traverse multiple modes of production and have suffered social dislocation.

The historic structural transformations imposed upon the Puerto Rican jibaro translate statistically into a tragic profile of unemployment, substance abuse, broken families, and devastated health in U.S. inner cities. No other ethnic group except perhaps Native Americans fares more poorly in the official statistics than do mainland U.S. Puerto Ricans. This is most pronounced for the majority cohort living in New York City where Puerto Ricans have the highest welfare dependency and poverty rates, the lowest labor force participation rates, and the fastest growing HIV infection rates of any group (Falcon 1992; Lambert 1990).

THE ETHNOGRAPHIC SETTING

These contemporary expressions of historical dislocation formed the backdrop for my five years of participant-observation fieldwork on street culture in the "crack economy" during the late 1980s and early 1990s. For a total of approximately three and a half years

I lived with my wife and young son in an irregularly heated, rat-filled tenement in East Harlem, better known locally as El Barrio or Spanish Harlem. This two hundred-square-block neighborhood is visibly impoverished yet it is located in the heart of the richest city in the western hemisphere. Its vacant lots and crumbling abandoned tenements are literally a stone's throw from multimillion-dollar condominiums. Although one in three families survives on public assistance, the majority of El Barrio's 130,000 Puerto Rican and African-American residents comprise the ranks of the "working poor." They eke out an uneasy subsistence in entry-level service and manufacturing jobs in a city with one of the highest costs of living in the world.

In my ethnographic research, I explored the ideologies (i.e., the power-charged belief systems) that organize "common sense" on the street—what I call "street culture." Consequently, over the years, I interacted with and befriended the addicts, thieves, dealers, and con artists who comprise a minority proportion of El Barrio residents but who exercise hegemony over its public space. Specifically, I focused on a network of some twenty-five street-level crack dealers who operated on and around my block.

On the one hand, such an intensive examination of street participants risks exoticizing the neighborhood and may be interpreted as reinforcing violent stereotypes against Puerto Ricans. On the other hand, case studies of the "worthy poor" risk "normalizing" the experience of class and racial segregation and can mask the depths of human suffering that accompanies rapid economic restructuring. Furthermore, the legally employed majority of El Barrio residents has lost control of the streets and has retreated from daily life in the neighborhood. To understand the experience of living in the community, the ideologies of violence, opposition, and material pursuit which have established hegemony over street life—much to the dismay of most residents—have to be addressed systematically. Furthermore, on a subtle theoretical level, the "caricatural" responses to poverty and marginalization that the dealers and addicts represent provide privileged insight into processes that may be experienced in one form or another by major sectors of any vulnerable working-class population experiencing rapid structural change anywhere in the world and at any point in history. Once again, there is nothing structurally exceptional about the Puerto Rican experience except that the human costs involved are more clearly visible given the extent and rapidity with which Puerto Rican society has been absorbed by the United States and the particularly persistent virulence of American ideologies around "race" and culture.

My central concern is the relationship of the street dealers to the worlds of work—that is, the legal and illegal labor markets—that employ them and give meaning to their lives. The long-term structural transformation of New York from a manufacturing to a service economy is crucial to understanding this experience. Although economists, sociologists, and political scientists have argued extensively over the details of the statistics, most recognize that the dislocations caused by the erosion of the manufacturing sector are a driving force behind the economic polarization of urban America (Wilson 1987). They also specifically recognize that Puerto Ricans are the most vulnerable group in New York's structural adjustment because of their over-concentration in the least dynamic subsector within light manufacturing and because of their fragile incipient foothold in public sector and service employment (Rodriguez 1989).

Through my ethnographic data I hope to show the local-level implications of the global-level restructuring of capital and, in the process, give voice to some unrepentant victims. In a nutshell, I am arguing that the transformation from manufacturing to service employment—especially in the professional office work setting—is much more culturally disruptive than the already revealing statistics on reductions in income, employment, unionization, and worker's benefits would indicate. Low-level service sector employment engenders a humiliating ideological—or cultural—confrontation between a powerful corps of white office executives and their assistants versus a mass of poorly educated, alienated, "colored" workers.

SHATTERED WORKING-CLASS DREAMS

All the crack dealers and addicts whom I have interviewed worked at one or more legal jobs in their early youth. In fact, most entered the labor market at a younger age than the typical American. Before they were twelve years old they were bagging groceries at the supermarket for tips, stocking beer off-the-books in local *bodegas,* or shining shoes. For example, Julio, the night [10] manager at a video games arcade that sells five-dollar vials of crack on the block where I lived, pursued a traditional working-class dream in his early adolescence. With the support of his extended kin who were all immersed in a working-class "common sense," he dropped out of junior high school to work in a local garment factory:

> I was like fourteen or fifteen playing hooky and pressing dresses and whatever they were making on the steamer. They was cheap, cheap clothes.
>
> My mother's sister was working there first and then her son, my cousin Hector—the one who's in jail now—was the one they hired first, because his mother agreed: "If you don't want to go school, you gotta work."
>
> So I started hanging out with him. I wasn't planning on working in the factory. I was supposed to be in school; but it just sort of happened.

Ironically, little Julio actually became the agent who physically moved the factory out of the inner city. In the process, he became merely one more of the 445,900 manufacturing workers in New York City to lose their jobs as factory employment dropped 50 percent from 1963 to 1983 (Romo and Schwartz 1993). Of course, instead of understanding himself as the victim of a structural, transformation, Julio remembers with pleasure and even pride the extra income he earned for clearing the machines out of the factory space:

Them people had money, man. Because we helped them move out of the neighborhood. It took us two days—only me and my cousin, Hector. Wow! It was work. They gave us seventy bucks each.

Almost all the crack dealers had similar tales of former factory jobs. For poor adolescents, the decision to drop out of school and become a marginal factory worker is attractive. It provides the employed youth with access to the childhood "necessities"—sneakers, basketballs, store-bought snacks—that sixteen-year-olds who stay in school cannot afford. In the descriptions of their first forays into legal factory-based employment, one hears clearly the extent to which they and their families subscribed to mainstream working-class ideologies about the dignity of engaging in "hard work" versus education.

Had these enterprising, early-adolescent workers from El Barrio not been confined to the weakest sector of manufacturing in a period of rapid job loss their teenage working-class dream might have stabilized. Instead, upon reaching their mid-twenties they discovered themselves to be unemployable high school dropouts. This painful realization of social marginalization expresses itself generationally as the working-class values of their families conflict violently with the reality of their hard-core lumpenization. They are constantly accused of slothfulness by their mothers and even by friends who have managed to maintain legal jobs. They do not have a regional perspective on the dearth of adequate entry-level jobs available to "functional illiterates" in New York City and they begin to suspect that they might indeed be "vago bons" (lazy bums) who do not *want* to work hard and help themselves. Confused, they take refuge in an alternate search for career, meaning, and ecstasy in substance abuse.

Formerly, when most entry-level jobs were found in factories the contradiction between an oppositional street culture and traditional working-class, shop-floor culture was less pronounced—especially when the worksite was protected by a union. Factories are inevitably rife with confrontational hierarchies; nevertheless, on the shop floor, surrounded by older union workers, high school dropouts who are well versed in the latest and toughest street-culture styles function effectively. In the factory, being tough and violently macho has high cultural value; a certain degree of opposition to die foreman and the "bossman" is expected and is considered appropriately masculine.

In contrast, this same oppositional street identity is nonfunctional in the service sector that has burgeoned in New York's finance-driven economy because it does not allow for the humble, obedient, social interaction—often across gender lines—that professional office workers impose on their subordinates. A qualitative change characterizes the tenor of social interaction in office-based service sector employment. Workers in a mailroom or behind a photocopy machine cannot publicly maintain their cultural autonomy. Most concretely, they have no union; more subtly, there are few fellow workers surrounding them to insulate them and to provide them with a culturally based sense of class solidarity.[1] Instead they are besieged by supervisors and bosses from an alien, hostile, and obviously dominant culture. When these office managers are not intimidated by street culture, they ridicule it. Workers like Willie and Julio appear inarticulate to their professional supervisors when they try to imitate the language of power in the workplace and instead stumble patfietically over the enunciation of unfamiliar words. They cannot decipher the hastily scribbled instructions—rife with mysterious abbreviations—that are left for them by harried office managers. The "common sense" of white-collar work is foreign to them; they do not, for example, understand the logic for filing triplicate copies of memos or for postdating invoices. When they attempt to improvise or show initiative they fail miserably and instead appear inefficient—or even hostile—for failing to follow "clearly specified[3]" instructions.

Their "social skills" are even more inadequate than their limited professional capacities. They do not know how to look at their fellow co-service workers—let alone their supervisors—without intimidating them. They cannot walk down the hallway to the water fountain without unconsciously swaying their shoulders aggressively as if patrolling their home turf. Gender to barriers are an even more culturally charged realm. They are repeatedly o reprimanded for harassing female co-workers.

The cultural clash between white "yuppie" power and inner-city "scrambling jive" in the service sector is much more than a difference of style. Service workers who are incapable of obeying the rules of interpersonal interaction dictated by professional office culture will never be upwardly mobile. In the high-rise office buildings of midtown Manhattan, newly employed inner-city high school dropouts suddenly realize that they look like idiotic buffoons to the men and women they work for. Once again, a gender dynamic exacerbates the confusion and sense of insult experienced by young, male inner-city employees because most supervisors in the lowest reaches of the service sector are women. Street culture does not allow males to be subordinate across gender lines.

"GETTIN' DISSED"

On the street, the trauma of experiencing a threat to one's personal dignity has been frozen linguistically in the commonly used phrase "to diss" which is short for "to disrespect." Significantly, back in the coffee-hacienda highlands of Puerto Rico in 1949, Wolf had noted the importance of the traditional Puerto Rican concept of *respeto:* "The good owner 'respects' [*respeta*] the laborer." Wolf pointed specifically to the role "respect" plays in controlling labor power: "It is probably to the interest of the landowner to make concessions to his best workers, to deal with them on a respect basis, and to enmesh them in a network of mutual obligations" (Wolf 1956£, 235; see also Lauria 1964).

Puerto Rican street dealers do not find "respect" in the entry-level service sector jobs thatNhave increased twofold in New York's economy since the 1950s, On the contrary, they "get dissed" in their new jobs. Julio, for example, remembers the humiliation of his former work experiences as an "office boy," and he speaks of them in a race and gender-charged idiom:

> I had a prejudiced boss. She was a fucking "ho'," Gloria. She was white. Her name was Christian. No, not Christian, Kirschman. I don't know if she was Jewish or not. When she was talking to people she would say, "He's illiterate." So what I did one day was, I just looked up the word, "illiterate," in the dictionary and I saw that she's saying to her associates that I'm stupid or something! Well, I am illiterate anyway.

The most profound dimension of Julio's humiliation was being obliged to look up in the dictionary the word used to insult him. In contrast, in the underground economy, he is sheltered from this kind of threat:

> Big Pete (the crack house franchise owner] he would never disrespect me that way. He wouldn't tell me that because he's illiterate too. Plus I've got more education than him. I got a GED.

To succeed at Gloria Kirschman's magazine publishing company, Julio would have had to submit wholeheartedly to her professional cultural style but he was unwilling to compromise his street identity. He refused to accept her insults and he was unable to imitate her culture; hence, he was doomed to a marginal position behind a photocopy machine or at the mail meter. The job requirements in the service sector are largely cultural—that is, having a "good attitude"—therefore they conjugate powerfully with racism:

> I wouldn't have mind that she said I was illiterate. What bothered me was that when she called on the telephone, she wouldn't want me to answer even if my supervisor who was the receptionist was not there. [Note how Julio is so low in the office hierarchy that his immediate supervisor is a receptionist.]
>
> When she hears my voice it sounds like she's going to get a heart attack. She'd go, "Why are you answering the phones?"
>
> That bitch just didn't like my Puerto Rican accent.

Julio's manner of resisting this insult to his cultural dignity exacerbated his marginal position in the labor hierarchy:

> And then, when I did pick up the phone, I used to just sound *Porta'rican* on purpose.

In contrast to the old factory sweatshop positions, these just-above-minimum-wage office jobs require intense interpersonal contact with the middle and upper-middle classes.

Proximal contact across class lines and the absence of a working-class autonomous space for eight hours a day in the office can be a claustrophobic experience for an otherwise ambitious, energetic, young inner-city worker.

Willie interpreted this requirement to obey white, middle-class norms as an affront to his dignity that specifically challenged his definition of masculinity:

> I had a few jobs like that [referring to Julio's "telephone diss"] where you gotta take a lot of shit from bitches and be a wimp.
>
> I didn't like it but I kept on working, because "Fuck it!" you don't want to fuck up the relationship. So you just be a punk [shrugging his shoulders dejectedly].

One alternative for surviving at a workplace that does not tolerate a street-based cultural identity is to become bicultural: to play politely by "the white woman's" rules downtown only to come home and revert to street culture within the safety of one's tenement or housing project at night. Tens of thousands of East Harlem residents manage this tightrope, but it often engenders accusations of betrayal and internalized racism on the part of neighbors and childhood friends who do not have—or do not want—these bicultural skills.

This is the case, for example, of Ray, a rival crack dealer whose black skin and tough street demeanor disqualify him from legal office work. He quit a "nickel-and-dime messenger job downtown" to sell crack full-time in his project stairway shortly after a white woman fled from him shrieking down the hallway of a high-rise office building. Ray and the terrified woman had ridden the elevator together and coincidentally Ray had stepped off on the same floor as her to make a delivery. Worse yet, Ray had been trying to act like a "debonair male" and suspected the contradiction between his inadequate appearance and his "chivalric" intentions was responsible for the woman's terror:

> You know how you let a woman go off the elevator first? Well that's what I did to her but I may have looked a little shabby on the ends. Sometime my hair not combed. You know. So I could look a little sloppy to her maybe when I let her off first.

What Ray did not quite admit until I probed further is that he too had been intimidated by the lone white woman. He had been so disoriented by her tabooed, unsupervised proximity that he had forgotten to press the elevator button when he originally stepped on after her:

> She went in the elevator first but then she just waits there to see what floor I press. She's playing like she don't know what floor she wants to go to because she wants to wait for me to press my floor. And I'm standing there and I forgot

to press the button. I'm thinking about something else—I don't know what was the matter with me. And she's thinking like, "He's not pressing the button; I guess he's following me!"

As a crack dealer, Ray no longer has to confront this kind of confusing humiliation. Instead, he can righteously condemn his "successful" neighbors who work downtown for being ashamed of who they were born to be:

> When you see someone go downtown and get a good job, if they be Puerto Rican, you see them fix up their hair and put some contact lens in their eyes. Then they fit in. And they do it! I seen it.
>
> They turnovers. They people who want to be white. Man, if you call them in Spanish, it wind up a problem.
>
> When they get nice jobs like that, all of a sudden, you know, they start talking proper.

SELF-DESTRUCTIVE RESISTANCE

Third and second-generation Spanish Harlem residents born into working-class families do not tolerate high levels of "exploitation." In the new jobs available to them, however, there are no class-based institutions to channel their resistance. They are caught in a technological time warp. They have developed contemporary mainstream American definitions of survival needs and emotional notions of job satisfaction. In short, they are "made in New York;" therefore, they are not "exploitable" or "degradable." Both their objective economic needs as well as their personal cultural dignities have to be satisfied by their jobs. They resist inadequate working conditions. Finally, they are acutely aware of their relative depravation vis-a-vis the middle-level managers and wealthy executives whose intimate physical proximity they cannot escape at work.

At the same time that young men like Julio, Willie, and Ray recognize how little power they have in the legal labor market, they do not accept their domination passively. They are resisting exploitation from positions of subordination. They are living the unequal power struggle that a growing body of anthropological and ethnographic literature is beginning to address (Bourgois in press; Foley 1990; Fordham 1988; Willis 1977' Wolf 1990A, 590).

Unfortunately, for people like Julio and Willie, the traditional modes of powerless resistance—foot dragging, disgruntlement, petty theft, and so forth—which might be appropriate in traditional peasant or even proletarian settings (see Scott 1985) contradict the fundamental "technological" requirement for enthusiastic "initiative" and "flexibility" that New York's finance-driven service sector demands. In manufacturing, resistance can be channeled through recognized institutions—unions—that often reinforce class consciousness. In fact, oppositionally defined cultural identities are so legitimate on the shop floor that they even serve to ritualize management/worker confrontation.

In the service sector, however, there is no neutral way to express cultural nonconformity. Scowling on the way to brewing coffee for a supervisor results in an unsatisfactory end-of-year performance evaluation. Stealing on the job is just cause for instant job termination. Indeed, petty theft is the avenue for "powerless revenge" most favored by Willie and Julio. They both were skilled at manipulating the Pitney-Bowes postage meter machines and at falsifying stationery inventory to skim "chump change."

More subtle, however, was the damage to Julio's work performance due to his constant concern lest Gloria Kirschman once again catch him off guard and "disrespect" him without his being immediately aware of the gravity of the insult. Consequently, when he was ordered to perform mysteriously specific tasks such as direct mailings of promotional materials that required particular combinations of folding, stuffing, or clipping, he activated his defense mechanisms. Julio had rarely received direct mail advertisements in his project apartment mailbox; consequently, the urgency and the precision with which his supervisor oversaw the logistics of these mailings appeared overbearingly oppressive and insulting. Gloria appeared almost superstitious in the rigor and anxiety with which she supervised each detail and Julio refused to accept the "flexibility" that these delicate mailings required—that is, late-night binges of collating and recollating to make bulk-rate postage deadlines coincide with the magazine's printing and sales deadlines. Furthermore, to Julio, it was offensive to have to bring over the assembled promotional packets to Gloria's home for a last-minute late-night inspection:

> It would be late and I would be at the office to do these rush jobs: collate them, staple them, fold them in the correct way … whatever way she said, It was always different. And it had to be just the way she wanted it. I'd stuff them just the right way (making frantic shuffling motions with his hands] and then seal the shit.
>
> I used to hate that. I would box it and take it to the 38th Street Post Office at 10:30 at night.
>
> But then sometimes she would call me from home and I would have to bring papers up to her house on 79th Street and 3rd Avenue [Manhattan's silk stocking district] to double check.
>
> And she would try to offer me something to eat and I would say, "No, thank you," because she would try to pay me with that shit, 'Cause she's a cheap bitch.
>
> She'd say, "You want pizza, tea, or cookies?" She had those Pepperidge Farm cookies [wrinkling his face with disgust].
>
> But I wouldn't accept anything from her. I wasn't going to donate my time man.

She thought I was illiterate. She thought I was stupid. Not my boy, charge *every penny.* From the moment I leave the office that's overtime all the way to her house. That's time and a half.

I used to exaggerate the hours. If I worked sixteen, I would put eighteen or twenty to see if I could get away with it. And I would get away with it. I'm not going to do that kind of shit for free.

And that bitch was crazy. She used to eat baby food-I know cause I saw her eating it with a spoon right out of the jar.

If Julio appeared to be a scowling, ungrateful, dishonest worker to Gloria, then Gloria herself looked almost perverted to Julio. What normal middle-aged woman would invite her twenty-year-old employee into her kitchen late at night and eat baby food in front of him?

Julio's victories over his employer, Gloria, were Pyrrhic. In the cross-cultural confrontation taking place in the corridors of high-rise office buildings there is no ambiguity over who wields power. This unequal hierarchy is constantly reasserted through the mechanisms of cultural capital so foreign to participants in street culture. For example, when someone like Willie, Julio, or Ray is "terminated" for suspicion of theft, the personnel report registers an insulting notation: "lack of initiative," "inarticulate," or "no understanding of the purpose of the company." Julio correctly translates this information into street-English: "She's saying to her associates that I'm stupid!"

Willie and Julio have no frame of reference to guide them through service employment because their social network only has experience with factory work. In their first factory jobs, both Willie and Julio were guided by older family members who were producing the very same products they were making. Still today, for example, Julio's mother is a sweatshop /homework seamstress and Willie's uncle is a factory foreman in the Midwestern town where his metal-chroming company relocated. In contrast, the only socialization available to Willie and Julio in the service sector comes from equally isolated and alienated fellow workers. Willie, for example, who has always been precocious in everything he has done in life from dropping out of school, to engaging in street violence, to burglarizing, to selling drugs, to abusing women, to becoming a crack addict—immediately understood the impossibility of his supervisor's maintaining an objective quality control in the mailroom where he worked prior to being hired by Julio at the crack house:

I used to get there late, but the other workers wasn't never doing shit. They was *lazy* motherfuckers—even the supervisor.

They all be sitting, asking each other questions over the phone, and fooling with video games on the computer. And that's all you do at a place like that. My boss, Bill, be drinking on the sneak cue, and eating this bad-ass sausage.

Finally, the precarious tenure of entry-level jobs in the service sector is the immediate precipitating factor in Willie's and Julio's retreat from the legal labor market. When they were not fired for "bad attitude," they were laid off due to economic retrenchment. The companies employing them fluctuated with the unpredictable whims of rapidly changing "yuppie fashions." Julio, for example, lost two different positions in fragile companies that folded: (I) Gloria Kirschman's trendy magazine, and (2) a desktop publishing house.

Surprisingly, in his accounts of being laid off Julio publicly admitted defeat and vulnerability. On repeated occasions I had seen Julio brave violence on the streets and in the crack house. I knew him capable of deliberate cruelty, such as refusing to pay for his fifteen-year-old girlfriend's abortion or of slowly breaking the wrist of an adolescent who had played a prank on him. Downtown, however, behind the computer terminal where he had held his last job "in printing," he had been crushed psychologically by the personnel officers who fired him. Ironically, I registered on my tape recorder his tale of frustration, humiliation, and self-blame for losing his last legal job as a printer only a week after recording with him a bravado-laced account of how he mugged a drunken Mexican immigrant in a nearby housing project:

> I was with Rico and his girl, Daisy. We saw this Mexican He was just probably drunk. I grabbed him by the back of the neck, and put my 007 [knife] in his back [making the motion of holding someone in a choke hold from be hind]. Right here [pointing to his own lower back]. And I was jigging him *HARD* [grinning for emphasis at me and his girlfriend, who was listening, rapt with attention]!
>
> I said: "*No te mueve cabron o te voy a picar como un pernil* [Don't move motherfucker or I'll stick you like a roast pork]." [More loud chuckles from Julio's girlfriend.] Yeah, yeah, like how you stab a pork shoulder when you want to put all the flavoring in the holes.
>
> I wasn't playing, either, I was serious. I would have jigged him. And I'd regret it later, but I was looking at that gold ring he had. [Chuckle.]
>
> The Mexican panicked. So I put him to the floor, poking him hard, and Rico's girl started searching him.
>
> I said, "Yo, take that asshole's fucking ring too!"
>
> After she took the ring we broke out. We sold the ring and then we cut-out on Daisy. We left her in the park, she didn't get even a cent. She helped for nothing. [More chuckling.]

As a knife-wielding mugger on the street, Julio could not contrast mare dramatically with the panic-stricken employee begging for a second chance that legal employment had reduced him to:

I was more or less expecting it. But still, when I found out, I wanted to cry, man. My throat got dry, I was like ... [waves his hands, and gasps as if struck by a panic attack].

They called me to the office, I was like, "Oh *shit!*"

I couldn't get through to them, I even told them, "I'll let you put me back to messenger; I will take less pay; just keep me employed. I need the money; I need to work. I got a family."

But they said, "Nope, nope, nope." I left.

I just stood right outside the building; I was fucked, man. All choked up. *Me joduron* [They jerked me].

THE NEW IMMIGRANT ALTERNATIVE

The flooding of cocaine and then crack onto America's streets during the 1980s infused new energy into the underground economy, making drug dealing the most vibrant equal opportunity employer for Harlem youths, Normally, in order to fill jobs adequately in the expanding service sector, New York's legal economy should have to compete for the hearts and minds of the growing proportion of the inner city's "best and brightest" who are choosing to pursue more remunerative and culturally compatible careers in the underground economy. A wave of cheaper, more docile and disciplined new immigrant workers, however, is altering this labor power balance. These immigrants—largely undocumented—are key agents in New York's latest structural economic adjustment. Their presence allows low-wage employment to expand while social services retrench. This helps explain, for example, how the real value of the minimum wage could have declined by one-third in the 1980s while the federal government was able to decrease the proportion of its contribution to New York City's budget by over 50 percent (Berlin 1991, 10; Rosenbaum 1989, Al). The breakdown of the inner city's public sector is no longer an economic threat to the expansion of New York's economy because the labor force that these public subsidies maintain is increasingly irrelevant.

Like the parents and grandparents of Julio and Willie, many of New York's newest immigrants are from remote rural communities or squalid shantytowns where meat is eaten only once a week, and where there is no running water or electricity. In downtown Manhattan many of these new immigrants are Chinese, but in East Harlem the vast majority are Mexicans from the rural states of Puebla and Guerrero. To them, New York's streets are still "paved in gold" if one works hard enough.

Half a century ago Julio's mother fled precisely the same living conditions these new immigrants are only just struggling to escape. Her reminiscences about childhood in her natal village reveal the trajectory of improved material conditions, cultural dislocation, and crushed working-class dreams that is propelling her second-generation son into a destructive street culture:

> I loved that life in Puerto Rico, because it was a healthy, healthy, healthy life. We always ate because my father always had work, and in those days the custom was to have a garden in your patio to grow food and everything that you ate.
>
> We only ate meat on Sundays because everything was cultivated on the same little parcel of land. We didn't have a refrigerator, so we ate *bacalao* [salted codfish], which can stay outside, and a meat that they call old-meat, *carne de vieja*, and sardines from a can. But thanks to God, we never felt hunger. My mother made a lot of cornflour.
>
> Some people have done better by coming here, but many people haven't. Even people from my barrio, who came trying to find a better life [*buen ambiente*] just found disaster. Married couples right from my neighborhood came only to have the husband run off with another woman.
>
> In those days in Puerto Rico, when we were in poverty, life was better. Everyone will tell you life was healthier and you could trust people. Now you can't trust anybody.
>
> What I like best was that we kept all our traditions … our feasts. In my village, everyone was either an Uncle or an Aunt. And when you walked by someone older, you had to ask for their blessing. It was respect. There was a lot of respect in those days. [Original in Spanish]

Ironically, at sixty, Julio's monolingual Spanish-speaking mother is the only one of her family who can still compete effectively with the new immigrants who are increasingly filling Manhattan's entry-level labor market. She ekes out a living on welfare in her high-rise housing-project apartment by taking in sewing from undocumented garment industry subcontractors.

"Rather than bemoaning the structural adjustment which is destroying their capacity to survive on legal wages, street-bound Puerto Rican youths celebrate their "decision" to bank on the underground economy and to cultivate their street identities. Willie and Julio repeatedly assert their pride in their street careers. For example, one Saturday night after they finished their midnight shift at the crack house, I accompanied them on their way to purchase "El Sapo Verde" (The Green Toad), a twenty-dollar bag of powder cocaine, sold by a reputable outfit three blocks away. While waiting for Julio and Willie to be "served" by the coke seller, I engaged three undocumented Mexican men drinking beer on a neighboring stoop in a conversation about finding work in New York. One of the new immigrants was already earning five hundred dollars a week fixing deep-fat-fry machines. He had a straightforward racist explanation for why Willie—who was standing next to me—was "unemployed":

OK, OK I'll explain it to you in one word; Because the Puerto Ricans are brutes! [pointing at Willie] Brutes! Do you understand?

Puerto Ricans like to make easy money. They like to leech off of other people. But not us Mexicans! No way! We like to work for our money. We don't steal. We came here to work and that's all. [Original in Spanish]

Instead of physically assaulting the employed immigrant for insulting him, Willie turned the racist tirade into the basis for a new, generational-based, "American-born," urban cultural pride. In fact, in his response, he ridiculed what he interpreted to be the hillbilly naivete of the Mexicans who still believe in the "American Dream." He spoke slowly in street-English as if to mark sarcastically the contrast between his "savvy" Nuyorican identity versus the limited English proficiency of his detractor:

That's right, m'a man! We is real vermin lunatics that sell drugs. We don't want no part of society. "Fight the Power!"[2]

What do we wanna be working for? We rather live off the system. Gain weight, lay women.

When we was younger, we used to break our asses too. [Gesturing toward the Mexican men who were straining to understand his English] I had all kinds of stupid jobs too … advertising agencies … computers.

But not no more! Now we're in a rebellious stage. We rather evade taxes, make quick money and just survive. But we're not satisfied with that either. Ha!

CONCLUSION: ETHNOGRAPHY AND OPPRESSION

America was built on racial hierarchy and on blame-the-victim justifications for the existence of poverty and class distinctions. This makes it difficult to present ethnographic data from inner-city streets without falling prey to a "pornography of violence" or a racist voyeurism. The public "common sense" is not persuaded by a structural economic understanding of Willie's and Julio's "self-destruction." Even the victims themselves psychologize their unsatisfactory lives. Most concretely, political will and public policy ignore the fundamental structural economic facts of marginalization in America (see Romo and Schwartz 1993). Instead the first priority of federal and local social "welfare" agencies is to change the psychological—or at best the "cultural"—orientations of misguided individuals (Katz 1989).

Unfortunately researchers in America have allowed the gap to grow between their hegemonically "liberal" intellectual community and an overwhelmingly conservative popular political culture. From the late 1970s through most of the 1980s, inner-city poverty was simply ignored by all but right-wing academics who filled a popular vacuum with scientifically flawed "best sellers" on the psychological and cultural causes of poverty in order to argue against the "poisonous" effect of public sector intervention (cf. Gilder 1982; Murray 1984). Their analyses coincide with the deep-seated individualistic, blame-the-victim values so cherished in American thought.

There is a theoretical and methodological basis for anthropology's reticence to confront devastating urban poverty in its front yard. Qualitative researchers prefer to avoid tackling taboo subjects such as personal violence, sexual abuse, addiction, alienation, self-destruction, and so forth, for fear of violating the tenets of cultural relativism and of contributing to popular racist stereotypes. Even the "new advocacy ethnography" which is confronting inner-city social crises—homelessness, AIDS, teen pregnancy—in an engaged manner tends to present its "subjects" in an exclusively sympathetic framework (Dehavenon n.d.). The pragmatic realities of a new advocacy anthropology require published data to be politically crafted. A complex critical perspective therefore is often stifled by the necessity of contributing effectively and responsibly to a "policy debate." Defining policy as the political arena for engagement can demobilize both theory and practice.

Regardless of the political, scholarly, or personal motivations, anthropology's cautious and often self-censored approaches to social misery have obfuscated an ethnographic understanding of the multifaceted dynamics of the experience of oppression and ironically sometimes even have served to minimize the depths of human suffering involved. At the same time, there is a growing body of ethnographic literature at the intersection of education and anthropology—sometimes referred to as cultural production theory—which provides insight into how contradictory and complicated forms of resistance often lead to personal self-destruction and community trauma (Foley 1990; Fordham 1988; MacLeod 1987; Willis 1977). Nevertheless, perhaps even these more self-consciously theoretical attempts to grapple with an unpleasant reality tend to glorify—or at least to overidentify with—the resistance theme in order to escape a "blame-the-victim" insinuation (see Bourgois 1989).

Much of the problem is rooted in the nature of the ethnographic endeavor itself. Engulfed in an overwhelming whirlpool of personal suffering it is often difficult for ethnographers to see the larger relationships structuring the jumble of human interaction around them. Structures of power and history cannot be touched or talked to. Empirically this makes it difficult to identify the urgent political economy relationships shaping everyday survival—whether they be public sector breakdown or economic restructuring. For my own part, in the heat of daily life on the street in El Barrio, I often experienced a confusing anger with the victims, the victimizers, and the wealthy industrialized society that generated such a record toll of unnecessary human suffering. For example, when confronted with a pregnant friend frantically smoking crack—and condemning her fetus to a postpartum life of shattered emotions and dulled brain cells—it was impossible for me to remember the history of her people's colonial terror and humiliation or to contextualize her position in New York's changing economy. Living the inferno of what America calls its "underclass," I—like my neighbors around me and like the pregnant crack addicts themselves—often blamed the victim. To overcome such a partial perspective when researching painful human contexts it is especially important to develop a sensitive political economy analysis that "articulates the hidden histories" of the peoples raking themselves over the coals of the latest forms of capitalism.

NOTES

The author would like to thank the following institutions for their support: the Russell Sage Foundation, the Harry Frank Guggenheim Foundation, the Social Science Research Council, the National Institute on Drug Abuse, the Wenner-Gren Foundation for Anthropological Research, the United States Bureau of the Census, and San Francisco State University. Helpful critical comments by Jane Schneider and Rayna Rapp changed the shape of the article. Finally, none of this could have been written without Harold Otto's moral support and typing, as well as final work on the keyboard by Henry Ostendorf and Charles Pearson.

1. Significantly, there are subsectors of the service industry that are relatively unionized such as hospital work and even custodial work—where there is a limited autonomous space for street culture and working-class resistance.
2. "Fight the Power" is a song composed by the rap group Public Enemy.

PART V

THE FUTURE OF CULTURE

Peace Lessons from an Unlikely Source

Frans B. M. de Waal

U pon arrival from Europe, now more than two decades ago, I was taken aback by the level of violence in the American media. I do not just mean the daily news, even though it is hard getting used to multiple murders per day in any large city. No, I mean sitcoms, comedies, drama series, and movies. Staying away from Schwarzenegger and Stallone does not do it; almost any American movie features violence. Inevitably, desensitization sets in. If you say, for example, that *Dances with Wolves* (the 1990 movie with Kevin Costner) is violent, people look at you as if you are crazy. They see an idyllic, sentimental movie, with beautiful landscapes, showing a rare white man who respects American Indians. The bloody scenes barely register.

Comedy is no different. I love, for example, *Saturday Night Live* for its inside commentary on peculiarly American phenomena, such as cheerleaders, televangelists, and celebrity lawyers. But *SNL* is incomplete without at least one sketch in which someone's car explodes or head gets blown off. Characters such as Hans and Franz ("We're going to pump you up!") appeal to me for their names alone (and yes, I do have a brother named Hans), but when their free weights are so heavy that their arms get torn off, I am baffled. The spouting blood gets a big laugh from the audience, but I fail to see the humor.

Did I grow up in a land of sissies? Perhaps, but I am not mentioning this to decide whether violence in the media and our ability to grow immune to it—as I also have over the years—is desirable, or not. I simply wish to draw attention to the cultural fissures in how violence is portrayed, how we teach conflict resolution, and whether harmony is valued over competitiveness. This is the problem with the human species. Somewhere in all of this resides a human nature, but it is molded and stretched into so many different directions that it is hard to say if we are naturally competitive or naturally community-builders. In fact, we are both, but each society reaches its own balance between the two. In America, the squeaky wheel gets the grease. In Japan, the nail that stands out gets pounded into the ground.

Does this variability mean, as some have argued, that animal studies cannot possibly shed light on human aggression? "Nature, red in tooth and claw" remains the dominant image of the animal world. Animals just fight, and that is it? It is not that simple. First, each species has its own way of handling conflict, with for example the chimpanzee (*Pan troglodytes*) being far more violent than that equally close relative of ours, the bonobo (*P. paniscus*) (de Waal 1997). But also within each species we find, just as in humans, variation from group to group. There are "cultures" of violence and "cultures" of peace. The latter are made possible by the universal primate ability to settle disputes and iron out differences.

There was a time when no review of human nature would be complete without assertions about our inborn aggressiveness. The first scientist to bring up this issue, not coincidentally after World War II, was Konrad Lorenz (1966). Lorenz's thesis was greeted with accusations about attempts to whitewash human atrocities, all the more so given the Nobel Prize winner's native tongue, which was German. But Lorenz was hardly alone. In the USA, science journalist Robert Ardrey (1961) presented us as "killer apes" unlikely to ever get our nasty side under control. Recent world events have done little to counter this pessimistic outlook.

The opposition argued, of course, that aggression, like all human behavior, is subject to powerful cultural influences. They even signed petitions to this effect, such as the controversial *Seville Statement on Violence* (Adams et al. 1990). In the polarized mind-set of the time, the issue was presented in either-or fashion, as if behavior cannot be both learned and built upon a biological foundation. This rather fruitless nature/nurture debate becomes considerably more complex if we include what is usually left out, which is the ability to keep aggression under control and foster peace. For this ability, too, there exist animal parallels, such as the habit of chimpanzees to reconcile after fights by means of a kiss and embrace. Such reunions are well-documented in a multitude of animals, including nonprimates, such as hyenas and dolphins. They serve to restore social relationships disturbed by aggression, and any animal that depends on cooperation needs such mechanisms of social repair (Aureli and de Waal 2000; de Waal 2000). There are even indications that in animals, too, cultural influences matter in this regard. This may disturb those who write culture with a capital *C*, and hence view it as uniquely human, but it is a serious possibility nonetheless.

Nonhuman culture is currently one of the hottest areas in the study of animal behavior. The idea goes back to the pioneering work of Kinji Imanishi, who in 1952 proposed that if individuals learn from one another, their behavior may over time grow different from that of individuals in other groups of the same species, thus creating a characteristic culture (reviewed by de Waal 2001). Imanishi thus brought the culture concept down to its most basic feature, that is, the social rather than genetic transmission of behavior. Since then, many examples have been documented, mostly concerning subsistence techniques, such as the sweet potato washing of Japanese macaques (*Macaca fuscata*) and the rich array of tool use by wild chimpanzees, orangutans (*Pongo pymaeus*), and capuchin monkeys (*Cebus* spp.) (Whiten et al. 1999; de Waal 2001; Hirata et al. 2001; Perry et al. 2003; van Schaik et al. 2003). However, much less attention has been paid to *social culture*, which we might define as the transmission of social positions, preferences, habits, and attitudes.

Social culture is obviously harder to document than tool use. In human culture, for instance, it is easy to tell if people eat with knife and fork or with chopsticks, but to notice if a culture is egalitarian or hierarchical, warm or distant, collectivistic or individualistic takes time and is difficult to capture in behavioral measures. A well-documented monkey example of social culture is the inheritance of rank positions in macaque and baboon societies. The future position in the hierarchy of a newborn female can be predicted with almost one hundred percent certainty on the basis of her mother's rank. Females with relatives in high places are born with a silver spoon in their mouth, so to speak, whereas those of lowly origin will spend their life at the bottom. Despite its stability, the system depends on learning. Early in life, the young monkey finds out against which opponents it can expect help from her mother and sisters. When sparring with peer A she may utter screams that recruit massive support to defeat A. But against peer B she can scream her lungs out and nothing happens. Consequently, she will come to dominate A but not B. Experiments manipulating the presence of family members have found that when support dwindles dominant females are unable to maintain their positions (Chapais 1988). In other words, the kin-based hierarchy is maintained for generation after generation through social rather than genetic transmission.

Returning to the issue of aggressive behavior, here the effects of social culture can be felt as well. Without any drugs or brain lesions, one experiment managed to turn monkeys into pacifists. Juveniles of two different macaque species were placed together, day and night, for five months. Rhesus monkeys (*Macaca mulatta*), known as quarrelsome and violent, were housed with the more tolerant and easy-going stumptail monkeys (*M. arctoides*) (Figure 1). Stumptail monkeys easily reconcile with their opponents after fights by holding each others' hips (the so-called "hold-bottom" ritual), whereas reconciliations are rare in rhesus monkeys. Because the mixed-species groups were dominated by the stumptails, physical aggression was rare. The atmosphere was relaxed, and after a while all of the monkeys became friends. Juveniles of the two species played together, groomed together, and slept in large, mixed huddles. Most importantly, the rhesus monkeys developed peacemaking skills on a par with those of their more tolerant group mates. Even when, at the end of the experiment, both species were separated, the rhesus monkeys still showed three times more reconciliation and grooming behaviors after fights than typical of their kind (de Waal and

Johanowicz 1993). Primates thus can adopt social behavior under the influence of others, which opens the door to social culture.

Not unlike rhesus monkeys, baboons have a reputation for fierce competition and nasty fights. With the study by Robert Sapolsky and Lisa Share published in this issue of *PLoS Biology*, we now have the first field evidence that primates can go the flower power route (Sapolsky and Share 2004). Wild baboons developed an exceptionally pacific social tradition that outlasted the individuals who established it. For years, Sapolsky has documented how olive baboons (*Papio anubis*) on the plains of the Masai Mara, in Kenya, wage wars of nerves, compromising their rivals' immune systems and pushing up the level of their blood cortisol (Sapolsky 1994). An accident of history, however, selectively wiped out all the male bullies of his main study troop. As a result, the number of aggressive incidents dropped dramatically. This by itself was not so surprising. It became more interesting when it was discovered that the behavioral change was maintained for a decade. Baboon males migrate after puberty, hence fresh young males enter troops all the time, resulting in a complete turn-over of males during the intervening decade. Nevertheless, compared with troops around it, the affected troop upheld its reduced aggression, increased friendly behavior, and exceptionally low stress levels. The conclusion from this natural experiment is that, like human societies, each animal society has its own ecological and behavioral history, which determines its prevalent social style.

It is somewhat ironic that at a time when researchers on human aggression are increasingly attracted, albeit with a far more sophisticated approach, to the Lorenzian idea of a biological basis of aggression (Enserink 2000), students of animal behavior are beginning to look at its possible cultural basis. There is no reason for animals with a development as slow as a baboon (with adulthood achieved in five or six years) not to be influenced in every way by the environment in which they grow up, including the social environment. How this influence takes place is a point of much debate, and remains unclear in the case of the peaceful male baboons in the Masai Mara. Given their mobility, the males themselves are unlikely transmitters of social traditions within their natal troop. Therefore, Sapolsky and Share look at the females for an answer—female baboons stay all their lives in the same troop. By reacting positively to certain kinds of behavior, for example, females may be able to steer male attitudes in a new direction. This complex problem is hard to unravel with a single study, especially in the absence of experimentation. Yet, the main two points of this discovery are loud and clear: social behavior observed in nature may be a product of culture, and even the fiercest primates do not forever need to stay this way.

Let us hope this applies to humanity as well.

REFERENCES

Adams D. et al. (1990) Seville Statement on Violence. Am Psychol 45: 1167–1168.

Ardrey R (1961) African Genesis: A personal investigation into the animal origins and nature of man. New York: Simon & Schuster. p. 384.

Aureli F, de Waal FBM (2000) Natural conflict resolution. Berkeley, CA: University of California Press. p. 424.

Chapais B (1988) Rank maintenance in female Japanese macaques: Experimental evidence for social dependency. Behaviour 104: 41–59.

de Waal FBM (1997) Bonobo: The forgotten ape.

Berkeley, CA: University of California Press. p. 235.

de Waal FBM (2000) Primates: A natural heritage of confl ict resolution. Science 289: 586–590.

de Waal FBM (2001) The ape and the sushi master: Cultural reflections of a primatologist. New York: Basic Books. p. 448.

de Waal FBM, Johanowicz DL (1993) Modification of reconciliation behavior through social experience: An experiment with two macaque species. Child Dev 64: 897–908.

Enserink M (2000) Searching for the mark of Cain. Science 289: 575–579.

Hirata S, Watanabe K, Kawai M (2001) Sweet-potato washing revisited. In: Matsuzawa T, editors. Primate origins of human cognition and behavior. Tokyo: Springer. pp. 487–508.

Lorenz KZ (1966 [1963]) On aggression. London: Methuen.

Perry S, Baker M, Fedigan L, Gros-Louis J, Jack K, et al. (2003) Social conventions in wild white-faced capuchin monkeys: Evidence for traditions in a Neotropical primate. Curr Anthropol 44: 241–268.

Sapolsky RM (1994) Why zebras don't get ulcers: An updated guide to stress, stress-related diseases, and coping. New York: W. H. Freeman & Co. p. 434.

Sapolsky RM, Share L (2004) A pacific culture among wild baboons: Its emergence and transmission. PLoS Biol 2:e106. doi:10.1371/journal.pbio.0020106.

van Schaik CP, Ancrenaz M, Borgen G, Galdikas B, Knott CD, et al. (2003) Orangutan cultures and the evolution of material culture. Science 299: 102–105.

Whiten A, Goodall J, McGrew WC, Nishida T, Reynolds V, et al. (1999) Cultures in chimpanzees. Nature 399: 682–685.

"If I Look at the Mass I Will Never Act"

Psychic Numbing and Genocide

Paul Slovic

ABSTRACT

Most people are caring and will exert great effort to rescue individual victims whose needy plight comes to their attention. These same good people, however, often become numbly indifferent to the plight of individuals who are "one of many" in a much greater problem. Why does this occur? The answer to this question will help us answer a related question that is the topic of this paper: Why, over the past century, have good people repeatedly ignored mass murder and genocide? Every episode of mass murder is unique and raises unique obstacles to intervention. But the repetitiveness of such atrocities, ignored by powerful people and nations, and by the general public, calls for explanations that may reflect some fundamental deficiency in our humanity—a deficiency that, once identified, might possibly be overcome. One fundamental mechanism that may play a role in many, if not all, episodes of mass-murder neglect involves the capacity to experience *affect*, the positive and negative feelings that combine with reasoned analysis to guide our judgments, decisions, and actions. I shall draw from psychological research to show how the statistics of mass murder or genocide, no matter how large the numbers, fail to convey the true meaning of such atrocities. The reported numbers of deaths represent dry statistics, "human beings with the tears dried off," that fail to spark emotion or feeling and thus fail to motivate action. Recognizing that we cannot rely only upon our moral feelings to motivate proper action against genocide, we must look to moral argument and international law. The 1948 Genocide Convention was supposed to meet this need, but it has not been effective. It is time to examine this failure in light of the psychological deficiencies described here and design legal and institutional mechanisms that will enforce proper response to genocide and other forms of mass murder.

The following terms are discussed in this selection:

> *genocide*
> *compassion*
> *dual process theories*
> *affect*

To avoid further disasters, we need political restraint on a world scale. But politics is not the whole story. We have experienced the results of technology in the service of the destructive side of human psychology. Something needs to be done about this fatal combination. The means for expressing cruelty and carrying out mass killing have been fully developed. It is too late to stop the technology. It is to the psychology that we should now turn.

—Jonathan Glover, *Humanity*, 2001, p. 144

1 INTRODUCTION

My title is taken from a statement by Mother Teresa: "If I look at the mass I will never act. If I look at the one, I will."

These two observations capture a powerful and deeply unsettling insight into human nature. Most people are caring and will exert great effort to rescue "the one" whose needy plight comes to their attention. These same good people, however, often become numbly indifferent to the plight of "the one" who is "one of many" in a much greater problem. Why does this occur? The answer to this question will help us answer a related question: Why do good people ignore mass murder and genocide?

An internet columnist (Reynolds, 2005, p. 1) frames this question and the topic of my paper:

> For sixty plus years, since the liberation of the Nazi death camps, we've said "never again." Since then we've had mass exterminations of human beings, whether by deliberate malice or sheer, bloody-minded ideological stupidity, in China, Cambodia, Nigeria, Ethiopia, Kosovo, and Rwanda. Each time we tut tut, but … we do nothing. "Never again" has become "again and again."

And now there's Darfur, a region of Sudan, where the Janjaweed gangs, with the support of the corrupt national government, are carrying out yet another genocide. In a few years there'll be an HBO movie on Darfur. We'll vow "never again," once again, but the world being as it is, there will be another genocide under way even as we engage in the ritual of mild self-flagellation for Darfur. Again and again.

Why do we ignore mass murder and genocide? There is no simple answer. It is not because we are insensitive to the suffering of our fellow human beings—witness the extraordinary efforts we expend to rescue someone in distress. It is not because we only care about identifiable victims, of similar skin color, who live near us: witness the outpouring of aid to victims of the December 2004 tsunami in South Asia. We cannot simply blame our political leaders. Although President Bush has been quite unresponsive to the murder of hundreds of thousands of people in Darfur, it was Clinton who ignored Rwanda, and Roosevelt who did little to stop the Holocaust. Behind every president who ignored mass murder were millions of citizens whose indifference allowed them to get away with it. It's not fear of losing American lives in battle that necessarily deters us from acting. We have not even taken quite safe steps that could save many lives, such as bombing the radio stations in Rwanda that were coordinating the slaughter by machete of 800,000 people in 100 days, or supporting the forces of the African Union in Darfur, or just raising our powerful American voices in a threatening shout—*Stop that killing!*—as opposed to turning away in silence.

Every episode of mass murder is unique and raises unique social, economic, military, and political obstacles to intervention. But the repetitiveness of such atrocities, ignored by powerful people and nations, and by the general public, calls for explanations that may reflect some fundamental deficiency in our humanity—a deficiency that, once identified, might possibly be overcome.

This paper examines one fundamental mechanism that may play a role in many, if not all, episodes of mass-murder neglect. This mechanism involves the capacity to experience *affect*, the positive and negative feelings that combine with reasoned analysis to guide our judgments, decisions, and actions. Many researchers have begun to study the "dance of affect and reason" as it applies to decision making. I shall draw from this research to show how the statistics of mass murder or genocide, no matter how large the numbers, fail to convey the true meaning of such atrocities. The numbers fail to spark emotion or feeling and thus fail to motivate action. Genocide in Darfur is real, but we do not "feel" that reality. I shall conclude with suggestions about how we might make genocide "feel real" and motivate appropriate interventions. I shall also argue that we cannot only depend on our feelings about these atrocities but, in addition, we must create and commit ourselves to institutional and political responses based upon reasoned analysis of our moral obligations to stop the mass annihilation of innocent people.

Although I have attempted to fashion a compelling explanation for genocide neglect that has implications for action, the story is not complete. The psychological account, while based on theory and recent empirical studies, clearly needs further testing and development, particularly to examine more directly the relationship between imagery, affect, and sensitivity to numbers. The action implications remain to be elaborated by legal scholars and others.

2 THE LESSONS OF GENOCIDE

Dubinsky (2005, p. 112) reports a news story from *The Gazette* (Montreal; 29 April 1994, at p. A8):

> On April 28, 1994: the Associated Press (AP) bureau in Nairobi received a frantic call from a man in Kigali who described horrific scenes of concerted slaughter that had been unfolding in the Rwandan capital "every day, everywhere" for three weeks. "I saw people hacked to death, even babies, month-old babies. … Anybody who tried to flee was killed in the streets, and people who were hiding were found and massacred."

Dubinsky (2005, p. 113) further notes that:

> The caller's story was dispatched on the AP newswire for the planet to read, and complemented an OXFAM statement from the same day declaring that the slaughter—the toll of which had already reached 200,000—amounts to genocide.' The following day, UN Secretary General Boutros Boutros-Ghali acknowledged the massacres and requested that the Security Council deploy a significant force, a week after the council had reduced the number of UN peacekeepers in Rwanda from 2,500 to 270.
>
> Yet the killings continued for another two and a half months. By mid-July, when the government was finally routed by exiled Tutsi rebels, the slaughter had been quelled, and 800,000 were dead, reinforcements from the United Nations were only just arriving.

In his review of the book *Conspiracy to Murder: The Rwandan Genocide* (Melvern, 2004), Dubinsky (2005, p. 113) draws an ominous lesson from what happened in Rwanda:

> Despite its morally unambiguous heinousness, despite overwhelming evidence of its occurrence (for example, two days into the Rwandan carnage, the US Defense

Intelligence Agency possessed satellite photos showing sprawling massacre sites), and despite the relative ease with which it could have been abated (the UN commander in Rwanda felt a modest 5,500 reinforcements, had they arrived promptly, could have saved tens of thousands of lives)—despite all this, the world ignored genocide.

Unfortunately, Rwanda is not an isolated incident of indifference to mass murder and genocide. In a deeply disturbing book titled *A Problem from Hell: America and the Age of Genocide*, journalist Samantha Power documents in meticulous detail many of the numerous genocides that occurred during the past century, beginning with the slaughter of two million Armenians by the Turks in 1915 (Power, 2003, see Table 1). In every instance, American response was inadequate. She concludes, "No U.S. president has ever made genocide prevention a priority, and no U.S. president has ever suffered politically for his indifference to its occurrence. It is thus no coincidence that genocide rages on" (Power, 2003; p. xxi).

Table 1. *A century of genocide.*

Armenia (1915)
Ukraine (1932–1933)
Nazi Germany/Holocaust (World War II)
Bangladesh (1971)
Cambodia (1975–1979)
Countries in the former Yugoslavia (1990s)
Rwanda (1994)
Zimbabwe (2000)
Congo (Today)
Darfur (Today)
? (Tomorrow)

A second lesson to emerge from the study of genocide is that media news coverage is similarly inadequate. The past century has witnessed a remarkable transformation in the ability of the news media to learn about, and report on, world events. The vivid, dramatic coverage of the December 2004 Tsunami in South Asia and the similarly intimate and exhaustive reporting of the destruction of lives and property by Hurricane Katrina in September 2005 demonstrate how thorough and how powerful news coverage of humanitarian disasters can be. But the intense coverage of recent natural disasters stands in sharp contrast to the lack of reporting on the ongoing genocides in Darfur and other regions in Africa, in which hundreds of thousands of people have been murdered and millions forced to flee their burning villages and relocate in refugee camps. According to the Tyndall Report, which monitors American television coverage, ABC news allotted a total of 18 minutes on the Darfur genocide in its nightly newscasts in 2004, NBC had only five minutes, and CBS only three minutes. Martha Stewart and Michael Jackson received vastly greater coverage, as did Natalee Holloway, the American girl missing in Aruba. With the exception of the relentless reporting by *New York Times* columnist Nicholas Kristof, the print media have done little better in covering Darfur.

Despite lack of attention by the news media, U.S. government officials have known of the mass murders and genocides that took place during the past century. Power (2003, p. 505) attempts to explain the failure to act on that knowledge as follows:

> ... the atrocities that were known remained abstract and remote. ... Because the savagery of genocide so defies our everyday experience, many of us failed to *wrap our minds around it*. ... Bystanders were thus able to retreat to the "twilight between knowing and not knowing." [italics added]

I shall argue below that the disengagement exemplified by failing to "wrap our minds" around genocide and retreating to the "twilight between knowing and not knowing" is at the heart of our failure to act against genocide. Samantha Power's insightful explanation is supported by the research literature in cognitive and social psychology, as described in the sections to follow.

3 LESSONS FROM PSYCHOLOGICAL RESEARCH

In 1994, Roméo Dallaire, the commander of the tiny U.N. peacekeeping mission in Rwanda, was forced to watch helplessly as the slaughter he had foreseen and warned about began to unfold. Writing of this massive humanitarian disaster a decade later he encouraged scholars "to study this human tragedy and to contribute to our growing understanding of the genocide. If we do not understand what happened, how will we ever ensure it does not happen again?" Dallaire (2005, p. 548).

Researchers in psychology, economics, and a multidisciplinary field called behavioral decision theory have developed theories and findings that, in part, begin to explain the pervasive neglect of genocide.

3.1 Affect, attention, information, and meaning

My search to identify a fundamental deficiency in human psychology that causes us to ignore mass murder and genocide has led to a theoretical framework that describes the importance of emotions and feelings in guiding decision making and behavior. Perhaps the most basic form of feeling is affect, the sense (not necessarily conscious) that something is good or bad. Affective responses occur rapidly and automatically—note how quickly you sense the feelings associated with the word "treasure" or the word "hate." A large research literature in psychology documents the importance of affect in conveying meaning upon information and motivating behavior (Barrett & Salovey, 2002; Clark & Fiske, 1982; Forgas, 2000; Le Doux, 1996; Mowrer, 1960; Tomkins, 1962, 1963; Zajonc, 1980). Without affect, information lacks meaning and won't be used in judgment and decision making (Loewenstein, Weber, Hsee, & Welch, 2001; Slovic, Fin-ucane, Peters, & MacGregor, 2002).

Affect plays a central role in what have come to be known as "dual-process theories" of thinking. As Seymour Epstein (1994) has observed: "There is no dearth of evidence in every day life that people apprehend reality in two fundamentally different ways, one variously labeled intuitive, automatic, natural, non-verbal, narrative, and experiential, and the other analytical, deliberative, verbal, and rational" (p. 710).

Table 2, adapted from Epstein, further compares these two systems, which Stanovich and West (2000) labeled *System 1* and *System 2*. One of the characteristics of the experiential system is its affective basis. Although analysis is certainly important in many decision-making circumstances, reliance on affect and emotion is generally a quicker, easier, and more efficient way to navigate in a complex, uncertain and sometimes dangerous world. Many theorists have given affect a direct and primary role in motivating behavior. Epstein's (1994) view on this is as follows:

The experiential system is assumed to be intimately associated with the experience of affect, ... which refer[s] to subtle feelings of which people are often unaware. When a person responds to an emotionally significant event ... The experiential system automatically searches its memory banks for related events, including their emotional accompaniments. ... If the activated feelings are pleasant, they motivate actions and thoughts anticipated to reproduce the feelings. If the feelings are unpleasant, they motivate actions and thoughts anticipated to avoid the feelings. (p. 716)

Underlying the role of affect in the experiential system is the importance of images, to which positive or negative feelings become attached. Images in this system include not only visual images, important as these may be, but words, sounds, smells, memories, and products of our imagination.

In his Nobel Prize Address, Daniel Kahneman notes that the operating characteristics of System 1 are similar to those of human perceptual processes (Kahneman, 2003). He points out that one of the functions of System 2 is to monitor the quality of the intuitive impressions formed by System 1. Kahneman and Frederick (2002) suggest that this monitoring is typically rather lax and allows many intuitive judgments to be expressed in

Imagery

Feeling Helping

Attention

Figure 1: Imagery and attention produce feelings that motivate helping behavior.

behavior, including some that are erroneous. This point has important implications that will be discussed later.

In addition to positive and negative affect, more nuanced feelings such as empathy, sympathy, compassion, sadness, pity, and distress have been found to be critical for motivating people to help others (Coke, Batson, & McDavis, 1978; Eisenberg & Miller, 1987). As Batson (1990, p. 339) put it, "… considerable research suggests that we are more likely to help someone in need when we 'feel for' that person …"

One last important psychological element in this story is attention. Just as feelings are necessary for motivating helping, attention is necessary for feelings. Research shows that attention magnifies emotional responses to stimuli that are already emotionally charged (Fenske & Raymond, 2006; Villeumier, Armony, & Dolan, 2003). The psychological story can be summarized by the diagram in Figure 1. Research to be described in this paper demonstrates that imagery and feeling are lacking when large losses of life are represented simply as numbers or statistics. Other research shows that attention is greater for individuals and loses focus and intensity when targeted at groups of people (Hamilton & Sherman, 1996; Susskind, Maurer, Thakkar, Hamilton, & Sherman, 1999). The foibles of imagery and attention impact feelings in a manner that can help explain apathy toward genocide.

Although the model sketched in Figure 1 could incorporate elements of System 1 thinking, System 2 thinking, or both, a careful analysis by Haidt (2001, p. 818; see also Hume, 1777/1960 for an earlier version of this argument) gives priority to System 1. Haidt argues that moral intuitions (akin to System 1) precede moral judgments. Specifically, he asserts that

> … moral intuition can be defined as the sudden appearance in consciousness of a moral judgment, including an affective valence (good-bad, like-dislike) without any conscious awareness of having gone through steps of searching,

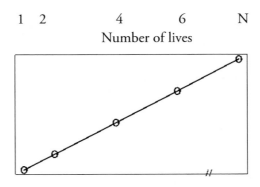

Figure 2: A normative model for valuing the saving of human lives. *Every human life is of equal value.*

Table 2. Two modes of thinking: Comparison of experiential and analytic systems

System1: Experiential System	System2: Analytic System
Affective: pleasure-pain oriented	Logical: reason oriented (what is sensible)
Connections by association	Connections by logical assessment
Behavior mediated by feelings from past experiences	Behavior mediated by conscious appraisal of events
Encodes reality in images, metaphors, and narratives	Encodes reality in abstract symbols, words, and numbers
More rapid processing: oriented toward immediate action	Slower processing: oriented toward delayed action
Self-evidently valid: "experiencing is believing"	Requires justification via logic and evidence

Seymour Epstein, "Table 1. Comparison of the Experiential and Rational Systems," from *The Relational Self: Theoretical Convergences in Psychoanalysis and Social Psychology*, Rebecca C. Curtis, ed. Copyright © 1991 by The Guilford Press. Permission to reprint granted by the publisher.

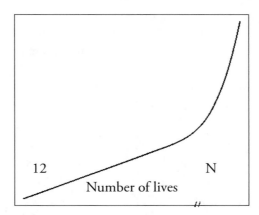

Figure 3: Another normative model: Large losses threaten the viability of the group or society (as with genocide).

weighing evidence, or inferring a conclusion. Moral intuition is therefore … akin to aesthetic judgment. One sees or hears about a social event and one instantly feels approval or disapproval.

4 AFFECT, ANALYSIS, AND THE VALUE OF HUMAN LIVES

How *should* we value the saving of human lives? If we believe that every human life is of equal value (a view likely endorsed by System 2 thinking), the value of saving N lives is N times the value of saving one life, as represented by the linear function in Figure 2.

An argument can also be made for a model in which large losses of life are disproportionately more serious because they threaten the social fabric and viability of a community as depicted in Figure 3.

How *do* we actually value humans lives? I shall present evidence in support of two descriptive models linked to affect and System 1 thinking that reflect values for life-saving profoundly different from the normative models shown in Figures 1 and 2. Both of these models are instructive with regard to apathy toward genocide.

4.1 The psychophysical model

Affect is a remarkable mechanism that enabled humans to survive the long course of evolution. Before there were sophisticated analytic tools such as probability theory, scientific risk assessment, and cost/benefit calculus, humans used their senses, honed by experience, to determine whether the animal lurking in the bushes was safe to approach or the murky water in the pond was safe to drink. Simply put, System 1 thinking evolved to protect individuals and their small family and community groups from present, visible, immediate dangers. This affective system did not evolve to help us respond to distant, mass murder. As a result, System 1 thinking responds to large-scale atrocities in ways that are less than desirable.

Fundamental qualities of human behavior are, of course, recognized by others besides scientists. American writer Annie Dillard, cleverly demonstrates the limitation of our affective system as she seeks to help us understand the humanity of the Chinese nation: "There are 1,198,500,000 people alive now in China. To get a *feel* for what this *means*, simply take yourself—in all your singularity, importance, complexity, and love—and multiply by 1,198,500,000. See? Nothing to it" (Dillard, 1999, p. 47, italics added).

We quickly recognize that Dillard is joking when she asserts "nothing to it." We know, as she does, that we are incapable of *feeling* the humanity behind the number 1,198,500,000. The circuitry in our brain is not up to this task. This same incapacity is echoed by Nobel prize winning biochemist Albert Szent Gyorgi as he struggles to comprehend the possible consequences of nuclear war: "I am deeply moved if I see one man suffering and would risk my life for him. Then I talk impersonally about the possible pulverization of our big cities, with a hundred million dead. I am unable to multiply one man's suffering by a hundred million."

There is considerable evidence that our affective responses and the resulting value we place on saving human lives may follow the same sort of "psychophysical function" that characterizes our diminished sensitivity to a wide range of perceptual and cognitive

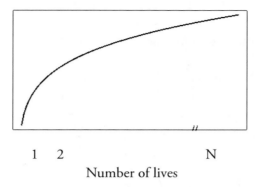

1 2   N

Number of lives

Figure 4: A psychophysical model describing how the saving of human lives may actually be valued.

entities—brightness, loudness, heaviness, and money—as their underlying magnitudes increase.

What psychological principles lie behind this insensitivity? In the 19th century, E. H. Weber and Gustav Fechner discovered a fundamental psychophysical principle that describes how we perceive changes in our environment. They found that people's ability to detect changes in a physical stimulus rapidly decreases as the magnitude of the stimulus increases (Weber, 1834; Fechner, 1860). What is known today as "Weber's law" states that in order for a change in a stimulus to become *just noticeable*, a fixed percentage must be added. Thus, perceived difference is a relative matter. To a small stimulus, only a small amount must be added to be noticeable. To a large stimulus, a large amount must be added. Fechner proposed a logarithmic law to model this nonlinear growth of sensation. Numerous empirical studies by S. S. Stevens (1975) have demonstrated that the growth of sensory magnitude (ψ) is best fit by a power function of the stimulus magnitude Φ, $\psi = \Phi^\beta$, where the exponent β is typically less than one for measurements of phenomena such as loudness, brightness, and even the value of money (Galanter, 1962). For example, if the exponent is 0.5 as it is in some studies of perceived brightness, a light that is four times the intensity of another light will be judged only twice as bright.

Our cognitive and perceptual systems seem to be designed to sensitize us to small changes in our environment, possibly at the expense of making us less able to detect and respond to large changes. As the psychophysical research indicates, constant increases in the magnitude of a stimulus typically evoke smaller and smaller changes in response. Applying this principle to the valuing of human life suggests that a form of *psychophysical numbing* may result from our inability to appreciate losses of life as they become larger (see Figure 4). The function in Figure 4 represents a value structure in which the importance of saving one life is great when it is the first, or only, life saved, but diminishes marginally as the total number of lives saved increases. Thus, psychologically, the importance of saving one life is diminished against the background of a larger threat—we will likely not "feel" much different, nor value the difference, between saving 87 lives and saving 88, if these prospects are presented to us separately.

Kahneman and Tversky (1979) have incorporated this psychophysical principle of decreasing sensitivity into prospect theory, a descriptive account of decision making under uncertainty. A major element of prospect theory is the value function, which relates subjective value to actual gains or losses. When applied to human lives, the value function implies that the subjective value of saving a specific number of lives is greater for a smaller tragedy than for a larger one.

Fetherstonhaugh, Slovic, Johnson, and Friedrich (1997) documented this potential for diminished sensitivity to the value of life—i.e., "psychophysical numbing"—by evaluating people's willingness to fund various life-saving medical treatments. In a study involving a hypothetical grant funding agency, respondents were asked to indicate the number of lives a medical research institute would have to save to merit receipt of a $10 million grant. Nearly two-thirds of the respondents raised their minimum benefit requirements to warrant funding when there was a larger at-risk population, with a median value of 9,000 lives needing to be saved when 15,000 were at risk, compared to a median of 100,000 lives needing to be saved out of 290,000 at risk. By implication, respondents saw saving 9,000 lives in the "smaller" population as more valuable than saving ten times as many lives in the largest.

Several other studies in the domain of life-saving interventions have documented similar psychophysical numbing or proportional reasoning effects (Baron, 1997; Bartels &

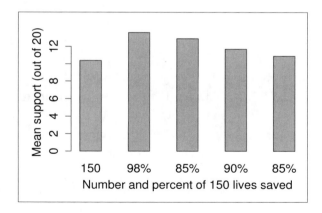

Figure 5: Airport safety study: Saving a percentage of 150 lives receives higher support ratings than does saving 150 lives.

Note: Bars describe mean responses to the question, "How much would you support the proposed measure to purchase the new equipment?" The response scale ranged from 0 (would not support at all) to 20 (very strong support; Slovic et al., 2002).

Burnett, 2006; Fetherstonhaugh et al., 1997; Friedrich et al., 1999; Jenni & Loewenstein, 1997; Ubel et al., 2001). For example, Fetherstonhaugh et al. (1997) also found that people were less willing to send aid that would save 1500 lives in Rwandan refugee camps as the size of the camps' at-risk population increased. Friedrich et al. (1999) found that people required more lives to be saved to justify mandatory antilock brakes on new cars when the alleged size of the at-risk pool (annual braking-related deaths) increased.

These diverse strategies of lifesaving demonstrate that the *proportion* of lives saved often carries more weight than the *number* of lives saved when people evaluate interventions. Thus, extrapolating from Fetherstonhaugh et al., one would expect that, in separate evaluations, there would be more support for saving 80% of 100 lives at risk than for saving 20% of 1,000 lives at risk. This is consistent with an affective (System 1) account, in which the number of lives saved conveys little affect but the proportion saved carries much feeling: 80% is clearly "good" and 20% is "poor."

Slovic, Finucane, Peters, and MacGregor (2004), drawing upon the finding that proportions appear to convey more feeling than do numbers of lives, predicted (and found) that college students, in a between-groups design, would more strongly support an airport-safety measure expected to save 98% of 150 lives at risk than a measure expected to save 150 lives. Saving 150 lives is diffusely good, and therefore somewhat hard to evaluate, whereas saving 98% of something is clearly very good because it is so close to the upper bound on the percentage scale, and hence is highly weighted in the support judgment. Subsequent reduction of the percentage of 150 lives that would be saved to 95%, 90%, and 85% led to reduced support for the safety measure but each of these percentage conditions still garnered a higher mean level of support than did the Save 150 Lives Condition (Figure 5).

This research on psychophysical numbing is important because it demonstrates that feelings necessary for motivating lifesaving actions are not congruent with the normative models in Figures 2 and 3. The nonlinearity displayed in Figure 4 is consistent with the disregard of incremental loss of life against a background of a large tragedy. However it does not fully explain the utter collapse of compassion represented by apathy toward genocide because it implies that the response to initial loss of life will be strong and maintained as the losses increase. Evidence for a second descriptive model, one better suited to explain the collapse of compassion, follows.

5 NUMBERS AND NUMBNESS: IMAGES AND FEELING

The behavioral theories and data confirm what keen observers of human behavior have long known. Numerical representations of human lives do not necessarily convey the importance of those lives. All too often the numbers represent dry statistics, "human beings with the tears dried off," that lack feeling and fail to motivate action (Slovic &

Slovic, 2004). How can we impart the feelings that are needed for rational action? There have been a variety of attempts to do this that may be instructive. Most of these involve highlighting the images that lie beneath the numbers. As nature writer and conservationist Rick Bass (1996) observes in his plea to conserve the Yaak Valley in Montana,

The numbers are important, and yet they are not everything. For whatever reasons, images often strike us more powerfully, more deeply than numbers. We seem unable to hold the emotions aroused by numbers for nearly as long as those of images. We quickly grow numb to the facts and the math. (p. 87)

Images seem to be the key to conveying affect and meaning, though some imagery is more powerful than others. After struggling to appreciate the mass of humanity in China, Annie Dillard turned her thoughts to April 30, 1991, when 138,000 people drowned in

Figure 6: The rescue of baby Jessica. Painting photgraphed by Bill Bentley, "The Baby Jessica Rescue Web Page," http://www.caver.net/j/jrescue.html, April 14, 2007.

Bangladesh. At dinner, she mentions to her daughter—seven years old—that it is hard to imagine 138,000 people drowning. "No, it's easy," says her daughter. "Lots and lots of dots in blue water" (Dillard, 1999; p.131). Again we are confronted with impoverished meaning associated with large losses of life.

Other images may be more effective. Organizers of a rally designed to get Congress to do something about 38,000 deaths a year from handguns piled 38,000 pairs of shoes in a mound in front of the Capitol (Associated Press, 1994). Students at a middle school in Tennessee, struggling to comprehend the magnitude of the holocaust, collected 6 million paper clips as a centerpiece for a memorial (Schroeder & Schroeder-Hildebrand, 2004).

Probably the most important image to represent a human life is that of a single human face. Journalist Paul Neville writes about the need to probe beneath the statistics of jobless-ness, homelessness, mental illness, and poverty in his home state of Oregon, in order to discover the people behind the numbers—who they are, what they look like, how they sound, what they feel, what hopes and fears they harbor. He concludes: "I don't know when we became a nation of statistics. But I know that the path to becoming a nation— and a community—of people, is remembering the faces behind the numbers" (Neville, 2004). After September 11, 2001, many newspapers published biographical sketches of the victims, with photos, a dozen or so each day until all had been featured.

When it comes to eliciting compassion, the identified individual victim, with a face and a name, has no peer. Psychological experiments demonstrate this clearly but we all know it as well from personal experience and media coverage of heroic efforts to save individual lives. One of the most publicized events occurred when an 18-month-old child, Jessica McClure, fell 22 feet into a narrow abandoned well shaft. The world watched tensely as rescuers worked for 2½ days to rescue her. Almost two decades later, the joyous moment of Jessica's rescue is portrayed with resurrection-like overtones on a website devoted to pictures of the event (see Figure 6).

But the face need not even be human to motivate powerful intervention. In 2001, an epidemic of foot and mouth disease raged throughout the United Kingdom. Millions of cattle were slaughtered to stop the spread. The disease waned and animal rights activists demanded an end to further killing. But the killings continued until a newspaper photo of a cute 12-day-old calf named Phoenix being targeted for slaughter led the government to change its policy. Individual canine lives are highly valued, too. A dog stranded aboard a tanker adrift in the Pacific was the subject of one of the most costly animal rescue efforts ever. An Associated Press article discloses that the cost of rescue attempts had already reached $48,000 and the Coast Guard was prepared to spend more, while critics charged that the money could be better spent on children that go to bed hungry (Song, 2002).

In a bizarre incident that, nonetheless, demonstrates the special value of an individual life, an article in the BBC News online edition of November 19, 2005, reports the emo-tional response in the Netherlands to the shooting of a sparrow that trespassed onto the site of a domino competition and knocked over 23,000 tiles. A tribute website was set up

---

Statistical lives

- Food shortages in Malawi are affecting more than 3 million children.
- In Zambia, severe rainfall deficits have resulted in a 42% drop in maize production from 2000. As a result, an estimated 3 million Zambians face hunger.
- Four million Angolans—one third of the population—have been forced to flee their homes.
- More than 11 million people in Ethiopia need immediate food assistance.
-

Identifiable lives

Rokia, a 7-year-old girl from Mali, Africa, is desperately poor and faces a threat of severe hunger or even starvation. Her life will be changed for the better as a result of your financial gift. With your support, and the support of other caring sponsors, Save the Children will work with Rokia's family and other members of the community to help feed her, provide her with education, as well as basic medical care and hygiene education.

Figure 7: Donating money to save statistical and identified lives. Deborah A. Small, George Loewenstein, Paul Slovic. Photograph taken from "Sympathy and Callousness: The Impact of Deliberative Thought on Donations to Identifiable and Statistical Victims," from *Organizational Behavior and Human Decision Processes*, Vol. 102, Issue 2; March 2007. Copyright © 2007 by Elsevier Science & Technology Journals. Permission to reprint granted by the rights *(Photograph has been altered.)*

---

and attracted tens of thousands of hits. The head of the Dutch Bird Protection Agency, appearing on television, said that though it was a very sad incident, it had been blown out of all proportion. "I just wish we could channel all this energy that went into one dead sparrow into saving the species," he said (BBC News, 2005). Going beyond faces, names, and other simple images, writers and artists have long recognized the power of narrative to bring feelings and meaning to tragedy. Barbara Kingsolver (1996) makes this point eloquently in her book *High Tide in Tucson*:

> The power of fiction is to create empathy. If lifts you away from your chair and stuffs you gently down inside someone else's point of view. … A newspaper could tell you that one hundred people, say, in an airplane, or in Israel, or in Iraq, have died today. And you can think to yourself, "How very sad," then turn the page and see how the Wildcats fared. But a novel could take just one of those hundred lives and show you exactly how it felt to be that person rising from bed in the morning, watching the desert light on the tile of her doorway and on the

curve of her daughter's cheek. You could taste that person's breakfast, and love her family, and sort through her worries as your own, and know that a death in that household will be the end of the only life that someone will ever have. As important as yours. As important as mine. (p. 231)

Showing insight into the workings of our affective system as keen as any derived from the psychologist's laboratory, Kingsolver continues:

Confronted with knowledge of dozens of apparently random disasters each day, what can a human heart do but slam its doors? No mortal can grieve that much. We didn't evolve to cope with tragedy on a global scale. Our defense is to pretend there's no thread of event that connects us, and that those lives are somehow not precious and real like our own. It's a practical strategy, to some ends, but the loss of empathy is also the loss of humanity, and that's no small tradeoff.

Art is the antidote that can call us back from the edge of numbness, restoring the ability to feel for another. (p. 231–232)

Although Kingsolver is describing the power of fiction, nonfiction narrative can be just as effective. *The Diary of Anne Frank* and Elie Weisel's *Night* certainly convey, in a powerful way, the meaning of the Holocaust statistic "six million dead."

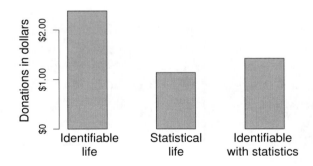

Figure 8: Mean donations. Deborah A. Small, George Loewenstein, Paul Slovic. Graph taken from "Sympathy and Callousness: The Impact of Deliberative Thought on Donations to Identifiable and Statistical Victims," from *Organizational Behavior and Human Decision Processes*, Vol. 102, Issue 2; March 2007. Copyright by Elsevier Science & Technology Journals. Permission to reprint granted by the rights holder.

6 THE COLLAPSE OF COMPASSION

Vivid images of recent natural disasters in South Asia and the American Gulf Coast, and stories of individual victims, brought to us through relentless, courageous, and intimate news coverage, certainly unleashed a tidal wave of compassion and humanitarian aid from all over the world. Private donations to the victims of the December 2004 tsunami exceeded $1 billion. Charities such as Save the Children have long recognized that it is better to endow a donor with a single, named child to support than to ask for contributions to the bigger cause. Perhaps there is hope that vivid, personalized media coverage of genocide could motivate intervention.

Perhaps. But again we should look to research to assess these possibilities. Numerous experiments have demonstrated the "identifiable victim effect" which is also so evident outside the laboratory. People are much more willing to aid identified individuals than unidentified or statistical victims (Kogut & Ritov, 2005a; Schelling, 1968; Small & Loewenstein 2003, 2005; Jenni & Loewenstein, 1997). Small, Loewenstein, and Slovic (2007) gave people leaving a psychological experiment the opportunity to contribute up to $5 of their earnings to Save the Children. The study consisted of three separate conditions: (1) identifiable victim, (2) statistical victims, and (3) identifiable victim with statistical information. The information provided for the identifiable and statistical conditions is shown in Figure 7. Participants in each condition were told that "any money donated will go toward relieving the severe food crisis in Southern Africa and Ethiopia." The donations in fact went to Save the Children, but they were earmarked specifically for Rokia in Conditions 1 and 3 and not specifically earmarked in Condition 2. The average donations are presented in Figure 8. Donations in response to the identified individual, Rokia, were far greater than donations in response to the statistical portrayal of the food crisis. Most important, however, and most discouraging, was the fact that coupling the statistical realities with Rokia's story significantly *reduced* the contributions to Rokia. Alternatively, one could say that using Rokia's story to "put a face behind the statistical problem" did not do much to increase donations (the difference between the mean donations of $1.43 and $1.14 was not statistically reliable).

Small et al. also measured feelings of sympathy toward the cause (Rokia or the statistical victims). These feelings were most strongly correlated with donations when people faced an identifiable victim.

A follow-up experiment by Small et al. provided additional evidence for the importance of feelings. Before being given an opportunity to donate study participants were either primed to feel ("Describe your feelings when you hear the word 'baby,'" and similar items) or to answer five questions such as "If an object travels at five feet per minute, then by your calculations how many feet will it travel in 360 seconds?" Priming analytic thinking (calculation) reduced donations to the identifiable victim (Rokia) relative to the feeling-based thinking prime. Yet the two primes had no distinct effect on statistical victims, which is symptomatic of the difficulty in generating feelings for such victims.

Annie Dillard reads in her newspaper the headline "Head Spinning Numbers Cause Mind to Go Slack." She struggles to think straight about the great losses that the world ignores: "More than two million children die a year from diarrhea and eight hundred thousand from measles. Do we blink? Stalin starved seven million Ukrainians in one year, Pol Pot killed two million Cambodians … " She writes of "compassion fatigue" and asks, "At what number do other individuals blur for me?" (Dillard, 1999, pp. 130–131).

An answer to Dillard's question is beginning to emerge from behavioral research. Studies by Hamilton and Sherman (1996) and Susskind et al. (1999) find that a single individual, unlike a group, is viewed as a psychologically coherent unit. This leads to more extensive processing of information and clearer impressions about individuals than about groups. Kogut and Ritov (2005b) hypothesized that the processing of information related to a single victim might be fundamentally different from the processing of information concerning a group of victims. They predicted that people will tend to feel more distress and compassion when considering an identified single victim than when considering a group of victims, even if identified, resulting in a greater willingness to help the identified individual victim.

Kogut and Ritov (2005a, b) tested their predictions in a series of studies in which participants were asked to contribute to a costly life-saving treatment needed by a sick child or a group of eight sick children. The target amount needed to save the child (children) was the same in both conditions, 1.5 million Israeli Shekels (about $300,000). All contributions were actually given to an organization that helps children with cancer. In

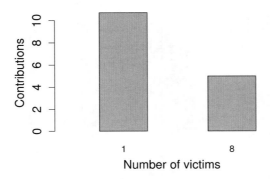

Figure 9: Mean contributions to individuals and their group. Tehila Kogut, Ilana Ritov. Graph taken from "The Singularity of Identified Victims in Separate and Joint Evaluations," from *Organizational Behavior and Human Decision Processes*, Vol. 97, Issue 2; July 2005. Copyright © 2005 by Elsevier Science & Technology Journals. Permission to reprint granted by the rights holder.

addition to deciding whether or how much they wanted to contribute, participants in some studies rated their feelings of distress (feeling worried, upset, and sad) towards the sick child (children).

The mean contributions to the group of eight and to the individuals taken from the group are shown in Figure 9 for one of the studies by Kogut & Ritov (2005b). Contributions to the individuals in the group, as individuals, were far greater than were contributions to the entire group. In a separate study, ratings of distress (not shown in the figure) were also higher in the individual condition.

But could the results in Figure 9 be explained by the possibility that donors believed that families in the group condition would have an easier time obtaining the needed money which, in fact, was less per child in that condition? Further testing ruled out this explanation. For example, Kogut and Ritov asked people to choose between donating to a single child of the eight or donating to the remaining seven children. Many more (69%) chose to donate to the group, demonstrating a sensitivity to the number of victims in need that was not evident in the noncomparative evaluations. Kogut and Ritov concluded that the greater donations to the single victim most likely stem from the stronger emotions evoked by such victims in conditions where donors evaluated only a single child or only the group.

Recall Samantha Power's assertion that those who know about genocide somehow "fail to wrap their minds around it." Perhaps this is a layperson's terminology for the less coherent processing of information about groups observed by Hamilton and Sherman (1966)

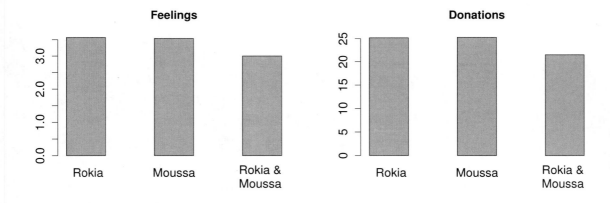

Figure 10: Mean affect ratings (left) and mean donations (right) for individuals and their combination. D. Västfjäll, E. Peters, P. Slovic, from Unpublished manuscript: *Representation, Affect, and Willingness-to-Donate to Children in Need.* Copyright © by Paul Slovic et al. Permission to reprint granted by the rights holder.

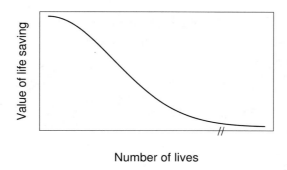

Figure 11: A model depicting psychic numbing—the collapse of compassion—when valuing the saving of lives.

and Susskind et al. (1999). And perhaps the beginning of this failure is evident with as few as eight victims.

Or, perhaps the deterioration of compassion may appear in groups as small as two persons! A recent study suggests this. Västfjäll, Peters, and Slovic (in preparation) decided to test whether the effect found by Kogut and Ritov would occur as well for donations to two starving children. Following the protocol designed by Small et al. (2007), they gave one group of Swedish students the opportunity to contribute their earnings from another experiment to Save the Children to aid Rokia, whose plight was described as in Figure 7. A second group was offered the opportunity to contribute their earnings to Save the Children to aid Moussa, a seven-year-old boy from Mali (photograph provided) who was similarly described as in need of food aid. A third group was shown the vignettes and photos of Rokia and Moussa and was told that any donation would go to both of them, Rokia *and* Moussa. The donations were real and were sent to Save the Children. Participants also rated their feelings about donating on a 1 *(negative)* to 5 *(positive)* scale. Affect was found to be least positive in the combined condition and donations were smaller in that condition (see Figure 10). In the individual-child conditions, the size of the donation made was strongly correlated with rated feelings ($r = .52$ for Rokia; $r = .52$ for Moussa). However this correlation was much reduced ($r = .19$) in the combined condition.

As unsettling as is the valuation of life-saving portrayed by the psychophysical model in Figure 4, the studies just described suggest an even more disturbing psychological tendency. Our capacity to feel is limited. To the extent that valuation of life-saving depends on feelings driven by attention or imagery (recall Figure 1), it might follow the function shown in Figure 11, where the emotion or affective feeling is greatest at $N = 1$ but begins to decline at $N = 2$ and collapses at some higher value of N that becomes simply "a statistic." In other words, returning to Annie Dillard's worry about compassion fatigue, perhaps the "blurring" of individuals begins at two! Whereas Robert J. Lifton (1967) coined the term "psychic numbing" to describe the "turning off" of feeling that enabled rescue workers to function during the horrific aftermath of the Hiroshima bombing, Figure 11 depicts a form of numbing that is not beneficial. Rather, it leads to apathy and inaction, consistent with what is seen repeatedly in response to mass murder and genocide.

7 THE MOURNFUL MATH OF DARFUR: THE DEAD DON'T ADD UP

The title of this section comes from the headline in a *New York Times* article (Lacey, 2005) describing the difficulty that officials are having in determining the actual death toll in Darfur. The diverse and savage methods of killing defy accurate accounting, with estimates at the time of the article ranging between 60,000 and 400,000. The point I have been arguing in this paper, that the numbers don't really matter because we are insensitive to them, is obviously not appreciated by those struggling to tally the dead. They are described as

> "… engaging in guesswork for a cause. They say they are trying to count the deaths to shock the world into stopping the number from rising higher …" An American professor leading the accounting effort on behalf of the Coalition for International Justice argues that calculating the death toll is important to "… focus the attention of people … to give them some sense of the scale of what's happening in Darfur."

If those attempting to count the dead are naïve about the impact the numbers may have, the writer of the story is not. He concludes:

> … eventually, when Darfur's violence mercifully ends, a number will be agreed upon. That number, like the figure of 800,000 for the Rwanda massacre, will be forever appended to the awful events. The rest of the world, slow to react to Darfur, will then have plenty of opportunity to think about it, and wonder why it was able to grow as large as it did. (Lacey, 2005)

8 FACING GENOCIDE

Clearly there are political obstacles posing challenges to those who would consider intervention in genocide, and physical risks as well. What I have tried to describe in this paper are the formidable psychological obstacles centered around the difficulties in wrapping our minds around genocide and forming the emotional connections to its victims that are necessary to motivate us to overcome these other obstacles.

Are we destined to stand numbly and do nothing as genocide rages on for another century? Can we overcome the psychological obstacles to action? There are no simple solutions. One possibility is to infuse System 1 with powerful affective imagery such as that associated with Katrina and the South Asian tsunami. This would require pressure on the media to do its job and report the slaughter of thousands of innocent people aggressively and vividly, as though it were real news. Nicholas Kristof, a columnist for the *New York Times*, has provided a model to emulate for his persistent and personalized reporting of the genocide in Darfur, but he is almost a lone voice in the mainstream American media. Another way to engage our experiential system would be to bring people from Darfur into our communities and our homes to tell their stories.

But, as powerful as System 1 is, when infused with vivid experiential stimulation (witness the moral outrage triggered by the photos of abuse at the Abu Ghraib prison in Iraq), it has a darker side. We cannot rely on it. It depends upon attention and feelings that may be hard to arouse and sustain over time for large numbers of victims, not to speak of numbers as small as two. Left to its own devices, System 1 will likely favor individual victims and sensational stories that are closer to home and easier to imagine. It will be distracted by images that produce strong, though erroneous, feelings, like percentages as opposed to actual numbers. Our sizable capacity to care for others may also be overridden by more pressing personal interests. Compassion for others has been characterized by Batson, O'Quin, Fultz, Vanderplas, and Isen (1983) as "a fragile flower, easily crushed by self-concern" (p. 718). Faced with genocide, we cannot rely on our moral intuitions alone to guide us to act properly.

A more promising path might be to force System 2 to play a stronger role, not just to provide us with reasons why genocide is wrong—these reasons are obvious and System 1 will appropriately sense their moral messages (Haidt, 2001). As Kahneman (2003) argues, one of the important functions of System 2 is to monitor the quality of mental operations and overt behaviors produced by System 1 (see also Gilbert, 2002 and Stanovich & West, 2002).

Most directly, deliberate analysis of the sobering messages contained in this paper should make it clear that we need to create laws and institutions that will *compel* appropriate action when information about genocide becomes known. However, such precommitted response is not as easy as it might seem. Shortly after World War II, on December 9, 1948, the U. N. General Assembly drafted and adopted the Convention for the Prevention and Punishment of the Crime of Genocide. Hopes were high as the world's states committed themselves to "liberate mankind from such an odious scourge" as genocide (Convention preamble). Yet it took 40 years for the United States to ratify a watered-down version of this treaty, which has been honored mostly in its breach (Power, 2003; Schabas, 1999). Objections have centered around lack of clarity in the definition of genocide, including the numerical criteria necessary to trigger action. Some feared that the act would be used to target Americans unjustly. Senator William Proxmire took up the cause in 1967, making

Refugees from Darfur

3,211 speeches in support of ratification over a 19-year period. However, only Ronald Reagan's backing, to atone for his politically embarrassing visit to a cemetery in Germany where officials of the Nazi SS were buried, tipped the political balance toward ratification in 1988 of a weakened version of the Convention. When the United States had its first chance to use the law to stop the destruction of Iraq's rural Kurdish population, special interests, economic profit, and political concerns led the Reagan administration to side instead with the genocidal regime of Saddam Hussein (Power, 2003).

In this paper I have drawn upon common observation and behavioral research to argue that we cannot depend only upon our moral feelings to motivate us to take proper actions against genocide. That places the burden of response squarely upon the shoulders of moral argument and international law. The genocide convention was supposed to meet this need, but it has not been effective. It is time to reexamine this failure in light of the psychological deficiencies described here and design legal and institutional mechanisms that will enforce proper response to genocide and other crimes against humanity.[1]

---

[1] A thoughtful reviewer of this paper questions my focus on preventing genocide. The reviewer asserts that numbers of preventable deaths from poverty, starvation, and disease are far larger than the

9 POSTSCRIPT

Roméo Dallaire, in recounting the anguishing story of his failure to convince the United Nations to give him the mandate and force to stop the impending slaughter in Rwanda observes that, "… at its heart, the Rwandan story is the story of the failure of humanity to heed the call for help from an endangered people" (Dallaire, 2005, p. 516).

The political causes of this and other such failures are rather well known. What I have tried to describe here are the psychological factors that allow politics to trump morality.

Dallaire (2005) challenges his readers with several questions: "Are we all human, or are some more human than others? If we believe that all humans are human, then how are we going to prove it? It can only be proven through our actions" (p. 522).

A final image: President George W. Bush stands by the casket of Rosa Parks in the rotunda of the U. S. Capitol, paying his respects. Why did the President and the nation so honor this woman? Because, by refusing to give up her seat on the bus she courageously asserted her humanity, answering Dallaire's questions by her actions. At almost the same time as the nation was honoring Parks, the U.S. Congress was stripping $50 million from the Foreign Operations Bill that was to help pay for African Union peacekeeping efforts in Darfur—another failure of the U.S. government to take meaningful action since September 2004 when Colin Powell returned from Sudan and labeled the atrocities there as "genocide." We appropriately honor the one, Rosa Parks, but by turning away from the crisis in Darfur we are, implicitly, placing almost no value on the lives of millions there.

"Are we all human?"

—Romeó Dallaire, 2005

ACKNOWLEDGMENTS

I wish to thank the William and Flora Hewlett Foundation and its president, Paul Brest, for support and encouragement in the writing of this paper. Additional support was provided by the National Science Foundation through grant SES-0241313.

Many individuals have provided constructive criticism and helpful suggestions on earlier drafts as well as other valuable intellectual and logistical support. A partial list includes Dan Ariely, Peter Ayton,

numbers of people killed in Darfur. The psychological account presented here clearly has implications for motivating greater response to humanitarian crises other than genocide and certainly such implications should be pursued. I focus on genocide because it is a heinous practice, carried out by known human antagonists, that could in principle be stopped if only people cared to stop it. Apathy toward genocide and other forms of mass murder moves us closer to the loss of humanity.

Jon Baron, Jon Haidt, Derek Jinks, Tehila Kogut, George Loewenstein, Ruth Marom, Ellen Peters, Ilana Ritov, Nils Eric Sahlin, Peter Singer, Scott Slovic, Deborah Small, Ola Svenson, Daniel Västfjäll, Leisha Wharfield, and an anonymous reviewer.

REFERENCES

Associated Press. (1994, September 21). 38,000 shoes stand for loss in lethal year. *The Register-Guard* (Eugene, OR), p. 6A.

Baron, J. (1997). Confusion of relative and absolute risk in valuation. *Journal of Risk and Uncertainty, 14*, 301–309.

Barrett, L. F., & Salovey, P. (Eds.) (2002). *The wisdom in feeling*. New York: Guildford.

Bartels, D. M., & Burnett, R. C. (2006). Proportion dominance and mental representation: Construal of resources affects sensitivity to relative risk reduction (Unpublished manuscript). Evanston, IL: Northwestern University.

Bass, R. (1996). *The book of Yaak*. New York: Houghton Mifflin.

Batson, C. D. (1990). How social an animal? The human capacity for caring. *American Psychologist, 45*, 336–346.

Batson, C. D., O'Quin, K., Fultz, J., Vanderplas, M., & Isen, A. (1983). Self-reported distress and empathy and egoistic versus altruistic motivation for helping. *Journal of Personality and Social Psychology, 45*, 706–718.

BBC News, UK edition. November 19, 2005. Sparrow death mars record attempt. http://news.bbc.co.uk/1/hi/world/europe/4450958.stm.

Clark, M. S., & Fiske, S. T. (Eds.) (1982). *Affect and cognition*. Hillsdale, NJ: Erlbaum.

Coke, J. S., Batson, C. D., & McDavis, K. (1978). Em-pathic mediation of helping: A two-stage model. *Journal of Personality and Social Psychology, 36*, 752–766.

Dallaire, R. (2005). *Shake hands with the devil: The failure of humanity in Rwanda*. New York: Carrol & Graf trade paperback edition.

Dillard, A. (1999). *For the time being*. New York: Alfred A. Knopf.

Dubinsky, Z. (2005). The lessons of genocide [Review of the book Conspiracy to murder: The Rwandan genocide]. *Essex Human Rights Review, 2(1)*, 112–117.

Epstein, S. (1994). Integration of the cognitive and the psychodynamic unconscious. *American Psychologist, 49*, 709–724.

Eisenberg, N., & Miller, P. (1987). Empathy and proso-cial behavior. *Psychological Bulletin, 101*, 91–119.

Fenske, M. J., & Raymond, J. E. (2006). Affective influences of selective attention. *Current Directions in Psychological Science, 15*, 312–316.

Fetherstonhaugh, D., Slovic, P., Johnson, S. M., & Friedrich, J. (1997). Insensitivity to the value of human life: A study of psychophysical numbing. *Journal of Risk and Uncertainty, 14*, 283–300.

Forgas, J. P. (Ed.) (2000). *Feeling and thinking: The role of affect in social cognition*. Cambridge, UK: Cambridge University Press.

Friedrich, J., Barnes, P., Chapin, K., Dawson, I., Garst, V., & Kerr, D. (1999). Psychophysical numbing: When lives are valued less as the lives at risk increase. *Journal of Consumer Psychology, 8,* 277–299.

Galanter, E. (1962). The direct measurement of utility and subjective probability. *American Journal of Psychology, 75,* 208–220.

Gilbert, D. T. (2002). Inferential correction. In T. Gilovich, D. fGriffin, & D. Kahneman (Eds.), *Heuristics and biases* (pp. 167–184). New York: Cambridge University Press.

Glover, J. (2001). *Humanity: A moral history of the twentieth century.* New Haven: Yale Nota Bene, Yale University Press.

Haidt, J. (2001). The emotional dog and its rational tail: A social intuitionist approach to moral judgment. *Psychological Review, 108,* 814–834.

Hamilton, D. L. & Sherman, S. J. (1996). Perceiving persons and groups. *Psychological Review, 103,* 336–355.

Hume, D. (1960). *An enquiry concerning the principles of morals.* LaSalle, IL: Open Court. (Original work published in 1777)

Jenni, K. E. & Loewenstein, G. (1997). Explaining the "Identifiable victim effect." *Journal of Risk and Uncertainty, 14,* 235–257.

Kahneman, D. (2003). A perspective on judgment and choice: Mapping bounded rationality. *American Psychologist, 58,* 697–720.

Kahneman, D. & Frederick, S. (2002). Representativeness revisited: Attribute substitution in intuitive judgment. In T. Gilovich, D. Griffin & D. Kahneman (Eds.), *Heuristics and biases* (pp. 49–81). Cambridge: Cambridge University Press.

Kahneman, D., & Tversky, A. (1979). Prospect theory: An analysis of decision under risk. *Econometrica, 47,* 263–291.

Kingsolver, B.(1996). *High tide in Tucson.* New York: Harper Perennial Edition.

Kogut, T. & Ritov, I. (2005a). The "Identified Victim" effect: An identified group, or just a single individual? *Journal of Behavioral Decision Making, 18,* 157–167.

Kogut, T., & Ritov, I. (2005b). The singularity of identified victims in separate and joint evaluations. *Organizational Behavior and Human Decision Processes, 97,* 106–116.

Lacey, M. (2005, May 18). The mournful math of Darfur: The dead don't add up. *The New York Times,* p. A4.

Le Doux, J. (1996). *The emotional brain.* New York: Simon & Schuster.

Lifton, R. J. (1967). *Death in life: Survivors of Hiroshima.* New York: Random House.

Loewenstein, G., Weber, E. U., Hsee, C. K., & Welch, E. S. (2001). Risk as feelings. *Psychological Bulletin, 127,* 267–286.

Melvern, L. (2004). *Conspiracy to murder: The Rwandan genocide.* London: Verso.

Mowrer, O. H. (1960). *Learning theory and behavior.* New York: John Wiley & Sons.

Neville, P. (2004, February 15). Statistics disguise a human face. The Register-Guard [Eugene, OR].

Power, S. (2003). *A problem from hell: America and the age of genocide.* New York: Harper Perennial.

Reynolds, M. (2005, June 7). Center line. Retrieved December 29, 2005 from http://www.mighty-middle.com/index.php?/archives/20050607.html

Schabas, W. (1999, January 7). The genocide convention at fifty (Special Report 41). Retrieved December 29, 2005 from http://www.usip.org/pubs/specialreports/sr990107.html)

Schelling, T. C. (1968). The life you save may be your own. In S. Chase (Ed.) *Problems in public expenditure analysis.* Washington DC: The Brookings Institute.

Schroeder, P. & Schroeder-Hildebrand, D. (2004). *Six million paper clips: The making of a children's holocaust museum.* Minneapolis: Kar-Ben Publishing.

Slovic, P., Finucane, M. L., Peters, E., & MacGregor, D. G. (2002). The affect heuristic. In T. Gilovich, D. Griffin, & D. Kahneman (Eds.), *Heuristics and biases: The psychology of intuitive judgment* (pp. 397–420). New York: Cambridge University Press.

Slovic, P., Finucane, M. L., Peters, E., & MacGregor, D. G. (2004). Risk as analysis and risk as feelings: Some thoughts about affect, reason, risk, and rationality. *Risk Analysis, 24,* 1–12.

Slovic, S., & Slovic, P. (2004). Numbers and nerves: Toward an affective apprehension of environmental risk. *Whole Terrain, 13,* 14–18.

Small, D. A. & Loewenstein, G. (2003). Helping a victim or helping the victim: Altruism and identifiability. *Journal of Risk and Uncertainty, 26,* 5–16.

Small, D. A. & Loewenstein, G. (2005). The devil you know: The effects of identifiability on punitiveness. *Journal of Behavioral Decision Making, 18,* 311–318.

Small, D. A., Loewenstein, G., & Slovic, P. (2007). Sympathy and callousness: The impact of deliberative thought on donations to identifiable and statistical victims. *Organizational Behavior and Human Decision Processes, 102,* 143–153.

Song, J. (2002, April 26). Every dog has its day—but at what price? The Register-Guard [Eugene, OR], p.1.

Stanovich, K. E., & West, R. F. (2000). Individual differences in reasoning: Implications for the rationality debate? *Behavioral and Brain Sciences, 23,* 645–726.

Stanovich, K. E., & West, R. F. (2002). Individual differences in reasoning: Implications for the rationality debate? In T. Gilovich, D. W. Griffin, & D. Kahneman (Eds.), *Heuristics and biases: The psychology of intuitive judgment* (pp. 421–444). New York: Cambridge University Press.

Stevens, S. S. (1975). *Psychophysics.* New York: Wiley.

Susskind, J., Maurer, K., Thakkar, V., Hamilton, D. L. & Sherman, J. W. (1999). Perceiving individuals and groups: Expectancies, dispositional inferences, and causal attributions. *Journal of Personality and Social Psychology, 76,* 181–191.

Tomkins, S. S. (1962). *Affect, imagery, and consciousness: Vol. 1. The positive affects.* New York: Springer.

Tomkins, S. S. (1963). *Affect, imagery, and consciousness: Vol. 2. The negative affects.* New York: Springer.

Ubel, P. A., Baron, J., & Asch, D. A. (2001). Preference for equity as a framing effect. *Medical Decision Making, 21,* 180–189.

Västfjäll, D., Peters, E., & Slovic, P. (In preparation). Representation, affect, and willingness-to-donate to children in need. Unpublished manuscript.

Villeumier, P., Armony, J. L., & Dolan, R. J. (2003). Reciprocal links between emotion and attention. In K. J. Friston, C. D. Frith, R. J. Dolan, C. Price, J. Ashburner, W. Penny, et al. (Eds.), *Human brain function* (2nd ed., pp. 419–444). New York: Academic Press.

Weber, E. H. (1834). *De pulsu, resorptione, auditu et tactu.* Leipzig: Koehler.

Zajonc, R. B. (1980). Feeling and thinking: Preferences need no inferences. *American Psychologist, 35*, 151–175.

EVOLUTION AND PUBLIC HEALTH

Gilbert S. Omenn[1]

Evolution and its elements of natural selection, population migration, genetic drift, and founder effects have shaped the world in which we practice public health. Human cultures and technologies have modified life on this planet and have co-evolved with myriad other species, including microorganisms; plant and animal sources of food; invertebrate vectors of disease; and intermediate hosts among birds, mammals, and nonhuman primates. Molecular mechanisms of differential resistance or susceptibility to infectious agents or diets have evolved and are being discovered with modern methods. Some of these evolutionary relations require a perspective of tens of thousands of years, whereas other changes are observable in real time. The implications and applications of evolutionary understanding are important to our current programs and policies for infectious disease surveillance, gene–environment interactions, and health disparities globally.

The following terms are discussed in this selection:

cultural evolution	*susceptibility to infection*
ecogenetics	*Western diet*
genome mapping	

[1]Center for Computational Medicine and Bioinformatics, Departments of Internal Medicine and Human Genetics, Medical School and School of Public Health, University of Michigan, Ann Arbor, MI.

Gilbert S. Omenn, "Evolution and Public Health," from *Proceedings of the National Academy of Sciences of the United States of America*, vol. 107, Supplement 1, January 26, 2010, pp. 1702–1709.

ublic health practice and public health research focus on protecting, enhancing, and understanding the health of communities and populations. The scientific disciplines of epidemiology, environmental and occupational health, and health behavior address causes and risk factors of disease over time and space. The substrate for the study of evolution in public health includes international patterns of incidence and prevalence of disease, influences of human and animal behavior, dramatic changes in diet, environmental sources of exposures to infectious agents and chemicals, diverse causes of migration of populations, and climate change. Advances in population genetics and evolutionary biology now facilitate in-depth analysis of gene–environment interactions in human populations and in other species whose life cycles are intimately linked with our own.

This Perspectives article addresses principles and examples of the roles of infectious diseases, cultural/social factors, and diet and metabolism in evolution and public health. It emphasizes implications for gene–environment interactions, global health, health disparities, and health policy.

PRINCIPLES OF EVOLUTIONARY INFLUENCES IN PUBLIC HEALTH

The accumulated and ongoing genomic and behavior variation in human populations makes us differentially susceptible to a broad range of disease agents, ranging from infections to obesity.

The interactions of disease agent, intermediate hosts or risk factors, and human host reflect variation and evolution over very different time scales—with microbes the most rapid by far, including microbes in our own microbiome.

Humans—through cultural, behavioral, and technological changes—have become the most disruptive and significant agents of change for the rest of life on the planet.

SUSCEPTIBILITY AND RESISTANCE TO INFECTIOUS DISEASES

Throughout human history, infectious diseases have been among the most important causes of mortality and morbidity for humans, including plague, smallpox, tuberculosis (TB), measles, and diarrheal infections (1). Studies of the origins and distribution of infectious diseases examine the geographic distribution, life stage, and evolution of the infectious agent [malaria parasites, TB mycobacteria, cholera bacteria, influenza, severe acute respiratory syndrome (SARS), and HIV]; the geographic distribution and life cycle of intermediate hosts (arthropod vectors for many diseases, birds for avian flu, bats for SARS, and deer and ticks for Lyme disease spirochetes); the geographic distribution of diseases they cause in humans and other species; and the key clues that some population subgroups are strikingly more or less susceptible than others. Infectious agents are also important factors in major "noninfectious" inflammatory diseases, like certain cancers, atherosclerosis, and arthritis (2).

Malaria

The protozoan parasite *Plasmodium falciparum* causes the most severe form of malaria. It causes more than 1 million deaths annually. It occurs over a wide geographic distribution of Africa, the Mediterranean, and south Asia. Altitude is associated with dramatic differences in rates of malaria infection, correlated with the distribution of the mosquitoes. The mosquitoes multiply in stagnant pools of water, a situation probably driven by agricultural practices involving deforestation both long ago and currently. *Plasmodium* species are excellent examples of infectious agents that have an obligatory intermediate host such that the status of humans is closely tied to the geographic distribution and activities of that species, which is the *Anopheles* mosquito in the case of malaria. Malaria particularly attacks children and young adults, providing the substrate for natural selection when genetic or behavioral factors provide differential resistance to infection or propagation of the parasite in humans. The most obvious means of avoiding infection are migration away from geographic areas with high prevalence of *Anopheles* and *Plasmodium* and elimination of the *Anopheles* host with antimalarial chemicals such as dichlorodiphenyltrichloroethane, which was very effective globally before its ban because of adverse effects on bird populations.

In addition, there are dramatic differences in susceptibility of individuals embedded in genomic variation. Children and adults with sickle cell trait (HbS) have red blood cells less hospitable to the life stage of the malaria parasite that infects and propagates in the blood than the red blood cells of individuals with normal HbA. Individuals with HbS are more likely than "normals" to survive infection with *P. falciparum*. In 1954, Allison (3) deduced that malaria was the selective factor that maintained the *HbS* gene in certain population subgroups in the face of high mortality from sickle cell anemia in individuals with a double dose of the *HbS* gene. Understanding that the life stage in red blood cells is critical, he and many other researchers examined the potential role of other genetic abnormalities of red blood cells, with dramatic findings. β-Thalassemias, other hemoglobinopathies (e.g., HbC, HbE), and glucose-6-phosphate dehydrogenase (G6PD) deficiency fit this same pattern of enhanced survival of heterozygotes (gene carriers) in the face of malaria as a negative selective factor (4,5). Sickle cell anemia (HbSS), sickle cell trait (HbS/HbA), and normal hemoglobin (HbAA) represent a balanced polymorphism. The incidence of sickle cell anemia in parts of equatorial Africa is as high as 1/25 of the population, compared with 1/400 among African Americans. People ill with malaria have reduced fertility. However, red blood cells of heterozygotes are more readily removed from the circulation than are normal (HbA/A) red blood cells parasitized with P. falciparum. A 20% increase in fitness for individuals with the trait could balance an 85% decrease in fitness of homozygous *HbSS* individuals (6).

An entirely different model for evolution of resistance and susceptibility emerged from international studies of blood group antigens on red blood cells. The Fy-allele of the Duffy blood group system on red blood cells is ubiquitous among Black Africans but is very rare or absent in Asian and white populations. Individuals who are Fy⁻/Fy⁻ have complete resistance against infection with Plasmodium vivax, the parasite responsible for a different form of malaria (1). The molecular mechanism of this clinical and public health association is of general importance: the Fy blood group is the receptor through which the P. vivax parasite enters erythrocytes. This biochemical polymorphism had sufficient survival advantage in West Africa that nearly the entire population became Duffy-negative. Combination with other infections and poor nutrition has been postulated to make it life-threatening, and hence selective (1). However, proof of causal relations after thousands of years is challenging; thus, another view is that the Duffy-negative allele might have become prevalent for reasons not observable now and acted to prevent this relatively mild form of malaria from becoming pandemic in West Africa.

HIV/AIDS

An analogous discovery of the defective-receptor mechanism of resistance explains the epidemiological observation that some men very highly exposed to the HIV/AIDS virus did not become infected. The most striking specific mechanism involves a mutant CCR5 receptor on lymphocytes with a 32-aa deletion. CCR5 is an essential component of the entry mechanism for HIV. If there is no entry, there is no infection and no transmission risk. There is no explanation yet for what natural selection force led to CCR5 mutations accumulating in the human population. Not all resistant individuals have this mutation; thus, there must be other explanations that could reveal additional important features of HIV infection and targets for prevention or therapy. Of course, the selective factor might have been some other agent altogether. From the pursuit of this line of research, we now know 20 polymorphisms of receptors, co-receptors, cytokine ligands, and HLA genes that influence susceptibility to HIV infection, replication, or relevant innate or adaptive immunity; the detailed modes of action reveal features of evolutionary selection (7). The presence of the CCR5 receptor seems to protect against West Nile virus (8); thus, public health use of CCR5 inhibitors to try to reduce risk for HIV/AIDS could lead to increased risk for West Nile Virus encephalitis. Viruses have a long history of coevolution with molecules of the immune system. Specific HLA-B alleles influence both the rate of progression to AIDS in HIV-infected individuals and the adaptation of viral sequences within the host and at large. There are homologies of human nonprogressors to chimpanzees that tolerate a strain of simian immunodeficiency virus (SIVcpz) without immunopathology. Chimps may have survived a selective sweep after a viral epidemic in the distant past.

Since the emergence of HIV/AIDS in the early 1980s, there has been intense interest in public health and lay circles about the origins of the virus (both HIV-1 and HIV-2).

Long-frozen serum samples from central Africa (from the malaria studies) were shown by Nahmias etal. (9) to harbor HIV in at least one case from 1959. Evidence now suggests that these viruses were introduced to humans only in the 20th century in central Africa from lentiviruses in nonhuman primates who suffer no pathology from the infection. Molecular phylogeny studies have compared and classified these viruses. HIV-1 evolved from a strain of SVIcpz in a subspecies of chimpanzees on at least three occasions, whereas HIV-2 originated in SIVsm of sooty mangabeys numerous times. Many other SIVs have not gained a foothold in humans to date (7).

The observation that 8% of the human genome consists of "endogenous retroviral sequences" suggests strongly that our species has a long history of infection with, responses to, and co-evolution and coexistence with retroviruses in what is thought to be a dormant state but could include some continuing pathology (10).

Influenza and SARS

With the recent and current international threats of influenza pandemics (H5N1 "avian" and H1N1/2009 "swine"), the public and policymakers realize again that the influenza viruses are highly mutable and capable of adapting rapidly to selective factors in their environments. The H5N1 flu seems to have originated via reassortment among avian flu strains in eastern Asia. The H1N1 strain(s) may have complex origins. Flu strains have variable potential to infect highly exposed humans from their reservoirs in other species and highly variable risk for human-to-human transmission. As reflected in the uncertainties annually about the morbidity and mortality risks from seasonal flu (200,000 hospitalizations and 36,000 deaths in an average year) and from a pandemic each generation or so, we know too little about the variation in susceptibility of humans to influenza viruses other than direct immunity to previously experienced strains. One major barrier limiting cross-transmission of avian influenza into humans (and vice versa) is the evolution of differences in sialic acid linkage binding specificity. The human and avian virus hemagglutinins prefer binding α-2–6- and α 2–3-linked sialic acids, respectively, on epithelial cells in target tissues. In addition, chimpanzees and other great apes do not express the human upper airway epithelial α -2-6-linked sialic acid targets for human influenza viruses (11). Current research utilizes reconstituted influenza strains and reverse genetics to discover the specific genes and gene combinations that may drive virulence and host range. Also, it is feasible to model the effects of vaccines and drugs on the evolution and dynamics of flu strains.

Another remarkable cross-species transmission, from mammals to humans handling infected animals and then to other humans, occurred with the coronavirus SARS in 2002–2003. Fortunately, modern genetic epidemiological methods led to rapid identification and control of this virus after outbreaks and economic disruption in Hong Kong and Toronto, linked by an air traveler. A compelling surveillance strategy was launched by Wolfe et al. (12) to set up stations in remote areas of the world where unusual infectious agents may exist among animals and might get their foothold in humans through infection of highly exposed animal handlers. In general, further mutations and selection would be necessary to make such viruses or other microbes capable of human-to-human transmission.

Microbiome

Our intestinal tract and every surface and orifice are rich sources of microbes in complex communities. There are many more microbial cells than human cells in our bodies. They perform critical functions in digestion and host defenses. We and our microbiota have coevolved; we provide unique habitats that have restricted colonization to a relatively small number of phyla (13). Our changing diet, hygiene practices, medical therapies, chemical exposures, and public health programs continue to lead to changes in the microbiome. Widespread use of broad-spectrum antibiotics has opened habitats to unique organisms. The National Institutes of Health launched a major initiative focused on genomics, ecology, informatics, and clinical implications of the microbiome (http://nihroadmap.nih. gov/hmp/workshop0407/index.asp).

Helminths (Worms)

Worms in the intestinal tract used to be "normal" before sanitation. There is some evidence that lack of worm loads has become associated with increased rates of autoimmune disorders, diabetes, and childhood leukemias (14). Public health programs to treat worm infestations have been associated with increased asthma and Crohn disease rates. Cross-reactivity between worm antigens and dust mites may contribute to high rates of asthma among African Americans (15). Conversely, genes that are associated with greater risk for asthma may be protective against worms. An evolutionary bioinformatics approach to worms has been employed by Divergence, Inc. using the worm genome sequences published by the Washington University Genome Center and comparative genomics to identify drug targets in worms that, because of divergent evolution, do not exist in the crops, livestock, or humans they infect (16).

ANTIBIOTIC RESISTANCE: AN ARMS RACE BETWEEN SPECIES–EVOLUTION IN ACTION

Within the microbial world, there is remarkable interspecies competition and cooperation. Microbes exchange genetic material, even with different genera. They compete for space and food sources, adapting to selective pressures. Fungi have been particularly adept at producing antimicrobial chemicals that protect them against bacteria. Starting with Fleming's use of the extract of *Penicillium* to kill Gram-positive bacteria, patients have benefited from these antibiotics from nature (17). These chemicals may be isolated and used directly, or they may serve as lead compounds for drug development. However, microbes are not passive agents. They respond promptly to negative natural selection in the form of antibiotics by developing genetically transmitted resistance to the action of individual antibiotics or sets of antibiotics. If these microbes are pathogenic to humans, our response is to create generations of antibiotics; hence, the "arms race."

Multiple-Drug-Resistant TB

One of the most threatening situations in public health during the past 20 years was the emergence of multiple-drug-resistant (MDR) TB mycobacteria, especially in patients with HIV/AIDS (18). Health care workers in New York City, New York State, and elsewhere were infected during care of patients with such TB and were at risk for untreatable illnesses. Fortunately, the public health community mobilized aggressively to identify and isolate such patients and provide them with whatever anti-TB therapy was still effective for their organisms in a setting of directly observed administration of the drug. Ensuring full dosage and full course of treatment is essential to avoid selecting additional resistance genotypes. The original outbreaks were contained, but MDR-TB remains a threat worldwide. TB was also an early application of genotyping methods to enhance epidemiological surveillance and discern patterns of transmission, which was a breakthrough for this organism that is so difficult to culture in the clinical laboratory (18).

Multiply Resistant *Staphylococcus aureus*

Among nosocomial or health care-associated infectious threats, multiply resistant *Staphylococcus aureus* (MRSA) is a prime example. The majority of cases of invasive infections in the United States now are acquired outside the hospital but mostly reflect recent hospitalization or surgery; community-acquired and hospital-acquired infections tend to be attributable to quite distinct strains monitored by the Centers for Disease Control and Prevention (CDC) Emerging Infections Program (19). These strains are highly adapted to the human host and are poised to invade wounds and the bloodstream. Infection control requires judicious use of our current arsenal of antimicrobials, excellent sanitary practices, and continued development of drugs. Parallel evolution of MRSA has been observed in different hospitals. Shifts to different antibiotics in the hospital formulary have stopped some hospital epidemics. More complex is the question of how to reduce the risk for and severity of these infections over long periods. Evolutionary biology and ecological theory were used to test the concept of alternating two or more classes of antibiotics over months or years. Bergstrom et al. (20) reported a mathematical model of cycling programs suited to S. aureus, Enterococcus, and other microbes with single-drug resistance. They concluded that cycling is unlikely to reduce either the evolution or the spread of antibiotic resistance. They proposed an alternative drug use plan called mixing, in which each treated patient receives one of several drug classes used simultaneously in the hospital. At the scale relevant to bacterial populations, mixing imposes greater heterogeneity than cycling does.

Acinetobacter

Evolution of microorganisms can proceed very rapidly in the ambient environment and not just in the laboratory or hospital. For example, Gram-negative Acinetobacter bacteria are prevalent in soils and water with only occasional infection of humans. However, in the 1980s, one species, Acinetobacter baumannii, emerged as a multidrug-resistant strain that contaminated field hospitals in Iraq during the first Gulf War and was introduced to U.S. hospitals by wounded U.S. Army personnel (21). This strain is highly resistant to drying and disinfectants, making decontamination difficult. Some lineages have acquired additional resistance mechanisms (22).

Effects of Immune Suppression

Another selective feature of modern society is the increasing prevalence of immunocom-promised individuals as a result of HIV infection, steroid therapies, cancer chemotherapy, and various genetic immune-deficiency conditions. These individuals are highly vulnerable when hospitalized. Very little investigated is the substrate of previous chemical exposures, especially occupational exposures, that impair immune defenses and lead to pathogenic emergence of otherwise innocuous microbial agents. An example is pneumonia attributable to ordinarily saprophytic organisms in the setting of silicosis of the lung. Among genetic disorders, cystic fibrosis patients are especially susceptible to infection with Pseudomonas species in the lung. Cystic fibrosis is a favorite subject for speculation about what selective factors could have led to its high prevalence, including much higher prevalence in white than African-American populations. In an experimental model, mice lacking cystic fibrosis transmembrane conductance regulator (CFTR) protein did not secrete fluid in response to cholera toxin, although heterozygotes experienced 50% less fluid loss from cholera toxin than the normal mouse (23). However, the responsible chloride channel apparently is not the rate-limiting step for fluid loss in humans (15); thus, the selection-by-cholera hypothesis remains quite speculative.

Vaccines Selective for Desired Microbial Characteristics

There are many examples of pathogens increasing in virulence in response to public health interventions (24), but treating infectious diseases or preventing pathogen spread need not result in an arms race. Treatments and vaccines can be designed that select for less rather than more virulence or for more desirable characteristics. The diphtheria toxoid vaccine selects against toxin production, which is what causes disease, rather than other features of Corynebacterium. Thus, diphtheria infections and clinical isolations still occur, but the extant strains lack toxin production (25). Vaccination using the seven-conjugate vaccine against Streptococcus pneumoniae has reduced carriage of penicillin-resistant serotypes (26) but not invasive isolates (27). A better understanding of the transmission patterns of invasive isolates could enhance vaccination strategies that already select against penicillin-resistant strains.

Immunization is the most important intervention to prevent infectious diseases and improve public health. For vaccine research and clinical usage, He et al. (28) have created a community-based vaccine ontology to standardize vaccine annotation, integrate information about vaccine types, and support computer-assisted reasoning (www.violinet. org/vaccineontology). Its literature-mining function can assist in capturing information about the evolution of the microbe and its responses to immunization and therapies.

Vector Control

Mosquitoes transmit numerous infectious diseases to humans, including dengue, yellow fever, and malaria. Disease can be prevented by immunizing or treating humans and by protecting humans from bites by infected mosquitoes with insecticide-treated bed-nets or spraying. Not surprisingly, mosquitoes have evolved resistance to insecticides. Read et al. (29) used mathematical modeling to propose a strategy to "evolution-proof insecticides by targeting older mosquitoes, which, if infected, are more likely to have mature malaria parasites in their salivary glands ready for transmission to humans; this scheme would control disease spread and generate only weak selection for survival and reproduction by resistant mosquitoes.

CULTURAL EVOLUTION—FROM OUR ORIGINS AS HUNTERS AND GATHERERS TO CONTEMPORARY SOCIETIES

Throughout 5–7 million years of human evolution, biological evolution and social evolution have been intertwined. Cultural conditions and technologies that affect our lives have been, and will be, a major driving force for biological changes in our species. One of the most remarkable examples was the beginnings of animal husbandry and agriculture 7,000-10,000 years ago; progressive domestication of sheep, goats, and cattle; and introduction of milk from animals as part of the human diet about 6,000 years ago.

Persistence of Intestinal Lactase Activity vs. Lactose Intolerance

The prominent biochemical features of milk are casein protein, calcium salts, water, and lactose (galactose-glucose disaccharide sugar). The ability to digest lactose declines rapidly in most humans after weaning because of a normal decline in the activity of the intestinal enzyme lactase. Before drinking of milk, there was no further need for this enzyme. Populations with a long history of cattle domestication and milk drinking selected for the "persistence of lactase" trait. The prevalence is >90% among northern Europeans (Swedes), ~50% in Spanish and Arab populations, 5–20% among African populations, and 1% among Chinese and Native Americans, and this is a source of health disparities in public health nutrition programs.

There are many interesting evolutionary questions about lactase persistence. How many times has a mutation occurred that was then selected positively to reach high prevalence today? How did the mutation or mutations spread globally? What is the mechanism for what seems to be a regulatory on/off mutation?

The inheritance is as an autosomal dominant gene *LCT* on chromosome 2q21, regulated in Europeans by cis-acting elements identified by SNPs just upstream of the *LCT* within introns of the adjacent minichromosome maintenance 6 *(MCM6)* gene (30). The SNP variant T-13910 in MCM6 appears to be the causal variant for lactase persistence in Europeans. It most likely arose in the Middle East and spread to Northern Europe (31). Itan et al. (32) used a simulation model incorporating genetic and archaeological data to conclude that this allele arose and was selected for among dairying farmers in the central Balkans and central Europe. In Africa, high prevalences do occur in pastoralist groups like the Tutsi (90%) and Fulani (50%), but that variant is absent in nearly all other African groups studied. Working with rural population subgroups in East Africa, Tishkoff et al. (30) reported three previously undescribed variants that account for 20% of phenotypic variation, leaving ample room to discover additional variants, especially with resequencing analyses. The chromosomes with these SNP variants show strong genetic signatures of natural selection. The search for variants was enhanced by choosing to genotype individuals with extremes of plasma glucose increase after ingestion of lactose; outliers are often clues to important mechanisms and risk factors. We must always consider that a trait of interest may be adaptive for more than one reason, and may therefore be selected for some other or additional benefit to reproduction and survival. In addition to protein, calcium, and sugar, milk provides water, which is especially important in arid regions, whereas lactose intolerance leads to water loss via diarrhea.

The social and public policy context of "nutrigenomics" can be illustrated with lactose intolerance. The dairy industry has had a long-running successful campaign with "Got Milk?" advertisements. Originally, the tag line was "Everybody needs milk." The Najavo Indian Nation painted their adobes with federal surplus powdered milk; the unkind comments of outsiders reflected ignorance of the unpleasant gastrointestinal symptoms the milk caused in these people, of whom >95% were lactose-intolerant. In response to objections on behalf of nonwhite U.S. populations, the tagline was changed to "Milk has something for everybody." This case also stimulates us to realize that "the normal state" depends on time and place and environmental conditions. Factors other than the primary gene variant contribute to variation in severity of symptoms, making population testing to identify susceptible individuals before they are symptomatic much more complex. Many cases of irritable bowel syndrome might be attributable to this condition in various populations. Finally, it is interesting that certain European cat breeds have a mutation similar to that in humans and that Asian breeds are particularly intolerant of lactose—apparently reflecting coevolution with humans.

Origins and Evolution of the Western Diet: Basis for the Epidemiology of Chronic Diseases

Many of the diseases associated with contemporary Western populations, and spreading across the globe, have arisen through discordance between our ancient genetically influenced biology and the dietary, cultural, and physical activity patterns of modern societies. There is a lively literature with titles like "Stone agers in the fast lane" (33) and "When the Eskimo comes to town" (34). Food staples and food-processing procedures that were introduced during the Neolithic Period have altered fundamentally seven critical nutritional characteristics of ancient hominin diets: glycemic load, fatty acid composition, macronutrient composition, micronutrient density, acid-base balance, sodium/potassium ratio, and fiber content (35). Most of the food types that dominate present diets were introduced quite recently: dairy products, cereal grains (especially refined grains that lack germ and bran); refined sugars (especially sucrose and fructose); refined vegetable oils (with low co-3 and high co-6 fatty acids); alcoholic beverages; salt; and co-6, saturated, fatty acid-rich mammalian meats. These foods have displaced the wild plant and animal foods of our predecessors. What Cordain et al. (35) call "the evolutionary collision of our ancient genome with the nutritional qualities of recently introduced foods" has contributed mightily to many chronic diseases of Western civilization: obesity, diabetes, cardiovascular disease, high blood pressure, dyslipidemias, osteoporosis, bowel disorders, inflammatory and autoimmune diseases, and several cancers. Several of these conditions are associated with insulin resistance; all remain rare among contemporary hunter-gatherer populations. Modern foods are also net acid generators, compared with net base-producing preagricultural diets. The latter are protective against osteoporosis, muscle wasting, calcium kidney stones, high blood pressure, and exercise-induced asthma. Inversion of the potassium/sodium and base/chloride ratios may cause growth retardation in children and accelerate aging (36). Modern diets are very low in potassium/sodium ratio, which exacerbates high blood pressure, kidney stones, osteoporosis, asthma, stroke, and other conditions. Finally, modern diets are strikingly fiber-depleted, leading to many gastrointestinal disorders. With these many major changes in the diet, including the diets of children, we may expect selection to be acting on numerous gene variants, most of which may have individual small effects. For example, a variant of the gene *FTO* is associated with increased body mass index and the complex phenotype of obesity (37). An engaging account of the nature and range of modern diets is *The Omnivore's Dilemma* (38).

Genetic variants may be selected positively or negatively to maintain traits that are the optimal average for a population with a stable environment or to move the average genome directionally to match permanently altered aspects of the environment. Changes that began even 10,000 years ago may be too recent to have reached an equilibrium of adaptation; the discordance emerges as diseases.

Evolution of the Thrifty Genotype in Relation to Diabetes

The human behavior of eating regular meals is itself a significant evolutionary change that contributes to our increased consumption of calories. Our "obesogenic environment" produces a mismatch between our evolutionary health status as a hunter-gatherer and present-day life, with many obesity-related diseases (39). Adipose tissue has emerged as an endocrine organ, secreting many hormones and peptides that control eating, metabolism, and storage of excess fat. The phrase "thrifty genotype" was introduced by human genetics pioneer James Neel (40) to describe the benefit of a sustained hyperglycemic response after an occasional hefty meal by hunter-gatherers. That sustained hyperglycemic response is associated now with peripheral resistance to insulin action and the development of diabetes and its complications in the kidney, nerves, arteries, and retina. Native-American populations vary notably in the prevalence and severity of diabetes and diabetic complications, a fertile subject for evolution-based clinical/translational research.

Diabetes also makes people more vulnerable to infections, partly through accumulation of reactive oxygen species, which require effective immune and inflammatory responses and antioxidants to overcome their effects. As Nesse and Stearns (15) have emphasized, our evolutionary legacy is a broad array of symptoms, defense mechanisms, and molecules that may have both protective and damaging features. A striking example is bilirubin, the end product of heme metabolism, which is neurotoxic at high concentrations, especially in infancy. Why, they ask, does the body make such a difficult-to-excrete toxin? It turns out that bilirubin is an effective antioxidant, which may help to delay atherosclerosis and aging. Lipophilic bilirubin and water-soluble glutathione have complementary antioxidant and cytoprotective roles (41). Bilirubin functions and is consumed at a concentration of 10 nM. Evolution has provided a steady source of intracellular bilirubin through the biliverdin reductase cycle, which amplifies bilirubin levels 10,000-fold. A clue comes from the benign genetic disorder Gilbert syndrome, a conjugation enzyme deficiency characterized by increased bilirubin levels, with 6-fold lower rates of heart disease and a 3-fold lower risk for carotid plaques. Sedlak et al. (41) claim that elevated bilirubin is a better index of disease protection than HDL-cholesterol. β-Carotene is another antioxidant that was proposed as a cancer chemopreventive agent, but it turned out to be carcinogenic (42).

ORIGINS OF RACIAL DIFFERENCES IN HUMAN POPULATIONS

Racial and ethnic differences have evolved through natural selection in adaptation to different environmental conditions, combined with reproductive isolation. During the most recent glacial period about 100,000 years ago, much of the earth's expanse was covered by ice, providing conditions for separate evolution of whites in the west, mongoloid populations in the east, and blacks in the south (1). Much migration has occurred since then, with admixture of genes. The most conspicuous racial difference is skin pigmentation. An obvious question is why are whites and Asians so lightly pigmented? A plausible hypothesis involves the adaptation in their latitudes to low levels of the UV radiation necessary for conversion of provitamin D to vitamin D in skin. Activated vitamin D is essential for proper calcification of the bones and avoidance of rickets in childhood. Furthermore, rickets in women impairs childbirth through pelvic deformation, leading to death of mothers and infants under primitive medical conditions, a strong selective pressure. An interesting experimental test of this explanation was performed with saddle pigs, which are darkly pigmented in mid-body and little pigmented in the dorsal and caudal regions; vitamin D formation after UV irradiation was shown to be greater in the unpigmented areas of skin. Exceptions may be instructive, too, specifically Eskimos and African Pygmies. They experience little UV irradiation in arctic regions and under the tropical rain forest canopy, respectively. Eskimos get activated vitamin D from fish and seal liver, whereas pygmies may get theirs from insect larvae in their diet (1). A gene-environment interaction involving the polymorphic p-2 serum protein Gc may be explained similarly because Gc2 is a more effective carrier protein for vitamin D than Gc1. Vitamin D deficiency is of high epidemiological interest because of increased colon cancer and heart disease risks; recently, the American Association for Clinical Chemistry reported a large increase in testing for vitamin D and its active metabolites.

In a HapMap analysis (43), some of the strongest signals of recent selection appear in five unlinked genes involved in skin pigmentation in Europeans (OCA2, MYO5A, DTNBP1, TYRP1, and SLC24A5), consistent with separate selective events. Embedded in SNP, haplotype, and sequencing study results are ample markers to assess population origins so that subjectively identified race need no longer be a confounding variable in the analysis.

EMERGING TOPICS WITH EVOLUTIONARY IMPLICATIONS

Revealing Natural Selection Potentially Important to Public Health Through Genome Mapping Studies

Genotyping and high-throughput genome sequencing are rapidly producing huge files of data that can guide studies of ongoing evolution relevant to public health. Voight et al. (43) published an analytical method for genome-wide scanning for SNPs that may be signals of recent selection. Their goal was to identify loci in which strong selection has driven mutant alleles to intermediate prevalence—on their way to fixation or to a balanced polymorphism. The key signal of strong directional selection is that the favored allele tends to sit on an unusually long haplotype of low diversity/high homozygosity attributable to a relatively fast increase in prevalence. Windows of consecutive SNPs that contain multiple extreme scores represent clusters attributable to "selection sweeps;" selection coefficients of 0.01-0.04 are sufficient to produce major regional population differences since the separation of African and Eurasian populations about 6,600 years ago (260 generations). The lactase region on chromosome 2 (in Europeans) and the alcohol dehydrogenase (ADH) cluster on chromosome 4 (in East Asians) were confirmed as highly selected by this method. In their application of tag-SNPs to the three-continent HapMap dataset, most signals, but not all, were specific to a geographic region subpopulation, consistent with emergence since the separation of these populations. Because genetic variants have different fitness, they should be loci (or should be in linkage disequilibrium with loci) that contribute significant phenotypic variation, possibly for complex traits and diseases. Among genes showing evidence of sweeps, enrichment was found for the gene ontology categories chemosensory perception, olfaction, gametogenesis, spermatogenesis, fertilization, carbohydrate/lipid/steroid/phosphate metabolism, electron transport, chromatin packaging/remodeling, MHC-1-mediated immunity, peroxisome transport, and vitamin transport (table 2 in ref. 43). This approach is a departure from the candidate gene approach reflected in the CCR5/HIV, HbS/malaria, and lactase persistence/lactose tolerance examples presented above. Behaviorally, modern human populations have experienced tremendous shifts in habitats, food sources, population densities, and pathogen exposures for long enough to produce selection of certain genes associated with specific complex trait phenotypes. Good examples are CY-P3A5 and salt-sensitive high blood pressure, ADH and alcoholism susceptibility, and 17q21 inversion and fertility (43).

It should be useful to combine these findings with genome-wide association studies (GWASs). There is a huge GWAS literature from the past few years, with numerous genomic variants associated with common traits and complex diseases. However, few of the variants are in protein-coding genes with identifiable functional consequences. Moreover, few studies have any assessment of exposures, which is essential for discovery of gene–environment interactions and identification of modifiable risk factors (44). Interactions of individual SNPs with environmental exposures have been reported. N-acetyl-transferase 2 (NAT2) genotypes are associated with differential detoxification of arylamines in dye industry occupational exposures and in tobacco smoke, leading to differential risk for cancer of the urinary bladder (45). Interestingly, *O*-acetylation by the same enzyme activates heterocyclic amines that lead to colorectal cancer; only weak main effects of well-done meat consumption (a source of heterocyclic amines), the genes CYP1A2 and NAT2 that are involved in their metabolism, or tobacco smoking (which can induce CYP1A2) were found for colorectal cancer, but a very high odds ratio of 8.8 was found for those who were both exposed and genetically susceptible, with no significant lower order interactions (46). A conceptual model for the role of genes involved in DNA damage response pathways for double-strand breaks caused by ionizing radiation is the basis for the Women's Environment, Cancer and Radiation Epidemiology (WECARE) study of second breast cancers after radio-therapy of primary breast cancers (47). A special symposium of the 2010 Annual Review of Public Health is devoted to genomics and public health, including articles on statistical (48) and epidemiological (49) methods to enhance GWASs.

Two central challenges in evolutionary biology are to understand the genetic and ecological mechanisms that drive adaptation and to recognize the effects of natural selection on a dynamic background of neutral processes of population history, bottlenecks, migration, mutation, recombination, and drift. Coop et al. (50) examined the role of geography and population history in the spread of selectively favored alleles using the Human Genome Diversity Panel of the Centre d'Étude du Polymorphisme Humain (Paris) (CEPH) and the Phase II HapMap. Over the past 50,000–100,000 years, humans have spread out from Africa to colonize essentially the entire planet, thereby experiencing a vast range of climates, diets, and environments as likely selective factors, together with sexual competition, viability selection, and resistance to evolving pathogens on an ongoing basis. Strong evidence of relatively recent adaptation by selection has emerged from haplotype sweep patterns of clusters of SNPs, homozygosity for extended distances, and selection coefficients >1% sustained for long periods for genes involved in resistance to malaria (G6PD and Duffy antigen), lighter skin pigmentation in non-Africans (SLC24A5, SLC45A2, KITLG, and EDAR), and diet and metabolism (lactase and salivary amylase). However, for most high-frequency SNPs that show extreme differentiation between pairs of the three Eurasian, East Asian, or African populations, geographic associations and neutral processes of ancestral relationships and migration still may be largely responsible for the local differences within regions (50).

The *P. falciparum* and *P. vivax* malaria examples (above) show how population genetics helps to reveal the evolution of parasite-host relationships. Population genetics is advancing remarkably through the elucidation of the human genome sequence and the development of high-throughput methods for SNPs, haplotypes, next-generation sequencing of exons, and, soon, the whole genome. A fascinating discovery with phylogenetic analysis has just appeared that radically revises our thinking about the origin of *P. falciparum* (11).

For at least 15 years, the evidence pointed to cospeciation of *P. falciparum* in humans and *Plasmodium reichenowi* in chimpanzees, evolved separately from a presumed common ancestor over 5–7 million years in parallel to divergence of their hosts. That was based on one isolate of *P. reichenowi*. With eight previously undescribed isolates, Rich et al. (11) showed that the global totality of *P. falciparum* strains is fully included within the much more diverse *P. reichenowi* variation. All extant *P. falciparum* populations seem to have originated from the parasite infecting chimpanzees by a single-host transfer, possibly as recently as 10,000 years ago. Furthermore, two critical genetic mutations have been elucidated. Inactivation of the gene *CMAH* in the human lineage blocked conversion of sialic acid neuraminidase 5Ac to Neu5Gc, making humans resistant to *P. reichenowi*. In addition, mutations in the dominant invasion receptor EBA 175 made *P. falciparum* prefer the overabundant Neu5Ac precursor. This combination may explain the extreme pathogenicity of *P. falciparum* in humans.

Global Climate Change

Global average surface temperatures have increased 0.8°C (1.4°F) over the past century, mostly in the past 30 years, with a "commitment" to further increases from carbon di-oxide already accumulated in the atmosphere (51). Looking forward, we can expect an increasing focus on modeling and predicting coevolution of humans and many relevant plant, microbial, invertebrate, and vertebrate species under the selective forces of global climate change and our attempts to mitigate and adapt to climate change. It is feasible to model and project geographic shifts with temperature and humidity for agriculture and for vector-borne diseases. The Arctic is particularly susceptible to climate change, with warming occurring at a rate twice that of moderate zones, leading to striking changes in the forests and viability of crops, appearance of unfamiliar insects and microbes, and thinning and breakup of the arctic ice. We can anticipate progressive major changes in temperature, humidity, habitats, vectors, and transmission for a host of infectious agents (52). A possible example is the appearance of the fungal pathogen *Cryptococcus gattii* in 1999 in the Pacific Northwest, with 200 human and 400 domestic animal cases now reported in normal individuals; previously, human cases occurred only rarely, mostly among immuno compromised patients.

Seasonality is another important climate variable for infectious diseases, recognized since the time of Hippocrates. Seasonality produces alternating periods of high transmission and population bottlenecks that limit strain diversity and cause rapid genetic shifts. Models show that small seasonal changes in host-pathogen dynamics, including host social behavior and contact rates (53), may be sufficient to create large seasonal surges in disease incidence, with exacerbations likely to arise from climate change (54).

The *term prevention* in public health is analogous to *adaptation* in the climate change literature, ranging from reduction of greenhouse gas emissions to redesign of cities to minimize heat islands and heat waves, to surveillance for diseases like tick-borne Lyme disease, and to mitigation of health disparities in human impacts of rising sea and river levels. Public health professionals will be critical to adaptation strategies, hopefully informed by an evolutionary perspective about the interrelations between living things and their environments.

Human Behavioral Phenotypes

Subjects involving a broad range of normal behaviors and mental illnesses are important in community public health and for initiatives to stimulate healthier choices in personal behavior. For example, genetic variation and evolutionary psychology may help to reveal underlying neural and social determinants of personality traits (55). Darwin was well aware of genetic influences on behavior, as reflected in his writing on the domestication of animals and comments on the distinctive mental qualities of dogs, horses, and other animals. The dog genome is under study, in part, because of the dramatic differences in behavioral traits among breeds. Humans and other mammals share basic emotion-motivation phenotypes of anger, fear, nurturance, curiosity, and sex-related behaviors shaped during human evolution by social adaptations.

A particularly interesting evolutionary perspective has been applied to uses and effects of psychoactive drugs (56). The use of pure psychoactive chemical agents as drugs and the i.v. and nasal routes of administration are specific evolutionary features of the contemporary human environment. They are "inherently pathogenic" because they bypass adaptive information processing systems and act directly on brain mechanisms that control emotion and behaviors. Drugs of abuse create signals in the brain that indicate falsely the arrival of a fitness benefit such that drug-seeking behavior displaces adaptive behaviors. Video game-playing and snacks high in fat, salt, and sugar were described in similar terms (56). Drugs that block anxiety, low mood, and other negative emotions can be analyzed by analogy to drugs that alter pain, cough, fever, diarrhea, vomiting, and related physical defense mechanisms.

CLOSING COMMENT

As illustrated in this article, important examples of practical applications of evolutionary understanding in modern public health include obesity, influenza, and appropriate uses of antibiotics. As documented by the Surgeon General and the CDC, the prevalence of obesity and overweight has increased sharply in the past 30 years, with huge consequences for the burden of chronic diseases and health care costs. The global epidemic of obesity represents a combination of rapidly changing, culture-based, behavior changes and discordant genomic predispositions that cannot be ignored. Meanwhile, we face simultaneous influenza epidemics from seasonal H1N1 strains, with enormous annual variation in impact, from H1N1/2009 swine flu strains with very differential susceptibilities in the human population, and therefore quite different high-risk target populations for prevention, vaccination, and therapy, and, lest we forget, from lingering H5N1 avian flu strains. Finally, we remain in an arms race with bacteria whose environments inside us and around us we are constantly changing, stimulating their own rapid evolution.

Evolution, natural selection, and population dynamics act over very long periods of time. We have learned in recent years, as highlighted by *Science* magazine's "Breakthrough of the Year 2005," that we can actually observe "evolution in action"—in the Galapagos, the Arctic and Antarctic, hospitals, rural and urban waste streams, and many other settings, with impacts on public health and implications for our public health research agenda. We can be confident that evolutionary perspectives will provide a useful foundation for research and communication in public health (57) as well as in medical care (58).

ADDITIONAL NOTES

Edited by Peter T. Ellison, Harvard University, Cambridge, MA, and approved October 23, 2009 (received for review September 11, 2009). This paper results from the Arthur M. Sackler Colloquium of the National Academy of Sciences, "Evolution in Health and Medicine" held April 2-3,2009, at the National Academy of Sciences in Washington, DC. The complete program and audio files of most presentations are available on the NAS web site at www.nasonline.org/Sackler_Evolution_Health_Medicine.

Author contributions: G.S.O. designed research, performed research, and wrote the paper. The author declares no conflict of interest. This article is a PNAS Direct Submission.

ACKNOWLEDGMENTS

I am grateful to my colleagues Professors Betsy Foxman, Randy Nesse, and Noah Rosenberg for specific inputs for this manuscript.

REFERENCES

1. Vogel F, Motulsky AG (1997) *Human Genetics: Problems and Approaches* (Springer, Berlin), 3rd Ed.

2. Ewald PW (2004) Evolution of virulence. *Infect Dis Clin North Am* 18:1–15.

3. Allison AC (1954) Protection afforded by sickle-cell trait against subtertian malareal infection. *Br Med J* 1:290–294.

4. Haldane J (1949) The rate of mutations of human genes. *Hereditas* 35(Suppl): 267–273.

5. Motulsky AG (1964) Hereditary red cell traits and malaria. *Am J Trop Med Hyg* 13 (Suppl):147-158.

6. Gelehrter T, Collins F, Ginsburg D (1998) *Principles of Medical Genetics* (Williams & Wilkins, Baltimore), 2nd Ed, p 51.

7. Heeney JL, Dalgleish AG, Weiss RA (2006) Origins of HIV and the evolution of resistance to AIDS. *Science* 313:462–466.

8. Lim JK, Glass WG, McDermott DH, Murphy PM (2006) CCR5: No longer a "good for nothing" gene—Chemokine control of West Nile virus infection. *Trends Immunol* 27: 308–312.

9. Nahmias AJ, et al. (1986) Evidence for human infection with an HTLV III/LAV-like virus in central Africa, 1959. *Lancet* 1:1279–1280.

10. Contreras-Galindo R, et al. (2008) Human endogenous retrovirus K (HML-2) elements in the plasma of people with lymphoma and breast cancer. *J Virol* 82:9329–9336.

11. Rich SM, et al. (2009) The origin of malignant malaria. *Proc Nat I Acad Sci USA* 106: 14902–14907.

12. Wolfe ND, et al. (1998) Wild primate populations in emerging infectious disease research: The missing link? *Emerg Infect Dis* 4:149–158.

13. Turn baugh PJ, et al. (2007) The human microbiome project. *Nature* 449:804–810.

14. Elliott DE, Summers RW, Weinstock JV (2007) Helminths as governors of immune-mediated inflammation. *Int J Parasitol* 37:457–464.

15. Nesse RM, Stearns SC (2008) The great opportunity: Evolutionary applications to medicine and public health. *Evolutionary Applications* 1:28–48.

16. McCarter JP (2008) Nematology: Terra incognita no more. *Nat Biotechnol* 26:882–884.

17. Lax E (2004) *The Mold in Dr. Florey's Coat: The Story of the Penicillin Miracle* (Henry Hold, New York).

18. Pearson ML, et al. (1992) Nosocomial transmission of multidrug-resistant Mycobacterium tuberculosis. A risk to patients and health care workers. *Ann Intern Med* 117:191–196.

19. Klevens RM, et al; Active Bacterial Core surveillance (ABCs) MRSA Investigators (2007) Invasive methicillin-resistant Staphylococcus aureus infections in the United States. *JAMA* 298:1763–1771.

20. Bergstrom CT, Lo M, Lipsitch M (2004) Ecological theory suggests that antimicrobial cycling will not reduce antimicrobial resistance in hospitals. *Proc Natl Acad Sci USA* 101:13285–13290.

21. Scott P, et al. (2007) An outbreak of multidrug-resistant Acinetobacter baumanniicalcoaceticus complex infection in the US military health care system associated with military operations in Iraq. *Clin Infect Dis* 44:1577–1584.

22. Dijkshoorn L, Nemec A, Seifert H (2007) An increasing threat in hospitals: Multidrug-resistant Acinetobacter baumannii. *Nat Rev Microbiol* 5:939–951.

23. Gabriel SE, Brigman KN, Koller BH, Boucher RC, Stutts MJ (1994) Cystic fibrosis heterozygote resistance to cholera toxin in the cystic fibrosis mouse model. *Science* 266:107–109.

24. Dronamraju K, ed (2004) *Infectious Disease and Host-Pathogen Evolution* (Cambridge Univ Press, Cambridge, UK).

25. Soubeyrand B, Plotkin SA (2002) Microbial evolution: Antitoxin vaccines and pathogen virulence. *Nature* 417:609–610, discussion 610.

26. Dagan R (2009) Impact of pneumococcal conjugate vaccine on infections caused by antibiotic-resistant Streptococcus pneumoniae. *Clin Microbiol Infect* 15(Suppl 3): 16–20.

27. Karnezis TT, Smith A, Whittier S, Haddad J, Jr, Saiman L (2009) Antimicrobial resistance among isolates causing invasive pneumococcal disease before and after licensure of heptavalent conjugate pneumococcal vaccine. *PLoS One* 4:e5965.

28. He Y, et al. (2009) VO: Vaccine ontology. *The First International Conference on Biomedical Ontology (ICBO 2009),* ed Smith B (National Center for Ontological Research, Buffalo, NY), p 172.

29. Read AF, Lynch PA, Thomas MB (2009) How to make evolution-proof insecticides for malaria control. *PLoS Biol* 7:e1000058.

30. Tishkoff SA, et al. (2007) Convergent adaptation of human lactase persistence in Africa and Europe. *Nat Genet* 39:31-40.

31. Hollox EJ, Swallow DM (2002) In *The Genetic Basis of Common Diseases,* eds King RA, Rotter JI, Motulsky AG (Oxford Univ Press, Oxford), pp 250–265.

32. Itan Y, Powell A, Beaumont MA, Burger J, Thomas MG (2009) The origins of lactase persistence in Europe. *PLOS Comput Biol* 5:e1000491.

33. Eaton SB, Konner M, Shostak M (1988) Stone agers in the fast lane: Chronic degenerative diseases in evolutionary perspective. *Am J Med* 84:739–749.

34. Schaefer O (1971) When the Eskimo comes to town. *Nutr Today* 6 (Nov-Dec):8–16.

35. Cordain L, et al. (2005) Origins and evolution of the Western diet: Health implications for the 21st century. *Am J Clin Nutr* 81:341–354.

36. Frassetto L, Morris RC, Jr, Sellmeyer DE, Todd K, Sebastian A (2001) Diet, evolution and aging—The pathophysiologic effects of the post-agricultural inversion of the potassium-to-sodium and base-to-chloride ratios in the human diet. *Eur J Nutr* 40: 200–213.

37. Cecil JE, Tavendale R, Watt P, Hetherington MM, Palmer CNA (2008) An obesity-associated FTO gene variant and increased energy intake in children. *N Engl J Med* 359:2558–2566.

38. Pollan M (2006) *The Omnivore's Dilemma: A Natural History of Four Meals* (Penguin Press, Penguin Books Ltd., New York).

39. Power ML, Schulkin J (2009) *The Evolution of Obesity* (Johns Hopkins Univ Press, Baltimore).

40. Neel JV, Weder AB, Julius S (1998) Type II diabetes, essential hypertension, and obesity as "syndromes of impaired genetic homeostasis": The "thrifty genotype" hypothesis enters the 21st century. *Perspect Biol Med* 42:44–74.

41. Sedlak TW, et al. (2009) Bilirubin and glutathione have complementary antioxidant and cytoprotective roles. *Proc Natl Acad Sci USA* 106:5171–5176.

42. Omenn GS, et al. (1996) Effects of a combination of beta carotene and vitamin A on lung cancer and cardiovascular disease. *N Engl J Med* 334:1150–1155.

43. Voight BF, Kudaravalli S, Wen X, Pritchard JK (2006) A map of recent positive selection in the human genome. *PLoS Biol* 4:e72.

44. Omenn GS (2009) From human genome research to personalized health care. *Issues Sci Technol* 25:51–56.

45. Vineis P, et al. (2001) Current smoking, occupation, N-acetyltransferase-2 and bladder cancer: A pooled analysis of genotype-based studies. Cancer Epidemiol Biomarkers Prev 10:1249–1252.

46. Le Marchand L, et al. (2001) Combined effects of well-done red meat, smoking, and rapid N-acetyltransferase 2 and CYP1A2 phenotypes in increasing colorectal cancer risk. Cancer Epidemiol Biomarkers Prev 10:1259–1266.

47. Bernstein JL, et al. (2004) Study design: Evaluating gene-environment interactions in the etiology of breast cancer—The WECARE study. Breast Cancer Res 6 (Suppl): R199–R214.

48. Thomas D (2010) In Annual Review of Public Health, ed Fielding JE (Annual Reviews, Palo Alto), Vol 31.

49. Witte JS (2010) In Annual Review of Public Health, ed Fielding JE (Annual Reviews, Palo Alto), Vol 31.

50. Coop G, et al. (2009) The role of geography in human adaptation. PLoS Genet 5: e1000500.

51. Ebi KL, Semenza JC (2008) Community-based adaptation to the health impacts of climate change. Am J Prev Med 35:501–507.

52. Last JM (1993) Global change: Ozone depletion, greenhouse warming, and public health. Annu Rev Public Health 14:115–136.

53. Altizer S, et al. (2006) Seasonality and the dynamics of infectious diseases. Ecol Lett 9: 467–484.

54. Fisman DN (2007) Seasonality of infectious diseases. Annu Rev Public Health 28: 127–143.

55. Bouchard TJ, Jr, Loehlin JC (2001) Genes, evolution, and personality. Behav Genet 31: 243–273.

56. Nesse RM, Berridge KC (1997) Psychoactive drug use in evolutionary perspective. Science 278:63–66.

57. Nesse RM, Stearns SC, Omenn GS (2006) Medicine needs evolution. Science 311:1071.

58. Nesse RM, et al. Making evolutionary biology a basic science for medicine. Proc Natl Acad Sci USA 107(Suppl):1800–1807.

LIFEBOAT ETHICS

MOTHER LOVE AND CHILD DEATH IN NORTHEAST BRAZIL

Nancy Scheper-Hughes

I have seen death without weeping. The destiny of the Northeast is death.
Cattle they kill. To the people they do something worse.

—Anonymous Brazilian singer (1965)

Why do the church bells ring so often?" I asked Nailza de Arruda soon after I moved into a corner of her tiny mud-walled hut near the top of the shantytown called the Alto do Cruzeiro (Crucifix Hill). I was then a Peace Corps volunteer and a community development/health worker. It was the dry and blazing hot summer of 1965, the months following the military coup in Brazil, and save for the rusty, clanging bells, of N. S. das Dores Church, an eerie quiet had settled over the market town that I call Bom Jesus da Mata. Beneath the quiet, however, there was chaos and panic. "It's nothing," replied Nailza, "just another little angel gone to heaven."

Nailza had sent more than her share of little angels to heaven, and sometimes at night I could hear her engaged in a muffled but passionate discourse with one of them, two-year-old Joana. Joana's photograph, taken as she lay propped up in her tiny cardboard coffin, her eyes open, hung on a wall next to one of Nailza and Ze Antonio taken on the day they eloped.

Nailza could barely remember the other infants and babies who came and went in close succession. Most had died unnamed and were hastily baptized in their coffins. Few lived more than a month or two. Only Joana, properly baptized in church at the close of her first year and placed under the protection of a powerful saint, Joan of Arc, had been expected to live. And Nailza had dangerously allowed herself to love the little girl.

In addressing the dead child, Nailza's voice would range from tearful imploring to angry recrimination: "Why did you leave me? Was your patron saint so greedy that she could not allow me one child on this earth?" Ze Antonio advised me to ignore Nailza's odd behavior, which he understood as a kind of madness that, like the birth and death of children, came and went. Indeed, the premature birth of a stillborn son some months later "cured" Nailza of her "inappropriate" grief, and the day came when she removed Joana's photo and carefully packed it away.

More than fifteen years elapsed before I returned to the Alto do Cruzeiro, and it was anthropology that provided the vehicle of my return. Since 1982 I have returned several times in order to pursue a problem that first attracted my attention in the 1960s. My involvement with the people of the Alto do Cruzeiro now spans a quarter of a century and three generations of parenting in a community where mothers and daughters are often simultaneously pregnant.

The Alto do Cruzeiro is one of three shantytowns surrounding the large market town of Bom Jesus in the sugar plantation zone of Pernambuco in Northeast Brazil, one of the many zones of neglect that have emerged in the shadow of the now tarnished economic miracle of Brazil. For the women and children of the Alto do Cruzeiro the only miracle is that some of them have managed to stay alive at all.

The Northeast is a region of vast proportions (approximately twice the size of Texas) and of equally vast social and developmental problems. The nine states that make up the region are the poorest in the country and are representative of the Third World within a dynamic and rapidly industrializing nation. Despite waves of migrations from the interior to tile teeming shanty towns of coastal cities, the majority still live in rural areas on farms and ranches, sugar plantations and mills.

Life expectancy in the Northeast is only forty years, largely because of the appallingly high rate of infant and child mortality. Approximately one million children in Brazil under the age of five die each year. The children of the Northeast, especially those born in shanty towns on the periphery of urban life, are at a very high risk of death. In these areas, children are born without the traditional protection of breast-feeding, subsistence gardens, stable marriages, and multiple adult caretakers that exists in the interior. In the hillside shantytowns that spring up around cities or, in this case, interior market towns, marriages are brittle, single parenting is the norm, and women are frequently forced into the shadow economy of domestic work in the homes of the rich or into unprotected and oftentimes "scab" wage labor on the surrounding sugar plantations, where they clear land for planting and weed for a pittance, sometimes less than a dollar a day. The women of the Alto may not bring their babies with them into the homes of the wealthy, where the often-sick infants are considered sources of contamination, and they cannot carry the little ones to the riverbanks where they wash clothes because the river is heavily infested with schistosomes and other deadly parasites. Nor can they carry their young children to the plantations, which are often several miles away. At wages of a dollar a day, the women of the Alto cannot hire baby sitters. Older children who are not in school will sometimes serve as somewhat indifferent caretakers. But any child not in school is also expected to find wage work. In most cases, babies are simply left at home alone, the door securely fastened. And so many also die alone and unattended.

Bom Jesus da Mata, centrally located in the plantation zone of Pernambuco, is within commuting distance of several sugar plantations and mills. Consequently, Bom Jesus has been a magnet for rural workers forced off their small subsistence plots by large landown-ers wanting to use every available piece of land for sugar cultivation. Initially, the rural migrants to Bom Jesus were squatters who were given tacit approval by the mayor to put up temporary straw huts on each of the three hills overlooking the town. The Alto do Cruzeiro is the oldest, the largest, and the poorest of the shantytowns. Over the past three decades many of the original migrants have become permanent residents, and the primi-tive and temporary straw huts have been replaced by small homes (usually of two rooms) made of wattle and daub, sometimes covered with plaster. The more affluent residents use bricks and tiles. In most Alto homes, dangerous kerosene lamps have been replaced by light bulbs. The once tattered rural garb, often fashioned from used sugar sacking, has likewise been replaced by store-bought clothes, often castoffs from a wealthy *patrão* (boss). The trappings are modern, but the hunger, sickness, and death that they conceal are traditional, deeply rooted in a history of feudalism, exploitation, and institutionalized dependency.

My research agenda never wavered. The questions I addressed first crystallized during a veritable "die-off" of Alto babies during a severe drought in 1965. The food and water shortages and the political and economic chaos occasioned by the military coup were reflected in the handwritten entries of births and deaths in the dusty, yellowed pages of the ledger books kept at the public registry office in Bom Jesus. More than 350 babies died in the Alto during 1965 alone—this from a shantytown population of little more than 5,000. But that wasn't what surprised me. There were reasons enough for the deaths in the miserable conditions of shantytown life. What puzzled me was the seeming indifference of Alto women to the death of their infants, and their willingness to attribute to their own tiny offspring an aversion to life that made their death seem wholly natural, indeed all but anticipated.

Although I found that it was possible, and hardly difficult, to rescue infants and tod-dlers from death by diarrhea and dehydration with a simple sugar, salt, and water solution (even bottled Coca-Cola worked fine), it was more difficult to enlist a mother herself in the rescue of a child she perceived as ill-fated for life or better off dead, or to convince her to take back into her threatened and besieged home a baby she had already come to think of as an angel rather than as a son or daughter.

I learned that the high expectancy of death, and the ability to face child death with stoicism and equanimity, produced patterns of nurturing that differentiated between those infants thought of as thrivers and survivors and those thought of as born already "wanting to die." The survivors were nurtured, while stigmatized, doomed infants were left to die, as mothers say, *a mingua*, "of neglect." Mothers stepped back and allowed nature to take its course. This pattern, which I call mortal selective neglect, is called passive infanticide by anthropologist Marvin Harris. The Alto situation, although culturally specific in the form that it takes, is not unique to Third World shantytown communities and may have its correlates in our own impoverished urban communities in some cases of "failure to thrive" infants.

I use as an example the story of Zezinho, the thirteen-month-old toddler of one of my neighbors, Lourdes. I became involved with Zezinho when I was called in to help Lourdes in the delivery of another child, this one a fair and robust little tyke with a lusty cry. I noted that while Lourdes showed great interest in the newborn, she totally ignored Zezinho who, wasted and severely malnourished, was curled up in a fetal position on a piece of urine-and feces-soaked cardboard placed under his mother's hammock. Eyes open and vacant, mouth slack, the little boy seemed doomed.

When I carried Zezinho up to the community day-care center at the top of the hill, the Alto women who took turns caring for one another's children (in order to free themselves for part-time work in the cane fields or washing clothes) laughed at my efforts to save Ze, agreeing with Lourdes that here was a baby without a ghost of a chance. Leave him alone, they cautioned. It makes no sense to fight with death. But I did do battle with Ze, and after several weeks of force-feeding (malnourished babies lose their interest in food), Ze began to succumb to my ministrations. He acquired some flesh across his taut chest bones, learned to sit up, and even tried to smile. When he seemed well enough, I returned him to Lourdes in her miserable scrap-material lean-to, but not without guilt about what I had done. I wondered whether returning Ze was at all fair to Lourdes and to his little brother. But I was busy and washed my hands of the matter. And Lourdes did seem more interested in Ze now that he was looking more human.

When I returned in 1982, there was Lourdes among the women who formed my sample of Alto mothers—still struggling to put together some semblance of life for a now grown Ze and her five other surviving children. Much was made of my reunion with Ze in 1982, and everyone enjoyed retelling the story of Ze's rescue and of how his mother had given him up for dead. Ze would laugh the loudest when told how I had had to force-feed him like a fiesta turkey. There was no hint of guilt on the part of Lourdes and no resentment on the part of Ze. In fact, when questioned in private as to who was the best friend he ever had in life, Ze took a long drag on his cigarette and answered without a trace of irony, "Why my mother, of course!" "But of course," I replied.

Part of learning how to mother in the Alto do Cruzeiro is learning when to let go of a child who shows that it "wants" to die or that it has no "knack" or no "taste" for life. Another part is learning when it is safe to let oneself love a child. Frequent child death remains a powerful shaper of maternal thinking and practice. In the absence of firm expectation that a child will survive, mother love as we conceptualize it (whether in popular terms or in the psychobiological notion of maternal bonding) is attenuated and delayed with consequences for infant survival. In an environment already precarious to young life, the emotional detachment of mothers toward some of their babies contributes even further to the spiral of high mortality—high fertility in a kind of macabre lock-step dance to death.

The average woman of the Alto experiences 9.5 pregnancies, 3.5 child deaths, and 1.5 stillbirths. Seventy percent of all child deaths in the Alto occur in the first six months of life, and 82 percent by the end of the first year. Of all deaths in the community each year, about 45 percent are of children under the age of five.

Women of the Alto distinguish between child deaths understood as natural (caused by diarrhea and communicable diseases) and those resulting from sorcery, the evil eye, or other magical or supernatural afflictions. They also recognize a large category of infant deaths seen as fated and inevitable. These hopeless cases are classified by mothers under the folk terminology "child sickness" or "child attack." Women say that there are at least fourteen different types of hopeless child sickness, but most can be subsumed under two categories—chronic and acute. The chronic cases refer to infants who are born small and wasted. They are deathly pale, mothers say, as well as weak and passive. They demonstrate no vital force, no liveliness. They do not suck vigorously; they hardly cry. Such babies can be this way at birth or they can be born sound but soon show no resistance, no "fight" against the common crises of infancy: diarrhea, respiratory infections, tropical fevers.

The acute cases are those doomed infants who die suddenly and violently. They are taken by stealth overnight, often following convulsions that bring on head banging, shaking, grimacing, and shrieking. Women say it is horrible to look at such a baby. If the infant begins to foam at the mouth or gnash its teeth or go rigid with its eyes turned back inside its head, there is absolutely no hope. The infant is "put aside"—left alone—often on the floor in a back room, and allowed to die. These symptoms (which accompany high fevers, dehydration, third-stage malnutrition, and encephalitis) are equated by Alto women with madness, epilepsy, and worst of all, rabies, which is greatly feared and highly stigmatized.

Most of the infants presented to me as suffering from chronic child sickness were tiny, wasted famine victims, while those labeled as victims of acute child attack seemed to be infants suffering from the deliriums of high fever or the convulsions that can accompany electrolyte imbalance in dehydrated babies.

Local midwives and traditional healers, praying women, as they are called, advise Alto women on when to allow a baby to die. One midwife explained: "If I can see that a baby was born unfortuitously, I tell the mother that she need not wash the infant or give it a cleansing tea. I tell her just to dust the infant with baby powder and wait for it to die."

Allowing nature to take its course is not seen as sinful by these often very devout Catholic women. Rather, it is understood as cooperating with God's plan.

Often I have been asked how consciously women of the Alto behave in this regard. I would have to say that consciousness is always shifting between allowed and disallowed levels of awareness. For example, I was awakened early one morning in 1987 by two neighborhood children who had been sent to fetch me to a hastily organized wake for a two-month-old infant whose mother I had unsuccessfully urged to breast-feed. The infant was being sustained on sugar water, which the mother referred to as *soro* (serum), using a medical term for the infant's starvation regime in light of his chronic diarrhea. I had cautioned the mother that an infant could not live on *soro* forever.

The two girls urged me to console the young mother by telling her that it was "too bad" that her infant was so weak that Jesus had to take him. They were coaching me in proper Alto etiquette. I agreed, of course, but asked, "And what do *you* think?" Xoxa, the eleven-year-old, looked down at her dusty flip-flops and blurted out, "Oh, Dona Nanci, that baby never got enough to eat, but you must never say that!" And so the death of hungry babies remains one of the best kept secrets of life in Bom Jesus da Mata.

Most victims are waked quickly and with a minimum of ceremony. No tears are shed, and the neighborhood children form a tiny procession, carrying the baby to the town graveyard where it will join a multitude of others. Although a few fresh flowers may be scattered over the tiny grave, no stone or wooden cross will mark the place, and the same spot will be reused within a few months' time. The mother will never visit the grave, which soon becomes an anonymous one.

What, then, can be said of these women? What emotions, what sentiments motivate them? How are they able to do what, in fact, must be done? What does mother love mean in this inhospitable context? Are grief, mourning, and melancholia present, although deeply repressed? If so, where shall we look for them? And if not, how are we to understand the moral visions and moral sensibilities that guide their actions?

I have been criticized more than once for presenting an unflattering portrait of poor Brazilian women, women who are, after all, themselves the victims of severe social and institutional neglect. I have described these women as allowing some of their children to die, as if this were an unnatural and inhuman act rather than, as I would assert, the way any one of us might act, reasonably and rationally, under similarly desperate conditions. Perhaps I have not emphasized enough the real pathogens in this environment of high risk: poverty, deprivation, sexism, chronic hunger, and economic exploitation. If mother love is, as many psychologists and some feminists believe, a seemingly natural and universal maternal script, what does it mean to women for whom scarcity, loss, sickness, and deprivation have made that love frantic and robbed them of their grief, seeming to turn their hearts to stone?

Throughout much of human history—as in a great deal of the impoverished Third World today—women have had to give birth and to nurture children under ecological conditions and social arrangements hostile to child survival, as well as to their own well-being. Under circumstances of high childhood mortality, patterns of selective neglect and passive infanticide may be seen as active survival strategies.

They also seem to be fairly common practices historically and across cultures. In societies characterized by high childhood mortality and by a correspondingly high (replacement) fertility, cultural practices of infant and child care tend to be organized primarily around survival goals. But what this means is a pragmatic recognition that not all of one's children can be expected to live. The nervousness about child survival in areas of northeast Brazil, northern India, or Bangladesh, where a 30 percent or 40 percent mortality rate in the first years of life is common, can lead to forms of delayed attachment and a casual or benign neglect that serves to weed out the worst bets so as to enhance the life chances of healthier siblings, including those yet to be born. Practices similar to those that I am describing have been recorded for parts of Africa, India, and Central America.

Life in the Alto do Cruzeiro resembles nothing so much as a battlefield or an emergency room in an overcrowded innercity public hospital. Consequently, morality is guided by a kind of "lifeboat ethics," the morality of triage. The seemingly studied indifference toward the suffering of some of their infants, conveyed in such sayings as "little critters have no feelings," is understandable in light of these women's obligation to carry on with their reproductive and nurturing lives.

In their slowness to anthropomorphize and personalize their infants, everything is mobilized so as to prevent maternal overattachment and, therefore, grief at death. The bereaved mother is told not to cry, that her tears will dampen the wings of her little angel so that she cannot fly up to her heavenly home. Grief at the death of an angel is not only inappropriate, it is a symptom of madness and of a profound lack of faith.

Infant death becomes routine in an environment in which death is anticipated and bets are hedged. While the routinization of death in the context of shantytown life is not hard to understand, and quite possible to empathize with, its routinization in the formal institutions of public life in Bom Jesus is not as easy to accept uncritically. Here the social production of indifference takes on a different, even a malevolent cast.

In a society where triplicates of every form are required for the most banal events (registering a car, for example), the registration of infant and child death is informal, incomplete, and rapid. It requires no documentation, takes less than five minutes, and demands no witnesses other than office clerks. No questions are asked concerning the circumstances of the death, and the cause of death is left blank, unquestioned and unexamined. A neighbor, grandmother, older sibling, or common-law husband may register the death. Since most infants die at home, there is no question of a medical record.

From the registry office, the parent proceeds to the town hall, where the mayor will give him or her a voucher for a free baby coffin. The full-time municipal coffinmaker cannot tell you exactly how many baby coffins are dispatched each week. It varies, he says, with the seasons. There are more needed during the drought months and during the big festivals of Carnaval and Christmas and Sao Joao's Day because people are too busy, he supposes, to take their babies to the clinic. Record keeping is sloppy.

Similarly, there is a failure on the part of city-employed doctors working at two free clinics to recognize the malnutrition of babies who are weighed, measured, and immunized without comment and as if they were not, in fact, anemic, stunted, fussy, and irritated starvation babies. At best the mothers are told to pick up free vitamins or a health "tonic" at the municipal chambers. At worst, clinic personnel will give tranquilizers and sleeping pills to quiet the hungry cries of "sick-to-death" Alto babies.

The church, too, contributes to the routinization of, and indifference toward, child death. Traditionally, the local Catholic church taught patience and resignation to domestic tragedies that were said to reveal the imponderable workings of God's will. If an infant died suddenly, it was because a particular saint had claimed the child. The infant would be an angel in the service of his or her heavenly patron. It would be wrong, a sign of a lack of faith, to weep for a child with such good fortune. The infant funeral was, in the past, an event celebrated with joy. Today, however, under the new regime of "liberation theology," the bells of N. S. das Dores parish church no longer peal for the death of Alto babies, and no priest accompanies the procession of angels to the cemetery where their bodies are disposed of casually and without ceremony. Children bury children in Bom Jesus da Mata. In this most Catholic of communities, the coffin is handed to the disabled and irritable municipal gravedigger, who often chides the children for one reason or another. It may be that the coffin is larger than expected and the gravedigger can find no appropriate space.

The children do not wait for the gravedigger to complete his task. No prayers are recited and no sign of the cross made as the tiny coffin goes into its shallow grave.

When I asked the local priest, Padre Marcos, about the lack of church ceremony surrounding infant and childhood death today in Bom Jesus, he replied: "In the old days, child death was richly celebrated. But those were the baroque customs of a conservative church that wallowed in death and misery. The new church is a church of hope and joy. We no longer celebrate the death of child angels. We try to tell mothers that Jesus doesn't want all the dead babies they send him." Similarly, the new church has changed its baptismal customs, now often refusing to baptize dying babies brought to the back door of a church or rectory. The mothers are scolded by the church attendants and told to go home and take care of their sick babies. Baptism, they are told, is for the living; it is not to be confused with the sacrament of extreme unction, which is the anointing of the dying. And so it appears to the women of the Alto that even the church has turned away from them, denying the traditional comfort of folk Catholicism.

The contemporary Catholic church is caught in the clutches of a double bind. The new theology of liberation imagines a kingdom of God on earth based on justice and equality, a world without hunger, sickness, or childhood mortality. At the same time, the church has not changed its official position on sexuality and reproduction, including its sanctions against birth control, abortion, and sterilization. The padre of Bom Jesus da

Mata recognizes this contradiction intuitively, although he shies away from discussions on the topic, saying that he prefers to leave questions of family planning to the discretion and the "good consciences" of his impoverished parishioners. But this, of course, sidesteps the extent to which those good consciences have been shaped by traditional church teachings in Bom Jesus, especially by his recent predecessors. Hence, we can begin to see that the seeming indifference of Alto mothers toward the death of some of their infants is but a pale reflection of the official indifference of church and state to the plight of poor women and children.

Nonetheless, the women of Bom Jesus are survivors. One woman, Biu, told me her life history, returning again and again to the themes of child death, her first husband's suicide, abandonment by her father and later by her second husband, and all the other losses and disappointments she had suffered in her long forty-five years. She concluded with great force, reflecting on the days of Carnaval '88 that were fast approaching:

> No, Dona Nanci, I won't cry, and I won't waste my life thinking about it from morning to night. … Can I argue with God for the state that I'm in? No! And so I'll dance and I'll jump and I'll play Carnaval! And yes, I'll laugh and people will wonder at a *pobre* like me who can have such a good time.

And no one did blame Biu for dancing in the streets during the four days of Carnaval—not even on Ash Wednesday, the day following Carnaval '88 when we all assembled hurriedly to assist in the burial of Mercea, Biu's beloved *casula,* her last-born daughter who had died at home of pneumonia during the festivities. The rest of the family barely had time to change out of their costumes. Severino, the child's uncle and godfather, sprinkled holy water over the little angel while he prayed: "Mercea, I don't know whether you were called, taken, or thrown out of this world. But look down at us from your heavenly home with tenderness, with pity, and with mercy." So be it.

CODE OF ETHICS OF THE AMERICAN ANTHROPOLOGICAL ASSOCIATION

I. PREAMBLE

Anthropological researchers, teachers and practitioners are members of many different communities, each with its own moral rules or codes of ethics. Anthropologists have moral obligations as members of other groups, such as the family, religion, and community, as well as the profession. They also have obligations to the scholarly discipline, to the wider society and culture, and to the human species, other species, and the environment. Furthermore, fieldworkers may develop close relationships with persons or animals with whom they work, generating an additional level of ethical considerations

In a field of such complex involvements and obligations, it is inevitable that misunderstandings, conflicts, and the need to make choices among apparently incompatible values will arise. Anthropologists are responsible for grappling with such difficulties and struggling to resolve them in ways compatible with the principles stated here. The purpose of this Code is to foster discussion and education. The American Anthropological Association (AAA) does not adjudicate claims for unethical behavior.

The principles and guidelines in this Code provide the anthropologist with tools to engage in developing and maintaining an ethical framework for all anthropological work.

II. INTRODUCTION

Anthropology is a multidisciplinary field of science and scholarship, which includes the study of all aspects of humankind--archaeological, biological, linguistic and sociocultural. Anthropology has roots in the natural and social sciences and in the humanities, ranging in approach from basic to applied research and to scholarly interpretation.

As the principal organization representing the breadth of anthropology, the American Anthropological Association (AAA) starts from the position that generating and appropriately utilizing knowledge (i.e., publishing, teaching, developing programs, and informing policy) of the peoples of the world, past and present, is a worthy goal; that the generation of anthropological knowledge is a dynamic process using many different and ever-evolving approaches; and that for moral and practical reasons, the generation and utilization of knowledge should be achieved in an ethical manner.

The mission of American Anthropological Association is to advance all aspects of anthropological research and to foster dissemination of anthropological knowledge through publications, teaching, public education, and application. An important part of that mission is to help educate AAA members about ethical obligations and challenges involved in the generation, dissemination, and utilization of anthropological knowledge.

The purpose of this Code is to provide AAA members and other interested persons with guidelines for making ethical choices in the conduct of their anthropological work. Because anthropologists can find themselves in complex situations and subject to more than one code of ethics, the AAA Code of Ethics provides a framework, not an ironclad formula, for making decisions.

Persons using the Code as a guideline for making ethical choices or for teaching are encouraged to seek out illustrative examples and appropriate case studies to enrich their knowledge base.

Anthropologists have a duty to be informed about ethical codes relating to their work, and ought periodically to receive training on current research activities and ethical issues. In addition, departments offering anthropology degrees should include and require ethical training in their curriculums.

No code or set of guidelines can anticipate unique circumstances or direct actions in specific situations. The individual anthropologist must be willing to make carefully considered ethical choices and be prepared to make clear the assumptions, facts and issues on which those choices are based. These guidelines therefore address *general* contexts, priorities and relationships which should be considered in ethical decision making in anthropological work.

III. RESEARCH

In both proposing and carrying out research, anthropological researchers must be open about the purpose(s), potential impacts, and source(s) of support for research projects with funders, colleagues, persons studied or providing information, and with relevant parties affected by the research. Researchers must expect to utilize the results of their work in an appropriate fashion and disseminate the results through appropriate and timely activities. Research fulfilling these expectations is ethical, regardless of the source of funding (public or private) or purpose (i.e., "applied," "basic," "pure," or "proprietary").

Anthropological researchers should be alert to the danger of compromising anthropological ethics as a condition to engage in research, yet also be alert to proper demands of good citizenship or host-guest relations. Active contribution and leadership in seeking to shape public or private sector actions and policies may be as ethically justifiable as inaction, detachment, or noncooperation, depending on circumstances. Similar principles hold for anthropological researchers employed or otherwise affiliated with nonanthropological institutions, public institutions, or private enterprises.

A. Responsibility to people and animals with whom anthropological researchers work and whose lives and cultures they study.

1. Anthropological researchers have primary ethical obligations to the people, species, and materials they study and to the people with whom they work. These obligations can supersede the goal of seeking new knowledge, and can lead to decisions not to undertake or to discontinue a research project when the primary obligation conflicts with other responsibilities, such as those owed to sponsors or clients. These ethical obligations include:

   - To avoid harm or wrong, understanding that the development of knowledge can lead to change which may be positive or negative for the people or animals worked with or studied
   - To respect the well-being of humans and nonhuman primates
   - To work for the long-term conservation of the archaeological, fossil, and historical records
   - To consult actively with the affected individuals or group(s), with the goal of establishing a working relationship that can be beneficial to all parties involved

2. Anthropological researchers must do everything in their power to ensure that their research does not harm the safety, dignity, or privacy of the people with whom they work, conduct research, or perform other professional activities. Anthropological researchers working with animals must do everything in their power to ensure that

the research does not harm the safety, psychological well-being or survival of the animals or species with which they work.

3. Anthropological researchers must determine in advance whether their hosts/ providers of information wish to remain anonymous or receive recognition, and make every effort to comply with those wishes. Researchers must present to their research participants the possible impacts of the choices, and make clear that despite their best efforts, anonymity may be compromised or recognition fail to materialize.

4. Anthropological researchers should obtain in advance the informed consent of persons being studied, providing information, owning or controlling access to material being studied, or otherwise identified as having interests which might be impacted by the research. It is understood that the degree and breadth of informed consent required will depend on the nature of the project and may be affected by requirements of other codes, laws, and ethics of the country or community in which the research is pursued. Further, it is understood that the informed consent process is dynamic and continuous; the process should be initiated in the project design and continue through implementation by way of dialogue and negotiation with those studied. Researchers are responsible for identifying and complying with the various informed consent codes, laws and regulations affecting their projects. Informed consent, for the purposes of this code, does not necessarily imply or require a particular written or signed form. It is the quality of the consent, not the format, that is relevant.

5. Anthropological researchers who have developed close and enduring relationships (i.e., covenantal relationships) with either individual persons providing information or with hosts must adhere to the obligations of openness and informed consent, while carefully and respectfully negotiating the limits of the relationship.

6. While anthropologists may gain personally from their work, they must not exploit individuals, groups, animals, or cultural or biological materials. They should recognize their debt to the societies in which they work and their obligation to reciprocate with people studied in appropriate ways.

B. Responsibility to scholarship and science

1. Anthropological researchers must expect to encounter ethical dilemmas at every stage of their work, and must make good-faith efforts to identify potential ethical claims and conflicts in advance when preparing proposals and as projects proceed.

A section raising and responding to potential ethical issues should be part of every research proposal.

2. Anthropological researchers bear responsibility for the integrity and reputation of their discipline, of scholarship, and of science. Thus, anthropological researchers are subject to the general moral rules of scientific and scholarly conduct: they should not deceive or knowingly misrepresent (i.e., fabricate evidence, falsify, plagiarize), or attempt to prevent reporting of misconduct, or obstruct the scientific/scholarly research of others.

3. Anthropological researchers should do all they can to preserve opportunities for future fieldworkers to follow them to the field.

4. Anthropological researchers should utilize the results of their work in an appropriate fashion, and whenever possible disseminate their findings to the scientific and scholarly community.

5. Anthropological researchers should seriously consider all reasonable requests for access to their data and other research materials for purposes of research. They should also make every effort to insure preservation of their fieldwork data for use by posterity.

C. Responsibility to the public

1. Anthropological researchers should make the results of their research appropriately available to sponsors, students, decision makers, and other nonanthropologists. In so doing, they must be truthful; they are not only responsible for the factual content of their statements but also must consider carefully the social and political implications of the information they disseminate. They must do everything in their power to insure that such information is well understood, properly contextualized, and responsibly utilized. They should make clear the empirical bases upon which their reports stand, be candid about their qualifications and philosophical or political biases, and recognize and make clear the limits of anthropological expertise. At the same time, they must be alert to possible harm their information may cause people with whom they work or colleagues.

2. Anthropologists may choose to move beyond disseminating research results to a position of advocacy. This is an individual decision, but not an ethical responsibility.

IV. TEACHING

Responsibility to students and trainees

While adhering to ethical and legal codes governing relations between teachers/mentors and students/trainees at their educational institutions or as members of wider organizations, anthropological teachers should be particularly sensitive to the ways such codes apply in their discipline (for example, when teaching involves close contact with students/trainees in field situations). Among the widely recognized precepts which anthropological teachers, like other teachers/mentors, should follow are:

1. Teachers/mentors should conduct their programs in ways that preclude discrimination on the basis of sex, marital status, "race," social class, political convictions, disability, religion, ethnic background, national origin, sexual orientation, age, or other criteria irrelevant to academic performance.

2. Teachers'/mentors' duties include continually striving to improve their teaching/training techniques; being available and responsive to student/trainee interests; counseling students/trainees realistically regarding career opportunities; conscientiously supervising, encouraging, and supporting students'/trainees' studies; being fair, prompt, and reliable in communicating evaluations; assisting students/trainees in securing research support; and helping students/trainees when they seek professional placement.

3. Teachers/mentors should impress upon students/trainees the ethical challenges involved in every phase of anthropological work; encourage them to reflect upon this and other codes; encourage dialogue with colleagues on ethical issues; and discourage participation in ethically questionable projects.

4. Teachers/mentors should publicly acknowledge student/trainee assistance in research and preparation of their work; give appropriate credit for coauthorship to students/trainees; encourage publication of worthy student/trainee papers; and compensate students/trainees justly for their participation in all professional activities.

5. Teachers/mentors should beware of the exploitation and serious conflicts of interest which may result if they engage in sexual relations with students/trainees. They must avoid sexual liaisons with students/trainees for whose education and professional training they are in any way responsible.

V. APPLICATION

1. The same ethical guidelines apply to all anthropological work. That is, in both proposing and carrying out research, anthropologists must be open with funders, colleagues, persons studied or providing information, and relevant parties affected by the work about the purpose(s), potential impacts, and source(s) of support for the work. Applied anthropologists must intend and expect to utilize the results of their work appropriately (i.e., publication, teaching, program and policy development) within a reasonable time. In situations in which anthropological knowledge is applied, anthropologists bear the same responsibility to be open and candid about their skills and intentions, and monitor the effects of their work on all persons affected. Anthropologists may be involved in many types of work, frequently affecting individuals and groups with diverse and sometimes conflicting interests. The individual anthropologist must make carefully considered ethical choices and be prepared to make clear the assumptions, facts and issues on which those choices are based.

2. In all dealings with employers, persons hired to pursue anthropological research or apply anthropological knowledge should be honest about their qualifications, capabilities, and aims. Prior to making any professional commitments, they must review the purposes of prospective employers, taking into consideration the employer's past activities and future goals. In working for governmental agencies or private businesses, they should be especially careful not to promise or imply acceptance of conditions contrary to professional ethics or competing commitments.

3. Applied anthropologists, as any anthropologist, should be alert to the danger of compromising anthropological ethics as a condition for engaging in research or practice. They should also be alert to proper demands of hospitality, good citizenship and guest status. Proactive contribution and leadership in shaping public or private sector actions and policies may be as ethically justifiable as inaction, detachment, or noncooperation, depending on circumstances.

VI. EPILOGUE

Anthropological research, teaching, and application, like any human actions, pose choices for which anthropologists individually and collectively bear ethical responsibility. Since anthropologists are members of a variety of groups and subject to a variety of ethical codes, choices must sometimes be made not only between the varied obligations presented in this code but also between those of this code and those incurred in other statuses or roles. This statement does not dictate choice or propose sanctions. Rather, it is designed to promote discussion and provide general guidelines for ethically responsible decisions.

VII. ACKNOWLEDGMENTS

This Code was drafted by the Commission to Review the AAA Statements on Ethics during the period January 1995-March 1997. The Commission members were James Peacock (Chair), Carolyn Fluehr-Lobban, Barbara Frankel, Kathleen Gibson, Janet Levy, and Murray Wax. In addition, the following individuals participated in the Commission meetings: philosopher Bernard Gert, anthropologists Cathleen Crain, Shirley Fiske, David Freyer, Felix Moos, Yolanda Moses, and Niel Tashima; and members of the American Sociological Association Committee on Ethics. Open hearings on the Code were held at the 1995 and 1996 annual meetings of the American Anthropological Association. The Commission solicited comments from all AAA Sections. The first draft of the AAA Code of Ethics was discussed at the May 1995 AAA Section Assembly meeting; the second draft was briefly discussed at the November 1996 meeting of the AAA Section Assembly.

The Final Report of the Commission was published in the September 1995 edition of the *Anthropology Newsletter* and on the AAA web site (http://www.aaanet.org). Drafts of the Code were published in the April 1996 and 1996 annual meeting edition of the *Anthropology Newsletter* and the AAA web site, and comments were solicited from the membership. The Commission considered all comments from the membership in formulating the final draft in February 1997. The Commission gratefully acknowledge the use of some language from the codes of ethics of the National Association for the Practice of Anthropology and the Society for American Archaeology.

VIII. OTHER RELEVANT CODES OF ETHICS

The following list of other Codes of Ethics may be useful to anthropological researchers, teachers and practitioners:

Animal Behavior Society
1991 Guidelines for the Use of Animals in Research. *Animal Behavior* 41:183–186.

American Board of Forensic Examiners
n.d. *Code of Ethical Conduct.* (American Board of Forensic Examiners, 300 South Jefferson Avenue, Suite 411, Springfield, MO 65806).

American Folklore Society
1988 Statement on Ethics: Principles of Professional Responsibility. *AFSNews* 17(1).

Archaeological Institute of America

1991   Code of Ethics. *American Journal of Archaeology* 95:285.

1994   *Code of Professional Standards.* (Archaeological Institute of America, 675 Commonwealth Ave, Boston, MA 02215-1401. Supplements and expands but does not replace the earlier Code of Ethics).

National Academy of Sciences

1995   *On Being a Scientist: Responsible Conduct in Research.* 2nd edition. Washington, D.C.: National Academy Press (2121 Constitution Avenue, NW, Washington, D.C. 20418).

National Association for the Practice of Anthropology

1988 *Ethical Guidelines for Practitioners.*

Sigma Xi

1992   Sigma Xi Statement on the Use of Animals in Research. *American Scientist* 80:73–76.

Society for American Archaeology

1996   *Principles of Archaeological Ethics.* (Society for American Archaeology, 900 Second Street, NE, Suite 12, Washington, D.C. 20002–3557).

Society for Applied Anthropology

1983 *Professional and Ethical Responsibilities.* (Revised 1983).

Society of Professional Archaeologists

1976 *Code of Ethics, Standards of Research Performance and Institutional Standards.* (Society of Professional Archaeologists, PO Box 60911, Oklahoma City, OK 73146–0911).

United Nations

1948 Universal Declaration of Human Rights.

1983 United Nations Convention on the Elimination of All Forms of Discrimination Against Women. 1987 United Nations Convention on the Rights of the Child.

Forthcoming United Nations Declaration on Rights of Indigenous Peoples.